BENT'S FORT

BENT'S FORT

David Lavender

University of Nebraska Press • Lincoln/London

International Standard Book Number 0–8032–5753–8
Library of Congress Catalog Card Number 54–7322

Bison Book edition reproduced from the
Dolphin Book edition by arrangement with
Doubleday & Company, Inc.

Manufactured in the United States of America

First Bison Book printing: March 1972

Most recent printing shown by first digit below:
7   8   9   10

FOR

M.M.L.

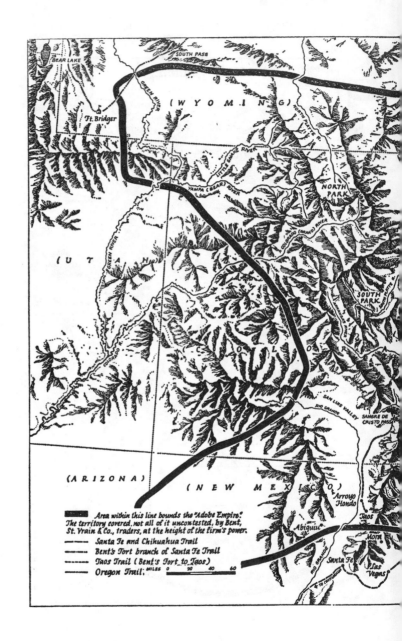

BEAR LAKE
SOUTH PASS
(W Y O M I N G)
GREEN RIVER
Ft. Bridger
NORTH PLATTE R.
LITTLE SNAKE RIVER
NORTH PARK
YAMPA (BEAR) RIVER
(U T A H)
GREEN RIVER
COLORADO (GRAND) RIVER
SOUTH PARK
COLORADO RIVER
C O L O R A D O
SAN LUIS VALLEY
RIO GRANDE
SANGRE DE CRISTO PASS
(A R I Z O N A)
(N E W   M E X I C O)
Arroyo Hondo
Taos
Abiquiu
Mora
Santa Fe
Las Vegas
RIO GRANDE
TO CHIHUAHUA

Area within this line bounds the "Adobe Empire."
The territory covered, not all of it uncontested, by Bent,
St. Vrain & Co., traders, at the height of the firm's power.
——— Santa Fe and Chihuahua Trail
——— Bent's Fort branch of Santa Fe Trail
——— Taos Trail (Bent's Fort to Taos)
——— Oregon Trail.   MILES 0   20   40   60

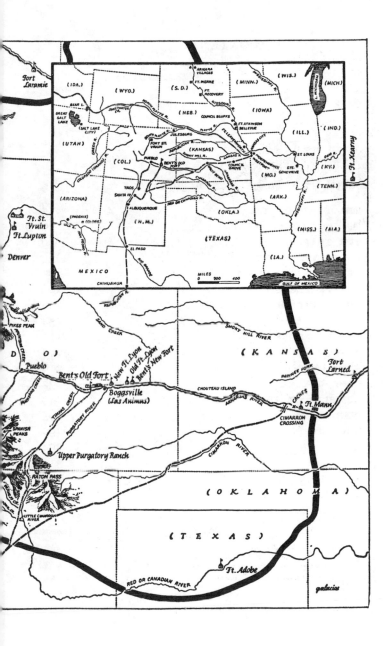

CONTENTS

THE PLACE CALLED PURGATORY

Northeast from the Spanish Peaks of Colorado a small creek flows toward the Arkansas River. Some miles from its mouth its canyon walls drop off into rich bottomlands where in olden days gnarled cottonwoods shaded the thick grass and reeds. Wild turkeys foraged in thickets of plum and grape, deer browsed among the sunflowers, and in the autumn huge bears snuffed at the chokecherries. To red men and white this spot of green was a welcome oasis in the sun-scorched plains of what is now southeastern Colorado. Yet the name by which three nations of whites called it was gloomy: El Rio de Las Animas Perdidas en Purgatorio—The River of Lost Souls in Purgatory.

The myth (or fact, if you will) that created the name is older than the landing of the Pilgrims on Plymouth Rock. In 1594 or thereabouts, even before the founding of Santa Fe, an expedition was sent out of Mexico, so the story says, to suppress the Indians beyond the border. Its leaders, Leiva Bonilla and Juan de Humaña, knew that Coronado fifty years before had gone in this direction, fruitlessly searching for fabled Quivara; and when their mission against the savages was completed, Bonilla and Humaña likewise began to dream of the unknown.

News of their intentions leaked back to Mexico, and the governor sent orders for them to return. Only six men obeyed, the remainder continuing with their truant captains. Soon the leaders quarreled and Bonilla was slain. Convinced by this that the illegal trip was accursed, the expedition's priests forsook it. Defiantly Humaña pushed ahead without them.

If arrogance admits of justification, these men had it.

Spain's early *entradas* into the New World drew the cream of
the nation. To them the endless plains were not the shock
they were to later Anglo-Saxons; for Spain, too, was semi-arid
and almost timberless, and Spanish horses, bred from Arabian
stock, were well fitted for crossing southwestern America's sun-
blasted, wind-swept land. The Indians whom the adventurers
met were mere foot creatures, beneath contempt as opponents.

On this occasion, however, the self-assured Spaniards grew
careless. One dawn, while the camp slept, the miserable, unmounted, unchivalrous savages set fire to the tall grass. In a
confusion of smoky flame, while stampeding horses neighed
shrilly and panicked men called back and forth, every person
perished save only a mulatto girl and a man named Alonzo
Sanchez, who, so the tale runs, later became a great chief
among the killers of his companions.

Years passed, Santa Fe was founded, and a roaming party
of explorers discovered near a small stream flowing from the
Spanish Peaks the rusted arms of what had once been a large
force. Only this remained of disobedient men who had died
abandoned by their own priests. In awe the discoverers named
the purling creek El Rio de Las Animas Perdidas en Purgatorio.

The name clung. More than a century later, as French
traders groped west and south from the Missouri, they found
the creek and shortened its resounding title to the single word
Purgatoire. Still later the Americans met it; some clipped the
Spanish down to Las Animas; others, wrestling the French
consonants, corrupted Purgatoire into Picketwire. Call it what
you wish. El Rio de Las Animas Perdidas en Purgatorio, Las
Animas, Purgatoire, Picketwire, or just plain Purgatory—it has
heard them all.

And it has watched nearly every major event in the winning
of the Southwest.

Pike forded it as his ill-equipped expedition marched westward to explore the lower reaches of Jefferson's Louisiana Purchase. Near its banks his men first glimpsed the dim blue
bulk of the Rockies and with one accord raised three cheers
for the Mexican mountains. It was a cheer that Spanish officials did not return. With diplomatic finesse Pike was arrested

and hustled out of the country. No finesse whatsoever greeted later intruders. Several stayed in prison for as long as nine years, and in 1817 De Mun, Chouteau, and their St. Louis trappers suffered confiscation of thirty thousand dollars' worth of furs.

During the course of rounding up the De Mun-Chouteau party, two hundred Mexican soldiers marched across the Raton Mountains toward the Arkansas. They were brave men if they believed their own story, for it was said that twenty thousand American troops were stationed in a strong fortification near El Rio de Las Animas Perdidas.

No fort was there—in 1817. But sixteen years later one came into being, conceived not by the military but by two St. Louis brothers, Charles and William Bent, recently displaced from the Missouri River by the violent trade wars to control its commerce. Here on the borders of a foreign land they found a field for a fresh start. Together with Ceran St. Vrain, a man who knew the Mexicans well, they built a vast mud castle that Mexico came to fear far more than she had its mythical predecessor. There was reason. For here was the spearhead of American expansion to the Southwest.

Call the roll of the pathbreakers—Carson, Beckwourth, Old Bill Williams, Maxwell, Walker, Wootton, Fitzpatrick of the broken hand, Frémont, and a forgotten host of others. Bent and St. Vrain gave them work or shelter as they opened the Southwest. Once the way was prepared, New Mexico, Arizona, and California were inevitably lost, not to twenty thousand American troops, but in large measure to seventeen hundred ragged soldiers of Stephen Watts Kearny's Army of the West marching out from their rendezvous at Bent's Fort.

In that quick and almost bloodless conquest (not completely bloodless: Charles Bent died horribly in Taos) the frontier leapfrogged past this fort which so long had stood in advance of the frontier. A whole way of life vanished, and the agonies of readjustment began. Bewildered and bereft, William Bent violently obliterated the post with his own hands, turned down the Arkansas a few miles east of the Purgatory, and there built another huge fort.

One sees in that rebuilding an unconscious effort to hold onto the singing past of a man's youth, of a nation's youth.

The effort failed. Seven years passed, and again William Bent left his fort, returning to the mouth of the Purgatory just as the Colorado gold rush began sweeping across the plains. There he built a stockaded ranch on ground where thirty years before, in another stockade of cottonwood pickets, he had first entered into alliance with the Cheyenne Indians, who were to become more nearly his own people than were the Missourians among whom he had been born.

Purgatory—so indeed it must have seemed during the '60s, when the Plains Indians rose against extinction and William's own sons, children of a red mother, joined her tribe to fight the white race of their father. Fight? It is too toneless a word for Chivington's guns pouring into the defenseless camp at Sand Creek; for young Charles Bent, named after William's beloved brother, lashing back at the whites with a savagery that led his father to disown him. Purgatory—there, in 1869, with most of the friends of the past already gone and the Cheyennes thrust from him onto a reservation, William Bent died.

This book attempts to reconstruct the story of that man, his brothers, his partners, and their forts. In many places it is a story built on surmise. Very little remains to us from the hands of the Bents or the St. Vrains. One must patch together the fragmentary records of their contemporaries and assume that if one thing was so, then another thing logically followed. It has not seemed expedient to delay the flow of the narrative by arguing out in front of the reader the sometimes tedious reconstruction upon which the many surmises are based. For those who are interested in such bits of historical patchwork, the data are reproduced in part in the Notes.

BENT'S FORT

CHAPTER I

THE TOWN ON THE RIVER

Toward noon on September 23, 1806, excitement swept the little village of St. Louis. Martha Bent, wearied by the long river trip from Ohio and harassed with the problems of moving into a new home, may have had no more than a glance for the throngs pouring toward the stone levees on the Mississippi. But it would have been strange indeed if her husband Silas had not caught up his coat and beaver hat; stranger still if the eldest of their four children, six-year-old Charles, had not scampered off, either alone or clutching his father's hand. He was a gray-eyed, black-haired youngster, small for his age, but never small in his energies. And this was a day to fire more than just a boy's imagination.

On the levee a motley group craned necks: French and Spaniards, Indians, Negroes, Canadians, and a sprinkling of "dose *Américains*"—Kentucky and Ohio backwoodsmen with long rifles in the crooks of their arms; canny-eyed traders from New England, and new officials of the United States Government, of whom thirty-eight-year-old Silas Bent was one. The amalgamation of races had not—and would not—proceed without frictions, but for the moment suspense held differences in abeyance. A flotilla of boats was nosing shoreward. Gunfire crackled welcome; "three huzzahs" rose through the sultry air. After an absence of two years and four months, Lewis and Clark had returned from the shores of the Pacific.

The Pacific! Even then the significance of the feat was sensed, and among the watchers jealousy mingled with admiration. For nearly half a century, under both French and Spanish dominion, some of those men and their fathers had been striving ever westward. Year after year, foot after toilsome foot, they had cordelled their keelboats up the tumultuous Missouri, had sweated out uncountable steps along the passavants. Under scorching sun, through shriveling cold, they had sought out the Indians, had fought, cajoled, dickered, betrayed. For a thousand miles or more they had gone, men whose names were household words in St. Louis, men whose names had been forgotten overnight. They knew that mountains lay at the end of the endless miles; they had heard of another vast river flowing westward to the Pacific. Riches waited for the trader who dared the road: Indians with beaver fur, otter skins, buffalo robes. And now dose Américains, those upstarts, had been all the way. Well, politics might change a city's flag, but it did not change values. St. Louis had been born facing west. It would keep its face that way, reaching long fingers up the Missouri toward the Shining Mountains, across the plains toward mysterious Santa Fe. Fur, robes—a way was known now, if the way could be held.

Charles Bent dawdled over his supper that September night. Seven years old, almost . . . Those burned and bearded homecomers in suits of rotting elkskin! Those crinkled eyes that undismayed had seen great bear and buffalo, had followed the trails of untamed tribes through deep forests of evergreen, past snowy peaks incalculably high, on and on into the never-never land, the American dream of the West. A dream cast in a boy's terms—yet not so different, after all, from what his elders likewise dreamed that day.

The Western itch lay deep in Charles Bent's young blood. In 1638, eighteen years after the sailing of the *Mayflower*, his ancestor, John Bent, had loaded a wife and five children aboard the brig *Covenant* and had fled from Charles I's ship-levy taxes to a new home in the new colony of Massachusetts.[1] There, with fifty-four other settlers, John had helped hew the town of Sudbury out of the forest west of Boston. With his son Peter he later laid out Marlboro. Indians burned the latter village on one occasion and during another attack scalped (but did not kill) one of Peter Bent's children—due bills of settlement which the St. Louis Bents would in their turn pay in full.

It was a prodigiously prolific family. By the time of the Revolution, Massachusetts teemed with Bents—farmers, yeomen, blacksmiths, mill operators, bakers, innkeepers, lawyers.

According to an unverifiable family tradition, Silas Bent, little Charles's grandfather, led one of the three bands of "Indians" who pitched British tea into Boston's harbor.[2] More verifiably, Silas joined the minutemen immediately after Lexington in 1775, served throughout the war, and afterward became a lieutenant colonel of the 7th Regiment of Massachusetts Militia.

Peace found him restless, ripe fodder for the ambitious plans of his Rutland neighbor and brother officer, General Rufus Putnam. Land in the West! Gripped by the vision, two hundred and eighty Revolutionary veterans joined Putnam in forming the historic Ohio Company of Associates. They purchased a million and a half acres of land along the northern bank of the Ohio River and signed with the federal government the Northwest Ordinance, destined to become the prototype for all later United States territorial organizations. Silas Bent held one share in the concern—worth 1173 acres. His circumstances considered, this self-uprooting appears reckless. He owned a good farm at the outskirts of Rutland and was soundly established in the respect of his community. He was forty-five years old, married, and the father of twelve children, the youngest not yet two. Nonetheless, he sold the farm and sent his eldest son, twenty-year-old Silas Jr., ahead to make known the unknown. The next spring, in 1789, the father loaded his goods and family into oxcarts for a racking trip across the mountains to a scow on the headwaters of the Ohio. Along the way he buried one of his offspring.

By a whisker Silas Jr. missed adding his name to one of history's footnotes, for on his scouting trip he reached Marietta, Ohio, shortly after Putnam's original forty-eight settlers had founded the future capital of Northwest Territory on the site of an ancient Indian mound. Nor did the Bent family stay long in the home the eldest son had located for them. Early in 1790 they moved from Marietta sixteen miles downstream and helped establish the town of Belpré, also known for a period as Bent's Post Office.

To what extent Silas Jr. may have been involved in the furious Indian wars that greeted the tide of emigration pouring down the Ohio is not known. It scarcely seems likely that he remained untouched. Although Putnam's formidable stock-

ade, named with classical defiance Campus Martius, protected
Marietta, the more distant clearings along the river burned
and bled. Two expeditions of regular soldiers and raw militia,
dispatched to punish the Indians, were hacked to pieces before Mad Anthony Wayne came from retirement and crushed
Chief Little Turtle's Miamis and their allies at Fallen Timber, near Lake Erie, in 1794.

To most of the settlers the resultant peace meant an opportunity to farm undisturbed. But young Silas Bent, scion of
farmers, apparently had little interest in the soil for which
his family had crossed the mountains. Sometime during the
mid-1790s he drifted north up the Ohio to another brand-
new village, Wheeling, Virginia—now West Virginia. There
he began a belated study of law. Finding no profit in the pro-
fession, he continued another twenty miles or so north into
the geographically odd fragment of land that lies between the
river and the Pennsylvania border. There, in a hamlet called
Charleston (not to be confused with the Charleston which
later became West Virginia's capital), he opened a store and
married Martha Kerr, ten years his junior.[3]

In Charleston, on November 11, 1799, their first son was
born and appropriately named Charles, though the fact that
the family tree was full of Charleses probably had more to
do with the name than did the birthplace.

As was characteristic among the Bents, a multitude of other
children followed. In time there would be eleven, seven sons
and four daughters; and neither storekeeping nor a brief term
as postmaster was proving more profitable for Silas than had
the law. After Juliannah's birth in 1801 and John's in 1803,
Silas applied for a job to his father's old friend, Rufus Putnam, now Surveyor General of the United States. Putnam responded with a place in the Marietta surveyor's office, and in
1803 Silas recrossed the river. He was either a good surveyor
or a good politician—or both. Although his sponsor, General
Putnam, was summarily fired by President Jefferson because
of a grievous mathematical error on an important plat, Silas
not only held his job but was elevated by Putnam's successor
to the rank of deputy. In addition, his legal training at last
paid off in the form of an appointment as associate judge of
the Washington County Court of Common Pleas. The success

was overdue. Silas was thirty-seven years old now, and his fourth child, Lucy, had been born on March 8, 1805.[4]

The next year the big break came. In July, Albert Gallatin, Secretary of the Treasury, appointed Silas Bent principal deputy surveyor in charge of Louisiana Territory. On September 17, 1806, six days before the return of Lewis and Clark, the family arrived in St. Louis.

In theory Silas's jurisdiction reached almost indefinitely through lands largely unknown. In practice his labors stopped with the frontier settlements along the Mississippi and Missouri rivers. Even this was more than he could manage. By 1810 Albert Gallatin was reading his deputy's complaint of having "to execute surveys at a distance of 500 or 1000 miles, which it is impossible for him to do," and was suggesting that Silas's commissioners explore avenues that would not "require from the principle [sic] Surveyor services which, though within the letter of the law, he cannot reasonably be expected to perform." To complicate matters still further, land titles were a hodgepodge of haphazard French claims and even more haphazard Spanish grants, many of them hotly contested by high-handed American settlers crowding westward across the Mississippi.

Troublesome though his duties were, they did not prevent Silas Bent from capitalizing on his other talents. At various times he was auditor of territorial accounts. In 1807 he became justice of the Court of Common Pleas, a position that at one period or another associated him with three of the most distinctive French leaders in Missouri—John Baptiste Lucas, Bernard Pratte, and resplendent Auguste Chouteau, the latter two among the wealthiest men in the territory and already, or soon to be, dominant figures in the Missouri fur trade. These French connections are of some significance. Though most of the interloping Americans were held in contempt by the older residents, Silas Bent was accepted.

At what date Silas abandoned surveying entirely in favor of the judiciary is uncertain. It was after 1810 and probably before 1813, when he was appointed by President Madison as judge of the Supreme Court of the territory, a position he held until the office was abolished in 1821 by the admission of Missouri as a state. Thereafter, until his death on Novem-

ber 20, 1827, aged fifty-nine, he functioned as clerk of the St.
Louis County Court. A pioneer in three states, he was remembered by his contemporaries, so it is said, as never having had
either his ability or his integrity questioned by the fierce parti-
sans among whom he worked.

Obviously, Silas's eleven children did not grow up in the traditional semi-literate, semi-indigent cabin-in-a-clearing. They
knew, as few other American youngsters did, the proud French
houses set amid deep lawns and fragrant fruit trees, where
sumptuous breakfasts were served alfresco on wide galleries
overlooking the Mississippi. Inside the iron-studded doors
they tiptoed decorously across gleaming inlaid floors and beside massive mahogany furniture brought from homes across
the sea. Down in the cool, paved cellars they dipped deep
drinks of water, clarified by alum and burnt almonds, from
red stone jars almost as tall as their heads. It was gracious
living at the edge of the wilds—but it is hard to believe that
it was the Bent boys' kind of living. To Charles and later to
his favorite brother, William Wells Bent, born on May 23,
1809, the vibrant town and its surroundings were far more
exciting.

As yet the whole of St. Louis lay between the river and the
bluffs. Its three main thoroughfares, running north and south,
took their names from their functions: the Rue Royale or
Principale, closest to the bustling levees; the Rue de l'Eglise,
fronting the cathedral; and on higher ground, bounding the
odorous, busy barns, the Rue des Granges. (As more and more
Yankees began pushing in, particularly after the War of 1812,
these streets would become Main, Second, and Third.) Such
sidewalks as existed were mere strips, yet always there was
room along them for rows of St. Louis's beloved locust trees.
Under the deep green shade rattled huge dray wagons and
tiny French carts loaded with firewood and driven by men
with calico handkerchiefs tied about their heads. Peasant
women rustled by in white caps and red petticoats. In the
tiny shops blanketed Indians, Negroes, sombreroed Spaniards,
black-clad priests and Sisters of Charity, Canadian trappers
and American hunters traded shoulder to shoulder, their all-
metal currency a bewildering melange of dollars, guineas,
doubloons, pistoles, piasters, crowns, and shillings. As the coins

clinked, bellmen strode among the carts and wagons outside, crying out news of meetings and lost children. Idlers lounged in the corner dram shops and billiard parlors, and even a judge's son would know where lay the brawling haunts of the water front.

Northeast of the town lay a fenced common where villagers could rent a plot for tillage. Not many did. Home agriculture and even manufacturing were so completely eschewed in favor of trade that St. Louis, importing most of its foodstuffs, earned from its neighbors the contemptuous nickname Paincourt (short of bread). There was, however, one mill, owned by the Chouteaus, its pond a favorite picnic place—except in the late summer of 1819, when the dam broke and so many fish were stranded that the thrifty French hauled away half a hundred cartloads and three times that many had to be raked up and buried by order of the afflicted commissioners.

Beyond the common, beyond the millpond, stretching immensely westward, was the Grande Prairie, savannas and timber and crystal creeks. Here St. Louis boys learned to hunt and jumped out of their skins when periodic alarms of hostile Indians swept down the rivers. In this lush land, fragrant in spring with blossoms of wild plum and wild crab apple, the wealthier citizens had farms. Life was a delight—blooded horses, hounds innumerable, beehives, dovecotes, orchards. Slaves set laden tables under the walnut trees; after the outdoor meal came laughter and brandy, cigar smoke and tales of the West to make a youngster's hair stand straight on end.

And always there were the rivers. Seldom has another city dominated the commerce of half a continent as completely as St. Louis did western America's in the early nineteenth century. From all the East merchandise funneled into her ports, there to be transshipped for the headwaters of the Missouri and the Mississippi, the marts of Mexico. Here was the outfitting point for government explorers and soldiers, gentlemen hunters and naturalists, trappers and traders. The peltries which the city gathered in from the Indian nations of the Arkansas, the Missouri, and the upper Mississippi, she flung down the tawny tide to New Orleans. By sail, oar, and back-breaking cordelle—no steamboat reached her docks until 1817 —settlers toiled upward from the Ohio. Down-current drifted houseboats, floating stores, sprawling rafts, sharp-nosed keel-boats, pirogues, canoes, all carrying a wild and heterogeneous population. A gabble of tongues, an effluvium of smells . . . last flings before leaving civilization, first ones on reaching it . . . fighting, gaming, whoring—nor was all of it confined to the water-borne riffraff. Refined violence was part of every gentleman's code; across the yellow river, near the Illinois shore, lay the notorious dueling grounds of Bloody Island. In one of its more sensational affairs of honor, Tom Benton, future senator, killed a son of Judge Lucas, Silas Bent's great good friend and associate, and all St. Louis rocked with scandal.

The rivers and the men of the rivers—Charles and William Bent grew up with the yarns of the Missouri as close to them as their ABCs. They knew of, and quite possibly saw across their father's own table, that tough and wily prince of the bloody waters, the Spaniard Manuel Lisa. Within months after the return of Lewis and Clark, while other traders were content to gossip in wonder, Lisa had started dragging his keelboats toward the mountains two thousand miles away, laying the foundations for the Missouri Fur Company. During the next two hectic decades the shifting, oft-reorganized concern would take many a St. Louis youth beyond the frontier, Charles Bent among them. The way to the future lay there, so men thought—if only the way could be held. Almost at once, however, Blackfoot Indians drove Lisa back, and British intrigue among the savages kept him back. Yet he never lost the dream. And it never occurred to him that there might be another way.

Tales of Lisa's doings filled St. Louis. Everlastingly driving his snail-paced, hand-hauled keelboats up and down the river, he traveled enough miles on the Missouri to have circumnavigated the globe, enduring privations that cracked nearly every one of the partners who tried to follow him. His personal life was equally fantastic. His first wife, whispers said, was a white girl whom he married out of pity for her condition after Indians had raped her. While she yet lived he wed, for reasons of trade policy, the daughter of a Mandan chief. The Indian woman worshiped him. In return Lisa forcibly took their first child from her to St. Louis, ordered the mother out of his fort near Council Bluffs when he journeyed there with his second white bride, and would have appropriated the Indian's second child too had not a government agent forbidden the act. All through the harrowing scenes his second white wife, Mary, remained devoted to him, although they could scarcely converse, for Mary spoke neither French nor Spanish and Lisa only a few words of atrocious English.

Today he seems an enigmatic man, as contrary as his river. Though his costly failures to open the upper river would have broken most traders, he somehow managed to keep re-forming his Missouri Fur Company and emerge prosperous. By his numerous enemies he was accused of the West's blackest treachery—deliberately setting Indians on rival parties. Meriwether Lewis, infuriated by his insolence, called him a scoundrel and a puppy. According to trader Thomas James, "rascality sat on every feature of his dark complexioned, Mexican face—gleamed from his black, Spanish eyes, and seemed enthroned in a forehead villainous low." Yet when the War of 1812 filled St. Louis with terror; when Bernard Pratte, Silas Bent's quondam judicial associate, was earning an honorary title of General by supervising the frantic defense efforts of the Committee of Safety, it was to Manuel Lisa that Governor William Clark turned. Could the one-time alien keep the British-aroused Indians of the North contained? Lisa could—and did. No honorary title of General rewarded the services, though they secured the northwestern flank of America. Indeed, there was little recompense of any kind. Yet the lack stirred no rancor. Equably Lisa told Clark, "I have suffered enough in person and property under a different government to know how to appreciate the one under which I now live." Then, still scheming of the upper river, he settled down at Council Bluffs to wait for a cooling off of the furies engendered by the war.

The rivers and the Indians who lived along the rivers—these were the pulse of St. Louis. So intertwined were they that General William Clark served not only as governor of the territory but as Superintendent of Indian Affairs as well. Troubles aplenty he had with the fierce sectionalism of his independent, hotheaded white citizens, but most of his energy and patience were devoted to his red charges. Even his personal life was inextricably mixed with theirs. In 1818, when he built his fine new two-story house at Main and Pine streets, he added to its southern end a high-vaulted council chamber hung with canoes, bows, arrows, shields, cooking pots, war bonnets, cradles, and scores of other trophies. Here the Indians visited him in full regalia, camping in his yard when there were not too many of them, spilling over to the "Beaver Ponds" at the city's edge when there were. Sometimes they got themselves gloriously drunk. Often, to entertain Clark's friends, they put on thunderous war dances, at one of which little Jessie Benton, destined to marry the West's greatest publicist, fell into such hysterics of terror that she had to be carried away and comforted. Other residents found the ubiquitous visitors sources of cruder amusement: Dr. Antoine Saugrain, the French physician who had made the thermometers for Lewis and Clark by scraping the mercury off the back of his wife's cherished mirror, laid endless booby traps with electric batteries so his friends could watch the curious redskins jump and howl. Yet Saugrain, pioneer inoculator against smallpox, also vaccinated the Indians free of charge.

The rivers, the trade, the Indians—all these tugs led west. Yet Charles Bent first went east. Sometime during his teens he was sent to school at Jefferson College in Canonsburg, Pennsylvania. His brother John, four years younger, also went there, though whether they attended simultaneously cannot be determined.

Offhand, Canonsburg seems an odd choice. It was a tiny place in the hills of southwestern Pennsylvania. Those few St. Louis youths who went from the local schools to college generally chose a Catholic institution, a favorite one being St. Thomas's at Bardstown, Kentucky. For the French this was all very well. Silas Bent, however, hailed from Puritan Massachusetts, and Canonsburg's two academies, Washington and Jefferson, had first carried the light of Presbyterian education to the frontier at about the time the Bent family was moving into Marietta. Silas had come into contact with the schools when living at Charleston, only twenty-five miles away; the fact that Grandfather Silas was still alive in Belpré and that numerous Bent cousins were scattered about eastern and southeastern Ohio may also have influenced the choice. Moreover, one of Judge Lucas's sons was at Jefferson—a wild lad, precipitantly removed not only from that Presbyterian institu-

tion but from Catholic St. Thomas's as well. Association with
young Lucas may have had its effect on John Bent, who was
supposed to be preparing for the law but whose "genial and
social habits interfered greatly with his studies." John was
never awarded a diploma—nor was Charles.[5]

How long Charles attended the college or what he studied
is not known. Later legends from New Mexico suggest, but
do not prove, both a mathematical and medical education.
Indeed, little is on record about the education of any of the
Bent children. Yet it was a family that respected learning,
and the boys, at least, had an opportunity to swallow as much
classroom work as they desired. Though William Bent, for
example, probably did not possess as much education as did
his two elder brothers, he stayed with his books long enough
to be able to figure shrewdly, express himself with a roughhewn directness, and spell after a phonetic fashion which, al-
beit extraordinary, was no worse than his brother's or Governor
William Clark's.

Perhaps while Charles was still at college the first of the
Bents went west. It was not one of the boys, but Juliannah.
Sixteen years old in 1817, she married Lilburn Boggs, a young
man who had come out of Lexington, Kentucky, only a year
before and almost immediately had won a choice job as cashier
of the new Bank of Missouri.

He had silver on his tongue, this Boggs, the glint of op-
portunism in his eye. When a land boom began in the Boone's
Lick country two hundred miles up the Missouri, he resigned
his bank position and joined the rush with his pregnant bride.
The birth of his first son and the utter failure of his store in
the settlement of Franklin occurred almost simultaneously.
But by now the frontier had its hold on Boggs. Instead of
returning to St. Louis, he stayed in the wilderness as deputy
factor and Indian agent at Fort Osage and New Harmony Mission, where a lank, redheaded ex-Baptist circuit rider named
Bill Williams was learning the way of the wilds and developing the peculiarities that soon would stamp him as the Rockies' weirdest eccentric. There at Fort Osage, among the Indians and trappers, Juliannah, not yet out of her teens, bore
her second son. A month later, in St. Louis, she died.[6]

It may be that the activities of his brother-in-law first took

Charles Bent into western Missouri. He was eighteen years
old when Juliannah married, and it is not unlikely that by
now he knew what he wanted. Unauthenticated references
place him on the river well before the time of his sister's death.
Unfortunately the brief statements do not say where he was
or what he did. By the time his name bobs up in contemporary
records he was twenty-five years old and well established in
the Missouri Fur Company that Manuel Lisa had founded.[7]

Manuel Lisa, still dreaming of the way to the West—if the
way could be held. By 1818 events seemed to promise that it
could be. The United States Government was at last making
a full-dress show of doing something about its neglected
frontier.

CHAPTER II

THOSE BLOODY WATERS

Through all of young America's thinking about the frontier, water flowed with the inexorable force of habit. Chan-
neled first by centuries of search for a mythical river that
would lead to the Western Sea, the habit persisted long after
the dream had run dry and left the colonies landlocked behind the Alleghenies. For water was the only easy way to conquer the heavily forested lands of the East. The panacea it
offered sent Robert Fulton's steamboat thrashing up the Hudson, put scores of laborers to digging the Erie Canal, and,
once the Alleghenies had been breached, founded the lusty
little shipbuilding towns of the Ohio.

Westward, however, the pattern of the land changed. Most
conspicuously, no forests grew to block travel. Yet cleaving
the prairies was the Missouri, route of Lewis and Clark. More
capricious, more deadly than any of the eastern rivers, it was
also as plain as the nose on a boatman's face. And so, year
after year, clumsy keelboats fought the vicious, snag-filled current with oar, towrope, and sail, trying to reach the beaver
wealth that lay between the Rockies and the Pacific.

There were hints (easy to see with hindsight) that another

way might exist. In 1813, after Robert Stuart's Astorians had returned from Oregon through a land gap later known as South Pass, the *Missouri Gazette* plainly said, "By information received from these gentlemen it appears that a journey across the continent of North America, might be performed with a wagon." The natives of the land were daily implying the same fact. As trading posts crawled up the Missouri, swarms of Indians poured into them, not afoot or in canoes like the savages of the forested East or Canadian North, but astride far-ranging horses which also, when occasion demanded, dragged whole villages across the plains. Though traders sometimes followed the villages on horseback, it was only as an adjunct to getting their goods back to the habitual highway. In order to maintain preconception, men spent hundreds of thousands of dollars, bled and died rather than turn to anything so radical as a caravan of pack animals, so unheard of as a wagon road two thousand miles long.

Even the government lent its weight. By 1818 the war with England was three years over. Peace with the British should also have brought peace to the British-inspired Indians of the upper Missouri. Affairs, however, had not worked out that way. Although Manuel Lisa had taken forty-three chiefs to St. Louis in an effort to convince them that the Great White Father, American version, still commanded the river, raiding parties went right on terrorizing the outlying settlements. The tribes farther north, slyly abetted by English fur gatherers, continued to attack all American parties bound for the upper waters. Finally, in response to frontier pressure that something be done, the government decided to send a military and scientific expedition as far as the mouth of the Yellowstone, there to establish a military post that would keep the highway open. Exultantly a St. Louis paper predicted, as the Bents read, "It [the post on the Yellowstone] will go to the source and root of the fatal British influence which has so many years armed the Indian nations against our Western frontier. The Northwest and Hudson Bay Companies will be shut out . . . A million [dollars in commerce] per annum will descend the Missouri, and the Indians . . . will learn to respect the American name."

Preparations began in a style befitting the scale of the expedition. Traders might haul themselves along by sheer muscle, but Colonel Atkinson, in command of the military, determined to do better for his soldiers. Five steamboats were contracted for on a lush cost-plus basis—despite the fact that no steamboat had yet assayed the Missouri to learn whether standard designs were appropriate. For the scientific arm of the venture an even more awesome transport was built, the *Western Engineer*, a seventy-five-foot stern-wheeler mounting three brass cannon and belching smoke through a black figurehead carved to resemble a serpent. On seeing the vessel and hearing its goal, a reporter for the *Missouri Gazette* cried, November 13, 1818, "It is intended to take the steam boat to pieces at the mountains, and rebuild her in [the Columbia]. The expedition is to traverse the continent by water!"

By water! Many men now knew the extent of the Rockies. Yet habit still held sway.

During the fall of 1818 and the spring of 1819 the disjointed, ill-managed force began moving up the Missouri. Inevitably Manuel Lisa's old dream flamed again—with additions. With the army behind him he would not stop now at the Missouri's headwaters. Like the *Western Engineer*, he too would cross the continent by water, stringing his posts to the Pacific. To implement the plan and to raise part of the necessary capital (the rest would come from furs pouring into new posts) he again reorganized his Missouri Fur Company. Among the new directors were the veteran trappers Robert Jones; huge-bodied Moses Carson, one of Kit's many elder brothers; and hot-tempered Joshua Pilcher, recently ejected from a top position in the Bank of Missouri during a bitter quarrel. By this time twenty-year-old Charles Bent probably was also working for the company, serving, as most educated young men on the river did, in the capacity of clerk—a more responsible position in the trading hierarchy than the word connotes today.

Still another new face went in 1819 with Lisa to his fort at Council Bluffs on the west side of the river, some miles above the present city of the same name. This was his second white wife, Mary Hempstead Keeney, who had for company one other white woman, name unknown. In St. Louis, Manuel's enemies sniffed that he had taken the pair along, farther than any other white woman had gone before, "in order to attract to his home the protection of the officers . . . It is necessary for him to treat them well so that he can hope to draw advantages from them."

The advantages turned out less potent than anticipated. One by one the army's five steamboats collapsed. In straggling detachments the grumbling soldiers limped on foot to Council Bluffs and there, in an injudiciously chosen camp, fell sick by scores. The *Western Engineer* was able, partly because of its stern propulsion, to thrust upstream as far as Lisa's post, but then bogged down. In short, a year's effort, a quarter of a million dollars, half a dozen lost boats, and scores of sick and dying soldiers had pushed the expedition scarcely one third of the way to its goal. Congress reacted by cutting appropriations to the bone. As a weak compromise for a British-defying fort on the Yellowstone, the army built Fort Atkinson near Lisa's headquarters, in a region comparatively untroubled. The exploratory part of the enterprise dwindled to Major Long's 1820 summertime trip with a handful of men to the Colorado Rockies, during the course of which Long wrote off the entire plains region as "almost wholly unfit for cultivation and of course uninhabitable by a people depending upon agriculture for their subsistence." British trappers and Blackfoot warriors, more contemptuous than ever, roamed the North unchallenged. If Lisa was to hold the waterway, he would have to do it unaided.

Before he could make the attempt he sickened, and on August 12, 1820, not yet fifty years old, he died.

The management of the Missouri Fur Company now devolved on a man as firmly wedded to the river as Lisa had been. This was Joshua Pilcher, competent, excitable, and given, like his predecessor, to tempestuous enmities that would soon result in charges of treachery. Although his company's Pacific aspirations died with the Yellowstone expedition, the drive to control the upper river remained unshaken. Pushing northward as far as present Chamberlain, South Dakota, Pilcher's men, perhaps late in 1820 or in early 1821, threw up a square stockade of cottonwood pickets with a blockhouse in one corner and, diagonally across the enclosure, a cannon-equipped tower. On this spot Lisa had once suffered a staggering blow when fire had destroyed fifteen thousand dollars' worth of pelts. An omen? The Missouri Fur Company defied it. Significantly they named the new post Fort Recovery, and from it veteran trappers Robert Jones and Michael Immell led a party to the mouth of the Yellowstone. This was dangerous land, bordering territory roamed by the Blackfeet, who had already been tutored in trapping by the British and who were certain to resent the American intrusion. At first Jones and Immell stayed clear of them, however, and during the fall of 1821 traded thirty packs of beaver from the friendlier Crows.[1]

This distant trade—indeed, all of the Indian trade—was soon to be fiercely contested. In 1821 American commerce with the western tribes was still supervised by the War Department, which granted stringently limited licenses to only a few private individuals—and then competed with them at government posts called factories. The next year, however, virulent frontier criticism, cleverly exploited by the Washington lobby of John Jacob Astor's American Fur Company, led Congress to junk the factory system. Nothing now controlled the trade except licenses issued almost wholesale by the Superintendent of Indian Affairs.

The result was a wild scramble of exploitation. Among the first to challenge Pilcher's hold on the upper river was a singularly able pair. One was Andrew Henry, who had learned the upper Missouri during Lisa's abortive prewar efforts to reach the Rockies; the other was Henry's partner, William Ashley, ambitious lieutenant governor of Missouri and brigadier general of the state militia. Throughout February and March 1822, General Ashley advertised in the St. Louis newspapers for "one hundred men to ascend the Missouri to its source, there to be employed for one, two, or three years."

Behind that appeal lay a lively imagination. Always before the big companies had relied on trade in order to obtain their peltries, even training Indians in the art of trapping; and though bands of white trappers might supplement the activities, the effort was always subordinate to barter. But Henry knew, and convinced Ashley, that the distant tribes of the mountains were far too uncivilized to be relied on as steady sources of furs, no matter what geegaws might be held out as inducement. Accordingly the pair decided to eschew trade, except for incidental benefits, and rely on the catches of their own men. When Henry started upriver with a powerful brigade in 1822, Pilcher knew he faced a serious threat.

Nor was that the only threat. The French traders of St. Louis—Chouteau, Berthold, and Bernard Pratte, Silas Bent's former judicial associate—moved in force into the Council Bluffs region, Lisa's erstwhile stronghold. So, too, did Astor's new Western Department. This last invasion was irony; years before, Lisa had refused Astor's backing, and now the successors of the Spaniard must reap the bitter fruit of that rejection.

To meet these attacks Pilcher stretched his credit wiretight. Soon three hundred of his men were dotted along almost a thousand miles of the river, from Council Bluffs to the Yellowstone. Among them, in addition to Robert Jones and Michael Immell, were such redoubtable hands as Andrew Drips; Moses Carson; moody Lucien Fontenelle, reputedly of noble birth; stout William Vanderburgh, schooled at West Point—and Charles Bent, by now firmly established in the lower echelons of the company.

Records do not reveal Charles's whereabouts during this critical period. Possibly he was at Council Bluffs; perhaps he was on the Yellowstone with Jones and Immell. Or he may well have spent the summer of 1822 with Pilcher himself as the tireless head of the company tried to assert dominion over the river tribes in North Dakota. Straightway, as the expedition neared the present border between the Dakotas, it ran into trouble—the twin mud villages of the Arikara Indians.

The Arikaras were an unsavory lot, disliked and mistrusted by every trader. They lived on the river shore in two contiguous towns, each village composed of about seventy odorous, earth-covered lodges that from a distance looked like enormous potato hills. Log pickets some twelve feet high and six to eight inches thick fortified both towns. Though successful as agriculturists, particularly in growing corn for barter with other tribes, the inhabitants, according to trader Edwin Denig, were lazy, lousy, dirty, flagrantly loose in their sexual relations, and riddled with venereal disease. They filled their household needs by catching fish in basket traps, lassoing driftwood from

the river, and eating drowned buffalo whose flesh was so putrid
it could be dipped with a spoon. From the moment of Pilcher's
appearance they were continually embroiled with the Missouri
Fur Company. Twice they attacked the trading houses he
tried to establish nearby, then won his trust by turning friendly
—and repaid his confidence by trying to kill him one day as he
floated downstream past their villages. In spite of them, however, the company managed, during the summer of 1822, to
push on into Mandan territory in central North Dakota, and
there anchored itself by building Fort Vanderburgh.

The effort had been made none too soon. Behind Pilcher the
French traders were thrusting northward from Council Bluffs.
Brazenly these invaders cordelled a short thirteen miles beyond
Fort Recovery and there, near the looping curve of the river
known as Grand Detour, built Fort Kiowa, a direct challenge
to the Missouri Fur Company's would-be monopoly over the
powerful Sioux. Meanwhile Andrew Henry had reached the
confluence of the Yellowstone and the Missouri and built a
stockade. At about the same time, Jones and Immell led a
second party of Missouri Fur Company men two hundred
miles farther on up the Yellowstone, to the mouth of the Bighorn.

Both companies made fall hunts. Prior knowledge of the
country served Jones and Immell well; their men gathered another thirty packs of beaver. These they cached and, made
optimistic by the success, settled down to wait out the bone-
cracking cold of the northern winter. When spring came and
the race for the headwaters of the Missouri began, let the
devil take the hindmost.

The devil turned out to be Blackfeet, inspired, so Pilcher
always believed, by the British. As the rival groups of white
hurried along the thawing streams and through the gaunt
hills of the badlands toward the Rockies, the savages struck.
Henry's turn came first, on May 4, 1823. Four of his men were
killed, the rest driven back to the Yellowstone stockade. For a
time Jones's and Immell's twenty-nine hunters fared better.
Up toward the Three Forks country they took another twenty
packs of beaver, despite the fact that Indians had trapped the
streams ahead of them. Then, thinking of home and celebra-

tion, they swung their treasure-laden pack horses downstream toward the furs they had cached the previous fall.

On May 30, near Pryor's Fork, they reached a spot where the trail narrowed to a single-file path between the river and a precipitous hillside. There they rode into an ambush. Seven of them died as the Blackfeet charged, including Robert Jones and Michael Immell, both of them hacked literally to pieces. Before the survivors could build rafts and escape across the stream, they had lost every horse and trap, every one of the twenty bales of furs. It would be interesting to know where Charles Bent was that bleak May day. But the records remain silent.

Hurrying desperately ahead to apprise Pilcher of the disaster, William Gordon and another survivor reached Fort Vanderburgh on June 15, so exhausted that they had to halt and send a messenger on toward Council Bluffs. Before the unwelcome courier reached Pilcher, however, word came downstream of still another defeat, this one suffered by General Ashley at the Arikara villages.

On March 10 Ashley had left St. Louis with another hundred men to join Andrew Henry on the headwaters of the Missouri. Toward the end of May, ignorant of his partner's debacle, the general halted at the Arikara villages to trade for pack horses which he could use as feeders for his keelboats. The Arikaras were in a sullen mood. Only a few weeks before, a hundred of them had attacked one of the Missouri Fur Company's trading houses some sixty miles downstream in an effort to recover certain female Sioux prisoners who had sought refuge there. Beaten back, they had lost two chiefs killed and several men wounded. Now the tribe was spoiling for trouble.

William Ashley knew this. But he was a bold man and he needed horses. Anchoring his keelboats in midstream, he went ashore with two companions and persuaded the Indians to open trade—guns and ammunition for horses, which in itself should have been a warning. The warriors were so good-natured, however, and the women so cordial that several of the whites camped on the shore, where they could watch the horses. Some of them actually went inside the town to sample the entertainment, and toward midnight one of them was killed. Though alarmed, Ashley decided to postpone settling matters until morning.

The Arikaras moved first. At dawn, sheltered behind their barricades, they poured their new fire power into the camp on the beach. Within fifteen minutes nearly every one of the dearly bought horses was dead. So were eleven or twelve men. Completely routed, Ashley picked up the living and dropped downstream. His hurt pride wanted another fling at forcing a way past the villages, but his panicked boatmen refused. Either he got reinforcements or he went back down the river. Reluctantly he sent runners overland to ask help from his partner Henry, of whose defeat he was still ignorant. Other urgent appeals were dispatched, together with a boatload of wounded and quitters, down the river to Agent Benjamin O'Fallon and Colonel Henry Leavenworth.

What followed was not just another pioneer uproar. It was the culmination of nearly two decades of trying to turn the Missouri into the highway to the West, and, if definite results could be obtained, the resultant battle would be decisive in frontier history. Well aware of this, Leavenworth on June 22 ordered out of Fort Atkinson's garrison all the force he could muster—more than two hundred and fifty soldiers and two six-pound cannon. The supplies and some of the troops moved by water, but there weren't enough boats for all. Most of the soldiers marched.

The Indian agent Benjamin O'Fallon thought there should be still more power and appealed to Joshua Pilcher, who agreed to add forty of his men to Leavenworth's forces. O'Fallon wanted still more. Knowing that the Sioux were at war with the Arikaras and that the Missouri Fur Company had great influence with the Sioux, he asked Pilcher to enlist their aid. The ethics of such internecine use of Indians was perhaps dubious, but in every trader's mind the time had come to teach the Arikaras a lasting lesson. Pilcher promised to talk to the Sioux at Fort Recovery and then set about gathering his own men. After adding a small army howitzer to their equipment, the eager traders hurried after Leavenworth, whom they overhauled on June 27.

It was a devilish trip. The river was swollen. Marchers on the shore waded waist-deep through flooded bottomlands;

the boat cordeliers wallowed from sunup to sundown in mud and ooze and brush. One of the military's craft broke in half on a snag, drowning a sergeant and six privates. In order to salvage part of the sunken boat's cargo, Pilcher took aboard his own laden vessels eleven barrels of supplies. He also loaned Leavenworth ten rifles to replace guns lost in the river. In return, because the Missouri Fur Company men were short of provisions, Leavenworth gave Pilcher two barrels of pork and one of wet beans. So far the commanders had been assiduous friends.

Somewhere along the river William Gordon's express met the command with word of the disasters suffered by Henry and by Jones and Immell. To Pilcher the latter revelation was a staggering blow. The horses, traps, and other equipment which his party had lost would be difficult and expensive to replace up there in the wilderness. Far worse, the best of his leaders were dead, the morale of his men was shattered, and fifteen thousand dollars' worth of furs, desperately needed to relieve his straitened credit, were irretrievably lost. Gloomily he told Leavenworth that he would probably have to abandon the upper river trade which he had worked so hard to open.

On July 19 the expedition reached Fort Recovery. Here, unless he was elsewhere on the upper river or already with Pilcher's group, Charles Bent probably met the command, though whether he continued with it cannot be said. Here, too, while wind and water damage to the boats was being repaired, the full significance of the triple victories by the Blackfeet and Arikaras became apparent. All the river tribes were excited; unless their ardor was immediately dampened by Leavenworth's campaign, new attacks would follow. Writing O'Fallon, Pilcher declared, "A decisive blow is indispensable for the safety of every white man on the river above Council Bluffs."

As his part in making sure that the blow was decisive, Pilcher summoned in a few bands of Sioux for war talks over a kettle of boiled dog meat and sent runners out for more Indians to support the attack on the mud villages. About seven hundred responded. Meanwhile Ashley's men, together with reinforcements brought downstream by Andrew Henry, swelled the complement. Thus in early August some eleven hundred well-armed fighters were moving against the Arikaras. Pilcher's mounted Sioux pranced in front, wearing white bands of muslin around their heads to enable the whites to distinguish them from the enemy.

Savagely the Arikaras rode out to meet the attacking horsemen. The battle was still indecisive, live Indians swarming in every direction and dead ones dotting the plain, when the whites, marching double time, hurried into view. The Arikaras fled into their villages. The soldiers had no chance to fire because of the intervening Sioux, who now set about trying to taunt the enemy into coming back into the open and fighting like braves. One Sioux of the Grizzly Bear clan, snorting and growling like the totem of his group, crawled on hands and feet to an Arikara corpse and with his teeth tore out mouthfuls of flesh from the dead body. Other bodies were hacked to pieces and the dismembered parts dragged mockingly about on cords. One chief offered the consummate insult of having his wife pound with a club on an Arikara corpse in full sight of the outraged town. And still the enemy, though screaming with fury, could not be enticed into the open. Unfortunately the whites did nothing to help. Leavenworth, quite justifiably impressed by the villages' stockades, ordered his men to hold back any assault until the artillery arrived via boat.

The next morning West Point-trained William Vanderburgh of the Missouri Fur Company and Lieutenant Morris of the military began a bombardment with a little cannon. Although Chief Gray Eyes and a small number of other Arikaras were killed, the besieged villagers soon learned to lie flat and let the round shot plump over their heads into the easily repaired mud huts. Meanwhile the Sioux had withdrawn and were amusing themselves by pilfering the Arikara cornfields. Seeing that artillery was ineffective, Leavenworth ordered a charge, called it off, discussed "sapping and mining." After hearing Pilcher's report that the temperamental Sioux could not be relied on to support a siege, he let matters dwindle off to inconclusiveness. Bored with the whole thing, the Indian allies stole thirteen horses and mules from the whites and left.

Finally the Arikaras came out, begging for pity. Leavenworth, prompted by an odd fear that the disgruntled Sioux might swing over to the side of the enemy, consented to talk terms. His demands were lenient: the restitution of property

destroyed or taken during the attack on Ashley, promises of
future good behavior, and the surrender of hostages. When
the peace pipe reached Pilcher, however, he refused to smoke.
Walking wildly back and forth, he stormed that the punishment was not adequate. Later, professing to think Leavenworth in danger, Pilcher, Vanderburgh, and one or two other
men opened fire on the red emissaries. The Arikaras fired back,
nicking Pilcher on the neck, but before serious bloodshed resulted the melee was broken up. Uneasy night fell on a pandemonium of wails from the women in the village, shrieks from
the men, the din of drums, howling of dogs, braying of livestock, and the eerie *whoo-whoo* of owls floating above the
stench of death.

So alarmed were the Indians by Pilcher's anger and by the
shooting that the next morning the treaty had to be renegoti-
ated. The Arikaras then professed inability to replace more
than a fraction of Ashley's property. Suspecting that the stall
was false, the trappers and Colonel Leavenworth's own officers
recommended an immediate attack. In his report Leavenworth
says that for the good of his reputation he too wanted to fight,
but for the good of his country he decided against it: excessive
punishment would only breed hostility among the Indians, who
had already been humbled enough. He ordered that the
Arikaras be given another twenty-four hours in which to comply. Pilcher was furious. So was Captain Bennet Riley; denied
permission to lead the charge, he stormed that he "had been
laying at garison at Council Bluffs for 8 or 10 years [hardly;
the garrison was less than four years old] doeing nothing but
eating pumpkins and now a small chance for promotion oc-
cured and it was denied him."

Perhaps the Arikaras were merely tricky; perhaps they really
could not replace Ashley's goods and dreaded the consequences. Anyhow, while the whites slept that night, the
Indians abandoned their villages, and efforts to overtake them
for further parleys proved unavailing. On August 15, amid
ugly recriminations, the embarrassed attackers started back to
their respective camps. Although Leavenworth ordered that
the villages be unmolested, he was scarcely out of sight when
Angus McDonald and William Gordon led a party of Missouri

Fur Company men into the deserted compounds and set them afire.

Irreparable ill will had been bred. On August 26 Pilcher wrote from Fort Recovery an intemperate "open" letter to the colonel. Published in the *Missouri Republican,* October 15, 1823, it cried at Leavenworth for all the West to read, "You came (to use your own language) to 'open and make good this great road'; instead of which you have, by the imbecility of your conduct and operations, created and left impassable barriers." Leavenworth retorted by blaming the Missouri Fur Company men—excepting Vanderburgh and Moses Carson—with deliberately wrecking the peace talks. (Vanderburgh and Carson immediately wrote Pilcher that they were mortified at having been selected as objects of Leavenworth's praise.) Meanwhile Leavenworth's supporters hurled charges of treachery against the Missouri Fur Company, claiming that Pilcher, on seeing he could not hold the upper river for himself, had tried like a dog in the manger to defeat Leavenworth's campaign so that no trader would be safe.

Whatever the truth may be, the battle certainly did nothing to inspire the Indians with awe of America's armed might. Pilcher was forced to abandon his new Fort Vanderburgh, Henry's party was attacked again on its way back to the Yellowstone, and ten long years later Edwin Denig, noting the high-handed attitude of both the Sioux and Arikaras, criticized Leavenworth for not having struck a summary blow when it was most needed.

Most needed—there was the crux. Had victory been clear-cut, all the tribes would have been impressed, Ashley would have gone to the mountains via the Missouri, and unguessable numbers of other trail blazers, Pilcher included, would have followed him there. As it was, Ashley and Henry dropped back to Fort Kiowa, thirteen miles above Pilcher's Fort Recovery, and halted to think things over. Henry soon returned upstream to further the original plan, but Ashley was not satisfied. Was the river the only route to the mountains? These bloody waters with their incredible labors, their endless battles! Surely there was some other way—across land, perhaps. Hadn't traders far south gone to New Mexico with their goods on horseback? Why couldn't it be done up here?

Ashley had with him a man who knew at least part of the northern plains—Edward Rose, a dangerous mixture of Negro, Cherokee, and white blood, marked by a flaming scar on his forehead and a nose whose tip had been bitten off in some brawl. After accompanying Lisa's first venture to the Bighorn in 1807, Rose had joined the Crow Indians and had become a chieftain among them. In between adventures on the plains, which included such exploits as selling squaw prisoners to lonely-bedded white traders along the Missouri, he had operated with a gang of New Orleans river pirates. Trustworthy, no. But he could find the way to the land of the Crows, where still more geographical information might be obtained. In September 1823, yielding to Ashley's solicitations, Rose agreed to take out a small party to see what could be done. Captain of the group was Jedediah Smith; among those with him were Irish Tom Fitzpatrick, scar-faced Bill Sublette, and lank Jim Clyman, an ex-surveyor who had helped Ashley recruit *voyageurs* in St. Louis's "grog shops and other sinks of degredation." As yet few people had heard of any of these young men, but the growths that resulted from this seedling trip would eventually make their names household words in western America. After bidding them Godspeed, Ashley returned to St. Louis to face his creditors and wait for word. Not for twelve months of suspense would it reach him.

Pilcher had no intention of waiting that long to learn what his rivals were up to. Promptly he sent Charles Keemle and William Gordon, two of the survivors of the Immell-Jones massacre, westward on Jedediah's tracks. Somewhere beyond the Black Hills of South Dakota, the Missouri Fur Company party caught up with their predecessors and wintered either with or near Smith's group in the Crow villages along Wyoming's frozen Wind River. But Pilcher's men lacked the drive of their rivals. River-trained, they did not believe that Ashley's scheme could work without water transport, a conviction that was strengthened by the difficulty both parties had had in obtaining horses.

Smith, Sublette, and Fitzpatrick, on the other hand, were not bound by prior experience to static forts sprinkled conveniently beside the river. Also, their wages and those of their companions would be a share of whatever they could find.

Before winter had relaxed its grip, they were moving again, their eyes ever westward. This time Keemle and Gordon did not follow. Why should they? There was beaver here—Crow beaver, well known throughout the trade for its superior quality. So the Missouri men sat where they were, dickering in the habitual way—until the Crows ended their hospitality by stealing the white men's horses. Afoot, the dispirited adventurers sought the familiar waterways and started down the Bighorn on a long, roundabout boat ride back to Fort Recovery. If Ashley's men wanted this kind of business, they were welcome to it.

That same winter of 1823–24 Charles Bent spent at Fort Recovery. During the icy evenings, while firelight flickered on the log walls of the cramped quarters, he speculated idly with the other traders about what lay westward beyond the ill-known Bighorn Mountains, on and on to the mythical lands of the Rockies. But, like Keemle and Gordon in the field, Charles was river-bound; he saw no particular reason for worrying about Jedediah Smith's novel trip. Besides, there were the immediate concerns of the daily trade to occupy his mind and hands, and his winter passed neck-deep in red strouds and buffalo robes.

It was a successful winter. In April, long before word had come in about Keemle's or Gordon's troubles, he helped load a treasure in peltries aboard two keelboats for transport to St. Louis. With him, sharing the command, were the two "Mc-Donels," one of them the Angus McDonald who had burned the Arikara villages. Also aboard was Jonathan Bean, who in 1836 would wed Mary Bent, now a child of thirteen.

The trip was no more eventful than the usual spring descent of the flooded waters. Occasional undermined sandbanks collapsed with startling thunder; drifting logs threatened; whirlpools growled. Buffalo lumbered off through the ooze, were pursued and killed; clouds of water birds whirled away from the boats with shrill protest, then settled back again. Now and again mounted Indians watched curiously from the shores, perhaps sending an experimental shot winging across the silt-choked current.

On the cool morning of May 13, as a south wind drifted across the greening prairies, the two craft put ashore at the government's Fort Atkinson. Dutifully the clerks, as leaders of the tiny flotilla, paid their respects to the officer of the day, Captain John Gantt, who had served in the Arikara campaign and who would one day forsake the army for the western mountains. Then Charles crossed to the sutler's store to visit James Kennerly and his wife, relatives of General William Clark. With characteristic graciousness he left the young couple as choice a gift as he could, "ten buffalow tongues of good quality."

Near Fort Atkinson, at the post of the French traders, where J. P. Cabanné was now in charge, another newsworthy expedition was shaping; and Charles may well have picked up word of it. A hundred men were soon to be assembled there for an overland trip to the southern Rockies and the mountains of New Mexico. Its leader was to be Sylvestre Pratte, son of Bernard Pratte. So now another of the Missouri Fur Company's sternest competitors was going to strike out overland! Thoughts of Jedediah Smith and of Keemle and Gordon must have flickered into Charles's mind. And there was food for more thought farther down the river at Franklin, Missouri, where a young man named Ceran St. Vrain was helping outfit the first big wagon caravan for Santa Fe.

But home was too near now for other considerations to intrude for long. On the keelboats went, Charles unaware that his little brother Edward was even then dying. Grief met him at his home in St. Louis, but it could not completely quench the welcome interlude of city clothes and city talk, nor the excitement of the horde of young brothers and sisters hanging onto his coattails and calling for stories. William was especially importunate. Small in stature like Charles, but tough as an oak knot, he begged to be allowed to go back up the river with his elder brother. But he was only fifteen, and with the memory of Edward's death still fresh in their minds, it is not likely that his parents acceded.

In midsummer the brief visit ended, and Charles started back upstream with the annual supply boats. By the middle of September he had most probably reached the company's headquarters fort at Council Bluffs. There he certainly heard with sinking heart that Pilcher was in financial straits again and was pulling his trading parties off the upper river, where the Indians were still raising hob. Incidental to this, Charles learned also of Keemle's and Gordon's failure. So much, the men of the Missouri Fur Company thought, for horseback trading to the Rockies.

The notion soon received startling contradiction. Jim Clyman of Jedediah Smith's exploring party came tottering into Fort Atkinson, a ragged skeleton with tales of wonder. Eighty days before, six hundred miles away on the sources of the North Platte, Indians had cut Jim off from his companions. With only eleven bullets in his gun he had started afoot for civilization. Miraculously he had made it. Nor were miracles finished. Ten days later Tom Fitzpatrick and two other men of the same party came dragging into the fort in even worse shape than Clyman had been.[2] Almost their first call was for an express to go to Ashley. They had found a new route to the West—the Southern Pass—and had gone through it to a successful hunt in the valley of the Green River, on the watersheds of the Pacific. The express dispatched, Fitzpatrick sold to Lucien Fontenelle the furs he had cached the previous July high on the Platte, and with mules supplied by Fontenelle returned to fetch back the pelts.[3]

An untouched source of beaver west of the mountains! The electrifying word reached Ashley about the time that he heard from his partner, Andrew Henry. Henry's men had also succeeded in crossing the Continental Divide, but their luck had been poor and Henry had had enough bloodshed and trouble. He dropped out of the partnership, and General Ashley, on his own now, hastily organized a supply caravan which reached Fort Atkinson on October 21.

The operation he intended was the logical culmination of earlier experiments on the headwaters of the Missouri, a full break with the established pattern of trading from fixed posts and the flowering of the land-supplied, free-trapper system which would revolutionize the industry. How much of this upheaval was foreseen by the traders along the river cannot be guessed. Probably not much. Habit patterns are hard to break; and although Fontenelle's purchase of Fitzpatrick's beaver may have prompted Pilcher to further speculation about the mountain trade, he was unable to act on those speculations. Complete collapse faced the Missouri Fur Company. Here at

Council Bluffs, Astor's American Fur Company and the St. Louis French had forever shattered what Manuel Lisa had fondly considered his company's private preserve. Farther up the river, Bernard Pratte's traders had cut so deeply into the commerce with the Sioux that Pilcher could not raise enough capital for the company to hang onto bravely named Fort Recovery. The post was abandoned and inevitably the Missouri Fur Company went into bankruptcy.

Though the company was gone, its chief lieutenants were not. The river was their life and they refused to quit it. Somehow—the details are not known—five of them effected a new organization known as Pilcher & Company. In addition to Joshua Pilcher, the partners were Andrew Drips, Lucien Fontenelle, William Vanderburgh—and Charles Bent, only twenty-five years old when the group's license was issued by William Clark on July 4, 1825. One reason for Charles's elevation was undoubtedly his proven ability. Another may have been St. Louis connections which enabled him to raise part of the $7712.82 capital with which the new company set about trying to re-establish the old pattern.[4]

Back up the river they went, to the vicinity of the French company's Fort Kiowa (also called Fort Lookout), not far from the already crumbling remains of Fort Recovery. According to the not entirely reliable testimony of James Beckwourth, a mulatto *engagé* who had gone west with Ashley's supply caravan, Pilcher was at Fort Kiowa—and perhaps Charles Bent was with him—when the general appeared at the post in the summer of 1825 with an enormous load of furs. Off beyond the mountains, in the valley of the Green, Ashley had reaped a fortune. Packing the furs on horses, he and fifty of his men, including Beckwourth, had crossed South Pass and then, to save expensive horse transport, had swung northeast to the Bighorn River. There they had built boats. While half the company returned to the mountains, the other half floated downstream until they met General Atkinson, who had just led a military expedition up the Missouri to complete Leavenworth's job of awing the Indians. Under the soldiers' protection Ashley passed the Arikara villages unmolested, and at Fort Kiowa both parties, civilian and military, stopped to spend the night.[5]

During the festive evening, while Ashley's mountain men got

drunk on whiskey smuggled from the soldiers' rations, Pilcher
and perhaps Charles Bent must have felt envy. A fortune! And
they had seen every move in the gambit. If only Keemle and
Gordon had not let Jedediah Smith's party pull away from
them in the valley of the Wind River. If only . . . But the
world was full of lost chances. Keeping their new company
alive here on the river would demand the full energies of all
five partners. The Rockies would have to wait.

It was probably during this grim stuggle for survival that
young William Bent came up the river and went to work for
his brother.[6]

Although William was nine and a half years younger than
Charles, the two were much alike, so dark of hair and complexion, so fluent in river French and Indian dialects that more
than one later observer would mistake these offshoots of
Massachusetts Puritans for French Canadians. Both were below medium height, Charles five feet seven inches tall according to an 1831 passport to Mexico, and William so slight that
for several years both the Sioux and Cheyenne Indians called
him "Little White Man." Size notwithstanding, the courage
of each became marked, even in a trade where physical bravery was a staple.

They needed bravery. Even more, they needed tenacity to
survive there on the river. Of necessity the partners of Pilcher
& Company worked themselves and their men with the relent-
lessness of desperation. Their summer months were spent as
galley slaves to the loads of cloth, knives, powder, lead, beads,
mirrors, and smuggled whiskey which, during winter, would
be translated into fur and buffalo robes. For the cordeliers (and
for the employers who swore at them, chanted, exhorted,
and on need swung whips) the twisting current was a living,
clawing, never-resting antagonist. Oars the boats had, and
sails, but their main dependence was the long towrope attached to the mast. Daily the voyageurs dragged the heavy
strand ashore, winning each forward inch by wallowing
through mud and thorn-spiked brush, scrambling across bluffs,
stumbling over rocks and tangled driftwood, toiling, so one appalled observer said, "as I have never seen men toil before."
Grizzlies, Indians, snags, and quicksand were normal expect-
ancies. Thunderstorms boomed; insects whined. And under the

blistering sun the mud left by high water dried into golden granules which fierce winds hurled into parched mouths as the tiny men gasped onward beneath the blue, blinding glare of a sky enormous beyond all saying.

The permanent forts were specks in the vast loneliness. Within each log stockade twelve or fifteen men constituted the normal working force. Another two or three hands looked after each temporary post that was set up among the tribes during the trading season. There was little time for idleness. In Pilcher's words, the days were filled with "procuring wood, building houses, sawing planks, building boats, farming" (each fort tried to grow as much garden as conditions and Indians would allow), "running from one post to the other, traveling through the country for the purpose of aiding those who have charge of the goods, collecting furs and peltries, and supplying the Indians." In spite of the gardens, the bulk of the food was obtained either by the fort's own hunters or, more often, by bartering with the Indians for pemmican and dried buffalo meat.

Ostensibly each trade item sold to the savages represented a profit of 200 to 2000 per cent. Actually the net was considerably less. Expenses were astronomical, partly because of the need of carrying excessive numbers of men on the pay roll for the sake of protection. Credit was another drain. The Indians were improvident. When the fall hunting season arrived, the reluctant trader was compelled to outfit his now-destitute customers with enough traps, powder, ball, blankets, strouds, knives, tobacco, and so on, to keep each hunter's entire family going throughout the winter, gauging the amount risked on the uncertain character of the recipient. In return, the Indian was supposed to sell his furs, if any, to the outfitter. No surety existed, however, particularly in the case of bootleg alcohol, which the savages were quick to demand on credit but slow to repay during their hangover miseries. Furthermore, any debt, alcoholic or otherwise, was regarded as without force after a year's time. Added to these difficulties were the matters of fluctuating fur prices (a loan was based on a given number of skins, regardless of what next season's price on those skins might be) and the rigors of British competition. The Indians, canny judges of quality, preferred English beads, vermilion, blue and scarlet strouding, and particularly English blankets, to similar articles of American manufacture. To satisfy demand, United States traders had to import these goods from overseas under a tariff impost of 40–60 per cent, whereas their British rivals got them through Canada duty-free.

In the face of all these handicaps and by means of brazen exploitation, well oiled with alcohol, a few traders did succeed. But for each triumph there was an unguessable number of failures, all accompanied by frightful physical toll. When Congress in 1831 demanded a survey of the fur trade, the Secretary of War collected scores of reports from leading participants and then summed them up: "The whole operation . . . is laborious and dangerous, full of exposures and privations, and leading to premature exhaustion and disability. Few of those engaged in it reach an advanced stage of life, and fewer still preserve an unbroken constitution. The labor is excessive, subsistence scanty and precarious; and the Indians are ever liable to sudden and violent paroxysms of passion, in which they spare neither friend nor foe."

So. A man might kill himself going broke. But beyond that dry pessimism shone the unchained roll of the river, the endless sweep of the plains—the golden glow of the West. Charles Bent, a judge's son, chose the glow, and in choosing committed not only himself but his brother William.

But all his optimism and all his doggedness were not enough. Even the cords of matrimony were helping to tie up the Missouri River as a private package. In 1825 a daughter of Bernard Pratte had married Ramsay Crooks, one of John Jacob Astor's most powerful lieutenants. It seems hardly coincidence, therefore, that in 1827 Astor and the French traders, Pratte and Pierre Chouteau, ceased their war and amalgamated their lower river trade into the American Fur Company's burgeoning Western Department. Next the new combine turned to the upper Missouri and absorbed the Columbia Fur Company, which under Kenneth McKenzie had already made serious inroads into what was left of Pilcher & Company's northern trade. Now the monopoly was complete. Sooner or later the five partners and the other small independent traders on the river would be strangled by that iron grip.

In a frantic hope of raising money through a regular salary,

Charles Bent applied for a position as sub-agent to the Ioway Indians. On March 29, 1827, the appointment became official, a matter of enough personal interest to General William Clark, Superintendent of Indian Affairs, that he passed word of it along to his son Meriwether, a cadet at West Point. Charles, however, was never able to fill the office he had requested. The exigencies of the trade chained him tighter than he had anticipated to the posts he was supervising on the upper river, and a few months later the agency job was given to his future brother-in-law, Jonathan Bean.

Charles had reason to be busy. His company was all but dead now, and as the five partners struggled for salvation they remembered the Rockies. Well and bitterly they knew that within the short space of two years William Ashley had reaped a fortune from the beaver streams of the distant mountains. Eager to foster his political ambitions, Ashley had then, in 1826, sold out to three of the men who had made his success possible—Jedediah Smith, William L. Sublette, and David Jackson. Ashley had also agreed, for a price, to send in to the new company the merchandise it would need at the following year's rendezvous. Early in 1827, accordingly, he dispatched the caravan. With it went a small, wheeled cannon drawn by two mules. Wheels up the Platte Valley, over South Pass! The stamp of the future was ineradicable now; but the men who crowded after the caravan were not looking any farther ahead than tomorrow's balance sheet. The first of the West's many brutal rapings was entering the ruthless stages which would reach full climax during the next few years.

Belatedly Charles and his partners decided to enter the race. Actually, they were four years late; the big chance had been lost in 1823, when Keemle and Gordon had stayed behind Jedediah Smith's party in the land of the Crows. Pilcher & Company must have realized by now the penalty of tardiness; yet once again, in 1827, they moved too slowly. Raising capital may have caused the delay. Anyhow, it was September before the partners gathered together at Council Bluffs forty-five of their best men and one hundred horses loaded with trade goods. All five of the partners accompanied the caravan, and there seems no cogent reason against assuming that young William Bent talked his way into going along.[7] It was the sort of trip to appeal to his adventurous nature, and he was old enough now—eighteen—to hold down a man's job on the trail. In this late season it would be no easy job, as all of them realized.

Knowing that winter was near, the forty-five men rode as fast as their loaded horses could go. Straight across the browning prairies they drove, to the shallow twistings of the crazy Platte. The plains gave way to rounding hills that somehow would become known as the Coasts of Nebraska (that is, the Coasts of the Shallow Water), and then the hills turned into stark bluffs and gaunt buttes monstrously eroded. They were in the land of little rain now, of eye-smarting dust and chapping wind, of pungent sage that smelled like turpentine, of shimmering alkali flats whose blowing grains tormented their skin and fouled their drinking water. Distances were even more tremendous than was apparent, for the dry, crystal air destroyed perspective. And each day the thread of cottonwoods along the river grew more golden, the cold of the lengthening nights more intense. The trip had turned into a headlong race with the early winter of the mountains.

The party did not make it. Snow was falling as the caravan left the North Platte and turned up its tributary, Sweetwater Creek, toward South Pass. As the blizzard lashed and the men struggled to find warmth in one of their overnight camps, Crow Indians caught them with their guard down and, in Pilcher's words, stampeded away "the last of our horses." Unable now to transport their precious trade goods, the glum, chilled men dug a jug-shaped hole in the soggy earth. There they cached the precious bales of merchandise and replaced the turf with scrupulous care, so that chance marauders would not discover the hiding place. Then they wallowed on through deep drifts, crossed the Continental Divide, and toiled downward into the ice-cold valley of the Green.

Consider a circle with a hundred-mile radius. Place its center on the spot where today the boundaries of Wyoming, Utah, and Idaho come together. It is a region of occasional forests and lakes, of many swift streams carving the high, bleak sweep of the limitless plains. Into the inhospitable circle, during the gale-ridden winter of 1827–28, the trappers of three nations poured. Americans under Smith, Jackson, and Sublette were radiating out in every direction from Bear Lake, lying athwart the Utah-Idaho border. Ranging farther north, along Idaho's Portneuf, Snake, and Salmon rivers, were Canadians whom Peter Skene Ogden and his associates had led southeastward from Fort Vancouver. And up through Colorado from the south, up from the Mexican town of Taos, came a motley, hard-luck group led first by Sylvestre Pratte, Bernard's son, and after Sylvestre's death, by Ceran St. Vrain.

It must have been November when Charles and his companions were bucking snow and Indians along the Sweetwater. It was November also when Ceran St. Vrain's party reached the North Platte and had its own bloody brush with savages. From this sprawling river both parties, moving via different routes, crossed the Divide to a miserable winter in the Green.

In the vast, cold-cramped valley, while wolves howled disconsolately, the two groups met.[8] Meeting, the Bents and St. Vrain talked—pure trade talk, beyond doubt, with no recognition of the course of empire. But immanent in it lay a tiny seed that one day would flower more luxuriantly than ever Joshua Pilcher's Missouri Fur Company had. Since this is so, it is perhaps well to look at the trapper just up from Taos, with his euphonious name drawn straight from the highhanded nobility of Louis XVI—Ceran de Hault de Lassus de St. Vrain.

CHAPTER III

THE TRAPPER FROM TAOS

When the United States acquired Louisiana and garrisoned troops at Bellefontaine, fourteen miles above St. Louis, an ex-nobleman named Jacques Marcellin Ceran de Hault de Lassus de St. Vrain opportunely built a brewery nearby. It seems an incongruous occupation. Jacques's father, the Chevalier Pierre Charles de Hault de Lassus de Luzière, had once been a member of the council of the King of France, with a reputed income of thirty thousand crowns a year—until revolution turned the chevalier's world upside down.

At that juncture Joel Barlow and other promoters had come into seething France. They bore with them what purported to be clear title to a great block of American land purchased by the Scioto Company from Rufus Putnam's Ohio Associates. Joel Barlow, author of *The Vision of Columbus* and member of the so-called Hartford Wits, was no more businesslike than poets are reputed to be. Worse, some of his land-selling colleagues were downright dishonest. Many Frenchmen, suspecting this, cried warning. But others saw in Barlow's *"Plan des Achates des compagnies de l'Ohio et du Scioto"* an idyllic newworld haven where they could rebuild their shattered lives. Among them were the fifty-two-year-old Chevalier de Hault de Lassus de Luzière and his wife, the Demoiselle Domitille Joseph, daughter of the one-time Seigneur of Beaufort and Echevin of the city of Bouchain. Raising what money they could, they purchased land from Barlow and in 1790 sailed for America with two of their younger children and four servants. The older children, including Jacques, now twenty, and his elder brother, Charles Auguste, stayed behind.

Some six hundred French emigrants, most of them utterly unfit for frontier life, were heading toward the same goal, the "city" of Gallipolis in southern Ohio. Disaffections cut the number considerably before the remainder reached the great river and with sinking hearts floated past Marietta, named for their queen, Marie Antoinette; past Belpré, where the Bents were building a new home; and on past mile after stern mile of forested wilderness. At Gallipolis they found eighty crude, whitewashed cabins. That was all. The lands that had been represented as ready for cultivation were choked with trees and swamps.

These *émigrés* were city mechanics, city tradesmen, clerks, shopkeepers, a few noblemen—a far different breed from the voyageurs who had wrenched open Canada. Helplessly they watched bad go to worse. Then the Scioto Company, which had sold them the land although possessing only an option on it, went bankrupt. Promptly the Ohio Company reasserted title, and now the colonists found that their investment had bought nothing but toil, sickness, and semi-starvation. In despair some of them purchased their homesteads a second time from the Ohio Company; a few accepted grants from the embarrassed Congress of the United States; others straggled off toward the French settlements around Detroit and Kaskaskia, Illinois.

Utterly ruined even before the final crash came, the chevalier in 1793 left Gallipolis for New Orleans, where his childhood friend, the Baron de Carondelet, was serving as governor of Louisiana. (Spain employed many French to help administer the vast territory she had acquired at the Treaty of Paris, 1763. The same situation prevailed even after Louisiana was secretly returned to Napoleon in 1800: Spain retained *de facto* control, with displaced Frenchmen doing most of the administrative work.) In New Orleans the chevalier obtained land grants along the Mississippi in what is now southeastern Missouri. His plan was to move French settlers there from Gallipolis; to mine lead for the army; to build gristmills and furnish flour to Havana and New Orleans. The new settlement, located a mile below Ste. Genevieve, was to be known as Nouvelle Bourbon, and he was appointed its commandant. But a severe stroke of illness and the apathy of the destitute French at Gallipolis kept the scheme from flowering. In 1797, when Moses Austin visited the spot, Nouvelle Bourbon consisted of twenty small houses clustered around a sugar camp. After listening to memories of the halcyon days in France, Austin reported with dry understatement, "Madame de Luziere did not appear to support the change of situation so well as the Chevalier."

During the same period two of the chevalier's sons, Jacques and Charles Auguste, also came to America—one of them in style. This was Charles, who had escaped from the Revolution to Madrid, where he served as an officer in the guard of the King of Spain, a hotbed of ineffectual royalist intrigue. Rising high in his employers' esteem, the adaptable expatriate was appointed lieutenant governor of Louisiana, assuming office in 1799.

Concerning Jacques, less is known. At some point or other, perhaps before the Revolution, he had served as a junior officer in the French Navy. Perhaps he too saw Spain. Wherever he was, he'd had enough of it by 1795. A disillusioned young man of twenty-five, he fled to his father's settlement at Nouvelle Bourbon. Later he moved to St. Louis, where he was given

various public offices, including command of a swift little royal
galliot on the Mississippi. He met and married Marie Félicité
Dubreuil. Presumably through the influence of his brother he
obtained sizable land grants in southeastern and northeastern
Missouri, and also in the northeastern part of St. Louis County.
Here, at Spanish Lake, he built his home. And here his fourth
child (and third son), Ceran, was born. Ceran St. Vrain. The
surname came about when Jacques Marcellin Ceran de Hault
de Lassus, son of the chevalier, added "de St. Vrain" to his
patronym in order more clearly to distinguish himself from his
brother, the lieutenant governor. What legality the addition
had or from where it derives is uncertain.

Two years after Ceran's birth the fortunes of politics once
again deserted the family. America had bought Louisiana. In
March 1804, with Charles de Lassus officiating, the Spanish
flag came down from the staff in St. Louis, was replaced briefly
by the French tricolor to symbolize that nation's fleeting control, and then was superseded by the Stars and Stripes.[1] The
chevalier was no longer commandant of Nouvelle Bourbon
(two years later he died); Charles was no longer lieutenant
governor. And now beer must support plain Jacques St. Vrain,
his wife Marie, and their growing numbers of children—eventually there would be ten.

There is no telling how well the brewery thrived. In time
Jacques and his partner were advertising their strong beer in
St. Louis at ten dollars a barrel cash or twelve dollars in
produce, their table beer at half those prices. But in 1813 the
establishment burned down, and probably most of Jacques's
resources with it. Other pursuits, notably land speculation,
also failed. He frittered away the land grants, and in 1818,
when his son Ceran was sixteen, he died insolvent.

After Jacques's death his widow seems to have lived with, or
near, her brother-in-law, ex-Lieutenant-Governor Charles de
Lassus, on a farm at St. Charles, not far above the mouth of
the Missouri.[2] But ten children—the youngest, Marcellin, had
been born in 1815—were more than she could care for. Some
of them had to be provided for in foster homes. One was Ceran,
whose future was foreshadowed when he entered the establishment of Indian-trading Bernard Pratte, one-time judicial associate of Judge Silas Bent.

Of Ceran's boyhood nothing is known. Though most of frontier Missouri was illiterate, he evidently had some schooling, for he could write rather barbarous English. (For whatever the fact may imply, it was in English that he wrote as a young man to his French mother and to his French benefactor, a language choice not followed by his brothers Charles and Felix in their personal correspondence.) But most of his education certainly came from the goods counters, the odorous warehouses, the torturous keelboats of Pratte, Cabanné, & Company. Apparently he performed well, for by the spring of 1824, when scarcely twenty-two, he was occupying a position of some responsibility in the firm. As part of his duties he almost certainly visited the fort at Council Bluffs, where Cabanné was already threatening Pilcher, Charles Bent, and their company. That Ceran St. Vrain and Charles Bent met somewhere along the river is not unlikely—if, indeed, they had not already known each other as boys in the tight-knit community of St. Louis.

Circumstances, however, turned Ceran's eyes to the Southwest rather than up the Missouri. After a stumbling start the Mexican trade was booming into prominence.

There had been attempts to reach the northern settlements of New Mexico ever since Charles de Lassus had watched the Stars and Stripes replace the tricolor on the flagstaff in St. Louis. Almost at once William Morrison, a partner of Lisa's in the first version of the Missouri Fur Company, had sent his man, Baptiste La Lande, to Santa Fe with a load of goods. La Lande sold them—and then neglected to return with the profits. Lisa, too, in conjunction with a harem-maintaining Portuguese named Jacques Clamorgan, in 1807 dispatched a now almost forgotten expedition to the New Mexico capital. After that, however, troubles began. Spain, stubbornly clinging to the theory of economic monopoly that was killing her empire, slammed the door on foreign trade. Despite its official nature, Pike's exploring party was arrested, searched, and hustled out of the country for straying, accidentally or otherwise, onto Mexican land. McLanahan's traders, aroused by Pike's account, were imprisoned for taking goods across the border. So, too, were Robert McKnight's ten men, who stayed in various jails for nine years. Auguste Chouteau and Jules de Mun suffered forty-eight days of confinement and the confiscation of thirty thousand dollars' worth of furs, which, so they insisted without avail, had been taken north of the Arkansas River in American territory.

But Spain's dead fingers were slipping. Iturbide's revolution cut them off, and on September 27, 1821, Mexico became an independent nation. When the news reached Santa Fe, the officials of the remote province all but fell over their own feet in a hurry to show the new bosses that their hearts approved the change. Since the old government had scowled on Americans, the new, as a necessary corollary, would reverse the policy. The prisoners of the Robert McKnight party were released, and new groups were hastily welcomed.

By good fortune there were no less than three parties of Americans hovering near the border to be invited in and wildly welcomed as symbols of the new liberty[3]—which on January 6, 1822, was more formally symbolized, according to Governor Malgares's purring letter to Iturbide, by a double-file parade of all the little town's excited citizens. Leading the procession was a "charming tot dressed as an angel, with a sword in her right hand," and behind her two more angels, richly adorned, carrying between them a baby dressed as a virgin, "representing Independence and the Purity of our Cause." Eager to produce still further tokens of devotion to the Cause, Malgares appealed for ideas to one of the visiting Americans, Thomas James, who obliged by helping splice pine trees into an appropriate liberty pole seventy feet tall. Salutes of artillery were fired, the Tesuque Indians performed a dance in the plaza, and then the freedom-conscious populace took over in ways which the pole-raising Mr. James considered somewhat less than appropriate: "No Italian carnival ever exceeded this celebration in thoughtlessness, vice, and licentiousness of every description."

Of the three parties of traders who capitalized on their welcome, the five men headed by William Becknell of Franklin, Missouri, were the first to reach home. Becknell was on fire. The enormous profits realized on his first dab of goods were but a harbinger. Procuring three wagons, he at once set about organizing a return trip—and incidentally inspired a neighbor of Boone's Lick, Colonel Benjamin Cooper, to hurry out ahead of him. The next fall two of Robert McKnight's prison companions, Samuel Chambers and James Baird, also recruited a party and with a big pack train of goods happily started back to the land where they had spent more than nine years in jail.[4]

Between them the Becknell and Chambers groups gave bitter forecast of the troubles that would plague later wayfarers along the Santa Fe Trail. Osage Indians might have ended Becknell's venturing almost before it began had not A. P. Chouteau ridden to the rescue. And then, when the group tried to blaze a short cut across the arid plains between the Arkansas and Cimarron rivers, thirst caught them. Futilely they killed their dogs and cut off the ears of their mules to drink the hot blood; the nauseous expedient closed their throats still tighter. Only by killing a buffalo that had been to water and draining the fluid from its stomach were they able to survive. A few months later the Baird-Chambers caravan had its turn with misfortune. A furious blizzard drove them for shelter to a wooded island in the Arkansas River, near the present town of Cimarron, Kansas. For three months of murderous cold they starved there. Nearly every horse and mule they owned perished. When spring came, they cached their goods in great earthen pits and made their way to Taos for fresh pack animals. For years afterward the gaping holes, known as the "Caches," gave mute warning of what could—and often did—happen along the way to Mexico.

In spite of all this, each of the 1822 parties reached Santa Fe and dazzling profits. New dreams caught the nation. In Baltimore, *Niles' Weekly Register*, reporting the new trade with more enthusiasm than geographical knowledge, predicted prematurely on November 23, 1822, "It is very possible that citizens of St. Louis on the Mississippi may eat fresh salmon from the waters of the Columbia! for distance seems annihilated by science and the spirit of adventure."

Ceran St. Vrain met William Becknell at least as early as the spring of 1824. Having returned the previous fall from racking his three wagons across the plains, Becknell was now determined, in company with M. M. Marmaduke, Augustus Storrs, and "other gentlemen of intelligence," to wheel a full-sized caravan across the plains—twenty dearborns, two wagons, two carts, and a small cannon. Wagons would do away with the devilish twice-a-day packing and unpacking of mules, and the company could handle enough hardware, cutlery, hats, shirting, French calicoes, German linens, cotton shawls and hose to make a real killing. Thirty thousand dollars' worth of goods was the group's order, and Bernard Pratte supplied at least part of it. Ceran St. Vrain helped supervise the sweaty work of delivering the merchandise to the traders and also acted as their agent in hiring some of the eighty-one men who accompanied the caravan.

One of the hands whom he fished out of a frontier grogshop was a wild, whooping, black-eyed, red-faced, bull-shouldered youth with the undistinguished name of Tom Smith. Call them symbols—those wheels rolling westward with American goods; that hung-over rowdy who in a few years, after a crippling accident, would be known fearfully throughout the northern provinces of Mexico as *El Cojo,* The Lame. Peg-leg Smith— he would steal more mules from California than any other man alive. The Mexicans could never stop him. Nor could they stop the penetration that started on May 16, 1824, when the West's first full-scale wagon caravan crossed the Missouri on Hardman's ferry, six miles above Franklin, and, having elected Alexander Le Grande their captain, belabored the reluctant mules on toward the dimly understood savannas of the future.[5] Shortly thereafter Charles Bent floated past the ferry on his way to St. Louis from the upper river. He must have heard of the caravan and quite probably talked to some of its outfitters— perhaps even to Ceran St. Vrain.

Possibly Ceran went with the party to Santa Fe. If so, he returned to Franklin in September with the remnants of it. Becknell and Marmaduke stayed in New Mexico; the others reached Missouri with $180,000 in gold and silver and $10,000 in furs—a 600 per cent gross profit on a few cartloads of Missouri hardware and dry goods. Or, as seems more likely, Ceran may have stayed on the river during the summer, attending to his duties for Bernard Pratte. At any event, he was in Missouri in November 1824, restless and eager to cut loose on his own.

The mountains of New Mexico were an itch under his skin. Only three months before, his good friend and almost foster brother, Sylvestre Pratte, had struck westward from Cabanné's post at Council Bluffs with one hundred and twelve men and three hundred mules. Though most of the mules were loaded with trade goods, the principal objective of the group was the forbidden beaver ground of New Mexico. Unless Ceran was in Santa Fe, he probably helped outfit the party and with envy in his heart watched the ill-broken cavalcade stream away from the fort under pluming canopies of dust.[6]

By fall he could no longer contain himself. Forming a partnership with one François Guerin, he talked Bernard Pratte into furnishing them goods on credit, and in November, with the threat of winter sharp in their faces, they started for New Mexico. It was a rough trip. What happened no one knows. Perhaps they stopped to trade with Indians; more probably they trapped; quite likely they were weather-bound for a time. Whatever caused the delay, they used up five months covering the same ground that Sylvestre Pratte's much larger party had recently crossed in less than half that time. Reporting later to Bernard Pratte, Ceran mentioned the journey only as "long and trublesome." For the dead of a Rocky Mountain winter, the description is undoubtedly an understatement.

It was about March 20, 1825, when the storm-whipped group crossed the Sangre de Cristo Mountains and saw below them, between the pine-covered foothills and the canyoned Rio Grande, the fertile valley of Taos. Dotting the fields were various mud-built hamlets, the most imposing of which was the blank-walled, multistoried pueblo of the Indians. Civilized Indians, they were called, though no New Mexican ever quite forgot that in 1680 they had arisen in fury to drive their conquerors from the land. Though subdued again and ostensibly converted to Catholicism, they remained potentially dangerous —as Ceran St. Vrain and Charles Bent in time would have reason to know.

Of the various Mexican settlements in the valley, the largest was San Fernandez (the name Taos was not attached to the village until later). Even to trail-weary newcomers it could not have looked prepossessing. All the buildings, great and small alike, were constructed of adobe, dull-looking indeed until the indolent inhabitants bestirred themselves to apply fresh coats of gypsum. Prosperous citizens shut themselves off behind high walls, allowing ingress to their courtyards by a single gate large enough to admit a carriage. The more numerous single-room houses of the poor had such niggardly doors that even a short man had to stoop to enter. Windows, if any, were mere portholes, either glassless or covered with translucent mica. Roofs were of earth. During rainy weather they leaked mud or even collapsed: at least one sleeping American trader in New Mexico, some years after St. Vrain's arrival, was killed by a falling, water-sodden ceiling.

In front of each house stood a cup-shaped mud oven in which the women baked excellent white bread and also a hard, porous sweet biscuit called *biscoche,* tasty with coffee and val-ued as a trade article with the Indians. The women, too, car-ried water to the houses from springs outside the town, balanc-ing the earthen jars with Biblical stateliness on their heads or shoulders. Picturesque they were, especially to a lonely trap-per. Their *rebozos* lay captivatingly about dusky hair and brown faces; bright skirts were cut short above tiny feet and shapely ankles; and low-necked *camisas* emphasized the grace of their supple backs and outthrust breasts. Picturesque, yes—but water carried that way was not wasted on personal cleanliness. Nor was wood, tediously packed from the foot-hills in tower-of-Pisa loads on creeping donkeys, wasted out-side the kitchen. On winter days men found warmth by wrap-ping themselves in vivid serapes and congregating on the sunny side of some house, where they napped, gossiped, smoked in-numerable cornhusk cigarettes, and picked lice off one another. Now and then a loose burro wandered by, long ears waggling as it munched on bones or other refuse thrown carelessly from the houses.

Articulate visitors (most of them Protestant and afflicted with the prevalent American priggishness of the time) found New Mexico benighted and contemptible. Gambling, they clucked, was a ruinous passion with both sexes. Chastity was sadly missing in the women; profanity served everyone as the common language. Justice could be marketed; taxes were crushing; the dangers from raiding Indians appalling. Fear and compulsion, they scoffed, were the only stimulants. Yet what else, one is tempted to ask, could stimulate where a laborer earned from two to six dollars a month while paying up to fifty cents a pound for coffee, a dollar a yard for calico—and where slavery for debt was not abolished until long after the American conquest?

Ceran St. Vrain was French, with all the adaptability of the French voyageurs who, more than any other race, wrested open the trans-Mississippi West. He was also Catholic. Hence he was not so likely to be captious about what some of his Anglo-Saxon contemporaries disdained as degradation, bigotry, and superstition. Yet even he, after having been in Taos for four months, wrote his mother gloomily that it was a "miserable place."

Nonetheless, he stayed.

The valley was a natural spot for trade. Long before any Americans had seen it, merchants had come from all directions to its annual summer fairs—strange merchants with exotic goods. From Chihauhua, hundreds of miles to the south, toiled wooden-wheeled *carretas* laden with shawls, dainty slippers, mantillas, and El Paso wine. Down from the northern mountains, leading muleloads of furs, beads, knives, and forbidden guns, rode the ubiquitous French. Native New Mexicans arrived with turquoise and bits of silver. Navajos carried blankets and pottery from their western deserts; Utes brought captive Indians to sell as slaves; arrogant Comanches from the plains offered buffalo robes for such horses as they could not steal. Capricious customers, these Indians—especially the Comanches. They traded one day, murdered the next. In 1760, for example, they had massacred numbers of their sometime hosts and had raced off with fifty women and children. Among the prisoners was a handsome girl named Villaponde. After amusing a Comanche chief for a time, she was bartered off to another tribe and eventually sold to a French trader named Lajoie, who took her as his wife to St. Louis, where she lived to a renowned old age, a familiar figure throughout the city. Ceran St. Vrain most probably knew her; certainly he remembered her story as he rode with Guerin and their gaunt men through the biting March wind to the town from which she had been abducted.

By the time the partners arrived, the annual fairs had been supplanted by diminutive stores. Already interlopers from the East were gaining control—Carlos Beaubien from Canada, for one. Missourians were already beginning to set up gristmills and a distillery that would soon turn a large portion of the valley's wheat crop into a blazing liquor notorious throughout the mountains as Taos Lightning. But more important for St. Vrain's purposes were the trappers who were making Taos their outfitting point.

Much has been written of the merchandising trade with New Mexico, but little of the Taos trappers, partly because those far-ranging, often illiterate and secretive men were not given to leaving records. Also, the southern Rockies were the land of individual effort. Small bands of independent trappers flitted ghostlike, dodging Indians, from creek to creek, with no St. Louis board of directors watching behind them, no suspicious clerks checking their balance columns with crabbed fingers, as was the case along the Missouri and in the cold valley of the upper Green. Could the full story be reconstructed, it might show that men from Taos had reached the brackish waters of the Great Salt Lake before Jim Bridger led a group of men to it down the Bear River. Certain it is that the sources of the Arkansas were known and trapped while men in the North were still stubbornly clinging to the Missouri as the only practicable route to the mountains. Certain, too, is the fact that trappers from these pioneer parties had illegally wintered in Taos years before Mexican independence opened the way to free intercourse.

With the coming of independence, trappers scattered through the land. Many of them, in order to get west, had hidden steel traps in their "possible sacks" and had signed on with the dry-goods caravans as mule-skinners. Only a few of their names have trickled down to us. Most notable is Ewing Young, who had come to Santa Fe with the second Becknell party in hopes of setting up a gunpowder manufactory. Failing because of lack of niter, he turned to fur. Within less than two years he and William Wolfskill, Isaac Slover, Joe Walker, Antoine Robidoux, and a shadowy legion of others had ravished the little streams behind Taos and Santa Fe. Now their eyes turned farther afield. In February 1824, Young, Wolfskill, and Slover led a party northwest to the tortuous, sand-choked San Juan. They were back by the time the Storrs-Marmaduke caravan arrived—the caravan which Ceran St. Vrain had helped equip in Missouri. If Ceran was along, which is unlikely but not impossible, it may have been the sight of Young's beaver that set him on edge.

It set others on edge. Men jumped the caravan to breach the unknown. In various groups sixty or seventy would-be trappers followed Young's faint trail toward the San Juan, each dreaming, according to Augustus Storrs, of at least a hundred and fifty pounds of beaver worth four dollars the pound. Among them, but working independently, was rowdy young Tom Smith. After leaving the caravan, Tom went to Taos, had himself a drunk, then threw in with three other trappers and three Mexicans and began zigzagging through the rugged San Juan Mountains of Colorado toward Utah. About the same time, Bill Huddart and fourteen men made their way to the Colorado River, where they found Antoine Robidoux already in the field; and undoubtedly other forgotten parties were poking and prying through the hitherto trackless valleys.

Alarmed by the surging exploitation, which had not been foreseen during the ready welcome extended hardware merchants, the Mexican Government in mid-1824 issued a decree banning the taking of beaver in the northern provinces. Arriving in the fall, Sylvestre Pratte's party, including Sylvester Pattie and his son James Pattie, side-stepped the interdict by opportunely rescuing from Comanches the beautiful daughter of a former governor, in return for which they were granted special licenses and frayed out in all directions. A small number of them, led by the Patties, took a significant turn southwest toward the headwaters of the Gila, in the great plateau that sprawls across the present New Mexico-Arizona border. Other Americans, with no high-placed maidens to succor, simply ignored the official decree, knowing that the undermanned army of New Mexico was powerless to enforce it. Etienne Provost and his partner LeClerc edged toward Salt Lake. William Becknell himself, outfitting in Santa Cruz, a village north of Santa Fe, piously wrote Governor Baca that although there were trappers in Taos he had "nothing to Dew with them"— and then blandly led his ten hunters northwest to a freezing winter along the Green.

Another item generally overlooked in tales of the Southwest is that these roving bands needed entrepreneurs to equip them and to absorb the furs they brought back. Matters were different in the big-business ranges of the North, where company men operated out of company forts or, later on, were supplied at an annual rendezvous by the company pack trains of William Ashley, Bill Sublette, Robert Campbell, and others, who reaped fortunes in the carrying trade. Down in the South, however, huge concerns like the Rocky Mountain and American Fur companies never took hold, partly because Mexican law precluded organized raping of such magnitude. This left the independent trapper with no means of getting his relatively small catch back to St. Louis, unless he wished to join one of the homeward-bound mercantile caravans. Many did. But most were too itchy of foot and too uncomfortable in civilized society to make a regular practice of the trip, so long as they could find in New Mexico some storekeeper who would buy their furs for the price of a debauch and then grubstake them for the next season's hunt.

Outfitting these wandering trappers seems to have been part of St. Vrain's and Guerin's purpose. In addition, they hoped to trade with the natives. Unfortunately, however, they reached Taos at an unpropitious time. The scattered hunters had not yet returned from the mountains, and the local residents were too poor to do more than yearn over their offerings. Currency was almost nonexistent. Mexican policy, based on the old Spanish custom of "favorable trade balances," drained hard money from the northern provinces, with the result that almost all commerce had to be conducted by barter. By the time Ceran and his men rode hopefully in from the frozen mountains, earlier parties had skimmed off the placer gold and beaver skins, and no new supplies had yet appeared. Mules were available, to be sure, and desirable in the Missouri market, but scarcity had shot their prices sky-high. For thirty-seven bleak days the partners twirled their thumbs, selling, as Ceran wrote Bernard Pratte, "verry fue goods and goods is at a verry reduced price at present."

Thirty-seven profitless days in a place like Taos were enough for Guerin. He sold out to St. Vrain for "one hundred dollars and 3 mulls [mules]," plus Ceran's assumption of his part of the debt due Pratte, and in disgust headed for home. At the same time Ceran sent back to Pratte the proceeds of the venture so far, "24 of bever" and one mule. Definitely the golden promises of Mexico were losing their luster. Taking note of reports from disillusioned hopefuls like Guerin, *Niles' Weekly Register* reported the 1825 trade as completely overdone: "Mexican villages are filled with goods from Missouri and there is no money to purchase them with."

In spite of the dreary prospects, Ceran was too stubborn to admit failure by returning home. Out here he was his own man; back in Missouri he would be just one more employee on the teeming river. Besides, there was a sustaining sanguineness in him. Confidently he wrote Pratte, "I am in hopes that when the hunters come in from there hunt that I will Sell out to Provoe & Leclere. If I doe not succeed to sel out to them and other hunters, my intention is to by up articles that will Sout the markit of Sonora to purchess mulls, but I Shall first doe all I can to Mak arrangement with Provoe & Leclere to furnish them with goods."[7] The resoluteness paid off, though perhaps not with Provost. (Etienne and LeClerc were having troubles of their own; shortly before Ceran wrote the letter, Indians fell on the Provost-LeClerc party near Salt Lake and killed seven of their men.) But someone showed up. In July, St. Brain triumphantly wrote his mother, "I have Sold the greater part of my goods at a verry good profite."

Moreover, another prospect was in the making. Tom Smith had reappeared with tales of a marvelous journey. His little group had found its way perhaps as far as central Utah's Sevier Valley, certainly as far as the fantastically eroded plateaus where the Green and Grand (now the upper Colorado) rivers pour together in a thunderous gorge. There the group had divided. With only a man named Maurice LeDuc for company, Smith somehow wormed a way south among those desolate buttes, across those vast red abysses where the Rockies tumble wildly down into the wastes of southeastern Utah. Utes stole five of their horses and sent the frightened pair fleeing across the San Juan to refuge with the Navajos. From there they had gone deep into Arizona along the Little Colorado River and at last, after visiting several days among the Moqui Indians, had circled back to Taos. Even today great stretches of the land, as stark as any in America, are almost impenetrable; but parts of it Tom Smith wanted to see again, particularly the towering peaks and the forested ridges of Colorado's San Juan

Mountains. He found seven men willing to follow him on a spring hunt along the Dolores, San Miguel, and San Juan rivers, and then asked Ceran for a stake. Ceran agreed. As he wrote his mother, if the venture succeeded, "it will be moste proffitable for me."[8]

While waiting for these different seeds to take root, Ceran may have done some trapping on his own. Or he may have loafed around Taos, a sturdy, convivial figure with a glossy black beard on his round face and wide-set dark eyes that were quick to crinkle in humor—or, occasionally, to flare in temper. He was learning the language. Perhaps he was even learning to like the native food.

It took learning. The principal dish was *atole*, a thin gruel made by stirring flour into boiling milk or water and so universally used that it was called *el café de los Mexicanos*. Equally universal were *tortillas*, made from lye-soaked corn ground Indian-wise on a stone, fried thin over the open fireplaces on a metal sheet called a *comal*, and used as an edible spoon for dipping up chile and *frijoles*. Meat was rare except when buffalo hunters returned from their dangerous forays into the land of the Comanches. In fact, food of all kinds was so scarce that prickly-pear cactus, neither palatable nor wholesome, was often resorted to. Whatever the dish, it was turned fiery with red peppers. When James Pattie and his father arrived in Taos with Sylvestre Pratte in October 1824, they could not down the first meal offered them; and how much of the hangdog yet violently excitable dispositions of the New Mexicans was due to their eating habits might make interesting speculation for some dietary study. The one gastronomic oasis in the Southwest's stomach-blistering deserts seems to have been a thick, aromatic chocolate which only the rich could afford and which early visitors recalled with extravagant affection.

Obviously so wretched a people could not be happy. Yet they were, a fact that affronted some of the loftier visitors from the East. New Mexican clothing might be poor, but it was gay clothing, garishly decorated. Amusements might be crude, but they were wholehearted, especially the fandangos. Any occasion was excuse enough for a fandango—a native feast day, the return of buffalo hunters, the arrival of foreign trappers, or even no occasion at all. The ringing of church bells summoned the entire village to an open court or to the *sala* of some larger house. (Cynics suggest that hosts were not wanting because their self-invited guests brought gifts and an abundance of the pale, mule-strong *aguardiente* of which both sexes freely partook.) Off the women's cheeks came the startling daubs of flour paste and the scarlet stains of *alegría* juice with which they protected their complexions during the workaday week. Their lustrous hair was plaited into long braids; their vanity sparkled with earrings, necklaces, heavy bracelets, massive crosses of gold and silver—jewelry for which more than one señorita or señora's husband had willingly accepted years of slavery. The orchestra consisted of one or more stringed instruments, perhaps an Indian drum, some singers, and the enthusiastic handclapping of both dancers and spectators.

Everyone attended. Albert Pike, future Confederate general and author of "Dixie," who came to Taos with Charles Bent in 1831, watched with disapproval "well-dressed women (they call them ladies) harlots, priests, thieves, half-breed Indians—all spinning together in the waltz. Here a filthy, ragged fellow with half a shirt, a pair of leather breeches and long dirty woolen stockings and Apache moccasins was hanging round with the pretty wife of Pedro Vigil; and there the priest was dancing with La Altragarcia, who paid her husband a regular sum to keep out of the way and so lived with an American." As for the dance steps (and other observers than Pike noted a familiarity of position that would have been frowned on in the States), if a trapper found himself unable to follow the intricate convolutions, he could substitute energy for skill and no one minded—except perhaps the jealous Mexican males.

The Americans had a way of taking over. Their obtrusiveness sprang partly from a self-confidence that found anything different from itself a challenge, partly from an exuberant young love of violence for violence's own gaudy sake. Deliberately they appropriated the prettiest girls and let the bereft men make of it what they would. The more the trappers were outnumbered, the more arrogantly they felt compelled to act. Inevitably many a Taos fandango ended in uproar and bloodshed. A knife would flash in the hands of an infuriated Mexican; an answering war whoop would bring the buckskin-clad trappers clustering back to back in the center of the room. There would be swirls of fists, screams from the women—then a timely evacuation by the mountain men and a fruitless chasing hither and yon by the local police. Seldom did the natives come out other than second-best. Yet to the Mexican males perhaps even a broken head seemed preferable to the sort of ending described by James Pattie after one New Year's fandango: "When the ball broke up, it seemed expected of us, that we should each escort a lady home, in whose company we passed the night, and we none of us brought charges of severity against our fair companions."

There were other portents of American absorption during Ceran's first summer in Taos, though naturally no one at the time noticed them as such. On July 4, 1825, a Dr. Willard made an American flag, drummed up a following of fellow citizens (Ceran, perhaps, included), and boisterously paraded around the plaza. Undoubtedly the brown, half-naked children scampered at their heels while the Mexicans and Pueblo Indians smiled in amusement. Perhaps there was a fandango afterward. If any philosopher in his cups felt inclined to moralize—and it is unlikely that any did—he probably would have coined phrases about the ties between nations. Why not? Hadn't a Mexican military expedition already crossed the plains to confer with Agent O'Fallon at Council Bluffs and make a treaty with the Pawnees in order to facilitate travel between the two countries?

In October more concrete evidence of the future appeared in the form of an official U. S. Government road-making expedition led by George Sibley and J. C. Brown, chief surveyor. This group also had signed a treaty of passage with the Indians, in their case the Osages. Interpreter for the pact-makers was long, stooped, redheaded, querulous William Shirley Williams. Old Bill—crazy as a coot, as independent and indefatigable as a wild jackass, more at home in the savage lands than the Indians themselves. Old Bill knew the Osages. He had traded and trapped among them for years, including the period when Juliannah Bent and her new husband, Lilburn Boggs, had lived at the agency post.

Bill had a friend in Taos, Paul Baillo, who likewise had

lived among the Osages, where both men had taken Indian wives now conveniently forgotten. Apparently in 1824 Baillo had left for Taos, possibly with Ceran St. Vrain. Perhaps already, and certainly by 1826, Baillo entered into partnership with Ceran, equipping trappers. It was Baillo who went out to meet Sibley's road markers (no one would ever pay much attention to the dirt mounds they had set up along the Arkansas for the wind to blow down) and led them across the pass into Taos Valley. Later he helped supply Sibley with food and forage during the fearful winter when measles swept the villages and children died like flies.

Sibley did not like San Fernandez. He took one nose-lifted look at its squalor and hurried outside town to rent two houses where the party could "live in our own way, for I . . . cannot easily reconcile myself to the living of the poor inhabitants here."[9] For Old Bill Williams, though, it was a good winter. Probably he had a rousing reunion with Baillo, and then, on November 14, he wheedled permission from Sibley to go trapping. In February he was back, laden with pelts. Two weeks later, after a howling gambling spree, he was dead broke— and happy. For what else than a spree did a man endure cold, toil, and fatigue? As for returning to his lackluster job with Sibley, nothing doing. Bill enjoyed the country out here and proposed to stay.

It was undoubtedly through Paul Baillo that St. Vrain first met Bill Williams, but whether the meeting occurred during the winter or the following summer cannot be said. Though in July Ceran had indicated to his mother that he might remain in Taos throughout the winter, there is evidence that he changed his mind and returned to Missouri on a quick cold-weather trip, probably for supplies. He was on the way back by May 1826 and had as a companion one of the great trailmakers of the West, Ewing Young, who also had made a hurried trip to the States for equipment.[10] Out of their talks came plans for the most widespread trapping expeditions yet conducted within the increasingly unfriendly borders of Mexico.

One can scarcely visualize what the long trip across the plains from Missouri was like. Records are scanty, particularly of the early days before wagons had grown monstrous in size, before patterns had shaken down into a standardized routine. The only satisfactory account is the little-known diary of Alphonso Wetmore, who crossed the plains in the early summer of 1828.[11] A few excerpts may give shape to the trail.

May 28. Reached the Blue Spring, the rendezvous of the Mexican traders, in season to attend to the election of officers; *ourself* elected captain of the host. "There may be some honor in it," as the deacon remarked on his own promotion, "but not much profit."

June 1 (Sunday) a tempest just as we were ready to set forward, the mules disengaged from the wagons in haste, and *double reefs* taken in the wagon covers. All hands employed in detaining the mules, who are disposed to take leave of *nos amigos*. At 9 o'clock under way, reached the Big Blue, all our spades in requisition to make the descent into the river practicable; the wagons eased down the bank by 20 men at a trail rope. . . . My Mexican servant furnished with a gun, proud as Franklin with his whistle. This character is today mounted on the *verbatim* copy of Rosinante, caparisoned in character.

June 6 . . . reached Elk creek, where we discovered the corpse of a wagon which had been left by the preceding caravan. O Temperance! O Ditch Water! Made 16 miles.

June 15th. Under way at 8 o'clock; made eight grievous miles [through mud]; a mutinous disposition repressed by bandit logic.

June 17th . . . extreme thirst . . .

June 19th . . . The antelope is a subject of speculation this morning, and one of our hunters has been occupied in decoying, with a flag, one of these nimble-footed animals. . . . We find buffalo grass today; and fresh traces of buffalo remind us of the approaching marrow-bone feasts that are to change the monotony of our meals. No fuel; made 18 miles.

June 21st. A little before day light, the mules made an abortive attempt to raise a stampido; half an hour later an alarm was created by a shot from one of the sentinels, and the cry of Indians aroused the whole camp. Killed and wounded, blank; alarmed, none.

June 22. At 5 o'clock A.M., after moving quietly forward three hours and a half, a team in the rear of the caravan took fright, and, in an instant, more than twenty were coursing over the prairie at Olympic speed . . . (June 24) . . . It is one of the foibles of mule teams, that, after they have travelled four or five hundred miles, and when it is supposed they are about to tire, to take fright from a profile view of their shadows, and run like the antelope of the plain.

June 25th. Reached the Arkansas at 4 o'clock, encamped and replenished our shot pouches. "Keep your eyes skinned now," said the old trapper. "We are now entering upon the most dangerous section of the trace, the war ground of Panis [Pawnees], Osages, and Kansas". . . . One of our hunters has filled the camp with smiles and buffalo meat: the first two buffalo which we discovered are slain.

July 1. During the day's march, the caravan bachi [the captain, Wetmore himself] shot his own mule through the head in a buffalo chase.

July 3rd. Our march today is through a plane and rolling country, surrounded with buffalo. A herd of these attempted to break through our column of teams.

July 6. Doubled teams and passed the river [the Arkansas]. Here we take on water for three days' march.

July 18 . . . Our camp is on the bank of a muddy pool, around which one hundred and sixty mules are pressing; a puddle is reserved for ourselves, which is deemed a luxury, after having drank unto pickling the salt waters of the Semiron [Cimarron River].

July 22. Sent a party of 8 men ahead to-day to make arrangements for payments of duties.

July 24. We were today gratified with a full view of the Rocky mountains, ranging along to the right. When our Mexican, from a hill top, caught a distant view of the mountain, he lept for joy, discharged his carabine, and exclaimed, "La luz de mis ojos, mi casa, mi alma, light of my eyes, my house, my love."

July 29 [Having reached a grove of pines], the whole
caravan of merchants and muleteers resolved themselves
into a committee of tar makers and long before night
every tar bucket was filled.

July 31st. Waiting the return of the advance party.
The Mexicans spinning rope yarn out of the foretops of
buffalo. . . .

If there was rope spinning on the 1826 caravan, St. Vrain
and Young did not see it, but hurried ahead to make arrangements for handling their wares. Presumably St. Vrain went
to Taos, but by August he was in Santa Fe, where an unusual
number of trappers were congregated, buying horses, repairing guns, restitching saddles—and no doubt finding time to
consider the monte games, the aguardiente, the smiles of the
girls, and the glowering looks of the Mexican men.

It was a notable gathering. Old Bill Williams and Tom
Smith were on hand. Alexander Branch appeared—perhaps the
same Branch or a relative of the Branch who had been with
Jedediah Smith and Tom Fitzpatrick at the opening of South
Pass two years before. Huge-muscled Milton Sublette showed
up. (Milton's brother, Bill Sublette, had also been at South
Pass with Fitzpatrick; far to the north by the blue reaches
of the Great Salt Lake, Bill was even now completing arrange-
ments with Jedediah Smith and David Jackson to buy out
Ashley's fur company.) Inevitably there were French about
Santa Fe, too, both voyageurs and their leaders—Sylvestre
Pratte, with whom Ceran had been in contact during the past
year and a half; and Michel Robidoux, of a clan almost as
ubiquitous as the Sublettes.

On August 29 Ceran and Old Bill Williams applied to Governor Narbona for passports to take thirty-five men on a "trading" trip to Sonora. The clerk had trouble with Ceran's name.
He put it down as Ceran Sambrano, in which form—or as
Seberiano Sambran—it would officially stay during the rest of
Ceran's years in New Mexico, until finally he adopted it himself in his dealings with the Mexicans. Ewing Young also procured a trade passport, his name being Hispanicized to Joaquin
Joon. And so it went, until Narbona became suspicious. A
quick check showed that the extraordinary numbers of south-

bound "traders" were carrying no goods and had been asking many questions about the streams. But each group had vanished immediately on obtaining its passport, and now it was too late to overhaul them. Ruefully Narbona wrote to the governor of Sonora, warning him to be on the *qui vive* for illegal trappers.

In October, Narbona's surmise received blunt confirmation from James Baird—the same Baird who had been imprisoned with Robert McKnight, had gone to the States after his release, and almost immediately had returned to New Mexico with Samuel Chambers on the winter-plagued trip of 1822–23. He had then secured Mexican citizenship by counting his jail term toward the requisite number of years residence. Baird's occupation was trapping as well as trading, and he was inclined to regard the Mogollon Mountains, where the Gila and San Francisco Rivers rise, as his private domain. With uneasiness he had watched the Patties move in with some of Pratte's men a year before and establish what amounted to a headquarters camp at the Santa Rita copper mines, which the elder Pattie was temporarily leasing. This new influx in 1826 roused Baird to write an angry letter to the prefect of El Paso:

> . . . I have learned that with scandal and contempt for the Mexican nation a hundred-odd Anglo-Americans have introduced themselves in a body to hunt beaver in the possessions of this state and that of Sonora to which the Río Gila belongs, and with such arrogance and haughtiness that they have openly said that in spite of the Mexicans, they will hunt beaver wherever they please. . . . I beg that your Excellency may make such provisions as you may deem proper, to the end that the national laws may be respected and that foreigners may be confined to the limits which the same laws permit them, and that we Mexicans [!] may peacefully profit by the goods with which the merciful God has been pleased to enrich our soil. . . .

Two months later James Baird died peacefully in El Paso. Meanwhile the troops he had been instrumental in stirring up were having no luck whatsoever in chasing down the trappers. Apparently there were five independent groups of them, some

of whom were reported variously at such scattered spots as
Santa Rita, Zuñi, Tucson, and the Apache country north of
the Gila. Others were so deep in the wilderness that no reports
at all came in concerning them.[12]

The leader of each band held an unenviable position. He
was chosen because his known qualities seemed to assure success. If he failed, no matter what the circumstances, the blame
would be written as his in every trappers' camp in the mountains. Jim Beckwourth, no shrinking violet, found it advisable
at about this same time to decline leadership of a band up
north on the grounds of youth. Yet Ceran St. Vrain, only a
little past his twenty-fourth birthday, was one of those who
led a crew south down the Rio Grande. Sharing the command
with him rode Bill Williams, twelve or more years his senior.

They were an oddly assorted pair: Ceran square-hewn,
black-headed, convivial; Old Bill gaunt, red-whiskered, and
solitary, mumbling to himself as he jogged along, his feet
thrust into wooden stirrups buckled so short that they thrust
his bony knees toward his slumped, pointed chin and his sharp,
pock-marked face. Every literate visitor to the West who saw
Bill described him with awe—all muscle and sinew, ambitious
to kill more deer and catch more beaver than any man about
him. Indestructible. At some time during this early period,
possibly on this very trip, a galloping horse tumbled downhill
with him, rolling over and over on his lank body while the
steel traps he carried over his shoulders hammered a vicious
tattoo on his hide. His companions picked him up half dead,
set him on his horse, and winked among themselves. This evening Old Bill would not beat them to the best beaver sets.
But he did.

Down the desolate valley of the Rio Grande—El Rio del
Norte—the pair led their men, probably as far as the mud
hamlet of Socorro. Then they swung west toward the Mogol-
lons, toward wide, grassy meadows and curling streams, toward cool aspen forests and the tall shafts of ponderosa pine.
After that . . . nothing is known. Not of St. Vrain; nor of
John Roles, who led another group of eighteen; nor of Sylvestre Pratte's party, who started with Michel Robidoux's
group but left them short of the Santa Rita mines and went

their own way. It is known, however, that Michel blundered into disaster.

One midnight on the desert, near the site of present Phoenix, Papagos Indians lulled Robidoux's fraternizing Frenchmen into complacence, then slaughtered all but three—James Pattie, whom the party had picked up at the copper mines; a voyageur who had crept out of the doomed camp with the mistrustful Pattie; and Robidoux himself, badly wounded. The next night, by sheerest luck, the destitute trio spotted campfires in the distance and so stumbled onto a party of twenty-nine trappers led by Ewing Young.[13]

It was a hard-bitten group, including at least two of Ceran St. Vrain's good friends, boisterous Tom Smith and big Milton Sublette. Grimly they listened to Robidoux's tale. What followed sprang from the same stern trappers' code that Joshua Pilcher had in vain tried to impress on Leavenworth at the Arikara villages: let no Indian depredation go unpunished! The next day the Papagos were lured into ambush and 110 of them killed, according to Pattie. The trappers then looted and burned the village and buried the dismembered remains of the Frenchmen. This done, business could be resumed.

It was extensive business. During the next months, despite Indian skirmishes that reduced Young's personnel by one third, different groups of the party trapped most of the major streams of Arizona, reached the Colorado River below the present California-Arizona border, reunited, and painfully followed the Grand Canyon northward toward Utah. They apparently reached American territory by crossing the Rockies either in Colorado or Wyoming and, if Pattie's geography is not confused, penetrated as far as the headwaters of the Columbia. The elapsed time does not seem to allow that many miles. It was a tremendous journey, nonetheless, before the gaunt men finally swung southward along the eastern base of the Rockies, fighting Indians and trapping the Platte and Arkansas as they went. In the spring of 1827 they gained Taos, but not the success they had labored for.[14]

Governor Narbona was out. In his place came crafty Manuel Armijo, intent on making a reputation for himself. For the first time since Mexican independence Americans were finding it wise to walk with circumspection.

Warned in Taos of the new state of affairs, Young secreted the company's twenty thousand dollars' worth of pelts in a desert-surrounded house belonging to one Cabeza de Baca, "a miserable fellow." The news leaked out. Armijo dispatched a squad of soldiers to seize the contraband. Baca was killed while resisting, and the furs were impounded in Santa Fe.

Some weeks later, while lawsuits over ownership were in process, Young won Armijo's permission for three men to take the furs to the plaza and beat out the dust and moths. Big Milton Sublette wandered by. With Young's connivance he suddenly seized two bundles marked with his own brand (a considerable feat if the "bundles" were the standard hundred-pound bales) and bolted into the house where he and other Americans were batching. After a furious uproar, during which troops and trappers hung hair-trigger on the edge of a pitched battle, the house was searched; but by that time Sublette and the furs had disappeared in the direction of Taos. Armijo now turned on Young, charging him with being Sublette's accomplice. By training loaded cannon on the house in which Ewing was barricaded, he persuaded the American to surrender. After that, a long-winded trial dragged out into anticlimax. Young apparently suffered no penalties, but neither did he or his men recover their furs.

Up in Taos, Sylvestre Pratte and his clerk, Ceran St. Vrain, reconsidered their plans for a fall hunt in the light of the governor's new hostility. New Mexico's streams were now not only overtrapped but officially dangerous. Northward, however, lay the high, peak-bordered valley of the upper Arkansas, marking the boundary between Mexico and America. By keeping to the mountains east of the river, their trappers could stay in friendly territory. Then, once beyond the vaguely identified forty-second parallel, Mexico's northern limit, they could swing west across the Divide into the vast reaches of the Green. Competition would be ferocious there from trappers working down from Canada and out from the Missouri; but probably Pratte and St. Vrain did not realize how ferocious it really loomed. In September they assembled their men, at least twenty-four of them, mostly French, but including also Old Bill Williams, Tom Smith, Alexander Branch, and Milton Sublette.

High on the mountains the aspens were showing yellow when they started out, Pratte in the lead, Ceran as clerk, or second-in-command. At about the same time, Charles Bent and his partners were saddling up to ride westward on a last-gasp effort to save their foundering company.

CHAPTER IV

MOUNTAIN WINTER

Lying along a north-south axis in central Colorado are four huge, mountain-cupped bowls. Grass-filled, softly rolling, almost treeless, they derive from their circling whale-backed peaks an austerity that makes the word "lovely" too gentle for describing them. The southernmost is called San Luis Valley; the others by the mountain name of park—North, Middle, and South parks, the latter the famed Bayou Salade of the fur hunters.

It was in North Park, called Park Kyack by the French fur trappers, that Sylvestre Pratte fell seriously ill in the fall of 1827, perhaps of the same disease that had troubled him previously in Santa Fe. After an anxious time of rude nursing, he died. Solemnly the trappers buried him and then took counsel among themselves. The result was a serious decision for Pratte's clerk and second-in-command.

The men were uneasy about their status. They had been out for some time now, had already caught about three hundred pounds of beaver. Some among them thought that in order to secure their wages they should seize the fur, together with personal property belonging to Sylvestre—his rifle, pistol, gloves, the cloth he had brought along for Indian trade, his seventeen traps, seven mules, eight horses. Then what? Should the party disintegrate into competitive groups, trying to beat each other to the best streams during what remained of the fall season? Should they then return to Taos and face the win-

ter with whatever they had managed to garner and hope for a
new *bourgeois* to sign them up in the spring?

Wiser heads said no. It was better to stick together.

But suppose the winter-long effort ended in failure? Who,
then, would guarantee their wages?

They turned to Ceran, a veteran of twenty-five. Would he
assume command—and responsibility?

The safe thing was to refuse. Keeping the men out through
the winter would cost six or seven thousand dollars in wages.
If the trip failed to net that amount, what was to prevent
the St. Louis executors of Pratte's estate from disclaiming the
account on the grounds that the expedition could have, and
should have, disbanded after Sylvestre's death? Yet Ceran returned the trust which his men held for him. They were good
hunters. They would stick to their jobs and the venture might
pull through. He decided to take the chance.[1]

Trapping as they went, the party moved along the sources
of the North Platte toward the present Colorado-Wyoming
border. By now they were shaken into trail shape. On a pack
horse each man carried the furs he had caught, his buffalo bed
robes, and a heavy skin sack (which could be boiled and eaten
in emergency) loaded with six five-pound traps costing from
twelve to sixteen dollars in St. Louis, the traps' three-pound
chains, spare springs, and tools for repair. On the rider's own
mount was a "possible sack" bulky with powder, galena lead,
flints, tobacco, sewing materials, occasionally a book or two,
and dressed deerskin for replacing his moccasins, which wore
out rapidly. About his person hung a skinning knife, whet-
stone, pipe case, awl holder, perhaps a tomahawk, scent con-
tainer, bullet pouch, and a powder carrier of black buffalo
horn scraped as thin as isinglass and stoppered with a wooden
plug. Always in hand was his gun—generally a heavy one,
eleven to twelve pounds, with a forty-inch barrel, .50-caliber,
firing a half-ounce slug with impact enough to drop a grizzly
or buffalo. A man loved his gun, named it (Ceran called his
Silver Heels), and had it rebored again and again to repair
damage from water and dust, until it looked as huge as a tunnel. His wiping stick was carried in the bore and served, in
addition to its intended function, as a rest on which the hunter
could lean the ponderous muzzle when he knelt to take aim.

In spite of affection for the gun, however, the men were not above using bows and arrows; the weapons conserved ammunition, gave no telltale report, and in the sightless night could be aimed by hunch better than a rifle.

Down to his shoulders hung the hunter's long hair, covered with a felt hat or perhaps the hood of a capote. He liked wool clothing, for it would not shrink as it dried and wake him, when he dozed beside the fire, by agonizingly squeezing his limbs. But wool soon wore out, and he then clad himself in leather, burdensomely heavy to wear, fringed on the seams with the familiar thongs which were partly decorative but mostly utilitarian, to let rain drip off the garment rather than soak in, and to furnish material for mending. Further waterproofing was added by wiping butcher and eating knives on the garments until they were black and shiny with grease. Upper garments might be of the pull-over type or cut like a coat, the buttonless edges folded over and cinched into place with a belt. No underclothing was worn, just a breechclout. "Trousers" were often nothing more than Indian-style, thigh-length leggings, the lower parts perhaps made of non-shrinkable strips of blanket. In extreme cold a Hudson's Bay blanket or a buffalo robe was draped Indian-wise over the entire costume.

Much of the hunter's life was spent in water. In the evening twilight he waded cautiously upstream, searching out good sets for his traps. These he placed under the icy water in the beaver's natural runway, chaining each trap in such fashion that the caught animal would be drowned before it could reach land and gnaw off its paw. Over each set he bent a twig baited with evil-smelling castoreum. The next dawn he examined his line, often having to reach deep to retrieve his prey, skinned the corpses, and packed the hides back to camp. There they were "grained" (the clinging bits of flesh removed) on slant-topped wooden blocks and then stretched on oval willow frames to dry, a process sometimes hastened by burning punky wood in a pit beneath them. In big-company brigades the handling of the skins was the work of the camp tenders; free trappers did it themselves. In either case there was little leisure. A thirty-man company could skim the cream off a circle of considerable radius during a single night, and therefore camp sites were moved every day or so.

When setting their traps the men split into twos or threes. Some individualists worked singly and jealously—Old Bill Williams for one, and evidently Tom Smith also, at least on Ceran's 1827–28 expedition. Indians found this habit an invitation to attack from ambush, and St. Vrain's party had already had a skirmish or two along the North Platte. A frontier maxim rightly held that the best Indian fighter was the one who avoided the most battles. Ceran was worried. When Tom Smith kept brazenly exposing himself, the captain rode out to the stream one day to tell him for God's sake to quit taking so many chances. As they were arguing about it, a discharge came from the brush—a gun, according to some accounts; an arrow, according to others. Probably it was a gun, because whatever struck Tom just below the knee had power enough to break both the leg bones.

Ceran flopped down to meet a charge, but the shot had been a typical skulking strike from ambush with no follow-up. He looked for Tom. The man had tried to jump to his rifle leaning against a nearby tree, but his leg had caved in. Now he was writhing on the ground.

They got him back to camp, choked down some of his cursing with a bolt of Taos Lightning, and cut away the legging. Splintered ends of the bones protruded through the flesh. The men glanced sideways at each other. They had seen enough mangled beaver limbs to know that Tom's lower leg would never be any good again. So had Tom.

"Cut it off," he said.

Amputating a beaver's leg and a man's are two different things. The group stood there hang-handed. Tom roared for Basil, the cook, to bring him a sharp knife. Reluctantly it was produced, and with his own hands Tom began slicing at the bloody flesh. His snarls brought the watchers hopping out of their trance for such accessories as they had—water, horsehair or perhaps buffalo sinews for ligatures, a tourniquet, more whiskey. The bone was a problem. Some stories have it that the camp possessed a keyhole saw which was pressed into service; others say that teeth were filed into a knife blade. But perhaps, if both tibia and fibula were shattered badly enough, no saw was necessary. At any rate, before the job was completed, Tom slid toward unconsciousness. Milton Sublette took the knife and finished.

There had been preparations to stop the gush of blood by searing the stump with a hot iron. But the sight of the glowing bar had made Tom bellow protest. Well, they thought, it wouldn't matter much what they did. Humor him along. Abandoning the projected searing, they tied up the arteries as well as they could, wrapped the stump in a dirty shirt, and swaddled Tom in a buffalo robe. After promising not to abandon him until they were sure he was dead (as young Jim Bridger, green to the trade, had abandoned Old Hugh Glass after Hugh was mangled by a grizzly), they went on about their work. Poor old Tom. He was as strident as a bull elk, as obstreperous a drunk as ever had cleaned out a Taos fandango. But he was a gone beaver now.

The weather was icy, the night a knife-edged glitter under the frozen stars. The cold seeped into Tom's bed. Perhaps that was what coagulated the blood. When Ceran and big Milton Sublette came the next morning to look at his corpse, the bleeding had ceased and Tom was perky enough to curse them soundly. Amazed, they stayed in camp another day, waiting for him to get his dying over with. When he strengthened instead, they stitched him up in a wrapper and a sugar-loaf hat made from red flannel trade cloth. Then they slung a litter tandem between two horses and loaded him in. Ceran appointed two men as his special attendants, and on they went. After all, business was business.[2]

They turned west from the North Platte across the Park Mountains, their horses floundering in the soft, still snow as they searched for openings through thick forests of spruce and among some of the most gigantic aspen trees on the continent. The rough going grew rougher when they dropped down through dense scrub oak into the narrow valley of the Little Snake, aptly named from its looping progress along the present Colorado-Wyoming border. The willows were thick, the hillsides rocky. In sleety weather the litter horses lost footing. Down the bank they rolled. Out of the tangle flew Smith, to land sitting in an ice-scummed pool. His nurses yelled for help. This time he was killed for certain. But no, there he sat in his red wrapper, his red hat askew and dripping as he bawled out his opinion of matters in general. The men began to laugh, and gradually Tom did too.

Leaving the Little Snake where it swung south toward the huge canyon of the Yampa, the party struck across southern Wyoming into the valley of the Green. There winter caught them—cruel, merciless, snow-heaped, the most rigorous, St. Vrain later wrote Bernard Pratte, that he had ever experienced. Either now or perhaps a little earlier Tom discovered that the bone ends left protruding by his shrinking flesh were loose. He had Sublette pull them out with a bullet mold used as pincers. Further cure was applied by a band of Ute Indians who moved in to share winter quarters with the trappers. Men, women, children—the whole howling, chanting, singing lot— chewed up roots and spat them on the stump. Obviously it was the proper remedy, for the flesh healed, and as Tom lay snugly in one of the lodges he began whittling out a wooden substitute. From now on he would be Peg-leg Smith, growing in time beyond the cramped confines of reality into a myth of a nation's youth. Youth propping itself against frontier bars, unstrapping a wooden leg, and with its very symbol of defeat joyously pounding its assailants into submission. Youth picking up, one summer in the desert, gold nuggets whose source could never be located again, and by the failure preserving the dream that took men west—everyman's dream of a lost Peg-leg mine, never quite found and so never quite pinching down and growing thin with truth. Tomorrow, always tomorrow, it would be there, gloriously waiting.

About the time that St. Vrain's party was lugging Tom Smith down the Little Snake, Charles Bent, his partners, and their horseless men were wallowing through South Pass, much of their hope for the future buried with their cached goods back on the Sweetwater. In the pass itself they noted with cold comfort that "the snow was deep, but the ascent and descent easy, being a depression in the mountains to such a degree that a carriage would cross without the least difficulty" —if they'd had a carriage. Unless Pilcher meant to except mules when he reported that Indians had stolen "the last of our horses," the men were carrying on their own backs an irreducible minimum of equipment, and their circumstances wcre even more desperate than their leader's terse account indicates.

Somehow they reached the Green. The land was strange, huge, and unfamiliar. Yet Charles had learned along the Missouri to pick a winter camp site with scrupulous care. The party would want a place against a south-sloping bluff or on the lee side of rocks which would turn storms and reflect the sun. They would make sure that wood and water were nearby and that their stock, if any, could find slopes where the wind would blow the grass clear of snow. Perhaps they built little shanties of cottonwood logs. Timber lacking, they may have contented themselves with deer and buffalo hides battened down over a frame of poles, the front ends left open to the fire. They would build racks high enough for storing beaver tails, buffalo hump ribs, and haunches of venison out of the reach of predators. Other racks would be erected over fire pits so that surplus meat, sliced thin and scored, could be smoked and dried into jerky. It is possible that Indians shared the quarters with them, as was the case with St. Vrain's brigade, for we know that sometime during the winter Pilcher secured from a band of Snakes horses to replace those that had been stolen.

Time did not lie heavy. There were clothes to mend with awls for needles and sinews for thread, and fur-lined moccasins to make—unless a man could pick up a squaw to attend to these domestic matters for him. He ate when he was hungry, slept when he was tired, regardless of the hour. A pot of herb-flavored meat boiled continuously on the fire, and also one of tea or coffee so long as such luxuries lasted. *Boudins* (intestines filled with minced tenderloin) sizzled on wooden spits; marrow bones roasted; tongues steamed in the coals. It was a greasy, all-meat diet, perhaps seasoned with a dash of gunpowder, and was supposed to "make a man shed rain like an otter and stand cold like a polar bear."

Endless yarns were spun, not just for entertainment but for the sharing of knowledge; there, in what mountain man Osborne Russell called Rocky Mountain College, young Bill Bent picked up bits of professional lore that would serve him well in the years to come. (Not all the education was pragmatic, however; Joe Meek learned to read from copies of

Shakespeare and the Bible in a winter camp and later named a half-breed daughter Helen Mar after a heroine in Jane Porter's *Scottish Chiefs*.) Hunting was a necessity, of course, and often possible only by means of improvised snowshoes. When there was stock, it required continual care. When streams froze tight, water holes had to be chopped for them (animals suffered more from thirst than from hunger during mountain winters); and when the grass was covered too deep for pawing, cottonwood branches had to be cut. Both horses and mules fared well on the juicy bark, though too much of it reputedly caused hair to fall out; and it was said that a winter camp's location could be recognized for years afterward by the numbers of peeled, whitened sticks lying about.

Blizzards did not roar endlessly. During clear, sparkling days there was much movement. As forage and game became depleted, the men searched out a fresh camp site. Hunters would spy the tracks or fires of another outfit and go over for a visit. Wandering Indians, insatiably curious, would roam from camp to camp, spreading news as they went. The whites also ranged far. Over on Idaho's Portneuf River, Peter Skene Ogden noted in his journal that on December 20, 1827, two Americans, probably from Smith's, Sublette's and Jackson's company, dropped by with word of Ogden's associates. A few days later more American trappers, these led by Samuel Tulloch, came by the Portneuf. When Tulloch wanted to buy snowshoes from Ogden, the Britisher refused lest the Americans use them to go to a camp near the Great Salt Lake and return with trappers and whiskey.

A terrible winter, Ogden says again and again. January and February were particularly bad. Ogden's American visitors failed repeatedly to reach Bear Lake; Ogden himself was unable to contact his associates. Yet there was travel, for somehow word reached Ogden, duly noted in his journal for Thursday, January 24, that "the Americans are in three different places starving, no Buffalo in that quarter This year, and were reduced to eat their Horses and dogs." In February men came in with reports of Indian skirmishes and rifled caches, and Robert Campbell's Americans were out with dog sleds—Indian-trained dogs almost certainly.

Ceran St. Vrain kept no journal to show movements on the

Creen that winter. Neither did Charles Bent. Yet there may have been as much traffic as existed along the Portneuf; and when Bent got back to Missouri he told J. P. Cabanné of Sylvestre Pratte's death. Charles, of course, may have picked up the word at the Bear Lake rendezvous during the following summer, but it is not illogical to guess that he got it straight from Ceran himself. And if their parties met, as seems likely, they certainly talked not only of deaths but of other things —of the old cabbages and the new kings of the trade, of Charles's company withering on the Missouri, and of New Mexico, where Ceran had done well.

With the coming of spring, the Pilcher partnership received its final blow. Having obtained horses from Snake Indians, one of the partners went back to the Sweetwater to retrieve the cached merchandise. The partner is not named. Drips, Fontenelle, Vanderburgh—or Charles Bent? Whoever it was discovered in dismay that seeping water had ruined most of the goods. Glumly the remnants were taken to the summer rendezvous at Bear Lake, where the mildewed pile looked picayune indeed compared to the fat offerings of Smith, Jackson, and Sublette.

So much for that last, lorn hope. Few of the company men had the heart to keep on trying. Not after seeing the powerful brigades of Jedediah Smith's company; not after realizing the extent of the Hudson's Bay Company's determination to keep its grip locked on the northern part of the region. Enough was enough. Only nine of Pilcher's original forty-five men agreed to stay with him as he moved northwestward toward Oregon. (Later on one of these men was killed by Indians and the others joined David Jackson in the Kutenai country. Pilcher himself wandered on through the Cascades to the Pacific, back through Canada to Missouri—and to a belated job with the American Fur Company, the rival which Lisa had once dismissed in scorn.) The hunters remaining behind simply scattered, some going home, some being swallowed into the brigades of their competitors or setting themselves up as free trappers. In those bleak circumstances, not knowing which way to turn next, Charles must have recalled more than once the things he had heard of the New Mexico trade.

Meanwhile Ceran St. Vrain's New Mexicans had likewise found only mediocre trapping. Worried perhaps by the thought of how Bernard Pratte would react to the poor showing, Ceran decided not to reduce profits still more by waiting to sell his pelts for cheap mountain prices at the Bear Lake rendezvous. In late April he headed his men eastward, intending to go to St. Louis. Along the way he changed his mind. The cause, so he and his engagés later declared at Taos, was a large war party of Indians whose traces the brigade intersected on the Platte. Outnumbered and short of ammunition, the group concluded that wisdom dictated a retreat to Taos.[3]

There is a certain convenience in the reasoning. Those men were used to dodging Indians when they wished, and it may be that the threat served mostly to make the green fields of Taos look still greener. After all, the town was by now home to many of them, and Ceran could write Sylvestre's father about the misfortunes rather than tell Bernard face to face. Whatever their real motives, they swung abruptly south and, following along the tawny base of the Colorado foothills, reached Taos on May 23, 1828.

There Ceran sold 1636 pounds of beaver for $5708.50. This was less than the pelts would have brought in St. Louis, and even when Sylvestre Pratte's personal property was tossed into the pot, the gross returns came to only $6393.75. This money Ceran disbursed to his men with meticulous honesty, drawing on some of his own share of the proceeds in order to complete the payments due them. When the returns reached Bernard Pratte, his clerks toted up the columns and found that the "expenses made for going for biver" reached $6915.41½. Thus one amputated leg and a rough winter had resulted in a net loss of more than $500. There was trouble about it. Pratte sent agents to Taos to check up. Their testimony, however, evidently convinced the company that Ceran had acted properly if not profitably. His stewardship was honored and he received the full $1910.02½ due him for approximately nine months' labor. Munificent enough. The salary of a top-ranking trader on the Missouri was $1000 a year, and the average laborer there earned $130 for a "wintering"—that is, for ten to eleven months' service.[4]

Soon Ceran was restless again. The meager returns and hard work of trapping were losing their charms, however, and when he fell in with two traders bound for Old Mexico, he decided to test the kindlier climes to the south. On September 30, 1828, he applied for and was granted, in spite of his spurious application in 1826, a passport to Chihuahua and Sonora. On the same day similar passports were granted to David Waldo, newly arrived from the East with the 1828 caravans, and to Richard Campbell, veteran trapper and New Mexico familiar.

They were a stout pair. Waldo was St. Vrain's age, twenty-six, and back in Missouri he had been sheriff of wild Gasconade County before reaching his twentieth birthday. Thereafter he had held an astonishing sequence of jobs for one so young—county clerk, county treasurer, justice of the peace, postmaster—all incidental to furthering a medical education whose first steps he had financed by cutting down a quantity of pine trees, lashing them into a raft, and floating them to St. Louis, where he had sold them for $500. In 1827 he had begun practice as a doctor, only to interrupt his own career the following year by a summer "vacation" trip that landed him in Taos. There he met St. Vrain and Richard Campbell.

Richard Campbell (no relation, apparently, of William Sublette's partner, Robert Campbell) had come to New Mexico at least as early as 1825 and since then had roamed even further than Ceran had. In 1827 Campbell seems to have traveled to San Diego with a group of Mexican traders, perhaps the first trip from Santa Fe across the fearful deserts of California to the Pacific Coast.[5] Later, in early 1828, Campbell and his associate, Ewing Young, had found it expedient, in view of previous difficulties with the government, to take out Mexican citizenship, a step which both St. Vrain and Waldo would soon duplicate. Possibly Campbell had also accompanied the 1828 expedition which Young had sent to the Gila and which had been soundly thrashed by the Apaches. Now Richard was back, looking for money to winter on.

Waldo was loaded with goods, and the other two bought up more from the 1828 caravans, for already American merchants were learning that it was possible to bounce their complaining wagons another 550 miles south and still undersell Mexican traders working in from the Gulf. It was a harsh trip, however: endless red tape about permits, a multiplicity of taxes, and then a monotonous jolting down the Rio Grande, in-

cluding one waterless *jornada* where Apaches habitually lay
in wait and once wiped out an entire party of American trappers. At El Paso there was the relief of pleasant farms and
good wines, but more exasperation from the hidebound customs officials. After that came Los Medanos, a horse-killing
series of sand hills so steep that goods had to be unloaded
from the wagons and portaged across on pack strings.

At least Chihuahua looked more like a city than Santa Fe
did. From afar wayfarers could descry the great stone arches
of the aqueduct and the soaring towers of the cathedral, whose
statue-embellished façade convinced many a Missouri back-
woodsman that it must be one of the world's great structures.
Smelting furnaces spewed smoke, the streets had some semblance of plan, and the better houses were actually built of
stone rather than of adobe. But traders had their troubles. If
they did not sell wholesale (as most tried to do), their retailing
brought in basketfuls of small-denomination copper coins that
had no worth outside the province and could be exchanged
for gold and silver only with the greatest inconvenience. Female shoppers, who strolled through the rented stores in the
evening by candlelight, created embarrassing problems with
their penchant for pilfering; and since Americans were not so-
cially acceptable, the only resorts after a tedious day were the
gambling houses and taverns.

In Chihuahua the trio may have traded their goods for a
drove of mules or for specie, which they sewed in leather hides.
After a thorough wetting the hides would shrink and com-
press the load into a solid, easily packed mass. Perhaps all
three rode the 550 miles back to Santa Fe together. Or perhaps Waldo left them in Chihuahua and, like many another
American, made his way to the coast, where he caught a ship
bound for New Orleans. However he traveled, he was in Missouri by the next spring, eager to go west again. So presumably
the expedition had been profitable.

Far to the north, meanwhile, Charles Bent sat through the
drunken revel of the rendezvous. Trading and trapping combined brought the remnants of his company less than twenty
packs of beaver. Loading these on horses, Charles, Fontenelle,
Vanderburgh, and, presumably, William Bent rode with their

men across South Pass and headed morosely down the Platte toward Council Bluffs. They may have been the party, or with the party, which callously abandoned sick Hiram Scott to die near the spectacular landmark ever afterward known as Scott's Bluff. More definitely, they had a set-to with Crow Indians on the North Platte and lost two hands. As if this denouement weren't dismal enough, they reached Council Bluffs to find the hold of the American Fur Company now complete. Already Kenneth McKenzie was forcing a keelboat upriver toward the Yellowstone, there to build Fort Union, the dominant post of the North. Already Etienne Provost was being readied for a trip among the Crows to entice their trade into the fold. Here at Council Bluffs shifty Joseph Robidoux, the last major holdout, had capitulated for $3500 and a salary of $1000 a year, transferring to his new employers not only a stock of excellent merchandise but "even an appearance of honesty." No, the picture could not be more clear—or more stark. If a man hoped to stay on the Missouri, he must dance to the American Fur Company's tune.

In addition Charles found private griefs at Council Bluffs. Silas Bent was dead—had died last November at about the time his sons were slogging over South Pass toward the Green. Thoughts of the bereft home tugged Charles toward St. Louis. But first, what was he to do about the future?

Unhappily he discussed the situation with William Vanderburgh, whose hope of being outfitted by Robidoux for a venture among the Pawnees had collapsed when Joe sold out to the Western Department. Should they now begin their careers all over again, accepting whatever position the American Fur Company might deign to give them? The thought tasted sour. Despite last winter's hardships, each remembered the clean, bold lines of the untracked land, the free sweep of the mountain winds in the mountain valleys. They wanted to go back.

Vanderburgh clutched at a straw. The American Fur Company was preparing to move into the mountain trade. Perhaps the partners—partners in nothing now—could use that as a means of obtaining an outfit and still avoid being totally submerged. Why not go to J. P. Cabanné, field manager of the Western Department, and ask if he would equip a party of

trappers for them to lead to the high country? There would be
strings attached, of course, but at least they would be on their
own once they left the river behind.

To Charles the prospect of mortgaging his future to this
reaching giant was not entirely heartening. Nonetheless, he
went with Vanderburgh to the post. Cabanné received them
graciously, listened to their news. So Pilcher & Company was
finally dead and Pilcher had gone to the Columbia! Cabanné
heard the news with a straight face, though doubtless it caused
him no distress. Word of Sylvestre Pratte's death was something else, however. Those tight-knit French were devoted to
one another and Cabanné grieved for his partner.

Preliminaries finished, business was broached. Behind his
beard Cabanné pondered Vanderburgh's proposal. He did not
want these two as competitors. On the other hand, the company's movements toward the mountains were still in the survey stage, and as yet he was unwilling to risk outfitting a large
party on sheer speculation. The pair had just returned from a
year in the mountains, and what did they have to show for
it? Slowly he shook his head.[6]

That was that. Somberly Charles rounded up William and
prepared to journey home. He was so short of cash that he
had to give Cabanné a draft. Perhaps Vanderburgh went to
St. Louis with him, perhaps not. In any event, the next winter
Vanderburgh accepted employment with the company and
soon was leading trappers back to his beloved mountains.
There, in 1832, four years after his separation from the Bents,
he was killed by Blackfeet, who stripped off his flesh and threw
his bones into the river.

Twenty-nine years old—and now Charles, utterly bankrupt,
must make a fresh start. On top of that was his responsibility
as the eldest son of the fatherless family. True, the oldest girls
were married; and John, already established as a lawyer, had
recently been elected to the state legislature. The youngest
boy, nine-year-old Silas Jr., would stay with their mother. But
what of William? Wherever Charles went the younger brother
would follow without question, which meant that Charles must
do the questioning for both. Then there were Robert and
George, twelve and fourteen, restless, impatient, afire with
yarns they had heard from the older pair. How long could

they be held at home, and what was to be done with them when the holding became impossible?

The more Charles wrestled with the problem, the more persistently his thoughts turned toward the New Mexico trade. A lone man had a chance there. No single company monopolized the field. Individuals bought what goods they could, loaded them in mule-drawn wagons, and in loose association with other small operators marched across the plains to the exotic-sounding city of Santa Fe. In the six years since Becknell had started the wheels rolling, the summer-long efforts had proved highly laborious, somewhat tedious—and safe.

This year, however, disaster had struck the homeward-bound caravans. As the details of death, brigandage, and unparalleled suffering trickled back to Missouri, Charles Bent must have wondered more than once whether this was a propitious time for starting a new venture into a new field. Yet he had to turn somewhere.

CHAPTER V

DEATH ON THE TRAIL

The detonator of the 1828 troubles on the Santa Fe Trail must have aroused the Bents' contempt. No man who had ever been on the plains or in the mountains with the fur brigades would have been guilty of such inanity.

On a sultry day late in August, the first group of homeward-bound Santa Fe traders, some sixty or seventy of them, were plodding toward the Cimarron, their wagons loaded with specie. Paralleling them came a herd of a thousand loose horses and mules of high potential value in the Missouri markets, but right now the source of fogging dust and tedium. Weary of the monotony, Daniel Munroe and a young companion named McNees rode ahead. They crossed what would today be the western boundary of the Oklahoma Panhandle and reached a nameless creek. Dismounting, they drank deeply and stretched out on the bank to wait for the caravan. In the drowsy heat they fell sound asleep!

When the caravan arrived McNees was dead and Munroe dying. Tracks told the story. A small band of Indians had ridden onto this irresistible opportunity and had counted coup with the whites' own unguarded guns. Though no Indians were in sight now, the traders grew panicked, despite the presence of such old hands as Colonel Marmaduke and Milton Sublette, city-hungry after his winter with St. Vrain on the Green.[1] Later the whites would commemorate the tragedy by naming the stream McNees Creek, but right now all they wanted to do was get away from there. After scratching out a grave for McNees they loaded the nearly lifeless Munroe into a wagon and pushed on as fast as the indifferent mules would go.

By the time they had turned down the Cimarron's sandy course Munroe was dead also. They had just finished burying him when half a dozen Indians appeared on the other side of the valley. It is not likely that these were the guilty savages, for they approached openly, probably hoping to beg tobacco. Some frightened or angry trader fired. An Indian horse fell, pitching his rider to the ground. More guns cracked. After the fusillade was over, only one startled savage was left alive. It was one too many, however, for he carried word of the slaughter to his tribe.[2]

Soon the Comanches struck back, making off with most of the caravan's thousand head of mules and horses. Appetites whetted by the success, two weeks later the Indians tried to stop a second caravan of thirty east-bound traders escorting another hundred and fifty animals and four or five wagons rattling with silver. The main body of the whites were able to cock their guns in time to bluff a way through, but the rear guard of three men did not fare so well. One of them, John Means, the captain of the caravan, was shot and scalped. From then on it was a running battle, until one night the Comanches managed to stampede every animal.

After suffering more casualties in a fruitless attempt to recover the missing stock, the party decided to load as much of the silver as they could on their backs—about a thousand dollars each—and head for Missouri afoot. Turning north in the darkness to avoid the Indians, who they believed were waiting to the east, they walked without sleep for forty-eight waterless hours to the banks of the Arkansas. By now the weight of their packs was intolerable. Caching their treasure on Chouteau's Island, they began a starving trek of more than four hundred miles. Finally the five strongest were sent ahead for help to the Big Blue, fifteen miles from Independence. They barely completed the thirty-two-day ordeal, and when rescuers hurried back for the stragglers, they found them strung out over fifty miles of trail, one of them, blinded by starvation, lying on his back and fighting off wolves with a stick.

What followed is an interesting commentary on the trade. The fur companies annually lost as many men—and, except in the disastrous spring of 1823, when many times three trappers died, they raised no fuss. Risk was part of their breathing. But these dead men were storekeepers, and now their colleagues yelled for a policeman like any hurt corner-store merchant. They commanded an audience, too. Munroe, McNees, and Means weren't something apart, as a fur trader dying on the Green was. They were the neighbor down the street. They were you, if you decided to hitch up for a summer's merchandising in Santa Fe.

Throughout Missouri demands rose for military protection. After all, did not the government protect maritime trade throughout the world? Why should not the dry-land flotillas to Mexico receive similar defense, furnishing, as they did, livelihood for hundreds, an outlet for the West's infant mercantile industry, and most of the silver coins that circulated on the frontier? The workaday world's commerce was involved, in other words, and not exotic furs, which one expected to carry a label of blood.

Finally, after frontier-conscious Andrew Jackson stepped into the White House on March 4, 1829, action of a sort was achieved. Old Hickory directed that four companies of soldiers escort the spring caravan as far as the Mexican border. (But no one escorted Bill Sublette's caravan toward the Green.) Assigned as their commander was Major Bennet Riley, who had been one of Leavenworth's more efficient captains during the latter's bumbling Arikara campaign of 1823. Perhaps at that ignominious battle, or certainly later at Fort Atkinson, Charles Bent had grown to know Riley well.

Riley's soldiers were infantry, not cavalry—there was no cav-

alry in the United States in 1829. Footmen against the finest
mounted warriors on the continent! Nor was that all. The
troops would walk only to the Arkansas, though last year's
depredations had occurred beyond that point, within Mexican
territory. After reconsidering the very arrangement which they
had so vociferously demanded, most of the traders decided to
keep their hair safe at home.

On May 1 a listless meeting was held at Fayette, hitherto a
center of investors in the trade. Only eleven people signified
their intention of risking the trail, promising to outfit nine
wagons and furnish nine extra hands—as compared to the two
hundred men who last year had taken out more than one hundred wagons. The thing would have withered on the vine right
then had not a handful of new recruits been gathering in St.
Louis and other counties along the river. Among them were
two pairs of brothers, Charles and William Bent, David and
William Waldo.[3]

Trail-seasoned David Waldo, who had missed last fall's debacle by going south with St. Vrain, was not the sort to be
impressed by frightened predictions that this would be the
most dangerous year the trade had yet faced. Nor, after half
a dozen or more years with the Missouri Fur Company, was
Charles Bent. Probably, too, they had sought out during the
winter persons who could give them a level-headed estimate of
the situation. Such a man was available: big Milton Sublette,
nicknamed the Thunderbolt of the Rockies by some awed journalist. Trouble in the Southwest? Yes, Milton had seen Munroe's and McNees's bodies. But after having helped Ewing
Young slaughter Papagos on the Gila, after having stolen his
furs from under the nose of the governor of New Mexico, after
having helped cut off Tom Smith's shattered leg, Milton would
have his own definition of trouble. Those linsey-woolsey storekeepers! They marched with none of the discipline of the fur
brigades, and when danger brightened they stampeded like
sheep. A Comanche was just another Indian. Not one of them
wanted that first bullet, and a man with a look of courage on
his face could stare them down every time. Hadn't Milton himself, leading a hunting party of only six men back there on the
Arkansas during the height of the caravan's harassment, out-
bluffed nearly two hundred of the red devils? Charles knew

the way of the mountain men; he could handle a storekeepers' trail. And those fandangos in Santa Fe . . . For a moment Milton was tempted. But his brother Bill was cleaning up in the North, and Milton liked the looks of the land enough to give it a try.[4]

How many wagonloads of goods the Bents possessed and how the purchase was financed remain unknown. Perhaps a little money had been left the brothers by their father. Other members of the family may have shared this most popular form of frontier speculation, and credit undoubtedly played a part.[5] Certainly by late April or early May 1829 the goods were ready on the packed wharves of St. Louis. Down past the clamorous warehouses the two brothers went, down beyond the reeking stone buildings where the great fur companies stored buffalo hides and rubbed rum into beaver skins to keep out the moths. The sight may have given Charles a momentary pang for the past, but it was forgotten as he saw their crates and barrels and bales trundled into the dark maw of the gilt-proud river steamer.

Swarming crowds overran the decks—sour-smelling Indians, hung-over trappers, soldiers, gamblers, and adventurers; fuzzy-chinned novice clerks bound for the trading posts that once Charles had reached by keelboat; rawboned emigrant families heading for the new clearings on the lower river with their stringy-haired children, haltered cows, and crated chickens, with their washtubs, cheese crocks, and bedsteads. An infinitesimal segment of the nation's century-long westering. Amid the chaotic mob, while the steamer bucked the yellow spring tide of the Missouri, William Bent may have celebrated his twentieth birthday; or, if not there, in equally chaotic Independence.

The town, a collection of log stores and taverns only two years old, was already achieving dominance as the starting place of the prairie trade. What it lacked in size it made up for in vigor. Here the high-bowed wagons were packed with scrupulous care, so that no joltings of trail or river ford could cause a shift in weight. Here double sheets of Osnaburg canvas were lashed over the deep beds, with Mackinaw blankets between the layers to help turn dust and rain—and for greater ease in smuggling. Here last-minute articles were obtained, last flings taken. On Sundays the local settlers would ride out to the camps to watch the proceedings, swap yarns, and engage the trappers and traders in shooting matches, with liquor, beeswax, fur caps, and bear tallow as prizes. Wherever a group gathered, horse trading was in order and dragged out interminably, for the mount a man trusted during the next 775 miles must be good. And with it all the half-wild mules had to be broken to harness.

Surrounding the camps on the outskirts of the village were scores of the beasts, mostly imported from Mexico. Tumultuously they were rounded up, roped, and tied for twenty-four hours within two inches of a wagon wheel, in hopes that starvation would induce tractability. The next day they were harnessed. Now and then one would bolt, tug chains flapping and bystanders scattering as horsemen raced in pursuit. Retrieved, the wheel span would be forcibly hitched on either side of the wagon tongue and the remainder of the team belabored into position in long, swinging iron traces.

Like the mules, many of the best muleteers hailed from New Mexico. Ludicrous-looking they were. Conical hats covered with oilcloth peaked above their hair. Their dusky heads were thrust through holes in coarse, bright-hued blankets, and their leather pantaloons were split down the sides, revealing a loose pair of cotton drawers beneath. Enormous spur rowels jingled on their heels; their saddles bore sweeping leather skirts and wooden stirrups three inches broad.

As soon as a rebellious team was hitched, one hired muleteer mounted the right-hand wheel mule. Another climbed aboard the left-hand mule of the span behind the leaders. The rest of the hands armed themselves with whips and took position on either side of the team. At a shout from the chief muleteer, all fell to, whooping, spurring, whipping. The mules brayed and plunged. Some tried to run away; some fell in the harness. Fantastic tangles resulted and the air smoked with oaths. Violently the tangles were straightened out; violently the rigorous training went on. Brutal—and effective. Within a few days the chastened teams were setting themselves into the collars in fine, smooth style.

On the seventh of June word reached Independence that Riley's escort of soldiers was approaching east of the river.

Charles Bent and Dave Waldo must have exploded on hearing that. Fort Leavenworth was on the west side of the Missouri. Had the fool pork-eaters crossed back over the river and marched forty miles down its boggy, ravine-split eastern bank, only to have to ferry it once again? With a handful of other traders they rode down to see.

Sure enough, the infantry had fouled itself up with faulty directions. Worse, the supply wagons were being pulled by snail-paced oxen. Cramped by the niggardly War Department, Major Riley's purchasing agent had outfitted the expedition with beeves, drawing part of his money from the subsistence department on the sophistry that as loads grew lighter some of the draft animals could be killed and eaten.

The subterfuge might look like economy to the quartermaster, but to most of the exasperated traders it seemed penny-foolish. An escort? Why, the caravan would spend half its time waiting for the would-be guardians to catch up. Raucous comments flew as the merchants traded jeers with the more than two hundred red-faced soldiers, riffraff of the settlements, who were serving out their enlistments at a wage of five dollars a month.

Amid the grumblings Charles Bent reserved judgment. In his scraping for funds he had learned all too well how expensive mules were, and from his fur-trapping days he knew what a temptation they offered to the Indians. Oxen were cheaper, safer. He would watch how they performed before he joined the condemnation. Crossing the river, he paid his respects to Major Riley. At the camp he also met an energetic, romantically inclined second lieutenant two years out of West Point—Philip St. George Cooke, possessor of luxuriant whiskers, a trenchant pen, and a waspish temper.

Etiquette observed, Charles returned to his wagons (or wagon) and gave the signal for starting toward Round Grove, thirty-five miles away through timbered creek bottoms and over spring-green meadows spangled with wild roses. Group by group, thirty-eight wagons and seventy-nine men rolled into the rendezvous—two thirds fewer than last year's numbers, but nonetheless a healthy increase over the assembly that had met at Fayette a month before. Among them were Milt Bryan and other survivors of the starving silver trek of 1828, returning to retrieve their treasure buried on Chouteau's Island.

The Grove shaded a noisy bustle. Necessary readjustments, revealed by the shakedown trip from Independence, were made. Spare hardwood axles, tongues, and reaches were cut and tied beneath the wagons. Young Bill Bent and others who knew the value that Plains Indians placed on hickory may have cut a supply for private speculation. A piece suitable for a bow would net a buffalo robe, and trappers in the mountains would pay a dollar for a gun stick. Indeed, it is a safe guess that Bill did his share of strutting at the rendezvous. He was an old hand, having visited the dangerous plains west of the Missouri and probably the mountains also. He knew how to talk the guttural language of the Sioux, how to lure antelope and kill buffalo. Those of the train not important enough to intrude upon his brother Charles or on David Waldo clustered around him with their untried guns and campfire courage, asking innumerable questions.

Waldo meanwhile was going from group to group to talk of more pressing matters—the election of a captain. It was an unenviable job. The man chosen had to organize the train, divide the messes for easier cooking, regulate the marches, select campgrounds, apportion the hated night rounds of guard duty, and otherwise try to pluck the pea of success from under the dubious shells of trouble. What would confound him most was the disposition of the very men who had elected him. Lieutenant Philip St. George Cooke, arriving with the military, soon sized up the situation. The office of captain was one "that experience had pronounced indispensable, but was nevertheless little honored; for danger itself, uncredited because unseen, could not overcome the self-willed notions and vagrant propensities of the most of these border inhabitants—self-willed and presumptuous because ignorant."

Because of prior experience on the trail Waldo might have seemed the logical choice. But he had witnessed a captain's tribulations and probably wanted none of them. Contenting himself with the office of secretary, he nominated for captain a man whose qualities had already become evident. Unanimously Charles Bent was elected.[6]

The soldiers and their ox-drawn wagons marched first, not

actually escorting the merchants but for some reason preceding them as a separate entity. A few miles behind, electric with the expectancy that marks the launching of any voyage, came the mélange of the caravan—singing French Canadians in gaudy calico shirts, Spaniards in serapes, hunters in leather, backwoodsmen in linsey, merchants in many-pocketed frock coats. They packed rifles, shotguns, pistols, and a bristling array of knives. Whips snapped, voices bawled, livestock chorused, and through it all rang the jangle of bells and trace chains, the creak and groan of the loaded wagons.

After seven years of experimentation the customs of the trail were beginning to solidify. Scouts rode ahead, hunters ranged out to the sides, loose livestock was herded in the rear. In order that corralling could be quickly accomplished, the wagons marched through dangerous country in two parallel lines, sometimes in four lines if the terrain allowed. Always a corral was formed at night, the wagon shafts slanting outside and the fore wheel of one vehicle abreast of the hind wheel of the next. Whenever one of the prairie's violent wind-and-lightning storms threatened, the adjoining wheels were chained together to keep the wagons from blowing over. Though later caravans picketed livestock, the one of 1829 hobbled theirs outside the wagon circle; and with so few men available for night guard, it must have seemed to William Bent that he spent a large part of the journey wandering about the grazing animals, listening for the sudden snort that might mean danger. In the morning the biting, kicking herd was driven inside the corral. Lariats spun, cries of "All set!" began to rise, and Charles's stentorian "Stretch out!" sent them along the way.

So they marched, plagued by mosquitoes, coughing in the dust or shivering in the rain, but exhilarated always by the endless sweep of the land. Creek banks were shoveled smooth; quagmires were covered with interlaced brush and grass. During the heat of the day noonings were made, and the afternoon's march sometimes continued until long after dark. To the amazement of all, the leg-weary soldiers and heavy-headed oxen stayed in the lead. More and more carefully Charles studied the ungainly beasts. Sometimes their sore hoofs had to be shod with buffalo hide; but though a mule's feet might not grow tender so quickly, they did wear smooth and slipped badly on the short dry grass. Assuredly mules were nimbler while in good condition, but day in and day out, as feed grew sparse, the oxen held up better.

A hundred and forty-five miles from Independence they paused to wash their shirts at lovely Council Grove, later to be famed as the great rendezvous of the trail. Some miles farther on, Charles spotted the first Indian sign and galloped ahead to warn Riley. As if to confirm the alarm, six of the military's few horses were stolen during the night, but pursuit overhauled nothing, and no savages were sighted as the men toiled on through blistering heat past the difficult fords of Cottonwood Creek and the Little Arkansas.

At Cow Creek the first buffalo were sighted. Pandemonium ensued, even among the troops. Officers raced away on the dozen horses remaining to the escort, enlisted men took off afoot, and green hands among the traders went berserk. A battlefield of shots echoed across the prairie—one lone bull fell dead. Later the men would grow accustomed to the moving mountains of meat. Enormous herds ranged the banks of the Arkansas, the bulls marching ponderously ahead of the cows and occasionally threatening the wagons by bawling, pawing, falling on their knees, and tearing the earth with their horns. When a stampede threatened to engulf Riley's escort, the troops turned it by firing in platoons, killing hundreds of the shaggy beasts. A plentiful supply of meat assured, wise hands prepared for future dearth by drying thin strips of flesh on cords stretched across the sides of the moving wagons. During the process of butchering William may have enjoyed shocking the novices by the Indian-trapper trick of gulping down raw liver sopped in bile and by retrieving the intestines for later roasting.

At Walnut Creek, Milt Bryan showed Charles Bent where a small cannon gleamed dully beneath the surface. Traders had dumped it there two years before, for what reason no record reveals. Charles had it pulled out and tinkered with it until it was in working order. While this was going on, others of the party wove seines from grapevines and caught a huge mess of fish. Moving on, they circled Pawnee Rock, future danger spot, but peaceful this day as William and others carved their names in its bold sandstone escarpment and listened to tales of how Comanches had once besieged and obliterated on the fortress-like top a small band of defiant Pawnees. Always on their left hand, south across the barren valley of the Arkansas, rose the low sand hills which Augustus Storrs five years before had described with unexpected imagery as looking like "a dim flame of fire." To the soldiers, one suspects, they looked like sand hills, at least on days when rain dampened the buffalo chips beyond burning and the vexed men had to splash through the river to the islands for firewood.

They were nearing the land of short grass now, heavy carpets of shallow-rooted sod where animals—buffalo, deer, antelope, jack rabbits, wolves—possessed amazing vitality and fleetness; where rattlesnakes and dwarfed owls seemed to share burrows in the mounded villages of the prairie dogs. It was a land of incredible distances, of searing winds and of bewildering mirages that made antelope look like horsemen, crows like Indians, buffalo like groves of trees. False ponds appeared, clouds and inverted hills clearly reflected on their nonexistent surfaces. Trying to explain the phenomenon a few years later, Josiah Gregg, classic authority on the trail, speculated that the cause was either gas emanating from the heated vegetation or a surcharge of carbonic acid precipitated by the action of the blazing sun.

At the Caches, Riley halted his troops, for he had been told that the caravan would cross the boundary here and follow the short dry route to the Cimarron. But now that the jumping-off place was at hand, the troop-inspired courage of some of the traders collapsed. To no avail David Waldo told them that continuing to the Upper Crossing would add thirty miles—two days' laborious travel—to their journey. Fruitlessly Charles Bent argued that if Comanches intended an attack, there would be ample opportunity, no matter where the crossing was made. The men would not listen. A longer trip meant longer protection.

Disgusted, Charles rode ahead and asked Riley if the escort would keep on up the river to Chouteau's Island. The major agreed. He was under orders to wait along the Arkansas until the caravan returned in the fall; where he waited made little difference. Grumbling as usual, his two hundred men marched

on through alternating wind and rain and sledge-hammer heat
to the upper ford, two or three miles below Chouteau's Island.

A series of conferences began. In the midst of them Milt
Bryan's departure with a squad of soldiers to recover the
cached silver on the island went almost unnoticed. Abjectly
the faint of heart begged Riley to ignore punctilio and accompany the caravan farther. Urbanely the major explained that
he lacked authority to take United States troops onto foreign
soil. Still trying to scratch up a grain of comfort, the traders
asked him to assume diplomatic functions by writing a letter
to the Mexican Government, suggesting that it emulate his
escort service with one of its own. To this Riley assented and
then told the group that whether they obtained a Mexican
escort or not he would expect them back on the Arkansas between October 5 and 10. To most of them it looked like a long
and dismally unprotected three months.

As they stood hesitant, Bryan's party returned with some
thirty bags of silver worth between $30,000 and $40,000.
Bryan had been lucky. A rise in the river had washed away
the sand covering the packs, but the Indians who frequented
the timbered island to utilize its white clay for painting their
buffalo robes had not detected the treasure. The sight of its
pale, cool glitter inspirited the traders considerably.

The next morning, July 10, they prepared for the river crossing, always a risky business. The broad stream, meandering
through a dozen shifting channels, was comparatively shallow,
but its bed was a hidden treachery of jarring potholes and
quicksand. Once forward motion ceased, a wagon began to
sink. Consequently teams were doubled, even tripled. Horsemen screeched and whipped on either flank, then brought the
teams back for the next in line. All day long the animals
plunged, the wagons lurched. By four o'clock all were across.
So far, so good.

In the evening Bennet Riley crossed to Charles's camp with
advice. From here on, Bent, keep the wagons bunched more
closely; send scouts out ahead; be sure to use flankers and a
rear guard. Charles shrugged wryly. The major had seen how
the men obeyed. Well, he'd do what he could. And by the
way, might he borrow a yoke of oxen in order to see how they

performed in the deep sand and waterless heat that lay ahead? Riley agreed and sent the animals over.

In the brief coolness of dawn the caravan started single file along the south bank of the river, then swung left into the sand hills. The going was heavy. The trail led through a narrow gut into a circular basin from which egress was gained by another pinched ravine. Wagons bogged down in the basin's sand, and the disjointed caravan stretched out over half a mile. A careless advance guard of three men rode on to the upper opening and there dismounted to wait. Charles rode along the train, fussing at the disorganization. Few took him seriously. Weren't there two hundred soldiers only nine miles away?

Somewhere out of sight of the caravan, either hunting or on guard, William Bent jogged along on a black mule whose split ears showed its Comanche origin. Suddenly the creature snorted. Out of a gully to one side, Indians materialized. Later the men would argue as to whether they were Kiowas, Comanches, or Gros Ventres. At the moment William did not care. He snapped one startled shot in their direction and raced for the caravan, yelling an alarm. The mule got what urging it needed from the ululating shrieks and the shower of arrows that followed.

In the basin Jacob Coates, veteran hunter, and young Bill Waldo heard the uproar and spurred up the slope to see what was afoot. Their abrupt appearance over the brow of the hill, with no indication of how many men might be behind, gave the Indians pause. Bent, however, sailed straight by in what seemed the precipitancy of terror. Actually, however, as Waldo and Coates realized when they stared after him, he had seen that his brother was in an even more precarious position.

Almost simultaneously with the attack on William another gang had howled down the ravine onto the dismounted three-man advance party. Instead of attempting a stand, the trio scrambled for their saddles. Two rode horses. The third, Samuel Lamme, rode a stiff-legged mule. Before he was well under way arrows struck him down. While the lead savages flung themselves onto his body to take his scalp, the others raced after the remaining quarry.

Instantly Charles perceived that the momentum of the pursuit would carry the Indians among the scattered wagons, where they could hack up the caravan unit by unit. Bluff the devils, Milton Sublette had said. It was the only chance now. Letting go a mountain-man yowl of defiance, Charles dashed straight at the attackers. Reloading on the run, William swept up beside him.

The unexpected opposition split the charge. The Indians veered wide, then regrouped for their famed circling attack, protecting themselves by leaning far over their mounts' sides as they fired under the animals' necks. The moment's hesitation caused by the brothers' head-on attack gave the frantic teamsters time to close ranks. Slowly the Bents dropped back, threatening the nearest savages with their guns but not making the fatal mistake of firing the lone shot each possessed. Enraged, the Indians tried to taunt them into recklessness by shaking Lamme's scalp and howling epithets. Finally the tense stalemate ended when a few cool hands among the traders brought the little Walnut Creek cannon into play. Its first hasty shot went wide, but the thunderous report and the spew of sand sent the dumfounded savages scurrying for cover.

Charles ordered the wagons corralled, stock secured, rifle pits dug. Then he called for volunteers to break through the besiegers with a summons for Riley. Nine men responded. Though available records reveal no names, William was perhaps among them: except for a notable handful, the traders had little stomach for that kind of service.

Striking under cover of the cannon for open ground and keeping a hedgehog bristle of rifles pointed in every direction, the messengers got through unscathed. By dark Riley's troops were mercilessly belaboring their oxen across the rising river and on into deep sand. Lieutenant Cooke, made gimpy by the spilling of a pot of boiling coffee on his foot, followed furiously with the baggage train. When dawn came and the Indians saw the formidable array, they decamped.

Remembering the battle years later, William Waldo declared that Charles Bent was a "military genius . . . equal to almost any emergency," and that only through his ability had a man escaped alive. Lieutenant Cooke, surveying the scene with West Point's books yet green in his memory, was less impressed. Battle—these sleepless, red-eyed traders cowering in their rifle pits while the besiegers kept out of range in the hills? A determined charge by either side would have carried the field. So it might have—with war's attendant casualties. But the besieged were not warriors. They were merchants bound for market, and military science, except as it applied to self-preservation, interested them not one whit. If there was profit in glory, let the troops have it.

While the rank and file of both groups bandied scurrilous remarks, Riley evaluated his tactical position. It was hopeless, and he ordered immediate evacuation. Lamme, hastily wrapped in a blanket, was buried in the abandoned breastworks.

For two days the combined parties slogged through a withering wind, their only water a stagnant pool. Already exhausted by the brutal river crossing and the labored dash through the sand, thirteen yoke of oxen collapsed. The others were in little better shape. When the parties reached a small pond, its surface putrid with heat-killed minnows, Riley called a halt. Further penetration of Mexican territory might create an incident and would certainly damage the well-being of his command. From here on, he announced, the caravan would have to manage without him.

One man killed, a few animals lost, but the merchandise intact—things might have been far worse. Charles Bent, mountain man, was astounded when a large portion of the traders refused to continue. Now what? If more than half of the caravan's eighty rifles deserted, the chance of the remainder winning through was negligible.

Sarcastically (and his later letters show that he had a mordant gift for sarcasm) he asked the deserters what they planned: sit on the banks of the Arkansas with Riley and try to trade velvet yard goods with the Indians, or go home, sell their outfits for what they could get, and write off the trip to experience?

The deserters were too terrified to be budged by that kind of talk. Swallowing pride, Bent, Waldo, and James Collins of Fayette went to Riley and begged him to continue. For the sake of the record they put their importunities in writing, a remarkable nine-page letter obviously penned at white heat. If the Indians "are so warlike at the onset," they demanded, "what must we not expect on reaching the center of danger, we expect nothing else Sir but to have our tracks marked with blood." Lest this sound too timid, they hastily added that some of the caravan would sooner "crimson the sands of the Semirone . . . than have their courage suspected." Next they cited examples of Andrew Jackson's penetration of foreign soil in Florida when circumstances demanded: "'Salus populi Suprema lex' the safety of the people always is and must ever be the supreme law of the land." Let Riley also consider the results of the caravan's failure: "Our property and that of our relations and friends would fall a sacrifice to the just demands of our creditors and our wives and children would be cast upon the cold charities of a friendless world, this must be the case with many of us." As for diplomatic niceties, Mexico would receive Riley with "open arms," for, as Charles would remember, had not a Mexican force five years before gone without rebuke across American territory to Council Bluffs in order "to form a treaty with the Pawnee Indians"? If Riley could not move his whole force, let him at least send twenty or thirty men, whom the traders would mount on mules and supply at their own expense. Even half measures "would give courage to the disheartened and prevent a division of the Company."

Riley, also writing out his answer for the record, said no.

One of the caravan's hired hands then tried to guarantee his safety by offering to enlist with the troops. Riley sent him packing with the public remark that he commanded soldiers, not cowards. The junior officers also offered pointed slurs about poltroons, and it began to occur to the reluctant members of the caravan that summering on the Arkansas with the scornful army might prove as uncomfortable as facing Indians. One by one they capitulated to the arguments of their captain. Satisfied that he had done all that circumstances allowed, Riley returned to the river and continual harassment by the savages, who in the next few weeks killed four of his men, wounded several, and ran off quantities of irreplaceable stock.

Scarcely had the soldiers left the sand hills when a mob of men and burros came panting in terror up to the caravan. They were Mexican *ciboleros,* buffalo hunters, more than a hundred of them, who had been out on the plains killing and drying meat. Their arms and equipment were primitive bows and arrows slung over their backs, crude lances bedecked with ribbons and carried perpendicularly in holders on the front of the saddles, a few ancient fusees whose barrels were stoppered against the weather by plugs of wood likewise fluttering with particolored streamers. From out of the hunters' tremendous gabble Waldo and Charles sifted the information that two thousand Indians were preparing for the warpath. The Mexicans had joined the caravan for mutual protection.

It was obvious that the mutuality would be one-sided, but being called on to succor persons even more frightened than they were helped encourage the traders. Slowly the caravan crawled on, racked by alarms. It was a horrible trip. According to William Waldo, "we seldom obtained more than three or four hours' sleep out of the twenty-four; men became so worn down with toil by day and watching by night that they would go to sleep and fall from their mules as they rode along. . . . In several instances men seized their knives in their sleep and struck them into the ground, and the men became afraid to sleep together, for fear of killing each other." For Charles Bent it was doubly trying. At all hours he was on the move, visiting the pickets, quieting jangled nerves, trying to amalgamate his singularly ill-assorted forces into some kind of sensible whole.

Meanwhile word reached Taos that an American caravan was being attacked east of the mountains. (These flashing mountain communications are tantalizing; one continually reads of amazing transmissions of news without discovering how they were made.) Ewing Young, busy outfitting trappers for a reckless and illegal trip to California, responded instantly with forty mountain men. The Indians proved to be no hyperbole. Driven backward, Young sent to Taos for reinforcements. Fifty-five more men turned out, and this time the rescuers were able to reach the beleaguered caravan.

It was a joyful meeting. Old friends like Ceran St. Vrain were pummeled noisily; new ones were made. Young Kit Carson was there, seven months younger than William Bent.[7] It was the beginning of a lifelong friendship. Both men were small of stature, reticent, instant in decision and action. In time Kit would name two of his sons after Charles and William Bent; and in the '50s, telling an interviewer of

Charles Bent and St. Vrain, Carson would declare, "Their equals were never in the mountains."

All they knew now, however, was that they were safe. Ninety-five Rocky Mountain trappers were a far better shield than five times that many traveling merchants or Mexican buffalo hunters. For the first time in weeks the Bents could bed down under their wagon for a night's uninterrupted sleep. In the morning they could wake up fancy-free and with Young's men start toward Taos, then swing on south to Santa Fe for business—and for fun.

CHAPTER VI

THE PEOPLE OF THE PLAINS

Word of the caravan's coming and of its experiences preceded it to Santa Fe; and as the freshly combed, freshly laundered teamsters rolled the dusty wagons smartly into the plaza, the annual excitement of *los carros! los Americanos!* swirled around them with heightened gaiety. Such arrivals were the climax to each starved New Mexican year. In time the caravans even assumed mythical powers: their arrival coincided roughly with the advent of the rainy season, and humbler minds came to believe that the wagons brought not only calico but life-renewing showers.

The wild welcome was gratifying. But as novelty wore off, the merchants, like the mountain men of Taos, began to look down their noses. In travelers' tales the epithets for Santa Fe grew increasingly derogatory. This prairie-dog town the capital city of a province? It looked more like a collection of brick kilns, a dry-land gathering of Mississippi flatboats. The "Palace of the Governors"? Why, it was nothing but a single-story, four-hundred-foot straggle of mud along the north side of the plaza, its portico held up by pillars of roughhewn tree trunks and its doors so low that a tall Missourian had to stoop to enter. And these indolent streets! People sauntered; donkeys crept. Snail-paced oxen wearily dragged squealing, two-wheeled carretas that looked like roofless bird cages. At twi-

light even this activity paused when the slow tolling of a huge
bell stopped the whole city for a whisper of prayers. Then
livelier bells jingled and business resumed as incomprehensibly
as it had ended.

By day and far into the evening heterogeneous mobs of Indians, peons, trappers, and teamsters thronged the central
square of the town, the plaza. Shrill vendors clustered at the
western extremity of the palace, beneath the squat tower
where petty criminals were confined. Here dark-complexioned
women in red skirts sat behind pyramids of soap, pats of goats'
cheese, eggs, onions, and sweet rolls, or dipped up fiery chile
and tamales from simmering braziers; and a popeyed farm
hand out West for adventure could gape at their brown breasts
as they leaned over to make change. Firewood, sacks of beans,
bundles of hay, even live animals could be bought; cuts of
buffalo and pork, limp-looking chicken carcasses, and bits of
liver and tripe stank under protective nettings of pink cloth.
By night the dusty (or muddy) square flickered with the red
light of bonfires, where men stood in circles, warming the seats
of their leather pants. In front of the palace, torches flared
smokily on long poles, and through the deep, narrow window
embrasures leaked the glow of rare, expensive candles.

The same "orchestra" of fiddle and guitar that played in-
discriminately in church or at fandangos led funeral proces-
sions jig time through the streets, especially if the corpse was
a child's, for rejoicing was in order when an infant went to
grace before being corrupted by the world. Sports seemed
equally outlandish: *el gallo,* wherein galloping riders tried to
pluck up a terrified rooster buried to its neck in sand; *el coleo,*
wherein yelling vaqueros seized a fleeing bull by the tail and
upset it with a violently dexterous twist. As in Taos, the chief
diversions appeared to be drinking, fornicating, and eternal
gambling—or so most visitors scoffed. But others found one custom "na sae bad": a woman's way of rolling a man's cornhusk
cigarette for him, lighting it from a flint-struck twist of cotton
carried in a little metal tube, and placing it between his lips,
"their magically brilliant eyes meanwhile searching one's very
soul."

This much of Santa Fe nearly every visitor saw. The Bents
saw more, thanks to Bennet Riley's letter of introduction to the

governor, which described Charles as "a gentleman of the first Respectability in our country"—a description so well filled that José Chavez, head of New Mexico officialdom, was soon calling him "my friend Charles Bent." All doors opened to them, and once inside the great *zaguán* gates of the fortlike houses, they must have been surprised to see that even the finest mansions had earthen floors slicked over with crude mortar and spotted by coarse woolen carpets. Gay bands of calico five or six feet high prevented the whitewash of gypsum on the adobe walls from rubbing off on the room's occupants. Furniture, difficult to transport, was largely limited to an ornate table, perhaps a crude settee, and a few high-backed chairs reserved for the men. An adobe bench covered with bright blankets sometimes circled the walls, and other seats were blanket-draped mattresses that also served as beds by night. The ladies of the household had no reluctance about completing their toilets in a room where male guests lay in bed on the floor— yet at mealtime the sexes generally dined decorously apart. Against such surroundings the beruffled clothing of the well-born seemed doubly resplendent and was often set off by barbaric displays of jewelry. Table service might be of solid silver, and women held their *cigarrillos* in golden pincers.

Business success must have sharpened the traders' appreciation of such hospitality as they had time to enjoy. But Riley's deadline for the meeting back on the Arkansas ruled out too much indolence. There were interpreters to hire, customs formalities to meet or circumvent, stores to rent, arrangements to make for the endless haggling that would translate dry goods and hardware into mules, fur, and gold bullion from the new placer mines south of the city. *Mañana* was a word that everlastingly exasperated. Tomorrow, tomorrow . . . all of it surrounded by a multiplicity of taxes and red tape. But whispered words in the right ear, a coin in the right hand were expediters long since standardized. What short cuts Waldo had not learned the previous year, Charles had probably picked up in Taos from St. Vrain, Ewing Young, and other veterans in the not very difficult art of Mexican smuggling.

The 1829 traders succeeded well. Within five weeks they had picked up merchandise which in Missouri would be worth perhaps $200,000. Moreover, Charles had succeeded in arranging with his new friend, José Antonio Chavez, *jefe político,* for an escort to the Arkansas of 219 soldiers, teamsters, and roustabouts commanded by Colonel Viscarra. In addition, thirty-odd American trappers decided to add their rifles to the caravan for the return trip to St. Louis. Ceran St. Vrain, who went to Missouri for fresh supplies sometime before the spring of 1830, may well have been among them.

Shortly before departure time Bent and Waldo were approached by several distraught families. Because of Spain's efforts to regain possession of Mexico, lost in 1821, the Mexican Government had issued an edict of expulsion against all Spanish nationals. Those in New Mexico who could not or would not bribe immunity from local officials entreated that they be allowed to accompany the Americans as far as Missouri. Permission was granted. In the forlorn group were ten men and six unprecedented women, and they carried with them every jot they possessed.[1]

As the ill-amalgamated cavalcade crept down the Cimarron River, a band of Gros Ventres appeared. The Americans reached for their guns, remembering last summer's attack. But the Indians held up a rude cross as a sign of peaceful intent, and Colonel Viscarra, eager to make a treaty, allowed them to approach. The Indians agreed to a parley, provided the Americans withdrew. Viscarra agreed. Well, it was his business. Reluctantly the traders and trappers moved away.

The moment the Americans were out of sight, the Gros Ventres fell on the Mexicans, killing a captain and two soldiers. Fortunately, out of sight was not out of hearing. Guessing the situation from the uproar, the Americans rushed back and turned the incipient battle into a rout. Exultant with victory and smarting to avenge the indignities suffered on the outward trip, some of the traders even skinned a few of their victims and nailed the red hides to the sides of their wagons.

Because of the battle, the group was late reaching the appointed rendezvous with Riley. Impatiently the major waited an extra day for them and then started his troops homeward down the Arkansas. Riding pell-mell, couriers dispatched by Charles Bent overhauled them and brought them back for an exchange of courtesies with the Mexican command. In fine good will the ragged military of each nation paraded in review; Viscarra's Indian militia from the Taos Pueblo put on a scalp dance, and the officers exchanged dinners. The only delicacy Riley could offer his guests after a summer on the Arkansas was salt pork. Viscarra, not so long from home, produced several raw onions, fried ham, foaming Mexican chocolate, and wine, all served from silver, while outside the tent two thousand horses, mules, and donkeys kept up an incessant braying. From this unmelodious herd Charles Bent furnished Riley's baggage train with draft animals to replace those stolen by the Indians during the summer. The yoke of oxen that Charles had borrowed could not be returned, however, for their keeper had lost them somewhere in the mountains.

This is the last mention of Charles Bent that occurs as the caravan toiled monotonously homeward.[2] Surely, however, there was no monotony in his plans. He had desperately cut himself away from the growing fur-trade competition farther north, and the surgery had brought him success. From now on his and his brothers' and Ceran St. Vrain's destiny would lie southwest. Here they would become vanguards of a nation that was on the move, it knew not where. Government policy, blinded by expediency, was setting up on the plains an Indian territory that was supposed to mark the boundary of the United States. North and South already were building disruption. But stronger than these crippling hobbles were the wagons rolling ever westward across policy-drawn map lines impossible to maintain.

Merchandise, which was part of the imperialistic motive, first brought the Bents and St. Vrain to Santa Fe; but if that was all, the story of the trail would be their story. The insatiable American hunger for land was another part of the onward drive, and in time it brought the partners grants of hill and plain and canyon whose size outstripped the belief of eastern men; but if that was all, a surveyor's plat would show it. Beyond these things, beyond the conception of the other merchants on the trail or the other land speculators and fur trappers in Taos, lay a memory of Joshua Pilcher's forts on the Missouri. The Indian trade—transplanted by Bent, St. Vrain & Company to the Arkansas, it filled the vacuum of the central plains, irrevocably tied the Southwest to St. Louis, and so

helped prepare the way for the final influx that would make
the nation whole.

Oddly, it was not the larger experience of either Charles
Bent or of Ceran St. Vrain that first touched on this significance. It was that of William, only twenty years old, and it
would be ridiculous to assert he caught any glimpse of the
future during that winter of 1829–30. He was simply a young
man looking for something to do.

Santa Fe bored him. He had no responsibility for the bartering of the caravan's goods; and the raw years of his late teens,
largely spent in Missouri River trading posts, had left him too
gauche to find enjoyment in the aristocratic salas where his
older brother shone. Trapper talk excited him more, and he
heard trapper talk a-plenty.

Big doings were in the air. The year before, in the fall of
1828, one of Ewing Young's hunting parties had been soundly
drubbed by Apaches down on the Gila (sickness had prevented Young from leading the group in person); and now
Ewing meant to recoup with an expedition to the forbidden
coasts of California. Rescuing the Bent caravan from the Indians on the Cimarron had delayed his preparations; and when
the combined parties returned to Taos, William almost certainly heard references to what was in the offing. Not the destination, perhaps. That was kept quiet lest Mexican officials
bring down an interdict. But there was no hiding the clink of
traps, the careful lashing up of bales, the horse swapping and
gun repairing. At last, when all was ready, the party clattered
falsely northward. Once beyond pursuit, they would swing
west and south toward the unknown. With them rode Kit Carson, no older, no bigger than William Bent. It was enough to
pull a young man's insides tight with envy.

Perhaps William was already on the road to Santa Fe with
his brother when Young's party left Taos. How much he saw,
how much he knew, is unguessable. But it was enough, together with other talk he heard of the mountains rising huge
and blue around him, to make him realize he did not want
to return to Missouri. When the wagons started east, he made
his way back to Taos, either with or without Charles's permission. There, as the golden shine of aspen leaves told that beaver
fur was turning glossy, he joined a group of the independent

trappers who were always hanging around town, ready for whatever developed. One of these men was a Frenchman named Charlie Autobeas, his vocal cords so scratchy that the Indians called him Hoarse Voice. Of the rest of the party nothing is known, but evidently they planned on meeting Indians as well as beaver, for they took trade goods with them.[3]

They worked northward and eastward. At some high pass in southern Colorado they crossed the front range of the Rockies through thick forests of fir and aspen, where icy streams froth in steep canyons. While the breath of winter hummed in the sharp, dry air, they dropped into the shaggy foothills bordering the plains. A world of country is there—stark hogbacks, gaunt buttes, and long pine ridges separating meadows of deep grass spotted by willow thickets. High above rise the twin Spanish Peaks, the Indian Huajtolla, or Wah-To-Yah, the munificent Breasts of the World. Stone dikes radiate from the Spanish Peaks like veins, and in the multitude of crannies thus formed was a frontier richness of grass, berry bushes, bears, deer, and vast flocks of wild turkeys. Once there had been quantities of beaver also; but by 1829 the cream had probably been skimmed, for the spot was too accessible to Taos to have remained untouched.

From the Spanish Peaks the drainage slips northeastward into increasing aridity. Oak brush and then black junipers and scrub piñon replace the tall upland trees, until finally no trees whatever can grow—just the grizzliness of sage, greasewood, cactus, and blade-leafed soapweed. The remnants of the streams grumble in drab, boulder-littered canyons that finally crumble away into the plains bordering the Arkansas River. It is a huge, austere, unprepossessing waste, but in olden days beaver could be found. And at the edge of the plains Indians might be lured in for trade.

Down one of the streams William Bent's little party went, pushing through the stony gorges where possible, crawling up to the plateaus when the going grew hopelessly rough. Eventually they reached the Arkansas River and went into winter camp. Perhaps the bivouac was at the mouth of Fountain Creek, which rises in boiling springs on the shoulders of Pikes Peak (hence the French-trapper name, Fontaine-quibouille) and reaches the Arkansas at the site of present Pueblo; or perhaps it was some miles farther east at the mouth of Huerfano Creek. George Bent, remembering tales his father told him, gives both locations. But the place doesn't matter as much as did the introduction to the Indians which occurred here.

The men were by no means sure of the temper of the savages; a party as small as theirs was always an invitation to attack. Accordingly they surrounded their camp with a stockade of cottonwood logs. Otherwise the layout probably looked much like the one on Bijou Creek, somewhat northward, which Ruxton described in 1847: "The camp had all the appearance of being a permanent one; for not only did one or two unusually comfortable shanties form a very conspicuous object, but the numerous stages [platforms] on which huge strips of buffalo meat were hanging in process of cure, showed that the party had settled themselves here in order to lay in a store of provisions, or, as is termed in the language of the mountains, 'make meat.' Round the camp were feeding some twelve or fifteen mules and horses, having their fore-legs confined by hobbles of raw hide, and, guarding these animals, two men paced backwards and forwards, driving in stragglers; and ever and anon ascending the bluffs which overhung the river, and, leaning on their long rifles, would sweep with their eyes the surrounding prairie. Three or four fires were burning in the encampment, on some of which Indian women were carefully tending sundry steaming pots; whilst round one, which was in the center of it, four or five stalwart hunters, clad in buckskin, sat cross-legged, pipe in mouth."

There may have been no Indian women cooking for William Bent's men (though the lack is not a safe bet), but it wasn't long before Indians appeared. These were a party of Cheyenne warriors out after Utes and traveling afoot. The white men's camp made them pause in avid curiosity. Over and over in their hands they turned the trade trinkets—to all Indians knowledge came more through touch than through sight—and whatever amazed them made them clap their palms to their mouths in wonder. When finally the group recollected its original martial purpose and went on, there were two who could not tear themselves away. They hung around the camp, undoubtedly pestiferous, and since for both Bill Bent and their tribe it was the beginning of an inextricable intertwining, it is perhaps well to digress for a look at these people of the plains, who were even then nearing the end of a long and weary road.

More than a century before, the Cheyennes had been a timid, earth-bound folk, living precariously in the lake country of northern Minnesota. Terrible pressures were on them. It was the time of the great displacements caused by the advance of the white men. The uprooted tribes of eastern Canada and the eastern United States, edging westward, warred furiously among themselves and with their farther neighbors in a contest not only for living room but also for the right to carry on into the wilderness, at a middleman's profit, the trade goods arriving from Hudson Bay and across the Great Lakes. Chippewas pressed against the Cheyennes; Sioux pressed them; Crees and Assiniboins harried them. Some of these tribes, living nearer white men, possessed guns. The Cheyennes did not, and the unequal odds forced them slowly southwestward across the Red River of the North and on to the Missouri. There they settled near the Mandans and from those most civilized of western Indians learned to grow corn and squash and to build large warm huts of earth.

In time, of course, the seepage of trade brought them guns. But legend, impatient of the slow monotone of commerce, crystallized the drama into a single event—the folk tale of the old woman and the Assiniboins. The setting was a great buffalo hunt, and the people, glutted with meat, had moved a few miles away from their village. One old woman, however, had stayed behind in her lodge to pound bones, boil them in her kettles, and skim off the grease. It was night. In order to have portable light and yet leave both hands free, she tied a torch to a stick and thrust the stick down her back, inside her dress. As she worked, no less than fifty Assiniboin warriors trooped inside the lodge and ordered food. Trembling, the old woman began roasting strips of fat on a stick. Suddenly she whirled the fat in a circle, spattering hot grease into the faces of the warriors. Away she scampered, the outraged Assiniboins in pursuit. Coming to the brink of a high bluff above jagged rocks, she hurled the torch over the edge and dodged to one side. The enemy, thinking they were chasing the torch down a negotiable slope, plunged over the brink onto the rocks below. The next morning the Cheyennes, summoned by the old woman, found all fifty either dead or maimed. After dispatching the living, the victors appropriated the vanquisheds' guns and ammunition. In spite of the new weapons, however, the Cheyennes feared retaliation and moved farther into the plains for safety.

And indeed the tribe did move onto the plains, but it was not a concerted migration. A group would leave the earth villages for a hunt or to trade with the tribes near the Black Hills of South Dakota. Commerce again. Hudson's Bay goods drifted in red hands toward the Rockies. Up from the Spanish settlements came Mexican traders, scared half out of their wits most of the time, yet driven by the only hope a poor man had of escaping peonage at home. To barter for dried meat, fur, robes, and moccasins they brought with them a sweet, porous hard bread which the Indians craved, salt, flint and steel, wood roughly shaped for manufacture into bows, and sheet iron that could be made into dozens of implements infinitely superior to the old stone tools. Slowly the articles of civilization worked back to the farther tribes—an emancipation that was also slavery. Though few of the Cheyennes had yet seen a white man, they were already becoming dependent on his goods. Who now can estimate the labor saved by so simple a thing as an iron awl, or by a kettle for boiling water in place of the old-fashioned buffalo paunch into which hot stones were dropped? How gauge the freedom of spirit that sprang from the ability to strike fire with flint rather than depend on twirling sticks or on precious coals apprehensively carried in a smoldering buffalo chip?

Some of the wandering Cheyennes stayed near the Black Hills, along the banks of the eastward-flowing river in South Dakota that still bears their name. Some returned to the earth villages. New groups formed, wandered, split, reamalgamated, and by now the old racial stock was highly infused with Mandan and Arikara blood. Despite the primitive agriculture they had learned, life remained precarious. Sometimes they caught antelope in pits or attacked buffalo floundering in deep snow. On other rare occasions footmen, ceremoniously painted with red earth, were able to slay buffalo by driving them over steep bluffs. Magic was important—the proper waving of eagle feathers, of circular willow wands. If the charm was right, a herd could be harassed into brush pens behind whose flimsy walls guards waving blankets got the beasts milling and thus approachable for slaughter. Such lucky chances were bright spots in a life of semi-starvation, an opportunity to dry jerky, to pound desiccated slabs of flesh into a powder, mix it with crushed berries, and seal it with melted fat against the future. But more normal days were filled with grubbing up roots, gathering the eggs of shore birds, hunting out the burrows of badgers and skunks.

A foot people, they could carry little until they learned to domesticate dogs. According to legend, this occurred after the Cheyennes had moved onto the prairies, where the creatures were noticed prowling around the camps. The animals, folklore says, were gentler and more particolored than true wolves (though it is hard to imagine what other genus they belonged to). Eventually, after infinite patience, someone learned how to lure the dogs by meat within hand's reach. Strings were tied onto them, and they were led into the camp, where they were of use in sounding alarms, keeping the grounds clear of refuse, and furnishing emergency rations during times of need. After a while someone else had the notion of putting packs on them, and then of attaching travois—practices that continued into historic times. A squaw might have as many as a dozen canines on which she packed small articles and to which she hitched diminutive travois, runaways being prevented by leashes. In olden days, patriarchs said, the dogs were bigger than the ones white men saw—inevitable degeneration!—yet bulky transport was beyond them. Although precious buffalo hides were now being used for shelter, not many could be dog-packed from place to place. As a result lodges remained mere hutches of bent willows over which the coverings were draped.

And then, somewhere near the Black Hills, the whole economy changed. The Cheyennes met the horse.

The animals came to the Plains Indians by trade with or theft from the Spanish settlements of Texas and New Mexico. By trade and theft they continued northward, tribe to tribe, until by the third quarter of the eighteenth century they had reached Canada. Along the way they became as complete a symbol of well-being as any that a people has ever worshiped.

Valuable of themselves, they could purchase whatever a man desired; but in larger measure they were an expression not merely of possession but of the heart's greatest joys, its most profound yearnings. When a young man wooed, his bringing horses to the lodge of his sweetheart's father was more than just a bribe. When husband and wife planned on a child, they often sent about the village crier to make public announcement of the happiness—and then distributed horses. When a man child was named or when a boy grew doughty enough to kill his first buffalo calf; when a girl passed through her first menstrual period and so achieved significance as the potential mother of warriors, the proud parents held feasts—and gave away horses. A warrior's outstanding feat might be signalized by his taking a new name—and passing around horses. When he died his favorite mount was slain with him. Should he break one of the few tribal rules of which village society as a whole took cognizance (such as violating the plans for a communal hunt), the supreme punishment was the killing of his horses.

This cultural dominance was but the pomp attendant on economic dominance. By bringing buffalo regularly within reach of arrow and lance, the horse made food surpluses possible for the first time. Life achieved a nobility above mere subsistence. Not the least of man's dignities lies in the shelter he occupies, and now a mounted warrior could provide ample material for one of the most functional dwellings ever devised, the mobile tepee of the Plains Indians. For the sake of their homes, savage women learned to tan buffalo hides and thus developed, by chance, a trade article that would bring the commerce of the whites sweeping over the prairies. That the commerce in time would mean extinction was, naturally enough, not recognized, its immediate luxuries being too dazzling to question.

Cheyenne women, so the tale runs, first learned the art of lodge making from the Kiowas, whom they met in the Black Hills of South Dakota. Cowhides, they discovered, were easier to work than the heavier bullhides, though the distinction is comparative; and winter was the best season. Under the shelter of cottonwood trees, the homemaker pegged the skin hair-side down to the hard earth and scraped away every particle of fat, flesh, and blood. She then flipped the hide over, laboriously removed the hair, and shaved the leather thin by chipping at it again and again and again with a curved elkhorn into which a flint or steel blade had been fixed. Both surfaces were next abraded by pounding them with the knobby end of a big bone, so that during steeping the skin would absorb the tanning mixture of brains, liver, pulverized soapweed, and grease obtained from boiled bones.

Now the lodge maker invited her friends to a feast; afterward each went home with a soaked hide and a softening rope of braided leather. This rope was stretched diagonally from a tree to a peg in the ground, and each friend cheerfully hauled one bulky hide back and forth, back and forth across the rope until the skin was pliable. Appreciation was expressed at another feast, to which a paid pattern maker was also invited. With appropriate ceremony this designer smeared grease mixed with paint onto her arms and face, put a pat of the same stuff into the part of her hair. The softened hides were laid out in a circle before her; she dipped into the pat in her hair with her forefinger and drew marks where cuts were to be made. How priceless now a white man's steel-bladed knife or a white man's quick-piercing awl for stitching the pieces together with sinew thread! With giggles, gossip, and intimate family talk that would have made a Hell Gate sailor blush, white clay was then rubbed into the sewn hides, and by evening the tepee was ready for pitching.

Generally the door faced toward the east, so that the back would be hunched against the prevailing west winds. In winter, when ground was frozen too hard for wooden pegs, the skirts of the lodge were held down with circles of stone. (Groups of these stone rings on the prairies puzzled some later travelers, who ascribed them to magic ceremonies.) Inside the tepee, an inner wall of hide five or six feet high deflected cold drafts above the heads of the occupants and carried smoke out through a hole in the top, a ventilation system furthered by ingenious upper flaps regulated by long outside poles. In summertime the bottoms of the lodges could be rolled up to catch the breeze. Household goods were stored in painted leather "trunks" shaped like large envelopes. Weapons and accouterments hung on the lodgepoles or from short tripods tied at the top with thongs. These tripods also supported backrests of willows woven horizontally between bands of leather. Beds of fur and robes were placed on mattresses of willow rods covered with mats of reeds. Dust was laid by sprinkling. A fire burned in the middle, pots simmered, friends dropped in to talk and boast and plan. And not one root grew from all this to tie the property to the ground or the owner to his property. An entire village could be dismantled in half an hour to go where it listed, free as the wind, as Francis Parkman saw a village go:

"One by one the lodges were sinking down in rapid succession, and where the great circle of the village had been only a few minutes before, nothing now remained but a ring of horses and Indians, crowded in confusion together. The ruins of the lodges were spread over the ground, together with kettles, stone mallets, great ladles of horn, buffalo robes, and cases of painted hide, filled with dried meat. Squaws bustled about in busy preparation, the old hags screaming together at the stretch of their leathern lungs. The shaggy horses were patiently standing while the lodgepoles were lashed to their sides, and the baggage piled on their backs. The dogs, with tongues lolling out, lay lazily panting, and waiting for the time of departure. Each warrior sat on the ground by the decaying embers of the fire, unmoved amid the confusion, holding in his hand the long trail-rope of his horse. . . .

"Everywhere glittered the iron points of lances. The sun never shone upon a more strange array. Here were the heavy-laden pack-horses, some wretched old woman leading them, and two or three children clinging to their backs. Here were mules or ponies covered from head to tail with gaudy trappings, and mounted by some gay young squaw. . . . Boys with miniature bows and arrows wandered over the plains, little naked children ran along on foot, and numberless dogs scampered among the feet of the horses. The young braves, gaudy with paint and feathers, rode in groups among the crowd, often galloping, two or three at once along the line, to try the speed of their horses. Here and there you might see a rank of sturdy pedestrians stalking along in their white buffalo-robes. These were the dignitaries of the village, the old men and warriors, to whose age and experience that wandering democracy yielded a silent deference."

Such rivers as the plains presented were taken in stride: "Numbers of these curious vehicles, *traineaux,* or, as the Canadians called them, *travaux,* were now splashing together through the stream," their baskets "well-filled with domestic utensils, or, quite as often, with a litter of puppies, a brood of small children or a superannuated old woman. Among them swam countless dogs, often burdened with miniature *traineaux;* and dashing forward on horseback through the throng came the warriors, the slender figure of some lynx-eyed boy clinging fast behind them. The women sat perched on the pack-saddles, adding not a little to the load of the already overburdened horses. The confusion was prodigious. The dogs yelled and howled in chorus; the puppies in the *traineaux* set up a dismal whine, as the water invaded their comfortable retreat; the little black-eyed children, from one year of age upward, clung fast with both hands to the edge of their basket, and looked over in alarm at the water rushing so near them, sputtering and making wry mouths as it splashed against their faces. Some of the dogs, encumbered by their load, were carried down by the current, yelping piteously; and the old squaws would rush into the water, seize their favorites by the neck, and drag them out. . . . Stray horses and colts came among the rest, often breaking away at full speed through the crowd, followed by the old hags, screaming after their fashion on all occasions of excitement. Buxom young squaws, blooming in all the charms of vermilion, stood here and there on the bank, holding aloft their master's lance, as a signal to collect the scattered portions of his household."

Utter freedom—but a man had to have horses to achieve it. Drawn by the magnet and pressed from behind by the Cheyennes and Sioux, the Comanches and Kiowas first drifted away from southeastern Wyoming southward toward the horse herds, both wild and domesticated, that ranged in Mexican territory. Similar motives later started the Cheyennes and their allies, the Arapaho, drifting south across the Platte. Raids, wanderings, probings—no one can say how long the restless movements continued. But folklore demands certainty, and again Cheyenne legend supplies an incident to represent an era.

During the first part of the nineteenth century, so the tale goes, Atsina Indians (sometimes called Gros Ventres and thus confused with other northern Gros Ventres) came from Blackfoot country, where they had been living, to visit their relatives, the Arapaho. With these Gros Ventres were eighteen or twenty Blackfoot warriors. These Blackfeet had lost relatives fighting the whites in Canada and were spoiling for a way to restore pride. In the combined camp of the Cheyennes and Arapaho they put on an arrogant show, marching abreast in a long line through the circle of lodges, singing and boasting that they were the best horse stealers in the land. The next day they vanished southward, to reappear in time with scores of captured mustangs. Flushed with success, they told the envious Cheyennes of huge buffalo and wild-horse herds between the Platte and Arkansas.

The boasts of the Blackfeet and the hope of booty were irresistible to the Cheyenne clan of Hairy Rope People, so called because they claimed to be the first to weave ropes from buffalo hair rather than from strips of leather. Led by their chief, Yellow Wolf, a wiry little wisp of a man and destined to be an influential friend of the Bents, they crossed the Platte and inaugurated half a century of wild horse running. Favorite places were the little lakes near the head of Sand Creek in east-central Colorado—Black Lake in particular, shallow and only five hundred yards in diameter, its waters too bitter for a man to swallow. Black Lake's minerals attracted horses, however. These not only drank the water but also rolled in it in sensuous frenzy. Deep trails led to the shore from all directions, and inevitably so notable a place developed myths. A great serpent was said to live in its bottom, creating the very water that was its habitat and devouring anyone foolhardy enough to bathe there. Eventually lightning killed the creature. A Cheyenne war party solemnly reported having found its body, and after that the lake of course began to dry up.

Before this time the Cheyennes had developed their technique of running wild horses. They soon learned that a ridden animal could seldom overhaul a free one, except in the spring, when the winter-starved mustangs lacked endurance. Accordingly wild horses were generally run before the new grass appeared, and even then were carefully surrounded. After the

ambush had been laid, one man concealed himself by lying
flat on his mount's back and cautiously approached the herd
against the wind. When he had come as close as he dared, he
suddenly sat up with a whoop and charged. The startled mustangs scattered. As they tried to regroup, other Indians bolted
out of hiding, ropes ready.

Lassos were not used; for some reason the Cheyennes were
slow learning that dexterity. Instead, they held their loops
open by tying them with light strings to a willow hoop. The
hoop was fastened to the end of a long pole, and the rider
had to gallop furiously to come close enough to his quarry to
drop the hoop over its head. The animal was then choked,
thrown, and hog-tied. Often the captor would breathe into its
nostrils while it was down, believing that he could thus impart
something of his spirit to his new possession.

The mustang was then tied close to the tail of a gentle mare
that had been brought along for leading purposes. For a week
or so it was kept tied to the mare, its feet often being hobbled
at night. After a particularly successful hunt a man's mare
might be the hitching post for eight or ten mustangs, and she
helped the Indian considerably in the gentling process. At all
times he stayed near his little herd, petting the mare first and
then the captives. Every inch of the wild ones' skins felt his
fingers before he began piling robes onto their backs and so
gradually induced them to let him mount.

Opinions differ as to the quality of the horses thus captured. There was, of course, no selective breeding in the wild
herds; nor, except for the Nez Percé Indians of the Northwest, among the Indians. Care was almost equally nonexistent.
The horses were overridden, underfed, never curried, and generally subject to careless brutality. The high-forked wooden
saddles which the Indians adapted from cruel Mexican models
often gouged such raw sores into an animal's back that when
it was turned loose at night it rolled in agony. Flies tormented
the wounds; magpies alighted to pick out chunks of flesh. Occasional protection was furnished by placing a pad over the
sore, but the mere presence of a festering back was never considered reason for not riding an animal.

Sizes of the mustangs ran small—about fourteen hands—and
on the Missouri and Illinois frontier, where farmers held the

typical American view that bigness meant quality, there is evidence, in lawsuits and bills of sale, that Indian ponies were considered scrubs. But among travelers who saw the savage horses worked in their native habitat the accounts change tune. Those little horses, stout-backed and nimble-legged, with tapering muzzles and proud concave heads that showed Arab origin, performed prodigies.[4]

Not the least of the prodigies was the transformation wrought in the Indian's spirit. In all man's history this has been true. Cavalier, chevalier, caballero, equerry—these are but a few of the titles deriving straight from the ownership of horses. To the Indians, however, the uplift came not slowly, but in a burst; not to one stratum of society, but to everyone. Physical prowess, already formidable, was infinitely increased; and war, as the Indians defined it, became the ultimate of every male's life.

Particularly was this true of the Cheyennes. They were a clean-limbed, hardy people, the tribe's average height of 68.7 inches topping that of every other plains group—and of most Europeans. (Next in size came their allies, the Arapaho, while shortest of all were the bandy-legged Comanches.) From childhood they were taught endurance. Jacob Fowler, in 1821, saw Indian children scampering through foot-deep snow to play on the ice of the Arkansas River, "all as naked as the [sic] came to the World . . . all tho the frost was very seveer . . . and Some that Ware too young to Walk Ware taken by the larger ones and Soot on a pece of skin on the Ice and In this Setuation kicks its [legs] Round and Hallow and laff." Some years later William Bent saw two Cheyennes, Crossing Over and Fine Horns, run a foot race from Sand Creek along the Arkansas to Short Timbers—a distance of *twenty miles*, and only ten feet separated them at the finish.[5] Indian stoicism in the face of pain has always been proverbial, and among the plains tribes self-immolation was a regular ritual. At their summer Sun dances both the Cheyennes and their relatives, the Sioux, were notorious for skewering the flesh of their chests with wooden pegs, attaching the pegs to ropes tied to a medicine pole, and then swinging around the poles until the pegs often ripped out of their bodies.

Courage matched hardihood. One example, famous among

the Cheyennes, tells of a warrior named Mouse's Road who
was cut off on foot from his companions by more than a hundred mounted Comanches and Kiowas. Thinking his broken
bow made him easy prey, a succession of the enemy charged
the Cheyenne. Mouse's Road pulled two of the attackers from
their horses and stabbed them to death with his knife. He
would have stabbed a third, also, but the knife broke on the
Comanche's silver hair ornaments, and the best Mouse's Road
could do was hack the man up with the stump of the blade.
When a fourth Comanche charged, Mouse's Road picked up
a lance from one of his victims, dashed the howling opponent
from the saddle, and left him dead on the ground. Seizing
the man's horse, the Cheyenne then hurled himself at the
whole ring of besiegers. Dumfounded by the ferocity, they
started to fall back. One Kiowa, however, had a gun. He broke
the Cheyenne's thigh with a ball. Unhorsed and crippled,
Mouse's Road then crouched defiantly on the ground with his
captured lance and was overcome only when a Kiowa crept
up behind and shot him in the back. Ever afterward his slayers
said he was the bravest man they had ever encountered.

Transferred to horseback, élan such as that made the Cheyennes a tremendous foe. Comanches, it is true, had a wider
reputation for fighting prowess because of their centuries-long
plaguing of New Mexico and because of the havoc they later
wrought in Texas. But an authority who knew both tribes,
Colonel Richard Dodge, said that the numerically inferior
Cheyennes possessed far more boldness and dash; and the veteran Indian fighter, Randolph Marcy, tells an incident that
serves as substantiation. In one cavalry encounter a white soldier fell flat on the ground from his horse. Riding onto him at
top speed, a Cheyenne caught the man up by his hair, beat
out his brains with a tomahawk, tore off his clothes, dropped
the body, and rejoined his red companions with "a fiendish
howl of exultation"—all without slackening his horse's pace
from a dead run.

For the kind of warfare they practiced, the Plains Indians
were powerfully equipped. Arrows were made with scrupulous
care to obtain absolute straightness, perfect balance, exact proportion between head, shaft, and feathers. Bows were seasoned, scraped, fitted, polished, and then given singing resili-

ency by attaching strips of tough sinew to the backs with a glue made from boiled chips of the hide off a bull's neck—a nutritious adhesive, incidentally, that tasted to one observer like boiled Irish potatoes. With these bows an Indian could drive an arrow completely through a buffalo; and although mulatto Jim Beckwourth, who lived long with the Crows, says that the savages were indifferent marksmen, Josiah Gregg has a different story. While Gregg watched, a Comanche arced an arrow in such wise that it killed a prairie dog out of sight behind a hillock, a trick Gregg obviously could not duplicate with a gun; and when Josiah tried to awe the Comanche by blazing away with a new Colt repeating pistol, the unimpressed Indian quickly fired a number of arrows with the same rapidity. Any warrior could shoot fast enough to keep four or five arrows in the air all the time, and painter George Catlin saw one Mandan put eight into flight before the first touched the ground. An Indian could carry a hundred of these arrows in his quiver; in battle he could hide himself by hanging to the side of his horse while shooting under its neck; and for further protection he carried a shield of thick, steam-shrunk parfleche, smoked and impregnated with glue until it was almost as impenetrable as iron.

Because of all this, the mountain men generally tried to avoid fighting the Indians they met. When battle did come, however, the whites were most times victorious. In small part the success was due to the fact that a Hawken rifle in a good shooter's hands was invariably deadly at a hundred yards, a bow at seventy or so. But in the main victory came from the whites' cool steadfastness under fire. The Indian mind, by and large, was powerless to devise consecutive tactics. The savages grew enormously excited, acted without concert, wasted their arrows in a frenzy of ill-aimed shooting (which accounts for Beckwourth's slur on Crow marksmanship). They had no stomach for a protracted siege, were averse to attacking at night. Omens and superstition overrode common sense— for example, the mystic paintings of birds, animals, and other designs on shields were deemed more potent protection than the parfleche itself. Mass panics boiled up out of nowhere. Anything not understood was a thing to flee from—the white men's little cannon, for instance. The Indians were petrified of them, believing the guns could shoot holes through the earth and kill on the far side of mountains.

The Indian fought for glory. His communal life exposed him to every eye in his village. Just as he dreaded contempt above all else, so he craved admiration as the highest of rewards. But he wanted to enjoy his glory personally. Though desire for revenge was a powerful motive in starting him on the warpath, neither this nor any other cause was worth dying for when battle was actually joined, and there was nothing contemptible in his mind about running away to fight another day. The result was Indian raiding parties rather than Indian armies, with emphasis on guile, stealth, swiftness, and, above all, a careful playing of the odds.

From this attitude developed the curious concept of counting coup. To count coup meant simply to touch an enemy with something held in the hand. If the enemy was killed, fine; if his scalp was taken, better still. But a touch was enough and elevated a neophyte into the rank of warriors. He need not even be the slayer of a touched foe; Cheyenne ritual allowed the first three men who reached a body to count coup on it, regardless of who had done the killing, and the more generous Arapaho allowed four counts. Disputes over order were settled by witnesses formally testifying around a painted buffalo skull whose eye sockets had been stuffed with grass and against whose staring bones guns and arrows rested ceremoniously. The touch need not be direct. One Cheyenne was formally allowed to count coup on a dead Shoshoni whom he touched with the end of a rope reached full length down a cliff. Coup on enemy women and children was as valid as coup on men. So were the coups of capturing an enemy's gun, shield—or horse.

Indeed, in early days horse stealing and war were synonymous terms, and some notable thiefs, like Chief Yellow Wolf of the Hairy Rope band of Cheyennes, were deemed celebrated warriors because they managed to avoid battles during their raids!

As in all things Indian, elaborate rites attended the horse stealing, especially in the case of a young man making his first venture. Ceremoniously dressed, the warrior visited the tribe's totem, the four medicine arrows, told the arrows his plan, and made an offering. Or he might fast for four days on a bed of sage or swing himself with pegs in his chest from a pole. Sometimes the leader and his companions went with medicine men into the sweat house, consecrated a lance or shield to carry with them, and snipped off bits of skin from their arms or legs to leave as a sacrifice.

During the night preceding departure the raiders circled the village to make sure everyone knew they were going and to collect useful gifts of moccasins, tobacco, arrows, perhaps powder and ball. On the trail to enemy country the warriors generally traveled afoot. Horses were a nuisance to care for, particularly during the actual raid, when the men would slip into the sleeping village of the enemy and silently cut free the prize horses picketed for safekeeping in front of the owners' lodges. Besides, it was a matter of triumph to leave home unmounted, return whooping and howling, faces painted black in triumph, with many horses.

Ritual followed the party down the single-file trail. A man must know when to eat, what to eat. Sometimes a special drinking cup made from the pericardium of a buffalo heart was toted along on a six-foot pole; and sign was often read in the blood of a slain badger. Any untoward trivia—the erratic flight of a bird, the unexpected howl of a wolf—might call the whole thing off. One reason for wiry little Yellow Wolf's notable successes was his un-Indianlike directness in demanding less ceremony and more attention to the business at hand.

Dogs shared with the men the carrying of equipment: a robe for bedding, emergency rations of dried meat, weapons, and extra moccasins to replace those swiftly worn out by the sandy, cactus-studded terrain. Each raider also carried a riding pad of leather a foot wide and four or five feet long. This could be stuffed with grass, laced shut, and put on the stolen horses for greater comfort during the return journey.

The group traveled cautiously through ravines and behind ridges, for a foot party caught in the open by mounted enemy stood little chance. Scouts called wolves ranged ahead and on the flanks. When they had news to impart, they ran back shaking their heads and howling like the animals for which they were named. In hostile country camp was made in quickly piled brush huts that hid the light of the tiny fires.

Somewhere along the Arkansas, near the mouth of either Fountain or Huerfano Creek, the scouts of such a party of Cheyennes came running back to the main group with astounding news. A stockade was there; white men were in it. The whites had horses, and undoubtedly the Indians calculated the odds before persuading themselves it was safer to walk out into the open, right palms up in the sign of peace. William Bent came forward to meet them. Perhaps they were the first Cheyennes he had ever seen—though his son George years later said that William had encountered Arapaho on the North Platte before coming to the Arkansas, and if this is true, William may have met Cheyennes also. At any rate, he could talk some Sioux, which most Cheyennes also knew because of the cultural relationship of the tribes, and he could use sign language. The meeting passed off pleasantly enough, and for the moment that seemed the end of it.

As has been noted, however, two of the Cheyennes stayed behind when the rest of the party went on. Soon these deserters had the fright of their lives. Over the hills from the south came a band of Comanches led by a chief named Bull Hump.

Normally the Comanches got their horses from Mexico, but this time Bull Hump was after Cheyenne stock. Bent's stockade diverted him temporarily. William scarcely had time enough to hide the two terrified Cheyennes among his bales of pelts and trade goods before the Comanches strode arrogantly into the enclosure. But though he had hidden the men, he could not hide their moccasin tracks. Instantly the Comanches recognized the distinctive pattern and demanded to know all about these Cheyenne footprints.

Right there a momentous decision confronted twenty-year-old William Bent. The Comanches ranged unchallenged through Texas to the Rio Grande, from Colorado's Platte River southward into Mexico. New Mexicans lived in mortal terror of them: "They are so skillful in horsemanship they have no equal; so daring that they never ask for or grant truces, and in possession of such territory that . . . they have no need to covet the trade pursued by the rest of the Indians whom they call, on this account, slaves of the Europeans, and whom they despise."[6] By the time William Bent met them, their horse and mule herds numbered into the tens of thousands, and already their raiding parties were leaving a broad trail into Mexico, "worn deep by the horses of countless travelers and . . . whitened by the bones of abandoned animals." Every hacienda in northern Mexico felt their strike. They stole young boys and girls as well as livestock, and in time the entire Comanche and Kiowa nations became infused with Mexican blood. Once a Mexican girl became pregnant, she was reluctant to face shame at home, and many declined ransom in order to stay with the Indians. The males, too, often preferred the not unkindly slavery of the Comanches to peonage at home; and these captives, many of whom achieved leadership in the different bands, added no little potency to the raids through their knowledge of the two countries.

A man interested in trade would think twice about overlooking the chance to conciliate customers so powerful. Two Cheyenne scalps would be tempting bait—or a source of danger if Bull Hump discovered that he was being hoodwinked. As yet, however, William Bent was not weighing trade policies. When he told Bull Hump that all the Cheyennes had departed from the stockade, his sole motive was probably an instinctive sympathy for the frightened underdogs. Nonetheless, whether planned or not, the move won him the gratitude of the Cheyennes. From now on he would be welcomed whenever he appeared.

The Comanches vanished; the two Cheyennes crawled out of hiding.[7] No one had any idea that a seed had been planted that would help influence the growth of America. The Cheyennes wanted to get home; the weather-weary trappers were probably thinking of Taos and its fandangos. As soon as the season was over, the whites gathered up such peltries as they had garnered and headed gleefully over the mountains. Even yet William Bent had no notion that within a year he would return.

CHAPTER VII

THE NIGHT THE STARS FELL

Though there was no reason to presume the Indians would be less murderous in 1830 than they had been in 1829, the War Department released no soldiers to escort the spring caravan toward Santa Fe. Nonetheless, inspired by 1829's profits, some 140 men lined 70 wagons and $120,000 worth of goods across the windy prairies.[1] Ceran St. Vrain was one of the 60 proprietors; Charles Bent was probably another.

In the hot days of late July, as the mountains beckoned cool and blue to the west, the tired teams reached the clear headwaters of the Canadian, or, as the New Mexicans called it, the Rio Colorado, Red River. There an unpleasant surprise appeared. As the proprietors were scheming the usual dodges to circumvent import duties, up rode the customs inspector with a troop of soldiers, miles farther than they had ever come before. Welcome to New Mexico, gentlemen, and of course no one would mind the formality of a guard to protect each wagon.

Glumly Ceran wrote Bernard Pratte, from whom he had again bought goods on credit, "We had all to pay full dutys which amounts to about 60 percent on cost."[2]

To make matters worse, although Ceran pushed his goods through the customs and onto the market ahead of the other traders, the merchandise "sold verry slow, so slow that it was discouraging. I found that it was impossible to meet my payments if I continued retaling. I there fore thought it was best to hole Saile & I have done so." The results of this "hole Sailing"—one wagon, eleven mules, one horse, and 653 beaver pelts—Ceran sent back to Pratte in charge of Lavoise Ruel and Andrew Carson, another of Kit's far-ranging brothers. (Kit himself was still in California with Ewing Young.) For the toils and possible perils of the trip Andrew was paid at the rate of fifty cents a day, fifteen dollars a month.

Sometime before Carson departed, Charles Bent likewise returned East. "I have also lent Mr. Charles Bent one wagon

which you will receive," Ceran wrote Pratte, not mentioning
the date of the loan. It was the beginning of a series of prodigious trips. Presumably Charles had reached Santa Fe on August 4 with the caravan. Now, perhaps less than a month later,
he was hurrying back to Missouri for more goods. In December, after a race with winter, he would be in Santa Fe again,
having covered more than twenty-three hundred strenuous
wagon miles in about nine months. Phenomenal energy and
extraordinary trail skill are implicit in these trips and in the
five crossings he apparently made the following year; if the
full story could be reconstructed it would probably reveal accomplishments unequaled by any other man on the Santa Fe
Trail.[3] Certainly it reveals the implacable drive of the man.
Forgotten now were the Missouri River and the cutthroat
fur-trade wars that so recently had defeated him in the North.
His future lay southwest, and he met it as if the whole vigor
of the explosive frontier were epitomized in his chunky, black-
headed frame.

William was in Santa Fe that August of 1830 and must
have known of Charles's plans for the flashing trip to Missouri
and back. But Missouri still did not interest the younger
brother. He had tasted the wilderness, the singing zest of a
morning world. Yonder, across each ridged horizon, beyond
the next river, lay new excitements in a land made indescrib-
ably bright by the daily awareness of danger. Beaver was the
excuse; yet to a youth of twenty-one beaver could scarcely
have been more than an excuse. Probably, unless his older
brother persuaded him to invest some of the profit of the
Arkansas venture in the fall caravan, William blew himself
to a stem-winding mountain-man spree. Then, shaking off his
hang-over, he threw in with three other foot-loose Missourians
named Joshua Griffith, Joseph Reynolds, and Robert Isaacs.

The quartet scraped up a riding horse each, nine pack
mules, twenty-four traps, a huge dog called Lolo, and a Mexican roustabout named Leone. With this picayune outfit they
proposed to risk the Gila, where Ceran St. Vrain had trapped
four years before. They may have talked to him about the
country, and if so he may have tried to dissuade them. Very
clearly Ceran would remember that all but three of Michel
Robidoux's party had been massacred there in 1826 and that

two years later a strong group of trained men sent out by
Ewing Young had been disastrously routed by Apaches. It
was not an easy land. But William and his three friends were
young; they would not listen. On August 25 they pointed their
horses toward Albuquerque and the south.

They went deep, perhaps as far as the stark borders of Sonora, near the present Arizona copper-mining towns of Bisbee
and Douglas. Finding poor trapping, they swung north along
the San Pedro River to its junction with the Gila, a little south
of modern Globe, then followed the barren bottoms of the
larger river westward toward the future site of Phoenix. At
last they found beaver. But they also found so much Indian
sign that belated caution dictated a retreat. Retracing their
steps past the mouth of the San Pedro, on December 17 they
reached a section of the Gila where beaver abounded. Eagerly
they set their traps, built their camp. Seven of their best animals they picketed by the fires, but the other six head were
so poor that the men decided to let them graze outside the
camp. It had been a long, hard haul. Now the partners were
going to cash in.

The night passed quietly—too quietly. The next morning the
loose horses and seventeen of the party's twenty-four traps
were gone. The moccasin tracks all around weren't necessary
to show what had happened; shortly after daylight several hundred Indians, women and children included, appeared on the
opposite bank of the river and signaled for a parley. Blandly
their Spanish-speaking spokesman admitted the thefts but
promised to return the horses and traps if the whites would
let the Indians come into their camp and trade.

This the overwhelmingly outnumbered trappers declined.
The Indian spokesman left in a rage; the whites forted up
behind their baggage. One hundred and eighty-three warriors,
by Robert Isaacs's count, strung their bows and swarmed
across the Gila. From then on matters developed with normal
lack of logic. Threats and execrations were yelled back and
forth. Finally the whites informed the Indians that on the
morrow they planned to trap up the stream between narrowing canyon walls and promised that if the Indians did not
molest them trade would be opened the following evening.

The savages howled back agreement, and the two groups spent an uneasy night some four hundred yards apart.

At dawn the trappers packed their remaining horses and started upstream. A mass of Indians followed. Neither side intended to keep its bargain. During the night the Indians had prepared an ambush in the canyon. Having anticipated this, the trappers veered suddenly toward the rimrocked top of a nearby hill. The Indians in the ambush leaped into view with howls of frustration. Together with the group following the whites they tried to execute a nutcracker squeeze, but the frantically spurring trappers broke through to the boulder-strewn hilltop. While the Spaniard Leone tied the horses together, the Missourians forted up in a ring, five men against forty times that many.

As usual, the Indians let fly a frenzied hail of arrows; the whites coolly waited for unmissable targets. Reynolds, who had a scatter-gun loaded with several balls, was told to hold his fire for a final emergency. The other three, "Griffith, Bent and myself," Robert Isaacs recounted later, "shot twelve times —eleven fell." The dog Lolo contributed by whipping two Indian curs, and Leone took a couple of pot shots that missed. After thirty minutes the Indians lost interest and withdrew, "carrying off their dead, and stuffing grass into the wounds of those whom they yet hoped to save."

The trappers caught their breath, calculated the odds in case the Indians returned to besiege their waterless rock pile, and pulled out fast for the nearest Spanish settlement. They arrived poorer than they had left—except in experience.[4] And in reputation. Though they had been foolhardy to risk the Gila with so puny a force, the fight that enabled them to emerge impressed the frontier. Echoes of the battle reached as far as St. Louis, and in time legend would ascribe to William Bent leadership of a three-day (instead of thirty-minute) defense against practically uncountable hordes. Actually, heroics weren't part of it. It was the old story of outnumbered mountain men standing back to back and learning, as so many others had learned, that in Indian warfare a few bullets and a lot of nerve went a long way.

If the party rode fast enough, William was back in Santa Fe in time to see Charles before his indefatigable elder

brother took off on still another trip. Charles, too, had learned
a lesson: continual time on the trail precluded the profits a
man might make if he were free to regulate selling according
to fluctuating demands. Particularly was this true of a person
operating on short-term credit; he had to dump his goods fast
and hurry home to pay off his notes. The obvious answer, provided enough volume could be handled, was a partnership in
which one member stayed in New Mexico to sell while the
other looked after transport.

Such was the arrangement Charles Bent proposed to Ceran
St. Vrain shortly after reaching Santa Fe in late December
1830. He found Ceran on the point of going to Missouri to
replenish his own stock. What sense was that? Charles asked.
He had just brought in plenty of goods. Let Ceran, who knew
the Mexicans well, market the merchandise while Charles hit
the trail. St. Vrain agreed, wrote Bernard Pratte of the plan,
and asked that Charles be given the mules Andrew Carson
had taken to Missouri the previous fall. The partnership
didn't excite Ceran. "There is," he wrote Pratte on January
6, 1831, "no news in this Cuntry worth your notice more than
money is verry Scrse, goods sells low and and [sic] duties
verry hie, but still the prospects are better here than at home."
And on that hardly sanguine note, which may have been just
a debtor grumbling to a creditor, the firm of Bent and St.
Vrain was launched.[5]

Charles seems not to have gone directly back to Missouri.
On January 5, 1831, he was issued in Santa Fe a passport for
the "interior states"—Chihuahua and Durango. Perhaps he
sent an agent in his place; more probably he racked his wagons
southward, as Ceran and David Waldo had done three years
before. After unloading his goods wholesale, he either returned to Santa Fe with his specie packed in shrunken rawhide; or, as many another Chihuahua trader did, he may have
crossed to a Mexican seaport and taken ship for New Orleans.
Whatever route he followed, he gathered no moss: in May
1831 his wagons were loading by the Missouri docks for the
775-mile trip back to Santa Fe.

This was the first great boom year of the trade. Half a million dollars' worth of goods flowed west. At least two sizable
caravans got under way before Bent, and through fortuitous

circumstances both have received more attention from history. One of these predecessors became famous years later when Josiah Gregg's minute description of its housekeeping and wayfaring (in *Commerce of the Prairies*, a classic of America's westering) stamped it on the nation's mind as the prototype of all Santa Fe caravans.[6]

The other became famous because of its tragedy. Its twenty-three or -four wagons belonged, in large part, to three of Ashley's former mountain men—Jedediah Smith, William Sublette, and David Jackson. After buying out Ashley in 1826, the trio had made modest fortunes for themselves and in turn had sold out to the Rocky Mountain Fur Company, composed of Ceran's erstwhile employee, Milton Sublette, and Jim Bridger, Henry Fraeb, Jean Baptiste Gervais, and Thomas Fitzpatrick. Now Smith, Sublette, and Jackson, together with various of their families, were investing part of the beaver profits in the Santa Fe trade. While they were making ready to leave Independence, Fitzpatrick arrived in need of supplies for his new company's first rendezvous. The traders welcomed him boisterously. Perhaps they had already agreed, the previous summer in the mountains, to provide the goods which their successors would need this year. In any event, it was arranged that Fitzpatrick would go with the caravan to Santa Fe, although the journey would take him several hundred miles out of his way, and there load his merchandise on pack mules for the trip north.

Smith, Sublette, Jackson, Fitzpatrick—openers of the North. Twice Jedediah Smith had crossed the continental United States—the first man in history to do so—and had beaten off staggering blows by desert, mountains, and ambushing Indians. No other quartet in America knew as much of wilderness survival as these four men. Yet on the dread jornada between the Arkansas and the Cimarron they became lost. As thirst began to strangle them, Smith and Fitzpatrick went ahead of the wagons to search for water. Tom's horse played out. With a telescope he watched America's greatest explorer cross a ridge and drop eternally from sight. Only Indian tales drifting later into Santa Fe told what had happened. Comanches had surrounded Smith and had frightened his horse. As it shied, they shot him through the back and lanced him to death—but not before he had killed their chief. The entire frontier was shocked. Gloomily Joshua Pilcher, now employed by the American Fur Company, wrote to the Secretary of War, "I confidently look forward to the time when a whole caravan will share the same fate, unless steps are taken to protect them."

Charles Bent, traveling behind both Gregg and the Smith-Sublette-Jackson caravan, was luckier.[7] Perhaps he was threatened by the Gros Ventres, as both his predecessors were, but no records have reached us. In the normal course of events he would have reached Santa Fe before Fitzpatrick left, and undoubtedly he knew that Tom bought for the rendezvous twenty-eight hundred dollars' worth of goods from Jedediah Smith's estate.

While Fitzpatrick was still fiddling around Santa Fe (and signing up as one of his trappers young Kit Carson, not long returned from California), Charles went back to Missouri. It must have been a hard-riding trip, unencumbered by wagons, because in August he was in St. Louis. Swiftly he made arrangements for still another caravan, and by early September he was loading his wagons in Independence. The trip was historic: for the first time a Santa Fe train was pulled entirely by oxen. Riley's escort to the Arkansas had demonstrated the possibility two years before, and perhaps Charles had experimented further during his 1830 trips. Now he was ready to make a full-scale test that would prepare the way for the gargantuan freight caravans that later sinewed the West. All Missouri watched with interest, and no less a man than Thomas Forsythe, dean of Indian agents, considered the experiment of enough import to write to the government: "In August last Mr. Charles Bent set out from St. Louis with a number of wagons, loaded with goods, etc., for Santa Fe, and drawn by oxen. His party consisted of from 30 to 40 men, and, if he succeeds with his ox wagons, the oxen will answer the tripple purpose of 1st, drawing the wagons; 2d, the Indians will not steal them as they would horses and mules; 3d, in case of necessity, part of the oxen will answer for provisions."[8]

Plodding along with the oxen but seeing across their lumbering backs to the wings of the western morning came a six-foot giant of boundless energy. He was twenty-one, his name was Albert Pike, and in a sense he, too, was an innovation. The land beyond the Mississippi was beginning to catch the imagination of young America—not as a field for selling dry goods or for taking beaver pelts, but as an attainable symbol of every young man's half-understood desirings. In increasing numbers they would go west, see the elephant, and come back to the patterned East with memories that would abide throughout their lives, color all their thinking. If they were literate (and sometimes if they weren't), they tried to put on paper what the venture had meant to them; and who now can gauge the mass effect of their stories in preparing the nation's mind for the long jump to the Pacific?

Such was Albert Pike of Massachusetts, educated and dissatisfied. Restlessly he had roamed into Tennessee, thinking to support himself by schoolteaching. Finding no school and not truly wanting one, he drifted on to St. Louis, encountered Charles Bent, and signed up for adventure. He got it. On the Cimarron a thunderbolt stampeded his horse, and most of the remaining miles to New Mexico he covered on foot. Then as the ox-drawn caravan labored up the Sangre de Cristo Mountains (this time Charles was headed toward Taos rather than Santa Fe) an early snowstorm immobilized it for a week. While sleet howled, the men heaped evergreen boughs around the wagon wheels, crept inside, and numbly waited for the weather to clear. Nearly all of them suffered frostbitten feet, and young Albert was awed to discover that he outlived a horse which froze solid a few yards from his bivouac. Later, after thawing out for a while in Taos, he joined Bill Williams and others on a fruitless, starving trip into Texas, and in 1834, in his *Prose Sketches and Poems*, he gave America the first and still one of the best pictures of that lank old eccentric. The literary discovery of the Southwest had begun.[9]

It is possible that William Bent was with Charles on one or more of these implacably hurried trips. It seems more likely, however, that after returning from the Gila he gathered a small party and ventured once more onto the high plains along the Arkansas. He knew the Cheyennes would receive him favorably because of his rescue of a pair of them from Bull Hump's Comanches the previous spring. Moreover, he was

soured on trapping. The profitless trip to the Gila and con-
versations with the mountain men in Taos had convinced him
of what was becoming apparent to more and more trappers:
the streams of the Southwest and of the eastern Rockies had
been skimmed and reskimmed until the few beaver remaining
did not justify the risk of hunting them. Probably, too, William was tired of the wet, hard work. If he had not been, he
could have gone into the Northwest with men like Kit Carson
and joined the internecine struggles for control even then
building toward their climax. But no. William Bent preferred
the Indian trade, in which he had first been tutored along the
Missouri during the impressionable years of his teens.

Only surmise can fill the next twelve or eighteen months.
For the ordinary Mexican mule and donkey caravans, existence was purely nomadic—the finding of an Indian encampment, the making of presents, then the spreading of trade
goods on the ground: bolts of calico and a few Navajo blankets; some knives and beads and mirrors; the hard, sweet
bread the Mexicans baked in their outdoor ovens; salt and
pepper; perhaps a little powder and lead; dried onions, beans,
and pumpkins, which the once agricultural Indians relished as
a change in their all-meat diet. Generally there was Taos whiskey, too, and it is not likely that William eschewed its use,
even though legend now blames another trader for introducing
alcohol to the Cheyennes.[10]

Once the goods were displayed, prices were set by the use
of counting sticks—this many pumpkins for a pair of moccasins; this many buffalo robes for a Navajo blanket. Haggling
was interminable. Every article was traded for individually,
never in lots. But finally the bartering was done and then
probably there was a feast in the lodge of the chief, storytelling, gambling at the game of hand, horse races, and quick,
urgent amours if the band were Arapaho, for their sexual
standards were notoriously lax compared to those of their
chaste allies, the Cheyennes. Then on the traders would go,
looking for the next village.

Some of this Mexican-like wandering William and his companions undoubtedly did. But he seems to have carried more
goods than the poverty-stricken nomads, for he also built a
headquarters stockade at the mouth of Fountain Creek, the

site of modern Pueblo. Here he could store his merchandise; here the customers could seek him out. By 1832 business had increased to the point where he began to think of a complete overhaul in his methods of operation. For one thing, pack trains were no longer adequate; he needed wagons. For another thing, he was dissatisfied with the inferior goods obtainable in Santa Fe and wanted to import a wide assortment of the merchandise that was prepared in St. Louis especially for the Indian trade. Undoubtedly he discussed the problems with his older brother. Charles, remembering his own trading days along the Missouri, was intrigued. The situation was worth looking into.

When Charles made the examination is impossible to say; however, the time and weather elements involved suggest the summer of 1832. Charles had taken to the trail again that spring, captain of the year's principal caravan. Little is known of the journey except that lightning forking out of a storm near the New Mexican mountains killed several of the train's huddled oxen. But there is no doubt that business was booming. The year before, St. Vrain had taken out Mexican citizenship in order to facilitate the firm's dealings, and in May 1832 he had dispatched agents to Chihuahua and Sonora with goods.[11] It was about this time, too, that the partners were thinking of opening a permanent store on the south side of the plaza in Taos. And now there was this Indian business of William's to expedite.

His Mexican affairs attended to, Charles started his wagon-loads of trade goods toward the Fountain Creek stockade, in country that probably never before had felt the touch of a wheel. From Taos he crossed eastward over the Sangre de Cristos, then left the ragged ruts to swing north across Raton Pass to the headwaters of Purgatory Creek—El Rio de Las Animas Perdidas en Purgatorio. A hellish, boulder-rolling, tree-chopping, earth-digging trip it must have been, and impressive indeed to the pair of youngsters who were along: George and Robert Bent. In that summer of 1832 George was eighteen, Robert sixteen—old enough to do men's work—and at last they had wheedled permission from their mother to go West with their now-famous elder brother.

The youngsters earned their keep. In those days no wagon

could travel directly north from the headwaters of the Purgatory to the mouth of Fountain Creek. The route had to be a circuitous one, and probably William rode out to show the way. For a few miles he led the train down the Purgatory, through vales where Trinidad now stands. Then, as the canyon walls pinched in, he veered leftward on an ageless trail used by Indians and Spanish explorers, striking at last the dry wastes of Timpas Creek, its rare potholes of water bitterly alkaline. When at last the wagons reached the Arkansas, they were seventy miles or so below the stockade, and now they must turn westward up the river, over sterile benches, past queer hills shaped like overgrown potato mounds—a roundabout route from New Mexico indeed, but one that stagecoaches between Santa Fe and infant Denver would retrace thirty years later.

What Charles saw at the stockade set his ever-active mind jumping fast—there seems no doubt that the primary concepts were his. Forget these log houses and picket stockades. In order to hold this unexploited country against the other traders already edging into it, the brothers would need a central fort as powerful as any on the Missouri River. Not a log fort—sufficient suitable timber would be hard to find—but one built of adobe. In New Mexico, Charles had learned the virtue of those sun-dried mud bricks. They kept houses warm in winter, cool in summer, and they were impervious to attackers using fire. In the dry climate of the Southwest adobe was even more durable than wood, and, equally important, was as cheap as the earth from which it was dug.

Talk buzzing with the prospects, the four brothers turned the wagons eastward down the Arkansas toward home. At the mouth of Purgatory Creek, on the south bank of the river, they went into camp. Feed was good in the lush bottomlands, and the trail-weary oxen needed rest. Apparently a small stockade was already there, or perhaps the men threw one up for protection during the layover. As they sat around their fires inside the paling, a guard shouted. Indians with a big herd of horses were boiling down the hills to the south. William recognized them—Cheyennes of the Hairy Rope clan, led by Little Wolf, Wolf Chief, and that astute, undersized horse thief, Yellow Wolf. The warriors were on their way home after a successful raid on the Comanches and were in high spirits.

The older Bents invited them inside. While George and Robert stared, presents were distributed, coffee—the sweetened "black soup" which the Indians were learning to enjoy inordinately— was set to boiling, and after ceremonious pipe-puffings talk began. Meeting William's brothers was of deep interest to the genealogically minded Cheyennes. Yellow Wolf sized up the quartet, decided they should have Indian names—an accolade. Charles was called White Hat, because, legend says, he was the leader, though actually the connotation is not clear. Slim, short-statured William probably already had his name, Little White Man. (When the Kiowas met William later, they would note the strong, beaked nose between his black eyes and name him Hook Nose.) George became Little Beaver; Robert, the youngest and handsomest of the Bents, was Green Bird.

In sign language and in Sioux, helped by William's interpolations in Cheyenne, Charles tried to explain the proposed new fort to the Indians. Big medicine. They popped their hands over their mouths in awe. Good, good. But not, Yellow Wolf said, properly located.

Unless Yellow Wolf had been to the Missouri, he probably could not visualize the proposed structure. But he was a notably intelligent Indian, as other whites than the Bents would eventually remark, and he knew that buffalo did not range in numbers close to the mountains. Fountain Creek was too far west. Why not build the new fort in the Big Timbers, a long belt of noble cottonwoods some twenty-five miles or so down the river from the mouth of the Purgatory? It was a favorite camping spot of such Cheyennes as dared venture that close to Comanche territory. There were shelter, good feed for ponies, plenty of firewood. Buffalo were thick. The warriors could provide and the women tan as many hides as the Long Knives had goods to buy. A fort there would be protection against the Comanches, and Yellow Wolf himself would guarantee to bring his whole clan to trade. The other chiefs grunted assent. In dignity Yellow Wolf drew his robe around him. He had spoken. His words were true.

Charles was impressed. He sensed, also, that more trade than that of the Cheyennes was involved. This stretch of the river was the heartland of the plains, the uneasy border between half a dozen or more tribes: Cheyennes, Arapaho, and

Prairie Apaches wandering the rolling uplifts between the South Platte and the Arkansas; the Utes of the mountains foraging after buffalo and horses; the Comanches and Kiowas south of the river; and roving bands of Crows, Gros Ventres, and Wyoming Shoshoni out to visit friends or raid enemies. Yellow Wolf had spoken good words. The brothers would think them over.[12]

In the end the fort's location was moved down-river from Fountain Creek, but not as far as the Big Timbers—and evidence exists that William later regretted not following Yellow Wolf's exact suggestion. Why the Bents did not choose Big Timbers cannot be said. Undoubtedly Charles wanted the fort located at a point where he could haul supplies to it and then go on to New Mexico without retracing his steps; for this reason he was interested in a spot near the ford that led to Timpas Creek and Raton Pass. Probably, too, he wanted to keep the fort as close as possible to the mountains without leaving good buffalo country, in order to make the establishment an outfitting center for the free trappers of the southern Rockies. The mouth of Purgatory Creek, with its trees and good grazing, would fit all the requirements. But unfortunately Purgatory Creek was on Mexican soil, open to interference from Santa Fe. Of necessity the brothers crossed to the American north bank of the Arkansas. Then they moved from the Purgatory a dozen miles upstream, between the sites of the future Colorado cities of Las Animas and La Junta. This brought them closer to the mountains and to the ford leading toward Raton Pass. Otherwise, it is difficult to account for the choice. The valley is sterile there; wood and grass were never abundant.

Indeed, the entire region is harsh, the center of what map makers long designated as the Great American Desert. Dry winds scour everlastingly; the evaporation rate is higher than at any other place in America save the deserts along the California-Mexico border. As a result more rain is needed to grow short grass on the southeastern plains of Colorado than, say, in Montana, and the rains are niggardly—a scant annual fifteen inches that come mostly from scattered, violent thunderstorms between April and June. Of the plains tributaries of the Arkansas River, only Purgatory Creek flows more than intermittently. The others, rising in timber belts far north and south of the river, dwindle away in the sand, reappearing only in occasional, often bitter pools—except when flash floods roll torrents of mud between the low banks. Back from the bottomlands, where willows, rushes, wild plums, grapes, and cherries grow, vegetation shrinks to blade-leafed yucca, dwarf cactus, and the thick, shallow sod that once nurtured incredible hordes of buffalo, antelope, prairie dogs—and the wolves, coyotes, foxes, and soaring vultures which one way or another subsisted on these inexhaustible larders of meat.

In winter northers howled. A sudden black cloud would pall the sky, prelude to screaming blasts of sand and temperatures that dropped as much as fifty degrees almost while a man was putting on his coat. There would come a whip of needle-like snow, then a swift clearing and dreadful cold. In summer temperatures climbed above the hundred-degree mark. Weird hot blasts, a few hundred feet to half a mile wide, flowed like invisible rivers between narrow belts of more moderate air. Spirits shriveled as respiratory organs dried; lips cracked and eyes burned. Loneliness, barrenness, glare, dreads real and dreads imaginary—it took a particular kind of spiritual iron to survive. And yet, and yet . . . in spring a softness touched the air. Cumulus clouds piled unbelievable turrets above the far line of the mountains; meadowlarks and lark sparrows dripped golden song where coreopsis, poppies, and sunflowers blossomed; and through the deep green light of twilight sounded the boom of diving nighthawks. Utter freedom, utter independence. Some twisted it into license, treachery, cruelty. But some found a self-realization they could not discover in kindlier, more restricted lands, a wholeness which words have never been quite able to describe.

In those winds, under that pouring sun, the Bents picked out the site for their mud castle. Southward across the river were low sand hills; along the north bank were small chalk bluffs and ledges of rock. Bordering the river were bottomlands that high water might flood but where in good seasons there might be enough grass for horses and perhaps even for cutting skimpy bits of hay. A hundred yards or so back from the stream (accounts vary, perhaps because the capricious Arkansas occasionally changed its channel) stood a gravelly bench com-

manding a long view of the valley. Here, the brothers said.
And far southwest they saw the magnificent humps of the
Spanish Peaks, and far northwest the dim helmet of Pike's
mountain, and north and south and east the edges of a rolling
immensity whose full extent no man had yet completely
grasped. Here. This was the heartland.

St. Vrain must have been consulted almost immediately and
found agreeable. Quite possibly he visited the site of the fort
and checked the plans before returning to Taos to make arrangements for such supplies and labor as were available
there. Meanwhile the four Bents turned their wagon train on
down the Arkansas. In early November they reached Independence with a cargo of silver bullion, mules, and furs which
the newspapers estimated as worth $190,000, "the avails of
nearly two years."

Strange stirrings tormented Independence. Members of a
sect called Mormons were pouring into Jackson County, setting
up a printing press, talking of a great temple, gaining control
of land, and in general putting the more orthodox Missourians
into dithers of resentment. Well, it was no affair of Charles or
William. Other information they gleaned struck closer home,
for it concerned the St. Vrains. While Ceran had been in New
Mexico, his older brothers, Charles and Felix St. Vrain, had
gone into the Indian trade on the Mississippi. There they had
won respect: when Thomas Forsythe had resigned in 1830 as
agent to the Sacs and Foxes, Felix had been appointed his
successor; and Charles St. Vrain worked with his brother as
agriculturist and as interpreter for Governor Reynolds during
the tense negotiations with Black Hawk's angry tribe. When
Black Hawk declared war, Felix St. Vrain was killed. The Indians cut off his hands and feet and ate pieces of his heart
so that they could say they had gained spirit from one of the
bravest Americans. It would be hard news to take back to Taos.

William Bent was probably the one who took the word back.
There was no need for him to await the assembling of the annual Santa Fe caravan, but it was desirable for him to reach
the upper Arkansas with dispatch so that work on the huge
fort could begin as soon as weather permitted. It was well he
hurried.[13] Behind him the regular caravan of 93 wagons and
183 men, of which Charles was again elected captain, ran into

torrential rains in western Missouri. Not until June were the
merchants able to start across the drying prairies.

Meanwhile William had got together with Ceran St. Vrain,
probably in Taos, and with gangs of hired laborers the two
young men crossed the mountains to launch the construction.
Plans had been thoroughly discussed. Although in later years
a few second-story rooms were added to the fort's southern
and western walls, every other essential feature of the great
bastion was in mind the day the first corner stake was driven.
It was a bold concept. In evaluating the fort's magnitude, one
must remember that in nearly two thousand miles from the
Mississippi to the Pacific there was no other building that re-
motely approached it. Only the American Fur Company's Fort
Pierre and Fort Union far up the Missouri were comparable;
and Charles Bent, who sketched the broad outlines of the fort,
had not seen these posts, though of course he was familiar with
the general plan of the Missouri River trading posts.

William and Ceran stepped off a space not quite rectangular,
not quite true with the compass. The fort faced a little east of
north and its western wall was slightly longer than the others,
though only careful measurements would show that the main
section of the fort was not a rectangle. Their plan set rooms
around the entire quadrangle, facing inward. There were about
twenty-five of these, with earthen floors and plastered walls,
averaging about fifteen by twenty feet in size. The trading
and storage rooms along the eastern side were somewhat
larger than the others, most of which served as dwellings. Because they were dwellings, most contained fireplaces for individual housekeeping, though only two of the hearths followed the Spanish tradition of being in a corner. Outside their
doors, which fronted a courtyard called the placita, ran a tim-
ber-supported veranda.

The main entry faced north and lay tunnel-like between two
rooms. It was large enough to pass freight wagons—nine feet
wide by seven high, and its outer gate was stoutly made of
iron-sheathed planks. Wickets were perhaps cut through the
walls from the bordering rooms to allow distribution of goods
without the necessity of admitting suspect savages to the inner
part of the fort, the placita.

This part of the structure was regular enough, but to the

south the layout grew complex. Behind the dwelling rooms on that side an alley ran east and west, and back of the alley was a long narrow building perhaps used for storing buffalo hides and for sheltering wagons. This long building projected eastward farther than the apartment rectangle, so that the wall which ran from it to the front corner of the fort left a curious triangular space behind the eastern trade and storage rooms. What purpose this triangle was designed to serve is hard to conjecture; perhaps the long building was extended as an afterthought and the wall was slanted out to its end in order to eliminate corners and improve defense. In any event, the fort thus became trapezodial, its dimensions 137 feet by 178 feet.[14]

The walls were fourteen or more feet high and thirty inches (three adobe bricks) thick. At the northeastern and southwestern corners of the trapezoid rose round towers eighteen feet tall and seventeen in diameter. Equipped with musketry and small fieldpieces, the towers enabled the defenders to sweep with fire all four walls in event of any attempt to storm the fortress. Sabers and lances also hung inside the towers for emergency hand-to-hand fighting, although actually no attack the Indians could mount was capable of forcing the place. A siege of course might starve out the garrison, but in view of the Indians' erratic nature, this was a chance the owners were willing to take—yet Farnham, passing by in 1839, reports that the possibility occasionally worried them.

Behind (south of) the main fort and adjoining the long building was an extensive corral. Its exact size is unknown but in area it was probably not much smaller than the fort itself. Its walls were lower—six to eight feet high. To prevent raiders from scaling them, their tops were planted thick with cactus, which in the spring produced a profusion of brilliant red and white blossoms.

Such was the ground floor. The second story was irregular. Another row of apartments, perhaps added as the fort's business and retinue grew, was built atop the western side of the square. Above the entry tunnel and forming its roof rose a squat watchtower with windows on all four sides; here a high-powered telescope would be mounted. Atop the watchtower was a belfry to hold the loud-tolling iron bell that summoned the men to meals; and rising above the belfry was a flagstaff from which floated the Stars and Stripes. Across the placita from the watchtower, on top of the southeast corner of the square, was a sort of blockhouse, perhaps an office for the clerks. West from it and oddly straddling the alley was the second-floor eyrie of the owners, a pretentious rectangular room that in time would be equipped with a billiard table and a bar.

In addition to its warehouses, the mud castle contained food storerooms, kitchen, dining hall, shops for blacksmithing, tailoring, carpentering. Within the main court, or placita, there would be a well of excellent water, a huge press for packing buffalo robes, and a brass cannon which each day was run out in front of the main gate. In short, as Lieutenant Abert remarked in notes made in 1846, the layout was "complex." Space was tightly utilized; Matthew Field, correspondent for the New Orleans *Picayune*, reported in 1839 that the place could garrison two hundred men and three to four hundred animals.

Except for some support timbers, beams, and the posts which held the narrow porch that lined most of the placita, everything was built of adobe. It added up to a lot of brick.

Perhaps a hundred or a hundred and fifty Mexican peons were brought from Taos to do the work. They were probably paid from five to ten dollars a month, much of it in calico, blue cloth, powder, lead, and coffee, all marked up at astronomical rates but still representing a higher net wage than was available at home. Also from Taos came dozens of wagonloads of coarse, cheap Mexican wool to be used along with marsh grass as binding for the mud. Water was hauled from the river in barrels and dumped into several huge pits. Other men dug and hauled clay. Yokes of circling oxen, prodded with long goads, tramped the mud to the proper stiffness for packing into molds perhaps a foot long, ten inches wide, and four to six inches thick. After being shaped in its mold, each brick was dumped out on smooth ground to dry—tens of thousands of them, heavy as sin after a long day of toting them up rickety, handmade ladders to the tops of the rising walls.

Before the work was well under way, smallpox swept the camp, introduced probably by the Mexicans. If the disease should reach the susceptible Indians, the results would be appalling. (A few years later the upper Missouri tribes would be decimated by one of the most virulent smallpox epidemics in American history.) William Bent, who seems to have suffered a comparatively mild attack, dispatched runners to warn the Cheyennes away from the stricken camp. Recovering, he nursed those who were too ill to move and sent the others home, including Ceran St. Vrain, who was packed to Taos in a mule litter.[15]

In isolation the disease burned itself out. Now lightly pock-marked for life, William destroyed every infected article and regathered the laborers. St. Vrain returned, round-faced, stocky, ebullient as ever, roaring orders through the hedge of whiskers that led the smooth-cheeked Cheyennes to name him Black Beard. Slowly the walls rose. Four feet lower than their tops, the roofs of the rooms were laid, Mexican-fashion—a corduroy of poles sloping gently from the fort's outer walls inward toward the central court. These ribbings were covered with brush and grass; then a thick layer of tramped clay was added, and the whole was topped with gravel. The almost flat roofs offered a position for defense behind the parapet of the walls, and also, on summer evenings, a fine promenade. As finishing touches, all floors were paved with a layer of beaten clay. Gravel was spread on the inner court to combat dust and mud.

Even before the structure was completed, it was named Fort William in honor of the man, not yet twenty-five years old, who had supervised most of the building and who would be its resident manager. For years the owners thus referred to the fort. But the mountain men who used the establishment and who spread its fame would have none of that. To them the refuge was always Bent's Fort (properly Bents' but never so written), and in time their custom became history's fact.

By the fall of 1833 the building was far enough advanced for business to start. In the East, Charles applied for and was granted, under date of December 18, an official U. S. Government trading license—a legality William seems to have ignored during the previous years when operating out of Mexican Taos. A $2000 bond was posted and the value of the trade goods involved was declared at $3877.28.[16] The move could not

have come at a more propitious time. The year before, John
Jacob Astor had noted silk hats on British men and had foreseen the end of the demand for beaver felt. Between the fall
of 1832 and October 1833 beaver prices in St. Louis skidded
from $6.00 a pound to $3.50. In the northern and central
Rockies, the Rocky Mountain and American Fur companies,
Wyeth, Bonneville, and a scattering of lesser men like Gantt
and Blackwell were cutting each other's throats over a dying
trade. From now on buffalo pelts would be the hinge that
swung the doors of the West, and the Bents and St. Vrain
were ready.

They had no intention of sitting on their laurels and waiting
for customers to come to their fine new fort. Their license shows
that. They asked for and were granted the right to trade not
only with the neighboring Cheyennes and Arapaho but also
with Snakes (the Wyoming Shoshoni, probably, and the Shoshoni's cousins, the Comanches), with Kiowas, Sioux, and even
Arikaras, who lately had been driven from the Missouri by the
Sioux. Trading points were designated along the eastern base
of the Rockies and "ten miles below the Black Hills"—not the
Black Hills of South Dakota, but the present Laramie Mountains of Wyoming. Still another post was named "near the
mouth of the Bear River" in northwestern Colorado, diagonally
across the state from the fort. This last point means that the
Bents were willing to cut in on the fur trade for as much as
they could get away with, and for the next decade their
traders would peck away at the fringes of the northern territory. Pursuant to this dangerous scheme, Kit Carson, who had
returned to Taos after the collapse of Gantt and Blackwell,
signed up in October 1833 with a Captain Lee and headed for
Bear River with a mule train of Bent, St. Vrain goods.[17]

Meanwhile William Bent and Ceran St. Vrain rode out from
the fort toward the Black Hills to find the Cheyennes and tell
them the smallpox danger was over. Of the meeting nothing
is known. But in time some 350 lodges, more than 2500 souls,
drifted after the traders back toward the Arkansas, thus making permanent the division of the Cheyenne tribe into northern and southern branches. Apparently no Missouri newspaper
noticed this shift that was to change the pattern of the plains.
But far up the Missouri River, at the American Fur Company's

new Fort Pierre in central South Dakota, trader William Laidlaw correctly evaluated the threat and wrote to Pierre Chouteau on January 10, 1834, "I understand from the Sioux that Charles Bent has built a Fort upon the Arkanzas . . . and if judiciously carried on it cannot fail to be very injurious to the trade in this part of the country. The Cheyennes have remained in that part of the country depending I have no doubt on that very establishment, and if kept up I have very little doubt but a great many of the Sioux will follow their example."

On November 12, 1833, while some of those Cheyennes were camped outside the fort's still unfinished walls, a dazzling shower of meteors blazed across the night sky. All America saw them. In Independence frightened Missourians were convinced that heaven was protesting against recent mobbings and whippings of the Mormons. In Santa Fe horrified Mexicans were sure that the state had brought a flaming curse on itself by denying certain privileges to the Church.

The Cheyennes read a different doom, one connected with the four medicine arrows which their culture hero, Sweet Medicine, had brought them at the beginning of time. These were totems of tremendous power: two buffalo arrows, assuring plentiful food; two man arrows, guaranteeing success in war. No woman, half-breed, or white man was permitted to look on objects so sacrosanct. They were kept wrapped in wolfskin in an extra-large lodge in the center of the village, and every night, supposedly, a specially chosen warrior armed with a long pole stood outside the tepee to drive prowling dogs away from this holiest of holies. The caretaker of the arrows was a powerful priest who, with his wife, always went about daubed with red paint. In the time of the building of Bent's Fort this priest was a man named Gray Thunder, or, as the name is sometimes translated, White Thunder. He was more than sixty years old, wrinkled, tough-minded, courageous, and, for an Indian, steadfast in his thinking. He was also, as William Bent had noted, the father of two pretty daughters, Owl Woman and Yellow Woman.

In 1832, at about the time the Bents were selecting the site for their fort, tragedy struck the Cheyennes. One of their war parties was discovered by Pawnees and obliterated. Later another Cheyenne party chanced on the mutilated bodies and furiously reported the discovery to their village. In grief women relatives of the slain men cut off their hair, hacked their faces and arms with knives. Blood streaming down their hands, they approached the warriors, ran bloody fingers over the men, and begged for revenge. Pipes were sent to other villages and even to the Sioux, and most of those appealed to signified, by smoking, their readiness to join a war party. Runners came from all the groups, and a council of elders decided that when cherries were red the following summer the entire tribe would move against the enemy behind the protection of the medicine arrows.

Portentous ceremony accompanied so rare and awesome a move. The huge cavalcade, women and children included, assembled near the Platte and finally, amid tremendous confusion, marched northeast into Nebraska. Scouts ranged ahead, looking for Pawnees. Four of these scouts were discovered and slain by the enemy, and now the wild anger being engendered by the nightly dances reached fever pitch. Meanwhile other scouts found the Pawnees gathered in a great village for some sort of ceremony of their own. The enemy camp was only a night's march away.

Here the soldier bands took over, exercising such discipline as could be imposed on the erratic and utterly individualistic Indians. Nearly every able-bodied, ambitious Cheyenne belonged to one of these four bands of soldiers: the Kit Foxes, Elkhorn Scrapers, Red Shields, and Dog Soldiers. (The last named, strictest in its discipline and, in later years, most feared by the whites, dwelt in a separate camp of its own, and on any march generally acted as the village's rear guard. Many Dog Soldiers were half Sioux, sometimes called Cheyenne Sioux.) Among them, these societies regulated the major dances, communal hunts, and the four-day ceremonies of "renewing" the medicine arrows; that is, attaching new feathers and rewrapping the shafts with fresh sinew. On a tribal move against an enemy the soldiers tried to keep some kind of order.

Every soul in the camp went on this last dark march against the Pawnees. All the lodges were left standing on the final campground, but each tepee's skirts were ceremoniously raised. Scaffolds were built for holding goods out of reach of coyotes and wolves. Meat was prepared and loaded with choice possessions on travois, to be dragged along with the marchers. Small children, too, rode the travois, being tied down so they would not tumble off in their sleep. As the women worked over the packing, the warriors prepared their weapons, sang their war songs, painted themselves and their horses. Then off through the night they went, the men riding, the women walking and leading the pack animals. Back and forth along the shadowy edges galloped the guards of the soldier societies. Before enemy blood could be shed, the ceremony of the arrows must be completed; and hence it was imperative that no young men, eager for the glory of counting the first coup, be allowed to slip off ahead on a secret raid of their own.

Dawn grayed over the weird scene. A short distance ahead lay the Pawnee village, roused to sudden turmoil by this unexpected appearance. And far off to one side a group of Cheyenne scouts saw a few Pawnee buffalo hunters. The scouts did not know that the ritual of the arrows had not yet begun. Besides, the opportunity was irresistible. They charged and killed.

Meanwhile the Cheyenne warriors drew up before the enemy village in two divisions, one division led by the totem of the buffalo cap, the other by the medicine arrows. In a great semicircle to the rear stood the wailing women and wide-eyed children. Now Gray Thunder came forward with Bull, the medicine man chosen to bear the arrows into battle. He raised the wolfskin packet. The women turned their backs lest they glimpse the awful charm. Gray Thunder removed the four arrows and faced the enemy, holding the notched ends in his left hand and resting the points across his right forefinger in a gesture imitative of shooting. He was chewing medicine root. Four times he spat toward the gathering Pawnees, to make them blind. Then, as he raised his left foot, the warriors gave four mighty whoops. They did not know that the slain Pawnee buffalo hunters were vitiating the magic. The ritual finished, Gray Thunder rewrapped the arrows in their wolfskin and tied the packet near the head of Bull's lance. In a loud voice the medicine priest warned the warriors to stay behind the arrows, which would protect the Cheyennes and turn the Pawnees helpless.

By this time the Pawnees had caught their horses and had drawn up in line of battle, watching the hocus-pocus with primitive uneasiness. What was going on? As they wondered, out in front of them walked a Pawnee who was ill or wounded and apparently desirous of death. Weakly he sat on the ground and waited. Seeing him, Bull charged to count the first coup with the arrow-bearing lance. And then, before the eyes of all the Cheyennes, the incredible happened. The sitting Pawnee ducked Bull's blow, caught the lance, and tore it from the bearer's grasp. Terrified, Bull wheeled back, chanting a lament. Realizing their man had captured something wonderful, the Pawnees rushed forward to see. The Cheyennes tried to counter. But the heart was gone from them. The charge faltered, broke, turned into a panicked retreat.

Later, at a solemn council, the chiefs and medicine men rationalized that Cheyenne magic in Pawnee hands would obviously lose its power and that the solution was to make four new arrows. With elaborate rites this was done. But the priest, Gray Thunder, grieved. He did not trust these substitutes. Somewhere, somehow, he would get the old ones back. Among others of the elders there was fear. The loss of what had been with them from the beginning of time could mean only the end.[18]

And now, on November 12, 1833, the very firmament was cracking open, tumbling down the stars. While the skies dripped fire, while William Bent and other traders watched from the fort's unfinished walls, the visiting warriors decked themselves in full battle regalia of feather and paint, lance and shield. They could not fight this fearful thing. But at least they could die like men. They mounted their horses. Women cried and children shrieked; in the fort the dogs howled back at the chorusing wolves. Chanting their death dirges above the din, the warriors rode in single file around the tepees, under the shadow of the great mud bastions.

The next morning the sun shone again. The young men laughed at their alarm, and stories of the night the stars fell passed into folk tale. Nonetheless, the symbol of death stood above them, unrecognized because from its vast walls seemed to come the luxuries of a fuller life. Better if the dirges had been for this, the white man's earthen fist henceforth clenched

unshakably about the people of the plains. Little though Bent,
St. Vrain & Company may have intended the doom, or even
thought about it, the arrows of an aboriginal faith were forever
blunted, the star of the Cheyennes could do nothing but dim.

CHAPTER VIII

ROBES, ALCOHOL, AND DRAGOONS

The Bents' Fort William had scarcely been completed
when Bill Sublette and Robert Campbell began building, in
the spring of 1834, a huge log post on southeastern Wyoming's Laramie River, not far from its junction with the North
Platte. Work progressed swiftly. By September, Lucien Fontenelle wrote Pierre Chouteau that the post had "men running
after these Indians [the Sioux and Cheyennes] to bring them
to the River Platte. Buffalo is in abundance on that river during all seasons of the year, and the situation may turn out to
be an advantageous one."[1]

Here was an immediate threat to the new firm of Bent, St.
Vrain & Company. From the beginning, as Charles Bent's trading license shows, the partners had planned to spread far up
into Wyoming. With the advent of Fort Laramie, they realized
more acutely than ever that to support the overhead of their
huge establishment they must search out every merchandisa-
ble buffalo robe at its source in the Indian villages.

Winter was the season when robes were prime, and so winter, with all its cruelties, became the trading season. As snow
gales blew and deep frost turned the prairie sod to iron, the
traders made their preparations. Indefatigable men—none more
so than William Bent. The burden of the field work was on
him. At first Ceran St. Vrain, too, was often out with trading
parties; but more and more frequently the New Mexico end
of the business took him to Taos, where the firm had opened
an adobe store on the south side of the plaza. Charles apparently made few trips among the Indians. Though he often
visited the fort and there became well acquainted with the
Cheyennes and their language, the bulk of his time was con-

sumed with the caravans rolling into Independence and back, and in handling commercial details both in St. Louis and New Mexico. Thus, though the senior partners retained control of policy making, the actual operation of the fort devolved on the man who had conceived the business in the first place. It was a fitting choice. Restless William, with an almost instinctive knack for handling Indians, was ill content to sit placidly inside any walls, however large. Always he was on the move. Such scanty records as exist show him ranging with his trade carts and pack mules from the Panhandle of Texas on the south, northward through Colorado and western Kansas into Wyoming, Nebraska, and the fringes of South Dakota.

It is one of the regrettable vacuums of our history that we know almost nothing of these trips nor of the men who helped William Bent implement the trade. When names bob up later —Uncle Dick Wootton, Mexican Sol Silver, Lucien Maxwell, Carson, Beckwourth, Blackfoot John Smith and a host of colorful others—the hard groundwork had been finished and the name of Bent's Fort was a talisman across the southwestern plains. But though we do not know details of specific trips nor anecdotes of the early trail blazers, we can reconstruct the methods by which they operated.

At the start of the season one of the firm's partners (or, in their absence, the chief clerk) carefully discussed with each trader his proposed route and the probable amount of goods he would need. Junior clerks, often young gentlemen from the States, apportioned the merchandise and charged it against the trader's account: white, blue, and red beads, red cloth, brass wire, hoop iron for making arrowheads, butcher knives, small axes, kettles, vermilion, lead, blankets of white, blue, and black—actually a very deep blue. Coffee and sugar, used mainly as good-will gifts, were measured out in three-pint Connecticut clay cups, as were the coarse grains of black gunpowder. Top luxury items included Navajo blankets and abalone shells. The latter, valued by the warriors according to their iridescence, were shaped into earbobs, leftover fragments being given to squaws and children for decorating their frocks. The tightly woven, boldly patterned Navajo blankets, highly prized by Cheyenne girls, were obtained by sending traders into the deserts of New Mexico and Arizona; transplanted to

Colorado, a single blanket would net up to ten buffalo robes
from an indulgent parent or husband.

All this material, together with illegal alcohol in small kegs
that the Indians called "hollow-woods," was loaded either onto
mules or carts, depending on the nature of the terrain to be
covered. Unless trouble was anticipated, the traders traveled
by twos or threes; and if a winter sun sparkled, the trips
weren't unpleasant. It was otherwise when blasts of sand and
sleet howled out of a leaden sky. Wise travelers carted wood
with them, for a heavy snowfall would bury buffalo chips, the
prairie's only fuel, beyond finding. To keep from freezing a
man often had to dismount and walk, breaking through the
crust, filling his moccasins with snow, falling, cursing, until he
grew too weary even for curses. His animals suffered cruelly.
The icy crusts cut their legs. At night they found what shelter
they could and stood hang-headed with their sterns to the
wind, too cold, sometimes, to paw for grass. As yellow twilight
faded above the camp—a hungry camp if no game had been
sighted—the sharp bark of a coyote would ring out, others
would answer, and in an instant the black sky seemed to ulu-
late. Always gaunt white wolves followed the travelers by day,
ringed them by night, and grew so bold that they would slip
into the camp itself to steal strips of leather or anything else
that was edible. Frozen branches cracked; gusts of wind
boomed crazily; spurts of fire under the black kettles ebbed
and died. A man folded one buffalo robe under him, spread
another on top, stretched his wet moccasins toward the fire,
and shivered out the night as best he could. Then on again,
wagon wheels screeching over the crust, and the breath of
horses and men alike freezing into beards of icicles.

Finally a village was found. Indians poured out, jabbering
welcome. If the traders contemplated a lengthy stay, they
might build a shanty of cottonwood logs. Otherwise they carried their goods into the lodge of the principal chief, who assigned them the place of honor to his left. Almost at once arrangements were made for "soldiers." The duty of these young
warriors, selected by the trader and chief, was to protect the
merchandise from pilfering and, in case the liquor situation
got out of control, to save the trader from bodily harm. Most
of the chosen young men were proud of the honor and cor-

respondingly responsible. To enhance the dignity, the traders often dressed their soldiers in uniforms. Dick Wootton, trading for Bent, St. Vrain & Company among the Sioux north of Fort Laramie in the winter of 1835–36, tells of using militia coats, shoulder straps, gilt-handled swords, and stovepipe hats bedecked with red feathers—incongruous enough above breechclout and leggings.

Before trade was opened there was a distribution "on the prairie"; that is, gifts of trinkets to key men. To express appreciation and to enlarge the scope of the "prairie," squaws might put on a begging dance. During the traders' first few nights in camp the leading warriors visited the lodge. Solemnly the Indians shook hands and then sat at the guests' left, being careful not to violate etiquette by passing in front of the fire, even though this meant circling the entire lodge to reach a seat. During the ensuing conversation no child dared whimper; if it did, the mother immediately hustled it outside. Dogs, however, were more difficult to control. Every so often the swarms of them scavenging through the village broke into terrible uproars; the half dozen or so inside the lodge would bolt full-cry across the squatted men to investigate, a chorus of wolves would answer, and throughout the village every conversation was stifled until the hideous din subsided.

When formal trade was about to open, the camp crier stalked through the village and in stentorian bellows announced what everyone knew: the name of the trader and the sort of merchandise he had brought. Now the squaws came, lugging in some of their robes to trade for necessities; the other pelts were held back by the warriors for their own personal desires. The first robes traded generally set the price for all, and long dickers ensued. An exception to the standard price might be a fine-haired, light-colored cowhide that gleamed like satin; these were called "silk robes" and commanded premiums. Even after prices were set, a squaw took forever making up her mind what she wanted, bartered her robes one by slow one, and fingered every commodity for minutes on end. Each bargain was generally sealed by the woman's sharing a few puffs with the trader on his pipe. In between transactions the whites might while away the time playing backgammon, and if business grew too slack they tried to lure customers by serving heavily sweetened coffee. As the hides piled up, the traders built a square crib of logs. Here they squeezed the robes into bales by hammering huge wooden wedges through the latticed sides of the crib.

Around them the village life revolved lazily. In between hours of scraping away at the endless buffalo robes, the women cooked, sewed clothes, cleaned house (the Cheyennes had the reputation of being the neatest housekeepers in the West), and cared for their children. Early each morning nearly every adult female in the village, accompanied by hordes of boys, girls, and harnessed dogs, went to the cottonwood groves to gather firewood and bark for their husbands' prize war horses. (Ordinary animals grazed as best they could on the nearby hills, under charge of the boys.) Laughing and screeching, the women climbed high into the trees and lopped off the upper branches. The wood, bulky rather than heavy, was strapped into ungainly piles. Part of it the squaws lugged home on their own backs. The rest was dragged on travois hitched to the huge, wolfish dogs. The animals did not like the chore. They growled and fought each other. Sometimes they ran away, women and children in vociferous pursuit. Every few yards they lay stubbornly down to rest, whining dismally under rains of blows.

Meanwhile the men sat in the sun making arrows or preening in front of small looking glasses while they decorated their faces with vermilion streaks or plaited their silver-ornamented hair, which among Cheyenne men sometimes grew well below their waists. Boys wandered about with miniature bows. Sometimes gangs of youngsters would pack up dogs, go a short distance from the village, pitch a mock camp, and play war, riding stick horses and leading stick war ponies into battle. They wrestled and held kicking matches, the object of the latter being to jump into the air and lash out at an opponent with one or both feet. Steep snow slopes provided coasting on sleds made from buffalo ribs, wood, or pieces of rawhide.

Throwing games were popular among old and young alike. In one, spike-headed darts were hurled with amazing accuracy at a mark fifty yards or so away. In another, played for distance on smooth ice, horn-tipped twigs, feathered bones, or bone-tipped willows were skidded along with a deft, underhand toss. Or two groups of men might line up facing each other forty or fifty yards apart and roll back and forth hoops laced with rawhide. The purpose was to claim an opponent's wheel by chucking a pronged stick through the interstices in the rawhide; as soon as one side possessed all the hoops, they chased the losers and tried to knock them down by heaving the hoops at them. A kind of shinny was played with curved sticks and a grass-stuffed deerskin ball. A variant, played by women, used a pair of balls connected by a short thong; each team piled trinkets at its goal, and the winning group collected all the goods.

Gambling was a passion. A woman's game had five marked plum seeds or flat bones; these were tossed in a small basket, and the tosser won or lost according to the combinations of marks that appeared. Most famous of all, because of its enthusiastic adoption by the mountain men, was the "game of hand." Though this had many variations, it consisted fundamentally of one player holding a small object between his hands and then, after much hocus-pocus, suddenly separating his fists and challenging an opponent to guess which palm held the marker. Teams would line up beside hider and guesser, make side bets, and chant gambling songs to the thump of small drums or sticks beaten on the ground. A sort of community hypnotism would build up a tense pitch of concentration, and a spirited contest, often lasting throughout the night, would utterly impoverish half of the players.

Such was the normal life that William Bent and his traders shared. With the advent of liquor, however, the whole tenor changed. On reaching a village, unscrupulous traders started business rolling by broaching a keg "on the prairie," and from then on barter in essentials became almost impossible. The men threw away every possession for alcohol; their squaws were lucky to hold back a pair of second-rate robes for necessary awls, kettles, or knives—and many of the women were as drunken as the men. One robe purchased, on an average, three three-gill cups of heavily diluted raw alcohol, and it did not take many cups to blast the Indian system into maudlin incoherence. Thereafter the drinker was cheated unmercifully. The more intoxicated he became, the more water was put into his alcohol. The quantity held by the cup was further reduced by the trader's holding his fingers inside as he filled it, or by substituting another whose bottom was thickened with a layer of wax. Sometimes, as the Indian neared unconsciousness, he was given nothing more than plain water hopped up with tobacco and pepper.

The orgies pass civilized belief. The Indians vomited over themselves and each other, grew lecherous and broke homes with almost public adulteries, sold their daughters for a night to the traders, howled, sang, and eventually began to fight. The women whooped, squealed, and pulled hair. Often the trader was endangered by the passions he unleashed. Occasionally the Indians would steal his horses and he would have to buy them back with more alcohol. Sage, bartering for Lupton in the early '40s, tells repeated tales of traders being shot or stabbed and of one white who was held over a fire until he was roasted alive. Many others were saved only by the intervention of their soldiers or of sensible squaws.

Out of self-interest, if nothing else, responsible traders deplored the horror. Though fly-by-night operators might be content to skim off the cream of a village's robes with alcohol, established concerns preferred the fuller, if slower, profits that came from more normal and leisurely operations. In addition, as foresighted whites began to realize, an unrestrained flow of alcohol could debauch every tribe on the plains to the point where the Indians no longer would be capable of sustained hunting and tanning operations. The tribes would then start living hand to mouth, and the trade might well dwindle to nothing more than the sporadic floating off of a few poor robes in puddles of alcohol.

No long-range operation could face the prospect with equanimity. And yet . . . one had to fight fire with fire. If firms like Bent, St. Vrain & Company did not meet the Indians' insatiable demand for alcohol, the business would go to the dozens of illegal operators hanging around the edges of the territory. This was bad enough. Unfortunately, the big companies also used the weapon in fighting each other. Although every contemporary account of Bent, St. Vrain & Company ascribes to them an honor in their Indian dealings far higher than the normal standard of the plains, they unquestionably resorted to liquor when circumstances demanded. Their virtue, if it is a virtue, lies in their having tried to hold the evil to a minimum. One of William's compromises was to credit the alcohol but not deliver it until trading was finished, sometimes sending the stuff out only once or twice a year and letting the chiefs distribute it among the red creditors according to markings of colored strings on each keg.

In that lonely land ethics all too often became whatever a man's caprice or power wanted them to become. Particularly was this true when he was motivated by revenge. In the early summer of 1834, for example, just about the time the fort had been completed, a band of Shoshoni wandered down from Wyoming to visit their relatives, the Comanches. Near Taos they fell on Charles Bent and stole a herd of mules from him. Later, on July 29, 1834, eight lodges of Shoshoni approached a log stockade on the Arkansas where William Bent was trading. In William's party were ten men, including three Delaware Indian hunters, and Alexander Le Grande, who had captained the pioneering Storrs-Marmaduke wagon train of 1824; Lucas Murray, a violent Irishman out of Canada; and Robert Fisher, who would be a Bent, St. Vrain stalwart for many years. Also present at the same stockade were John Gantt and a party, back from their unsuccessful invasion of the fur country to the north.

As the Shoshoni approached, William recognized them as some of the party that had stolen Charles's mules—or thought he recognized them, which was enough for his impetuous young nature.

"Boys," he told his men, "let's get 'em."

One of the other party protested. Even granting that the Shoshoni were guilty of the raid on Charles, they were arriving now in peace. If talks at the stockade didn't suffice for settlement, proper channels existed through the government—provided, of course, the government ever got around to acting on the claim.

"Damn the government," William snapped. "I'll settle it now."

Murray fired first on an unsuspecting Shoshoni standing only a few feet away. The Indian dropped dead and the battle was on. It was soon over—three Shoshoni killed and one wounded.

Also wounded in the scuffle was an Arapaho, an innocent bystander. No white was hurt.

Picking up the wounded man, the Shoshoni fled in terror—
there must have been forty or so of them, counting men,
women, and children. Behind them they left thirty-seven
horses, several guns, kettles, axes, ropes, and other possessions.
The whites also captured two women. The pair were turned
over to one of the uninvolved witnesses, who the next day
dispatched them to their main village. The rest of the plunder,
however, William and his men divided among themselves by
lottery.

The Shoshoni, so far as is known, sought no recompense,
either by direct attack or through the government. In time,
however, a report was made to the Indian Office by the outraged witness who had returned the two women to their people.[2] There is no evidence that any reprimand followed, perhaps because Charles was able to quiet matters. The sorry
affair, tuned to the mountain man's harsh key of teaching the
Indians to keep in line, constitutes the blackest mark on William Bent's record. No similar one appears again; and it may
be that from the wanton bloodshed came good, that William's
own unhappy conscience, undoubtedly helped by Charles's
angry reaction, swung him into henceforth diligently working,
as he did, to remove irresponsible warfare from the plains.

The affray did not, however, soften Bent, St. Vrain & Company's amoral view concerning stolen horses. Though the partners might resent having their own stock raided, they nonetheless did not question the ethics of the matter when the thievery
was committed on someone else. Readily they bought all animals offered for sale, without questioning the source. This of
course accorded with the Indians' concept. To them horse stealing was honorable and possession conveyed valid title.

Still, a man wasn't wise in every instance to insist on possession as the full ten points of the law. Not long after the
Shoshoni murder, a band of Yellow Wolf's Cheyennes stopped
by Bent's Fort on their way home from another successful raid
on the herds of the Comanche chief, Bull Hump. Feeling ex-
pansive, Yellow Wolf gave William Bent a mouse-colored
mule and a magnificent spotted stallion, then galloped on.
Shortly afterward Bull Hump rode angrily up with a large war

party. William smoked a pipe with the Comanches, probably passed out a few presents. Meanwhile the horse and mule were kept judiciously out of sight in the fort's adobe corral. Later the spotted horse became famous throughout the West—the best buffalo horse, Kit Carson subsequently told William's son, that Kit had ever seen.

As far as strictly Indian horses were concerned, the Indian view was the only pragmatic one. But often horses appeared with Spanish brands on hip or shoulder, showing clearly enough their general, if not their specific, point of origin—sometimes from as far away as northern Mexico. There is no record that the Bents ever brought up the matter. For one thing, such strange legality would only have bewildered and angered their customers.

Not all the thieves were Indians, however, and not all the Spanish horses came from Mexico. American trappers and traders, notably Ewing Young, had learned that the lush valleys of California were full of first-class stock. Young was honest about it. When he, David Jackson, and David Waldo led a combined beaver-trapping and mule-buying party out of Santa Fe in August 1831, they took with them several packloads of Mexican silver to facilitate purchases. Not so Old Bill Williams. Bill, it seems, in company with the Walker expedition which Bonneville sent to investigate California's beaver possibilities, reached the coast a little more than a year after Dave Jackson had begun buying stock for Young. The Walker party didn't strain itself trapping. But it did see countless horses ranging almost without supervision. Undoubtedly Bill snorted to himself when he heard that Dave Jackson had ridden as far up the coast as San Francisco, purchasing dibs and dabs of stock here and there until he'd bought about six hundred head. Why go to all that trouble?

Late in February 1834, Joe Walker started his party back eastward. By now Old Bill was, as usual, tired of regimentation. He cut loose with some others, and exactly what the group did remains unknown. But late in the summer of 1834, so the story goes, the lank old eccentric came riding down the Arkansas with a sorry-looking cavalcade. No one looked sorrier than Bill. His stringy body in its greasy buckskins was humped disconsolately over the long rifle resting across his saddle horn. His feet, burdened with huge iron spurs, were thrust into great wooden stirrups buckled so short that his bony knees bent like a grasshopper's. His long, sharp nose hobnobbed with his long, sharp chin, while his little eyes darted about and his querulous voice complained to itself. Behind him a few riders rollicked beside the remnants of a jaded herd of California horses. Hazing on the animals came half a dozen more men, their bedraggled bits of camp equipment loaded on a few pack animals. It had been a long, dry ride.

Charles Bent met them outside the fort. Old Bill's voice rose high and cracked.

"Roll out a barrel, old hoss. I'll kill it, or it'll kill me."

No barrel could kill Old Bill. The fort echoed to a tremendous carousal, Charles bought the horses, and Bill vanished with his hang-over, probably in the direction of Taos.[3] In time he would return, occasionally with more horses. Other men would follow—Joe Walker himself, Beckwourth, and, most indefatigable of all, Ceran St. Vrain's former engagé, Tom Pegleg Smith. Undoubtedly there were more. It was not the kind of trade to be fully reported. But it was a profitable trade back in Missouri, whither the Bents extended it with no twinge of conscience and perhaps with no notion that its ethics would be questioned by later standards.

Charles had brought interesting news with him to the fort that late summer of 1834. The year's principal Santa Fe caravan, of which his wagons were a part, had been escorted toward the border by sixty soldiers under command of a Captain Wharton.[4] These were not foot soldiers, as in the case of Bennet Riley's 1829 escort. They were mounted dragoons, the first American cavalry to see the plains. Not only that, but Charles had learned in Independence that three hundred more dragoons were marching toward Comanche territory along the Red River. General Henry Leavenworth, whom Charles remembered from the bumbling 1823 Arikara campaign on the Missouri, was in charge. Leavenworth's second-in-command was a Colonel Henry Dodge, one-time Missouri and Wisconsin lead miner who had grown up in the Ste. Genevieve district, near the hamlet of Nouvelle Bourbon, whose commandant had been St. Vrain's grandfather.

It is impossible to know how fully Charles grasped the short-sighted policies that lay behind this surprising military maneuver. Generally speaking, however, he was alert to whatever might affect his business; and like everyone on the frontier, he was aware that violent tribal emigrations, imposed by Washington, were disrupting the balance of power west of the river. For years an increasing influx of settlers into the South and into the eastern Mississippi Valley had been uprooting the Indian nations in those areas. Their lands were being negotiated from them by treaty, and now the problem arose of what to do with the homeless people.

To expediency-minded politicians the answer seemed obvious: put the displaced Indians on Louisiana Territory lands. This had been the suggestion of Thomas Jefferson, who had bought the western lands, and it became the active policy of Calhoun and Andrew Jackson. Out with the barbarians! Let them move beyond the western boundaries of Missouri and Arkansas and there form a permanent buffer between the United States and Mexico. And if the tide of settlement continued to roll toward the Pacific? . . . Ridiculous. The plains were uninhabitable by white men, and beyond the plains lay the mountains of Mexico. In the 1830s only a few wild visionaries dared predict a continental nation.

Moving the so-called civilized tribes westward entailed placating the tribes already living along the edges of the plains. It also meant, in order that peace could be maintained and the border protected, a complete overhaul of the United States' undermanned military organization. Widely separated forts were strung from Lake Superior and the upper Missouri down through Wisconsin and Iowa territories into Arkansas and Louisiana. Their nerve center was Jefferson Barracks, near St. Louis; their spearhead, near the junction of the Little Platte and Missouri rivers, was Fort Leavenworth.[5] Garrisoning, too, was revolutionized. Major Bennet Riley's 1829 venture to the Mexican border had demonstrated the folly of trying to police this huge area with foot soldiers. Riley was hardly back at Leavenworth when the War Department experimented with six companies of one-year volunteers, called rangers, who furnished their own horses and arms and were paid a dollar a day.[6] The militia scheme did not succeed. In 1833 the rangers were replaced by 1,832 enlisted dragoons.

Meanwhile, between 1829 and 1837, the government would negotiate ninety-four Indian treaties and, with varying degrees of force, persuaded several thousand eastern red men to move into the West—the southern Indians going into western Arkansas and eastern Oklahoma; the Delawares, Shawnees, Wyandottes, Potawatomi, Kickapoos, and others moving into eastern Kansas and Nebraska.

The legality of the treaties was a white sophistry. The Indians had little idea of what they were really signing. The very concept of individual landownership was foreign to their minds. So, too, was the notion of delegated authority. The whites might think it enough to round up a few chiefs, give them presents, glut them with food and oratory, and have them sign on the dotted line; but the young warriors of the tribes were disinclined to feel bound by what was done in their absence. Innumerable small frictions occurred. In 1833 a crisis seemed imminent. Pawnees killed some Delaware hunters; Chief Souwahnock of the Delawares retaliated by burning a Pawnee village to the ground. Fearing a widespread explosion, the army summoned representatives of half a dozen tribes to a great council at Fort Leavenworth and told the Indians to behave themselves. Inside the white man's stockade, ringed with the white man's gifts, the chiefs agreed to smoke a fraternal pipe.

This achieved, the government decided to impose a *Pax Americana* on the entire artificial, ill-amalgamated Indian nation it had created. The Plains Indians must learn that they were to live at peace not only with the unwelcome eastern red men but also with each other. They must promise, in addition, never again to attack caravans on the Santa Fe Trail. Behind these high-minded motives lay the further consideration of teaching the new dragoons the lie of the western land. After all, there was no telling what the army might be called on to do should the uneasy situation in Texas suddenly erupt into war. And so, pursuant to all these purposes, General Leavenworth's three hundred dragoons in 1834 marched southwest across Pawnee land toward Comanche territory.

At Bent's Fort, Charles's news of the march must have lifted several eyebrows. Peace? With the Comanches? The tribe was in no mood to feel friendly toward Americans. As William Bent had learned by now, Kit Carson, Joe Meek, Bill Mitchell, and three Delaware companions had recently given Comanche pride an infuriating blow.

The incident had occurred a few months before, when Kit's little party rode across the Sangre de Cristo Mountains onto the plains near the Cimarron River. There, where there wasn't even a bush or a gully for shelter, a large war party of Comanches had surprised them. Leaping to the ground, the six men cut the throats of seven mules. By holding onto the plunging animals, the trappers contrived to drop them in a rough circle. The gaps between the corpses they filled by throwing up shallow ridges of earth with their knives. Fortunately the Comanches were armed only with bows and with lances to which hair ropes had been attached so that the weapons could be retrieved after throwing. When the Comanches tried to charge close to the dead mules for a sure kill, the scent of the fresh blood made their mounts shy. Meanwhile the besieged fired in relays, keeping some of their guns loaded at all times. At each volley Comanches dropped, but for six men to beat off more than a hundred was unthinkable. The enraged Comanches kept circling all day long while the trappers parched under a merciless sun. By evening forty-two Indians were dead. That was enough. Howling their frustration, the attackers withdrew. Under cover of darkness the thirst-choked defenders started a seventy-five-mile trek toward water. Perhaps they went by Bent's Fort. It was the closest place where succor could be counted on and one logical route by which they could reach South Park, where records next pick Carson up. In any event, if William Bent had not heard of the battle directly from Kit himself, he soon learned about it through the quick-flashing gossip of the mountain men.

Could Leavenworth's dragoons come to terms with Comanches smarting from a defeat like that? There was no telling. Undoubtedly, however, the partners discussed every angle of the situation. They had been eying the Comanche trade, and it was possible that Leavenworth's show of force might rectify the harm done by the Carson episode. It would be well for William to weigh every rumor sifting up from the Red. If

truce talk sounded authentic, he might be justified in risking
a ride down south to see what he could see.[7]

Meanwhile the military's mission had started well, despite
Lieutenant Philip St. George Cooke's prediction that the march
would prove completely ill advised. Successful powwows were
held first with Pawnees and later with Kiowas, in whose camp
artist George Catlin, trailing along, was impressed by Chief
Dohasan's silver-bedecked hair (it reached to his knees) and
by the Smoked Shield, a seven-foot giant who reputedly killed
buffalo by running beside them on foot and stabbing them
with a short spear. By now, however, the summer heat of the
plains was growing intolerable. Under its hammering blows
malaria racked the dragoons. With a bitter I-told-you-so pen
Lieutenant Cooke wrote, "Nature would seem to have con-
spired with an imbecile military administration for the destruction of the regiment. On, on they marched . . . disease struck
them as they moved; with the false mirage ever in view; with
glassy eyes and parched tongues, they seemed on a sea of
fire."

Under the broiling sun Leavenworth sickened and died.
Command now devolved on Colonel Henry Dodge, whose ag-
gressive six-foot frame was the quintessence of the expanding
frontier. Born in 1782 at the outpost of Vincennes, Indiana,
Dodge had been taken as an infant by his family to Ste. Genevieve in Spanish Louisiana. At seventeen he was married. At
twenty-two he was sheriff of the Ste. Genevieve district and
not long thereafter became marshal of Missouri Territory. After
border skirmishing during the War of 1812, he returned to his
lead-mining interests in Ste. Genevieve. In 1827 new lead discoveries in southern Wisconsin sent him stampeding northward
with his wife and nine children. There he squatted on Winne-
bago land, discovered ore, built smelting furnaces and a shot
tower, and coolly defied the Indian agent's order that he leave
the ground. When the Black Hawk War broke out, he led a
company of mounted volunteers against the Indians. His men
being absorbed into the new dragoons, he stayed on as their
colonel.

Leavenworth's death posed Dodge with a difficult choice.
Should he continue the deadly march or take his tottering soldiers home? He was fifty-two years old now. His reputation

as fighter and his judgment as soldier were solidly established. If he decided to abandon the disastrous venture, there probably would be no severe censure. But Henry Dodge was not the kind of man to turn back. Though only half his troops were able to move, he cajoled and coerced them on and on up the Red River toward New Mexico. At the boundary, perhaps across the boundary in Mexican territory, his pitifully outnumbered command finally met a portion of the Comanche tribe.

Perhaps this group had not shared the Carson episode. Even if they had, the totally unprecedented appearance of more than a hundred fully armed soldiers was enough to give the Indians pause. Sick and grimy the whites might be, but to savages accustomed only to small bands of trappers or timorous Mexican traders they looked formidable enough. Amenably the Indians listened while Dodge extolled the olive branch. Of course they would behave themselves—they said. Surely Dodge was too experienced an Indian hand to take their promises seriously. But at least he had spoken the piece he had been sent out to speak. Gratefully he turned toward home, keeping his cynicism, if any, to himself. Lieutenant Cooke was more outspoken. The talks, he grumbled, were about "as availing as it would be to attempt to establish a truce between the howling wolf of the prairie and his prey."

News of the conference trickled back to Bent's Fort. Peace! If it didn't last . . . Well, that was one of the chances a man took. The next spring, probably while snow flurries still laced the air, William Bent loaded up a mule caravan and headed south into the Panhandle of Texas. For months there would be no word of how he fared.

Dodge was also on the move that spring of 1835. Wandering bands of the Arikaras, who had never been resettled after Leavenworth's 1823 campaign, were roaming the valley of the Platte, stealing Pawnee horses and raising hell in general. Pawnees were quarreling among themselves and with the Cheyennes, and a fresh alarm of warfare in the happy Indian nation gripped the army. Dodge was instructed to spread the message of peace with three companies of troops and two three-pound swivel guns. To help him find his way to the mountains he was given as his guide John Gantt of the short-lived firm of Gantt and Blackwell.[8]

First came a series of councils with the Otos, Omahas, Pawnees and Arikaras. Dodge distributed presents, gave his usual
oratorical admonitions, heard the chiefs' standard alibi that
their young men were difficult to control, and with a straight
face accepted promises of reform. The Pawnees went so far as
to declare their eagerness to make peace with the Cheyennes
and Arapaho. "They informed Colonel Dodge," wrote Lieutenant Kingsbury in his official journal of the expedition, "that
they would send one of their principal men with him for that
purpose."

(Far out on the plains the moccasin grapevine brought word
of the Pawnees' soft talk to Gray Thunder, keeper of the Cheyenne medicine arrows. Peace! Was it real enough for him to
recover the four arrows that had been lost the year the stars
fell? Should he ride east to see? If he gained the Pawnee village, he could probably count on the sanctuary that held a
guest inviolate. Reaching the camp and returning were something else, however. A large, armed party of Cheyennes crossing Pawnee territory would rouse suspicion; a small, unarmed
one would be fair game. But Gray Thunder was an old, old
man now—too old to fear death. Choosing as his companions
only two warriors and two women, one his own wife, he rode
eastward on a mission completely un-Indian-like in its open
courageousness.)

With John Gantt showing the way, Dodge's dragoons
marched up the browning valley of the South Platte. As the
men went into camp on the fifteenth of July, huge cloud banks
to the west suddenly dissolved and the startling wall of the
Rockies appeared ahead, sunset glitter flushing the snowcaps.
Swinging south along the base of the foothills, the command
passed the rearing bulk of Pikes Peak and toward the end of
July gained the Arkansas River. Here they found a small village of Arapaho and a party of Mexican traders. The latter,
Captain Ford of G Company sniffed in his journal, were "the
meanest looking race of people I ever saw, don't appear more
civilized than our Indians generally, dirty, filthy looking creatures." None of this, however, prevented some of the dragoons,
who were sated with buffalo meat, from swimming across the
river to the Mexicans' camp and swapping old clothes for flour.

Dodge sent Gantt out to find more Arapaho and bring them

to a council at Bent's Fort. Down-valley the command moved.
Indians and Mexicans followed in a seethe of excitement.
Loose horses created hubbub among the tired mounts of the
military; swarms of dogs pilfered merrily through the messes.
On August 6 the mud towers of the fort came into view. Scores
of white, conical Cheyenne lodges were clustered around its
adobe walls. Across the river, on the Mexican south bank, was
another Cheyenne village, where Taos traders were doing a
land-office business in whiskey that was forbidden on the
northern bank, less than a hundred yards away. Trappers
leaned over the battlements, staring down at the dusty soldiers.
Children scampered and whooped. Old squaws screeched;
young ones, gaudy in paint and beads, loped back and forth
on gaily caparisoned ponies. Horse herds grazed everywhere.
So jammed were the bottomlands that Dodge had to march
his men a full mile beyond the fort to find room enough to
camp.

While the command waited for Gantt to come in with his
Arapaho, the officers were entertained by Charles Bent and
Ceran St. Vrain. Probably the proprietors were dressed, as
Farnham saw them later, in Cheyenne moccasins, fringed
buckskin shirts and trousers. Nonetheless, they impressed Captain Ford: "The first white men we found living in the Indian
Country in a march of One Thousand Miles. they appear to
be much of a gentlemen." In the rectangular apartment above
the western wall, the gentlemen spread a lavish dinner. Dick
and Andrew Green, two Negro slaves owned by Charles and
William Bent, may well have been pressed into service as but-
lers. Black Charlotte, who was Dick Green's wife and who
called herself the "only lady in de whole damn Indian country," perhaps did honors as cook (assuming she was already
at the fort, as she was a few years later). Perhaps, too, the
icehouse had already been built near the river. If so, the august occasion probably sent riders hurrying miles up Purgatory
Creek for the wild mint that was one ingredient of a celebrated Bent refresher called "hailstorm."

Afterward the junior officers wandered about the place, gingerly eying a pet grizzly bear confined with a chain and noting
fifteen wagons loading for Independence with buffalo robes
which "they buy for about 25 cents worth of goods sell them

at St. Louis for five & six dollars." This detail of commerce did not escape the sharp eye of Lieutenant Lancaster P. Lupton of A Company, who had already discussed the Indian trade in detail with John Gantt. Unmilitary plans were beginning to brew in the lieutenant's ambitious mind.

Meanwhile the enlisted men were exploring the resources of the Indian villages. In a chief's huge lodge on the Mexican bank they found a tremendous revel. Appalled, Sergeant Hugh Evans wrote in his diary, "All (or nearly all) men women and children were drunk . . . filling their Bowls and horn spoons and hand it around with as much liberality as a candidate for office. Some reeling, stagering and hollowing, falling down and raising up, frothing and naked, and such gestures and grimaces looked as if they came from the fiends of the lower regions." So flagrant was the lust for liquor that Lieutenant Kingsbury clucked officially in his journal that the Cheyennes "will sell their horses, blankets, and everything else they possess for a drink of it. In arranging the good things of this world in the order of rank, they say that whiskey should stand first, then tobacco, third, guns, fourth, horses, and fifth, women."

Nonetheless, Dodge was able to hold his conference. Gantt returned on Monday evening, August 10, with various Arapaho, Gros Ventres, and even a couple of Blackfeet who had been visiting the Arapaho. The next morning Charles and Ceran turned the fort over to the military for a jam-packed gathering resplendent with barbaric color. Translators standing at his elbow, Dodge gave his usual speech, praised the Arapaho and Osages for having made friends with each other and with the Comanches, and urged the Cheyennes to follow suit. The Pawnee delegation was introduced, and now the Indians could indulge in the long-winded oratory so dear to their hearts. Speaking for the Cheyennes, Little Moon greeted the Pawnees warmly. Then he added wistfully to Dodge, "I wish you to tell the Pawnee to send each of us [Little Moon meant each band] a medicine arrow." To the whites it was a curious request. Lieutenant Kingsbury, reporting the conference, incorrectly explained the plea by saying, "It is customary among these wild Indians to exchange arrows in making peace; these are medicine arrows."

(Far to the northeast Gray Thunder had reached a Pawnee

village. In the lodge of a chief he had seen one of the four lost arrows. But would the Pawnees part with the souvenir?)

The oratory concluded, Dodge handed out as many medals as he had, each stamped with the likeness of the Great White Father, Andrew Jackson. Unfortunately there weren't enough to go around. Charles Bent noted that some of the chiefs had their noses out of joint; but good feeling prevailed and the Indians accepted Dodge's promise to send the medals later. Presents being distributed, the chiefs then professed undying love for the Americans.

Scarcely was this stir over when another rippled the fort. Out of the south, canopied by dust, streamed a huge herd of loose horses. Behind them, belaboring a train of heavily laden pack mules, rode a handful of sun-blackened men. It was William Bent's party, returning after no one knows how many months and how many hundreds of miles of dangerous travel among the Comanches.

At once Dodge sought William out for a report. What was the situation on the Red River?

The wiry little twenty-six-year-old trader nodded up at the handsome officer twice his age. Everything was fine, Colonel. William and his men had seen anyhow two thousand Comanches during their trip. No fighting. No trouble at all—yet. But it never paid to trust a Comanche too far.

Justifiably pleased with himself, Dodge ordered general recall sounded. As the bugles blew, a whoop of joy rose from the dragoons. Home! Down the valley they marched, into the Big Timbers. Here they found fifty lodges of Cheyennes, their camp "surrounded by a large number of horses; many of which they had just stolen from the Comanches." Peace, indeed! But Dodge repeated his set piece and told the Indians that if they would go to the fort, Ceran St. Vrain would distribute as many presents as had been given to the other bands.

Sudden rifle fire interrupted the talks. Startled, Dodge threw the dragoons into battle line. It was an unnecessary precaution. The shooting came from a hundred or so Pawnees and Arikaras, who were emptying their guns as a sign they arrived in peace. Couriers dashed back and forth. A swift, delirious joy filled the camp. Laughing Cheyennes rushed out to embrace the visitors, gave them horses, dragged them to the lodges for hastily prepared feasts. Intensely gratified, the jubilant Pawnees responded by presenting fifty or more of their guns to the Cheyennes. So it went all day long, and at night, within the circle of Cheyenne lodges, the Pawnees put on a howling dance.

Quite naturally Dodge assumed that the love feast arose from the peace he had been preaching. As he marched away the next morning, he did not notice a happy old Cheyenne who had arrived with the Pawnees, his wrinkled body smeared with the red clay of his office. It was Gray Thunder, and he had brought with him the single medicine arrow he had located in a Pawnee lodge. How much of his success was due to his own eloquence and how much to the recent passage of the troops cannot be said. In any event, Gray Thunder had persuaded many of the Pawnees and their visitors, the Arikaras, to journey with him to the Cheyenne village, there to return the precious totem in exchange for suitable gifts. The resultant hullabaloo was the glory Dodge had seen and, reasonably enough, had not understood.[9]

Still, the colonel had done well—and not just with the Indians.[10] As his commanding officer dryly added in a commendatory letter to Washington about the expedition, "The approaching disturbances in Texas would seem strongly to admonish us of the immense importance of our officers and men being thoroughly acquainted with the whole line of our southwestern frontier, from the Sabine bay to the Rocky Mountains." Thus, though politicians might think of the plains as a buffer state, the Western Department of the army was beginning to realize that pressures were building that might blow paper sophistries to bits. Political thinking prevailed, however. Not for half a dozen years would the army come west again. Like wind, it had rippled the plains; like wind, it passed. If the tribes were to be controlled and peace be secured, the follow-up would have to come through the unaided efforts of the traders themselves.

After the dragoons had left the fort, Charles turned toward Taos. It was a six-day ride, more or less—up the cactus-strewn wastes of Timpas, with hot cedar-freckled bluffs to the left and, far to the right, an occasional hill-framed glimpse of the gray peaks of the Rockies. Gratefully his little party dropped into the coolness of upper Purgatory Creek, followed it several miles, then climbed a twisting side creek under beetling cliffs, listened to the organ sound of wind in the pines. At the top the land leveled off into meadows, then dipped abruptly through immense bluffs to the austere foothills bordering the crystal headwaters of the Canadian or Red River. It was rough going. Each year, however, wagon drivers from the fort would make it a little smoother, knocking off a point of rocks here, leveling a sidehill there. Raton Pass, they would call the route, after the gray rodents that scuttled among its stones. They had no idea that eventually railroads would war over the right of way they were gouging out, nor that the name of the pass would become famous. All they wanted was to shorten their driving time to the Taos branch of the Santa Fe Trail, curving westward from the Canadian over the whale-backed humps of the Sangre de Cristos.

As he rode along, Charles may well have felt justified in taking time out to hunt through the tree-filtered sunlight for deer and wild turkeys, or just to lounge in camp an extra half hour during the cool mornings. No longer was there need for the pounding hurry of the past years. Business was good, and the company had new blood coming along to share in its management—debonair George and handsome Robert Bent, the first twenty-one now, the other nineteen. Also, there was Ceran's youngest brother, twenty-year-old Marcellin St. Vrain, a harum-scarum youngster, slighter than Ceran, but with the same curly black hair, the same hearty genius for making friends. As all three developed under William's watchful eye, Charles and Ceran could spend more of their time at the firm's store in Taos.[11]

Charles liked Taos. Its business—trading, distilling, even some of the farming—was dominated by a close-knit foreign colony: the Workman brothers and John Rowland from Missouri, the Branches and Steve Lee. Especially close to both St. Vrain and Charles Bent was shrewd, merry Charles Hipolyte Trotier, one-time Sieur de Beaubien, who during the early 1820s had come down from Three Rivers, Canada, and had married into the influential Lobata family.

For business reasons Carlos Beaubien, as he was now known, along with St. Vrain and most of the colony, had become a naturalized Mexican. Charles, however, clung to his United States citizenship. Also, he apparently stayed a Protestant, though there is no other evidence that he took his faith very seriously. Nonetheless, he was on good terms with most of his Catholic neighbors—excepting always the parish priest, Antonio Martinez. Heretic Charles might be, but he knew how to run survey lines for them, drawing, probably, on early experiences with his father. (When the government made an 1839 listing of the valley's foreigners, "Carlos Bentt" was classified not as a merchant but as a surveyor.) He knew some medicine. Perhaps he had studied a smattering of it at Jefferson College; perhaps he had learned it extemporaneously in the rough schools of the river and the trail; and probably he possessed a supply of the simple specifics of the frontier: calomel, quinine, various powders and salts. However skimpy his knowledge and equipment may have been, it amounted to more than his humble neighbors had. They flocked to him with their ailments, and he patched and improvised without accepting payment. Once, so the unlikely story goes, he opened a woman's abdomen, removed diseased portions of her intestines, sewed her up—and saw her recover.[12]

Then, too, there was Ignacia. Maria Ignacia Jaramillo, who in Missouri would have been called Ignacia Luna, for she was a widow of a man of that name. After a short marriage Luna had died, leaving her one daughter, Rumalda, now a child of four. As was the custom in New Mexico, the mother had resumed her maiden name. Quite probably she wasn't yet twenty and, like all the Jaramillo girls, she was strikingly beautiful—a handsome figure, luxuriant raven hair, enormous dark eyes, and a lighter complexion than most Mexican women boasted.

Because she was a widow, Charles perhaps did not have to endure the duenna-supervised courtship of the Spanish. Of that nothing is known. Even the date of the marriage is uncertain. But probably it was late in 1835 or early in 1836 that Charles Bent took his wife and stepdaughter to an adobe house north of the plaza, on the road leading toward the terraced Indian pueblo. It was not a pretentious home. Another house shared one wall with it. Under the roughhewn beams, the dusky rooms, each with a fireplace in one corner, were sparsely furnished by American standards. To one side was a courtyard, the single gate in its walls large enough to admit horsemen or even a carriage. Here, in this typically Mexican building, Charles taught his wife to speak English, to wear American clothes. Here, with perhaps her husband as her only doctor, Ignacia bore him five children, two of whom would die in infancy. And here, at last, the endless miles by keelboat, by horse, by lumbering wagon settled to a focus. From now on Taos would be home.[13]

CHAPTER IX

ADOBE EMPIRE

The honeymoon was short. In the spring of 1836 Charles was once more in Independence, loading seven wagons with the usual trade goods. Luxuries were added for trappers with loose money in their pockets: blue jars of imported Chinese ginger; hogsheads of black New Orleans molasses, which the Indians also relished; candies; and tins of Bent water crackers. These last, manufactured in Massachusetts by a distant cousin, would impress mountain men with the thought that the big lodge on the Arkansas had its own private brand of biscuit. Still another exotic item was included on this trip—a billiard table. Now that city-raised George and Robert Bent were at the fort, the big apartment atop the western wall was taking on refinements.

Although Charles had introduced oxen to the trail a few years before, he used mules this trip, ten or twelve to each wagon, and he needed skinners. One whom he hired was slow-drawling, broad-faced, twenty-year-old Richens Lacy Wootton, raised and fairly well educated on plantations in Virginia and Mississippi. Another was backwoods Jim Hobbs, only sixteen, who had run away from his stepmother in Shawnee country, twenty miles from Independence. Both were hard and craggy, but both were green. Before the trip was over, they would cause varying degrees of trouble.

The mules pulled well. In a few days the little train overhauled a Santa Fe caravan of fifty-seven wagons and decided to accompany it as far as the forks in the trail at Cimarron Crossing. Standing night guard at Little Cow Creek, green Dick Wootton roused the camp by blazing away at a shadow —and killing a mule. It was the mule's fault, he told the angry men, for pulling up its picket pin and straying. The next alarm was real. Near the bold escarpment of Pawnee Rock, Comanches tried to stampede the stock. The traders killed three, beat off the attack.[1] And now it was young Jim Hobbs's turn to get himself into a pickle—serious this time.

After the main caravan had swung across the river and the Bent wagons had plodded on alone beyond the Caches, a buffalo bull ran in front of the train. Jim snapped a shot at it with his pistol. The beast kept right on, and the men joshed the boy about his aim. Ruffled, Jim said he'd get that bull yet. Finding a rifle and another youth named John Baptiste to accompany him, he splashed hell-bent across the river in pursuit.

Charles yelled for the boys to come back. There was smoke in the sand hills—Indians. But the pair paid no heed. Furiously Charles gathered as many spare men as he could mount and took after them. Tracking slowed the party down, but at last they saw a carcass ahead. Jim Hobbs had gotten his buffalo. And then, as the sign showed, Comanches had gotten Jim and John Baptiste. Apparently the boys were prisoners; at least a scouting ride down the trail showed no corpses. Nothing could be done about it, however—too many Indians with too long a start. Reluctantly Charles returned to his wagons and rolled on toward the fort.

The plains lay brown and sere under the parching winds. Inside the fort, the sun smashed off the walls. Men gasped for breath. Fitful drafts in the tunnel-like entry afforded moments of relief; and at evening the workers, with their Mexican or Indian women, climbed to the rooftops to promenade along the battlements while sunset faded behind the mocking coolness of the peaks. Yet in heat or cold, work had to go on. The score or more hard-used wagons and carts under a pole shelter in the corral had to be readied for their next trips. At the rear of the placita, carpenter and blacksmith shops clanged continually. In another room a French tailor from New Orleans with a three-sided needle and sinew thread sewed buckskin into stacks of hunting shirts and leggings. Fuel, both buffalo chips and cottonwood, was a continual problem. So was water. Evidently the well inside the walls was insufficient, and every morning an old Irishman who had lost his toes to frostbite drove a cartful of water barrels down to the river. The rest of his time he spent carting trash to the rubbish pile outside the walls.

Plunging and kicking in their restless hunger, the horses and mules were driven each dawn from their night's safety in the corral to grazing land in the river bottoms, sometimes miles away. Mexicans herded them. Mexican vaqueros broke the wild animals that were brought in for trade. Old Juan was the boss, agile as a cat. To show off, he would sometimes sit his battered saddle with a Mexican silver dollar between each boot sole and stirrup. When the mule or horse had bucked itself out, the dollar would still be there. The oxen demanded care, as did the milk cows, chickens, turkeys, and pigeons that were imported to lend variety to the table of the chief traders and head clerks, a table presided over with memorable grace by Ceran St. Vrain when he was on hand. Hunters often brought in and tamed buffalo calves whose mothers they had killed. There were Mexican sheep and goats, and for a time George Bent raised peacocks, whose flamboyant tails and shrill screams astounded the Indians. The mountains of manure had to be hauled away regularly, partly because of fire hazard. Occasional attempts were made to use the stuff as fertilizer for a vegetable garden irrigated by water from the Arkansas, but Indian pilfering and loose stock doomed the sporadic farming.

Ragged Mexican traders brought meal and dried vegetables as supplements to the all-meat diet. During the late 1830s numbers of these vagabonds congregated at a spot four or five miles upriver from the fort. El Pueblo, they called the place, not to be confused with the Pueblo later founded at the mouth of Fountain Creek. Around a large oblong square they built thirty or so small houses, wall to wall, some with second stories. The whitewashed rooms were about twelve feet square, each with a fireplace in one corner. Goats, donkeys, dogs, buffalo calves, and children swarmed in the dust. Each night a loud bellow announced the penning of the horse herd. Scold-

ing women dragged their children to cover, and with a racketing rush the herd pounded into the oblong, there to spend
the night in odorous din with the other livestock and the
inhabitants. By day the wild-looking men, in full beards and
hair that hung below their shoulders, lounged in the shade,
smoking clay pipes and filing iron arrow points. Now and then
they aroused themselves for a hunt—hell-for-leather riders who
killed more buffalo with bows and arrows than many white
hunters did with guns. Part of their purpose in settling here
had been to raise produce and livestock for Bent's Fort, but
they used even less water in their alcohol than they did on
their gardens. Though trappers sometimes traded them valuable pelts for Taos whiskey, El Pueblo did not prosper. By and
large the Bents ignored it.

When time hung heavy around the great mud castle, yarn
spinning was the endless diversion. Warming their pants before a fire or squatting around a pan of dried meat on a dirt
floor in one of the rooms, visiting trappers and local employees
boasted of the coups they had counted and the grizzly bears
they had killed from California to Hudson Bay. Lore changed
hands. Strange doings were speculated on. Remember, Bill,
the time some Cheyennes jumped a Kiowa village near our
trading houses on Scout Creek (it was east of present Denver)
and captured a little white girl, two-three years old? Brown
hair, blue eyes, Irish-looking? Where do you reckon the Kiowas
picked her up? Texas, maybe? Do you suppose her folks know
she's alive—if they're alive themselves?[2] And speaking of kids,
remember that Cheyenne whose wife ran off with another
man? Darned if he didn't tote their baby more'n a hundred
and fifty miles from the Platte clear down here to the fort.
Killed buffalo with calves along the way, cut off their udders,
and let the child suck. Kept it alive until he found a village
down-river a piece and got a woman with milk to nurse it.
They're queer, these Injuns—what they'll do and what they'll
believe. Some of the medicine men beat everything—regular
ventriloquists, throwing their voices up to the smoke hole as
if they were talking to spirits, or having a prescription come
right out of their gourd rattles while they're doctoring some
patient. They say there's a Ree who shot his own son plumb
through with arrows, plastered the wounds with mud, and

brought the boy back to life without a mark on him. Of course it's all in knowing the tricks. Like Old Belzy Dodd right here in the placita the other day. He stomped around, glaring at the Injuns, then let out a yell and jerked off his wig. Some medicine—"White-man-who-scalps-himself!"

Violence was not confined within the telling of tales. These were passionate men, far removed from fear of legal retribution, and the raw alcohol of the trade was a wicked detonator. Larpenteur, at Fort Union on the Missouri, tells of putting laudanum in whiskey to quiet fights; of a hunter beaten and thrown into a fireplace to burn to death; of a lengthy feud in which friends of another murdered man used fire, muskets, and even a cannon to drive the opposition faction out of nearby buildings in which they had taken refuge. Perhaps the Bents and St. Vrain held a stronger hand over their men. When an employee named Tesson, angered by a boisterous charivari, shot at a Negro blacksmith, Ceran immediately sent him packing. Other derelictions were treated with the standard wilderness punishment of tying a man to a post and whipping him.[3] But more may have happened than we know. No one kept a daily record of life at Bent's Fort.

In the capricious nature of the firm's own customers existed the greatest potential for danger. Particularly was this true during summer, when Indian war parties crisscrossing the plains often stopped by the fort to demand powder and ammunition. The partners had to gauge their mood to a fine line: when to ignore insults; what gifts to present one swaggering chief without offending another; how far to yield to their importunities for liquor. It was never safe to let very many of a strange band inside the walls at once; and whenever a boisterous mob gathered, inside or out, William set armed patrols to pacing the battlements. Even the southern Cheyennes, who were generally allowed to roam about at will, were herded outside at sunset and the iron-studded gate was shut behind them for the night.

By making vigilance an ingrained habit, William forestalled unguessable difficulties. There is only one flare-up on record. A war party of Wyoming Shoshoni, denied admission, were hammering on the gates, yelling and shooting arrows over the wall. The head trader, Murray, lost patience. He was an irascible man, flat-nosed and Irish; the Cheyennes called him "Goddamn" because he used the oath so often. He ended the uproar by firing into the gang and killing one. There might have been repercussions had not the Shoshoni been so far from home. As it was, Murray made capital of the event by giving the scalp to a war party of Cheyennes and Arapaho, who promptly held a noisy dance over the trophy.[4]

Generally William demanded that all tribes be treated equally at the fort, lest favoritism rouse enmity. Sometimes, though, it was politic to share the joy of the Cheyennes, especially when a deliriously triumphant village of them came howling up to the gate with fresh scalps stretched on hoops that were carried at the ends of long willow wands. As a sign of victory they had painted their faces black with the ash of burned grass mixed in buffalo blood. Perhaps they came in formal parade—color, feathers, glitter; marshaled columns dipping, wheeling, caracoling. The shrill cries of the excited squaws, the racketing *ai-yai's* . . . Let them pour in; let them dance in the white man's lodge. The trappers liked the spectacle as much as the Indians did. As dusk deepened, the whites climbed onto the roofs to watch. Below, in the center of the court, fire glow brightened. Women formed a square, gaudy in blankets, some brandishing arms, some waving the scalps, their faces painted red and black. The glistening bodies of the men moved among them or squatted amid the thumping drums. Feet shuffled in little half jumps, bodies bent and jerked erect to the time of songs that sounded to white ears like chanted howls. Pure savagery, complete enjoyment—but the Pawnees, whose Dodge-inspired peace with the Cheyennes had been short-lived, would not relish having scalps of their tribesmen exulted over this way under Bent auspices. To the devil with the Pawnees! They were always kicking up trouble, harrying the caravans, and in the summer of 1838 killing two Bent herders and stealing stock within sight of the fort. It was time someone danced over a few of their scalps.

Within two years after its completion the mud fortress west of Purgatory Creek was the center of a primitive empire that spread across the entire watershed of the upper Arkansas. Inevitably challengers appeared. Northward, Fort Laramie had

passed into control of the American Fur Company.[5] In the
summer of 1836 that company's last major competitor, Nat
Wyeth, limped into Bent's Fort, completely beaten. Irony
here. From one end of the Northwest to the other, Wyeth,
Bonneville, and various others had fought themselves into
bankruptcy over a trade that was now scarcely worth having.
The American Fur Company was turning more and more to
traffic in robes; and it was to investigate the robe trade, plus
Santa Fe hauling, that Wyeth visited Bent's Fort. The partners plied him with mint juleps, fed him off a white table-
cloth in the big apartment. And they let him know, politely
but clearly, that an interloper could get his ears knocked down
here as well as in the North. Disconsolately Wyeth went home
to Boston and his ice business.

On his way he may have passed a new interloper rolling
west with laden wagons. It was Lancaster P. Lupton. An army
lieutenant until his resignation in March 1836, Lupton had
commanded Company A during Dodge's march across the central plains. All he knew of the trade was what he had learned
from talking to John Gantt and from using his eyes at Bent's
Fort. With the brashness of ignorance he now followed his
nose toward the magnificent hump of Long's Peak and finally
halted his wagons in a rich, well-timbered bottomland beside
the singing waters of the South Platte. He was squarely in the
heart of buffalo range frequented by the Arapaho and northern and southern Cheyennes and visited occasionally by the
Sioux, who were beginning to drift in from the northeast.

So strategic a spot had, of course, not been a vacuum. Bent,
St. Vrain & Company traders had visited the South Platte
profitably during at least three previous winters and must have
known that in the fall of 1835 it had been invaded also by
Louis Vasquez and Andrew Sublette, the latter a younger
brother of Bill and Milton and known as one of the best shots
in the land. On their arrival Vasquez & Sublette had started
building an adobe fort (financed in part by William Sublette,
to the annoyance of the American Fur Company), and now
Lupton was moving in a few miles south of them.

Even without Lupton a trade war probably would have
shaped up between Vasquez & Sublette, Bent & St. Vrain,
and the American Fur Company. Lupton's arrival made it

certain and immediate, as William Bent realized when he
rode up to the South Platte shortly after Lupton's appearance.
With William was Robert Newell, called "Doc," a far-ranging
mountain man who had first come west with William Sublette
in 1829 and who had signed on with Bent, St. Vrain in Independence the previous April. Perhaps their trip from the
fort to the South Platte was routine only, but it did not stay
routine. Less than twenty-four hours after their arrival the two
men heeled around and hurried more than two hundred miles
back to the Arkansas. In the laconic journal he had recently
started, Newell does not explain this haste. But the sight of
Lupton's wagons and of Vasquez & Sublette's new fort probably shocked William into speeding home to prepare urgent
countermeasures.

By fall his company's strategy was apparent (and in part
incorporated in their license of November 8, 1836, which for
the first time authorized their trading at a definite place on
the South Platte, at a point twelve miles above its junction
with the Cache la Poudre). Meanwhile a strong party that
included young Dick Wootton forged far north of Fort Laramie into territory claimed by the American Fur Company.
Doc Newell and five men, numbering one named Bill New,
were shifted from the Arapaho trade on Fountain Creek directly into the valley of the South Platte, taking with them, in
addition to the usual cloth, kettles, beads, tobacco, and flints,
an assortment of garden seeds, which suggests permanency—
"onion, turnip, pumpkin, cucumber, mellons, reddish, squash,
beets." Bent, St. Vrain evidently had already undertaken near
their Arkansas fort the first agricultural venture in the Rocky
Mountain West. Now they intended to stay long enough on
the South Platte to duplicate the experiment.

The American Fur Company also declared itself in the war,
sending John Albert and a party down from Fort Laramie.
The weather played a fierce accompaniment to the conten-
tion. Trapped by tremendous drifts at the junction of Cache
la Poudre Creek and the Platte, Albert's party lost most of
its horses, then lived on the frozen carcasses until spring. But
drifts or no, Doc Newell and Bill New were busy. Newell's
account book records in one place that he took in "246 new
robes, 4 horses, 4 mules, 15 cords, 6 saddles and lash ropes";

in another, that he had just sent to Fort William (Bent's Fort) another "86 robes, 12 horses, 1 mule, cords." Bill New meanwhile was on various occasions sending in from the Indian camps nearby "23 robes . . . 14 robes . . . 40 robes," plus meat and cords.

The spring of 1837 brought derelictions among the winter-pummeled employees. In May, perhaps leaving his garden unplanted, Newell took the results of his winter trade back to the Arkansas, resigned, and headed for Brown's Hole and eventual service with Drips and Fontenelle. John Albert, too, rode to the Arkansas fort and bought new horses to replace the ones which had frozen; then, instead of returning to the American Fur Company, he headed for Taos, where he began farming and later associated himself with Turley's distillery. A man had to keep warm somehow.

The employers themselves kept at each other's throats. The American Fur Company decided, in spite of the depression that was closing down on the West, to appropriate twelve thousand dollars for the erection of another fort within six miles of the post which Lupton planned. To run the subsidiary company they picked two old hands: Henry Fraeb, erstwhile partner in the Rocky Mountain Fur outfit, and Peter Sarpy, a squat, volatile, bushy-bearded Frenchman who had learned the Indian trade among the Omahas in Nebraska.

Exactly what details of these moves Charles Bent learned in the East that spring or what William Bent picked up during his own winter wanderings on the South Platte is impossible to say. But it was enough for them to know that Bent, St. Vrain & Company would also have to build a strong post on the Platte. A fine situation! Normally in this country a man had to ride hundreds of miles to find anything more than a trader's log stockade. Now, within a morning's gallop along one stream, there were going to be no less than four massive fortresses.[6]

But forts alone were not enough. There also had to be a way to bind the Indians to your establishment. One uncertain and troublemaking tie was alcohol. A sounder method was marriage into the tribe.

Such marriages were an old custom. When a trader took a red wife, he also took, in a sense, all of her relatives. In exchange for the in-laws he gained protection and comfort. He could forget the lonely, dangerous trapper's rat nest he used to hate to see at the end of a day. Now his squaw cooked for him in a comfortable lodge, sewed, tended to his horse, filled his pipe, brought hot water for his feet. The imperious demands of his body were quieted. For one or all of these conveniences some whites changed wives as often as they moved from one tribe to the next. But frequently affection grew, real and deep; and a man learned to his happiness that even on the lonely sweep of the savage plains it was possible to have a good and faithful wife.

It was probably early in the spring of 1837 that William Bent sought out and found a certain Cheyenne village, his sleek pack horses loaded with suitable gifts. The conical lodges, many painted with angular green, red, or black figures of men, animals, and symbolic designs, stood in a rough circle whose open mouth faced a stream. From the poles of many fluttered feathers, buffalo tails, or strings of little hoofs that clicked in the wind. Travois leaned against the frames. In front or back of each lodge slender tripods supported lances, shields, or medicine bags—the house number, so to speak, of the owner.

William needed no sign to find the lodge he wanted. Larger than the others, it stood alone within the circle, near the opening. Its occupant was Gray Thunder, keeper of the medicine arrows.

Gray Thunder's prestige, already high because of his position, had grown enormous following his recovery of one of the lost arrows from the Pawnees. As nearly as the Cheyennes had a headman, he was it. Though the exigencies of livelihood, primarily hunting, kept the tribe split into ever-shifting villages, each with one or more important chiefs, the arrows and the keeper of the arrows remained as a steadfast token of the nation's unity. Inevitably his two daughters, Owl Woman, or Mis-stan-stur, and her younger sister, Yellow Woman, came as near to being the princesses of dime-novel literature as the facts of Cheyenne social organization allowed.

Courtship? An Indian boy wooed by plucking at the robe of his inamorata, to get her attention as she went for wood or water. With other suitors he hung around the lodge entry, hoping for a word or smile. Lovelorn, he wandered at night outside the circle of lodges, playing plaintive songs on a flute he had made by hollowing out an eighteen-inch cylinder of juniper wood and burning six finger holes into it with a hot iron. If his suit was progressing, the girl would recognize his tune and slip outside, to stand for a moment with his robe wrapped around her shoulders as they whispered whatever it is lovers have always whispered. If the girl did not come, a medicine man might be entreated to lay a spell on the flute; or the aphrodisiac of a deer's white tail might be worn on the lover's shoulder, where the girl could get a whiff of its magic.

As soon as her consent was won (troth might be pledged by the exchange of horn or metal rings), the boy began worrying about his obligations to her family. Gathering every horse he could afford, he had his mother or some elderly friend tie them in front of the lodge of the girl's father. Perfectly aware of what was going on, her parents had already made their decision. Rarely did an unfavored courtship bud to the point where it was necessary to shame the suitor in front of the village by driving his horses away. Rarely, too, did lack of consent lead to elopements. From childhood, the proprieties were drilled into Cheyenne girls, and it was not unheard of for a disappointed lover to hang herself rather than overstep taboos.

The acceptance of horses was followed by a general exchange of gifts between the two families. There might be an engagement period during which the girl each day carried food to the lodge of her fiancé. She went in her finest buckskin gown, tanned white and belted with brass-studded leather. The soft material hung just below her knees, the right side longer than the left. There was a short right sleeve and a shoulder strap on the left; the diagonal slant across the breast was emphasized by a fold in the bodice. The whole was beaded, fringed, trimmed with red trade cloth, and ornamented with elk teeth. From knee downward her limbs were encased in yellow leggings decorated with black stripes. On her feet were the dainty, beaded moccasins which the Cheyennes made better than did any other tribe. Her hair, brushed glossy, either hung down her back in two braids, or perhaps was bunched behind and above her ears in buns wrapped in ornamented buckskin. Iridescent shells gleamed in her ears, brass bracelets on her arms. Vermilion shone on her cheeks and in the part of her hair. She was radiantly clean—the Cheyennes bathed every morning, winter or summer, in running water, which is more than can be said of the whites who visited them—and she had perfumed herself in the smoke of sweet grass and sage.

As she walked with the wooden bowl of food from her lodge to that of her betrothed, she was accompanied by a young girl friend or by her sister. If Owl Woman so went to William Bent, Yellow Woman was her companion. By polygamous Indian custom, a man marrying an elder sister was free to wed the younger also. Apparently William Bent did not do this, at least to the extent of having sexual relations with both, yet there is evidence that the younger sister, remaining unwed, occupied Bent's lodge much of the time.[7]

How much wooing William did can only be surmised. It is unlikely that he wandered in the hills playing a flute—even if he could play one. At the age of twenty-eight he was too old for the teen-age mooning of the village youths; as a trader he was obligated to act with formal dignity. Probably arrangements with Gray Thunder were aloof, precise, impersonal. Once they were completed, William may have bowed to the custom which had friends of the groom carry the bride into his lodge, where she was dressed in fine clothing he had provided and her neck and arms bedecked with his gifts.

Folklore says that after marriage a bride often retained her protective rope for ten or fifteen days, so that husband and wife could learn to see each other truly, without the distortions of passion. It was a curious device: a rope knotted about the waist under the clothing, its two ends wound about the thighs to the knees. Cumbersome, surely, and a symbolic rather than physical deterrent. A man respected it when it was worn; when it was gone, he knew he was welcome.

Owl Woman—a strange name to whisper at night. In English most Indian names sound ridiculous. The Cheyenne form was very little easier for white tongues—Mis-stan-stur. To dodge the clumsiness, trappers often used English pet names; Kit Carson, for example, called his Arapaho wife Alice, though her native Waa-nibe, Singing Wind, had more charm than most for white ears. William may likewise have devised a nickname.

Was she comely? All we know is that during Dodge's 1835 visit Lieutenant Kingsbury declared that the Cheyenne women "are remarkable for their beauty." And beyond beauty? This we know: on January 22, 1838, probably at Bent's Fort, the couple's first child was born, a girl. Looking at the little wrinkled flesh that was his flesh, William remembered the sister closest to him and named the baby Mary. Mary Bent —half Indian, but no less a Bent for all that. Unlike Charles, William named every one of his five children after a brother or sister. Bents all—or so in his fierce pride he tried to make them, unwittingly building for himself agonies of heartbreak that would have been less poignant could he have been more casual. Surely the devotion extended to and was returned by the mother. A marriage of policy, yes. But more than policy went into its fulfillment.

Policy, however, ruled his working days. Bent wagons rolled along the South Platte, northward past the future site of Denver, to a bench perhaps twelve miles below the mouth of another stream, which became known as St. Vrain Creek. There during the summer and fall of 1837 more thousands of adobe bricks were mixed, molded, and laboriously toted onto the walls. George Bent may have been in charge of construction, and the name he gave the post was Fort Lookout. (Later it would be called Fort George, and at various times when Marcellin was in charge, Fort St. Vrain, by which name history has chosen to record it.) Though smaller than the post on the Arkansas, Fort Lookout was nonetheless formidable, its walls running 130 feet north and south, 60 feet east and west. Bastions 19 feet in diameter frowned at the southwest and northeast corners. As at Bent's Fort, there was a well within the walls and a corral to the rear. Located only fifteen miles or so east of the foothills, it commanded a far more stupendous view of the snow-crowned mountains than did its prairie-lapped prototype.

Southward there were interruptions. Pawnees, raiding deep, hit twenty-two-year-old Marcellin St. Vrain and a party heading with twelve pack mules up Timpas Creek toward Raton Pass. It was a sound drubbing—one white man killed, three wounded. The attackers also captured three saddle horses, one rifle, nine laden mules. Since Pawnees were American Indians, the firm sent the government a claim for $3273 in damages; but because the attack occurred on Spanish soil, Washington was indifferent. There is no record of settlement.

Some of the loot must have amazed the Indians. The twenty-three robes they could use. But—ugh, ugh—what were these: two illuminated Latin missals valued at twenty dollars each, ten reams of printing paper, and twenty-five pounds of printer's ink? Evidently the last items had been intended for New Mexico's sole press, a small Ramage machine with iron bed and iron platen which had been brought across the plains in '34. On this press Padre Antonio Martinez had published at Taos, once a week for four weeks during 1835, New Mexico's first newspaper—*El Crepúsculo de la Libertad,* The Dawn of Liberty. The Pawnee attack apparently delayed further dawnings for several years; not until 1844 was another newspaper published in the province. But at least the Indians could signalize the victory by using the ink to paint their faces black.

It is possible, though unlikely, that the paper and ink were designed for revolutionary purposes. New Mexico simmered with unrest, some of it perhaps emanating from Texas, which in 1836 had won independence. In Washington there was thunderous talk of annexation; and on December 19 the Lone Star legislature, ignoring previous treaties and hundreds of miles of utterly unexplored territory, blandly claimed territory reaching clear to the Rio Grande—that is, well into New Mexico. Months before this, sparks of the uproar had set fire to the febrile imagination of one John Dickson, who recruited sixty shallow-brained filibusterers and set sail for Santa Fe via Buffalo, Detroit, and the upper Missouri. Dickson called himself Montezuma II and trumpeted that he was on his way to raise an Indian army, boot the Mexicans out of their northern provinces, and set up an aborigine paradise in California. Winter froze him out and he disappeared, but not before his rodomontade had appeared in eastern papers. From these papers and from astonished fur traders in the North, word of the doings leaked into Missouri. Mexican and American traders probably carried the tales to Santa Fe, together with the more solid facts of Texas freedom.

Did garbled whispers of all this help inflame the ignorant

Pueblo Indians and Mexican peons north of the capital? It cannot be said.[8] At any rate, when a new governor, Albino Perez, was sent from Mexico to replace the native governors the inhabitants were used to, they boiled over. It was Perez's fault, they said, that the impotent provincial soldiers did nothing to check the increasing fury of Navajo raids. The poverty-stricken Pueblos focused resentment on Perez's lace coat, on the red velvet curtains which the homesick man installed in the barren *palacio*, on the casks of wine he imported from the south. When local officials were replaced by Perez appointees and when the governor tried to reform the cumbersome tax system by imposing direct levies, Taos and the northern hamlets exploded. Direct taxes? The concept was ungraspable by simple minds. Wild rumor said that a man was to be taxed even for sleeping with his own wife.

With the connivance of Manuel Armijo, governor during the late 1820s and recently ousted as collector of customs, a revolutionary junta led a mob against the capital. Perez forced American merchants in Santa Fe to accept his notes for supplies, and with 150 men marched against the insurrectionists. They bowled his army over, ran him down, cut off his head. After horribly mutilating a few other officials, the Pueblo Indians moved into the palace. Disdaining its furniture and squatting on the floor, they elected as governor José Gonzales, a buffalo hunter from Taos.

Disappointed because he had not been elected, Manuel Armijo did a flip-flop. Rounding up an army in the south, he entered Santa Fe, laid still another requisition on the harried American traders, and set out after the rebels. The capital waited on tenterhooks. Wagons, carretas, horses, mules, burros, pigs, and goats milled with stark-eyed refugees around smoldering bonfires in the plaza. Two days crawled by. Then a wild pealing of cathedral bells announced that Armijo had won victory for the government—and for himself appointment as commander in chief of the army and governor of the province.

During these uneasy months (August 1837 to January 1838) Americans in New Mexico occupied a ticklish position. The Pueblo Indians thought them enemies because the merchants, through no choice of their own, had furnished both

Perez and Armijo with supplies. The loyalists charged that
Texas-inspired *gringos* had armed the Indians as a first step in
absorbing New Mexico. Charles Bent and other Americans
were imprisoned in Taos, by which party or exactly when is
uncertain. A courier raced to Ceran St. Vrain at Bent's Fort,
and soon a heavily armed rescue party was spurring toward
Raton Pass. Anticlimax. Down the hill toward them rode
Charles himself. Either by bribery or by threats of having his
men burn down the town, he had won his release.

Meanwhile the competitors on the South Platte were an-
noying each other as best they could. Sarpy and Fraeb, who
had named their American Fur Company-backed post Fort
Jackson, thumbed their noses at Bent, St. Vrain by sending
Jim Robertson and a party to the Arkansas with nearly a
thousand dollars' worth of trade goods. When in December
1837 a Spaniard stole some of Robertson's stock, the Arkansas
company could scarcely shed even crocodile tears.

No effort was lost to beguile the Indians. Early in 1838
Charles conveniently recalled that certain chiefs had never received the medals which Dodge, short of medals in 1835, had
promised to send them. In St. Louis he accordingly stopped in
to see William Clark, and on April 30, 1838, Clark obligingly
wrote the Commissioner of Indian Affairs for six large silver
medals: one each for Yellow Wolf, Whirlwind, and White
Cow of the Cheyennes; for Left-Handed Soldier, Buffalo Belly,
and Raven of the Arapaho. With an eye on Texas and the
restless Southwest, Clark added for the edification of the government, "Mr. Bent is an enterprising, respectable man . . .
and if occasion required would, from his knowledge of the
country, and of the Spanish and French languages, combined
with his general intelligence, prove useful."

Up on the South Platte, Sarpy and Fraeb tried to get rid of
Marcellin St. Vrain's competition by buying, in February 1838,
all the robes he had collected, perhaps taking advantage of his
inexperience during the dicker. This brought Fort Jackson's
winter take to 2761 robes worth $9318.37 and 53 beaver pelts
worth $193.37—a commentary on the position to which beaver
had declined in the trade. Expense, however, had been ter-
rific; and still very much in the picture were Lupton and Vasquez-Sublette. In hopes, perhaps, of cutting their throats,

Fraeb suggested to George Bent that they go into partnership, a strange wedding indeed.

The Bents had a better idea. Why not buy Fraeb's and Sarpy's Fort Jackson? It was the post with the powerful backing; when it was gone, they could focus on smaller competitors. In July, Ceran St. Vrain went to St. Louis and found the American Fur Company ready to listen. The depression of '37 had hit them hard, and with horror they were beginning to realize the full extent of the smallpox scourge which the previous fall had enfeebled nearly all the northern tribes, with a concomitant loss in trade. At this point Fort Jackson, which had had to purchase most of its robes from its own competitor, looked like a poor bet. Besides, the western department of the American Fur Company was about to undergo another upheaval, which would put Pratte out and bring Pierre Chouteau, Jr., into full control. Word was passed down to Sarpy and Fraeb that their backing no longer existed—in short, move on. (Sarpy went back among the Omahas; Fraeb hooked up again with Jim Bridger and in 1841 lost his scalp to the Sioux.)

The sale settled, the American Fur Company now proposed a cartel. Bent, St. Vrain & Company would not send trading parties into American Fur Company territory beyond the North Platte, where Honoré Picotte's Sioux Outfit held exclusive franchise. In return the American Fur Company guaranteed that none of its subsidiaries would encroach un the South Platte. And so in 1838 big business sliced up the western half of America, as the nation's boundaries then extended. After a little trouble during the subsequent winter, relationships would become increasingly cordial, and from now on the two gargantuas of the West would transact growing amounts of business together.[9]

Unaware of the deal, Louis Vasquez and Andrew Sublette rolled a big caravan out of Independence in the summer of 1838. With them rode a tall, yellow-skinned mulatto, Jim Beckwourth, lean-muscled, nerveless, violent of temper, and almost as brutally efficient in wilderness savagery as he claimed himself to be. After going to the mountains with Ashley in the early 1820s, Beckwourth had been adopted by Crow Indians, whose trade he helped keep within the orbit of the American Fur Company, and then, for a change of pace, he had gone to Florida to fight Seminoles for the United States Army. Now he was on his way back to the dry clarity of the mountains with his new employers. He was a good man for a cutthroat trade war, but he was not universally admired. When the caravan stopped brazenly at Bent's Fort for rest and repairs, irascible Mr. Goddamn Murray, the head clerk, looked down his flat nose at Beckwourth and told Sublette he had hired himself a rascal. Retorted Sublette (and as sure as buffalo have hides, he never used the words which Beckwourth's ghost writer put into Sublette's mouth), "Murray, it is unsafe for you to use such sentiments in relation to Beckwourth; should they reach his ears, he would surely make you rue it. I have heard these foul aspersions on his character before, and I am in a position to know they are all unfounded. Had I the least suspicion of his integrity, I should be the last man to take him in my employ." Then, full of honor—and its wagons full of alcohol—the high-minded caravan wended onward to the South Platte.

While Vasquez, Sublette, Beckwourth, and crew were cutting a jag of wild hay for winter, William Bent, on October 3, rode into Fort Jackson and told Abel Baker, the bourgeois in charge, that the place had changed hands. The next three days were spent in taking an inventory whose meticulous pages throw an interesting side light on the trade. Livestock: one yoke of oxen, one heifer, six horses, six mules, and one mare lame with the foot evil. Housekeeping items: a dozen pans, four sheet-iron kettles, eleven iron spoons, six table forks, six pewter plates, one coffeepot, and one pair of damaged candle snuffers. Tools: a grindstone, blacksmith tongs, carpentry and farming implements. Trade goods galore: blue and scarlet chiefs' coats, gilt coat buttons, ornamental brass tacks; pans, knives, lead, powder, cloth, blankets; a bale of tobacco; great heaps of beads, 380 pairs of earbobs, 350 clay pipes; awls, combs, and 300 sewing needles; 200 trout fishhooks; a dozen fox tails. The laboriously constructed buildings William didn't want, for Bent, St. Vrain's own Fort Lookout was only ten miles to the north. If the American Fur Company wished to destroy the post and thus preclude some fly-by-night from occupying it, that was their business. Destroy it they did. As soon as William had left with the merchandise, a party arrived from Laramie to raze Fort Jackson beyond usefulness.[10]

One down and two to go. The best way to handle remaining competition was to round up every vestige of business within hundreds of miles. Abel Baker was sent up to Fort Lookout to trade. A party was dispatched into Navajo country to obtain the blankets the Cheyennes prized. Agreements were violated; alcohol flowed far and wide. Hearing that a village of Cheyennes was camped on the North Platte, William hurried there with three cartloads of kegs. Frederick Laboue, trading in the village for the American Fur Company, rode angrily across the river to meet him. What about the cartel St. Vrain had signed, pledging that William's company would keep clear of the North Fork? Blandly the interloper replied that all he knew was that St. Vrain had written saying William could go wherever their Indians were. Pure bunk. William knew of the contract; he had just taken over Fort Jackson, whose sale was part of the transaction.

Using his alcohol freely, he pried sixty lodges of the Indians away from the others and was probably mortified at not winning the entire village. Still working the edges of American Fur Company territory, he swung north of the Colorado border into the Laramie Mountains. There he bumped into Jim Beckwourth pouring out rivers of Vasquez-Sublette firewater. A despicable business, Jim said piously, describing the orgies—and went right on pouring. He got the better of Bent (as Beckwourth tells it) and also nearly got his swart hide mortally punctured during the brawls he occasioned.

Bent, St. Vrain & Company was in no position to complain of such methods. At the far side of the "Black Country," Marcellin was going hog-wild. He was a slight youth, about five and a half feet tall and only 115 pounds or so in weight. He loved whiskey, horse racing, and hunting; among his accomplishments was that of luring curious antelope within gun range by standing on his head and waving his legs in the air. Made openhanded by liberal potions of his own trade alcohol, he was now offering one he-mule or one horse for ten robes. Outrageous prices—but the Picotte brothers, trading for the American Fur Company's Sioux Outfit and feeling the effect of Marcellin's prodigality, admitted he was raking in business. "We are obliged," Joe Picotte wrote his brother Honoré, "to

let go the hand [that is, be equally generous] if we want to
have a few hides."[11] So keen was the war that even Charles
Bent rode northward and muddied the waters still more by
trying to hire the American Fur Company's best men from
them.[12] Until the situation on the South Platte was stabilized,
the cartel agreement could wait.

The slack season of summer brought a brief respite. It also
brought several interesting visitors to Bent's Fort. The first were
hardly welcome—a war party of Comanches who in mid-June,
while the principal partners were still on the Platte, swooped
down on the horse herd, killed the guard, and made off with
more than fifty head of stock.[13] More intriguing were three
later parties of Americans, traveling separately and economically unconcerned, for a change, with the business of the
plains. One by-product of the visitations was the lifting of
Bent's Fort into the awareness of the nation, for a member of
each group wrote into an account of his travels an awed description of the color and scope of the great mud castle on the
Arkansas. Here was the best fort in the Rocky Mountain area,
declared Frederick Wislizenus, and he had visited them all.
It was, said Matt Field, correspondent of the New Orleans
Picayune, "as though an air-built castle had dropped to earth
. . . in the midst of the vast desert." Tourists, these two. The
third party, led by young Thomas Jefferson Farnham, was
more significant. When the group paused, quarreling among
themselves, in the shadows of the fort's "noble battlements"
("Peace again—roofs again—safety again . . . bread, oh! bread
again!"), they were on their way to the farmlands of Oregon.
The facts of expansion were at last overriding the shortsighted
expediency of the government. Not for much longer would
even congressmen talk of the Indian nations as forming the
"permanent" western boundary of the United States.

Legend whispers of another visitor—the first white girl, if
the tale be true, to see those gray-brown and most unfemi-
nine walls. She was sixteen-year-old Félicité St. Vrain, eldest
daughter of Felix, whom Indians had killed a few years before.
Shortly after reaching the fort with her uncle Ceran, she fell
in love with Kit Carson. Consternation resulted. Not that Ceran
disliked Kit. Among the free trappers still gouging the last
dangerous beaver pelts out of the Central Rockies, Carson was

the most efficient, hence the most prosperous. During the off season of summer he spent considerable time at the fort, lending a hand with the hunting and doing yeoman service in keeping the trail safe. But . . . he was a squaw man. Four years before he had killed another trapper over an Arapaho girl, had married her, and had brought her to Bent's Fort to live. She was lovely Waa-nibe, Singing Wind, and she bore Kit a beloved daughter, Adaline. Now she was dead and little Adaline needed a mother while Kit was away in the mountains.

A St. Vrain, scion of nobility, to mother a half-breed? Good God! Félicité was hustled back to St. Louis. Legend, true to the last sigh of 1839's conventions, says she took her broken heart into a convent.[14]

Another St. Vrain connection, being male and husky, was more readily absorbed. This was Lucien Maxwell, whose Irish father had married a daughter of Pierre Menard of Kaskaskia, Illinois, one of the greatest of the early fur traders and lieutenant governor of the state. Savinien St. Vrain, Ceran's brother, had also wed a Menard girl. Perhaps the remote relationship wasn't what brought Lucien west, but it didn't hurt him any when he hit the partners for a job. Nor did his appearance. He was twenty-one, brown-haired and blue-eyed, a little short of six feet tall, and built like a Greek wrestler. The partners sent him up to Fort Lookout, where the trade wars of the South Platte were being fought to a finish.

During the winter of 1839–40, Jim Beckwourth's unstinted alcohol and unbounded influence over the Indians had, according to Beckwourth, made Louis Vasquez and Andrew Sublette a fortune. Jim exaggerated. In the spring Vasquez and Sublette were able to float down the Platte, with dreadful effort, one thirty-six-foot boat loaded with their entire winter's take —seven hundred robes and four hundred buffalo tongues. On July 3 of the same year, according to the *Daily Missouri Republican*, Bent, St. Vrain & Company brought into St. Louis fifteen thousand robes and "considerable furs"—more than twenty times their rivals' haul. So much for Beckwourth's "immense profits."

Broke and discouraged, Vasquez and Sublette sold out to Lock and Randolph. The new partners fared no better. They never completed payments on their purchase, Sioux Indians stole forty-five of their horses, and in 1842 they gave up completely.

Only Lancaster Lupton clung on. While the other rivals fought, he quietly went about his business, married a Cheyenne, and in 1841 tweaked the nose of the American Fur Company by building Fort Platte within a mile or so of mighty Laramie. The move roused the company to rebuild its decaying log post out of adobe; but before the new Fort Laramie was completed, Lupton, having rolled the rock into the American Fur Company's garden, sold his new post to a subsidiary of Pratte and Cabanné. Now the alcoholic warfare shifted to the North Platte, where it sank to the depths of degradation. On the South Platte, Lupton apparently gave in and reached some sort of terms with Bent, St. Vrain & Company.[15]

From the North Platte southward the monopoly of Bent, St. Vrain was now complete. Working for them at their two forts were more than a hundred men, an extraordinary mélange of French, Mexicans, Americans, Indians, and all degrees of mixture. Beckwourth, out of a job after the collapse of Vasquez & Sublette, signed on in the summer of 1840. With Maxwell he traded out of Fort St. Vrain—saved the place, too, he says, when Indians attacked it in a fury because he would not give them alcohol on credit. More important in strengthening the position of the fort was Marcellin's 1840 marriage to a Sioux, relative of Chief Red Cloud.

Typical of the traders operating out of the Arkansas post were men like Mexican Sol Silver and Blackfoot John Smith. Silver was a Mexican captive whom Comanches had sold to the Kiowas; escaping from the Kiowas, Sol joined the Osages, led a raid during which he joyfully killed his former owner, and eventually drifted via Taos into the Bents' employ. Quicktempered, deadly with fist or gun, Sol Silver had the bushiest, blackest whiskers on the Arkansas. His own name he never knew; the one he went by came from the huge silver earrings that dangled by his swarthy cheeks. Yet even Sol's knowledge of Indians was surpassed by that of John Simpson Smith. A runaway tailor's apprentice of St. Louis, Smith had lived for a time with Blackfeet on the Missouri, wherefore the Cheyennes called him Po-ome, or Blackfoot. After killing some of his former friends in a quarrel, Smith fled for refuge among the Sioux, then married a Cheyenne and joined his wife's tribe. He was despot of the southern prairie. No Mexican pumpkin trader dared enter John Smith's "territory" without paying him tribute. When the governor of New Mexico put a five-hundred-dollar bounty on his head, not a single would-be taker dared risk Cheyenne wrath by trying to collect.

Added to such men were trappers thrown out of work by the dying beaver trade—Dick Wootton, Bill Mitchell, Bill New, and even such independent free agents as Old Bill Williams and Kit Carson. Most of these erstwhile trappers were employed as hunters, working with pack trains and retinues of butchers to supply the daily meat requirements of well over a hundred people. It was no sinecure. The buffalo had to be found, run down in wild chase, killed, and skinned—the last under a broiling sun where the only thirst chaser was a juicy hunk of raw liver laid on a buffalo chip and nibbled as a man worked up to his elbows in steaming blood. For this labor the chief hunters were paid one dollar a day, as compared to the ten to fifteen dollars per month earned by the Mexican workers around the fort.

Monopoly, manpower, resources, know-how—all these Bent, St. Vrain & Company had. The one great obstacle to complete control was the continual warfare waged by the Cheyennes and Arapaho, whose trade the company commanded, against the Comanches and Kiowas, whose trade it wished to clinch. Dodge's peace efforts had proved non-productive, and the sour temper of the Comanches toward friends of the Cheyennes had prevented repetitions of William's successful 1835 venture to the Canadian River. Throughout the latter part of the decade matters kept growing worse.

In 1837, not long after William's marriage to Owl Woman, a group of one of the Cheyenne soldier societies, the Bow Strings, decided to raid Comanche horses. When they went to the arrow lodge to get their medicine fixed, Gray Thunder told them they would have to wait; a Cheyenne had killed a tribesman and the arrows had to be renewed before their magic would be potent. Declining to tarry for what Gray Thunder said would be a propitious time, the young men beat the seventy-year-old priest until he promised to renew the arrows immediately. But, Gray Thunder warned, that kind of

ceremony was worthless. And sure enough, Comanches and
Kiowas under Chief Satanta wiped out every one of the forty-
two Bow String soldiers who went on the raid.

News of the disaster was brought back by a Sioux who
chanced to be with a party that recognized the braiding and
ornaments on two of the scalps the enemy were dancing over.
Runners were sent to all the Cheyenne villages, and the entire
tribe gathered for a council on the South Platte. They worked
themselves into a terrible frenzy. Women relatives of the slain
men hacked their legs and arms, ran bloody hands over the
faces of the warriors, and wailed for revenge. Matters weren't
helped any when Porcupine Bear, chief of the Dog Soldiers,
got hold of some American Fur Company whiskey. In a
drunken brawl Bear and some of his relatives sliced up another Cheyenne named Little Creek. For this murder, Porcupine Bear and his kin were, by tribal custom, stripped of authority and declared outlaws. It meant only that they and their
families moved off a way from the main village and camped
by themselves.

The result of the council was a decision to move the arrows against the enemy. The next spring, with Gray Thunder
and his wife in the lead, almost the entire southern Cheyenne
and Arapaho tribes poured into Bent's Fort to buy guns, flints,
powder, and ammunition. Owl Woman was certainly with
them. It was too momentous an occasion to miss. If William
was at the fort when the mob arrived, he probably tried to
remonstrate with her and her father. Wasted breath. On the
ragged column went.

Finally scouts located a Comanche-Kiowa camp on a tributary of the Cimarron. Again the attackers marched through
suspense-filled night—and again, exactly as in the case of the
Pawnee affray six years before, the magic of Gray Thunder's
ceremony with the arrows was vitiated. Porcupine Bear and
his outlaws, trailing along by themselves, prematurely am-
bushed thirty-one Kiowa men and women out after buffalo
and slew every one of them.

In spite of this misadventure, the first attack by the main
body went well. They caught several women out digging
roots with the pointed, fire-hardened sticks used by all the
plains tribes, and killed twelve of the females—perfectly valid

coups. But then the enemy warriors managed to group, the women threw up defensive breastworks, and a day-long series of scattered, unco-ordinated battles failed to carry the besieged camp. At sundown the Cheyennes withdrew. Gloom gripped them. Gray Thunder was dead, killed in one of the first charges, but at least his wife had recovered the precious bundle of medicine arrows. Howling and bloody, she carried them back to a camp near Bent's Fort, where another keeper was chosen. There was grief in the big lodge then. Indian mourning meant the cutting off of hair, the slashing of flesh, sometimes the amputation of a finger or two. Owl Woman—who knows? But undoubtedly William Bent was rendered heartily sick of the whole business.

In spite of their successful defense, the Comanches and Kiowas had been awed by the mass attack, something totally outside their prior experience. Meanwhile horse raids by the Cheyennes continued; the traders at the fort harangued the Comanches about the folly of unremitting warfare; and when smallpox appeared among the Kiowas during the winter of 1839–40, uneasiness rippled through the tribes. Suddenly the notion of peace took hold, and certain Prairie Apaches, married to Arapaho, were dispatched to sound out the enemy. After debates, hesitations, and preliminary meetings, a great council was agreed on, to be held during the summer of 1840 on the big flats three miles east of Bent's Fort.

The Cheyennes and Arapaho went into camp first, on the north side of the river. For three days, while curious traders, including Kit Carson and Peg-leg Smith, watched, drums thumped and dancers yowled. Horsemen laid bets and the game of hand twinkled in front of nearly every lodge. At the fort, business was tremendous as delegation after delegation poured in to buy presents for their erstwhile enemies. Next the Kiowas, led by Satanta and Little Mountain, swept onto the flats south of the river. As a token of good will they brought with them, wrapped in fancy Navajo blankets, the forty-two Bow String scalps they had taken three years before. The Cheyenne chiefs, however, rejected the offer, lest the relatives of the slain remember their grief and grow violent.

Now the Comanches and Prairie Apaches arrived, and the flats on both sides of the river were prickled with hundreds

upon hundreds of lodges. Thousands of people milled among
them and more than ten thousand horses grazed far and wide
on the hills. In the midst of the swarming conclave, a light-
skinned youth of perhaps twenty, dressed like a Comanche,
rode up to Kit. His name was Jim Hobbs, he said. Charles
Bent would remember that four years before Hobbs and John
Baptiste had left a Bent Caravan to chase a buffalo. Both lads
now belonged to a Comanche chief named Old Wolf. In fact,
Jim had won Old Wolf's confidence and had married one of
his daughters. Old Wolf held other white captives—two girls
named Brown who had been taken down near San Antonio,
one eighteen now, the other twenty-one. They were married,
if you wanted to call it that, to two of Old Wolf's sons. And
would Kit please get word to the Bents? Jim had a three-year-
old son, but just the same he was getting mighty tired of living
with Injuns, even in a chief's lodge.

The next day every Cheyenne—man, woman, and child—
waded the river and sat in a long row in front of their once
mortal enemies. Comanche boys and Mexican captives brought
horse after horse out of the hills and presented them to the
visitors, so many that the Cheyennes lacked ropes enough to
lead them all. To reciprocate, on their side of the river the
Cheyennes served a huge feast of white man's delicacies
bought at the fort—rice, dried apples, corn meal, and molasses.
Then they heaped guns, blankets, cloth, beads, and brass kettles in front of their guests. It was an exuberant love feast, re-
plete with storytelling, commodity swapping, horse racing,
gambling, and barbaric dancing. Inevitably alcohol was suggested, but up in the big lodge William Bent said no. The
potentials were already explosive enough.

A thousand howling Comanches, according to Hobbs, rode
three miles up the river to visit the fort. While Charles and
William, Kit and Blackfoot John Smith showed the headmen
around the interior, the others opened trade outside. Some alcohol slipped loose, a fight flared, and William got the stuff
back under lock and key in a hurry. Fascinated by his entertainment, Old Wolf stayed far into the night. Outside the
walls his worried warriors unleashed a fearful racket. To re-
assure them, Old Wolf, somewhat tangle-footed by now,
climbed up on the walls to let them see that all was well. So

it went for several days, the whites taking advantage of the occasion to impress the Indians by firing the cannon and almost scaring the visitors into headlong flight.

When Old Wolf was sufficiently warmed up, William ransomed Jim Hobbs from him for six yards of red flannel, a pound of tobacco, and an ounce of beads. John Baptiste, valued less highly, was let go for one old mule. Jim consoled his wife over his desertion with some beads and a bright red dress. But Old Wolf's sons refused to part with the Brown girls.

Peace with the Cheyennes, the Comanches decided, should also include peace with the owners of this wonderful storehouse of treasure. They begged for and received the Bents' promise to send traders once more into their country. The matter of horses was also touched on. Wisely Charles did not mention the animals which Comanches had stolen from the fort the previous summer, and perhaps he forgot that through Governor Armijo he had futilely tried to replevy some of the stock from New Mexicans to whom the Indians had later traded the animals. Now the bread was buttered on the other side. He told Old Wolf that the company would buy whatever surplus stock the Comanches had to sell—and would ask no embarrassing questions about sources.

Peace. Friendship. Profit.

But it was never safe to trust a Comanche too far.

The next year, in October 1841, a Bent train was plodding up the Arkansas. Sighting buffalo in the distance, twenty-five-year-old Robert Bent, youngest and handsomest of the four brothers, loped out to get some meat for dinner. Lurking Comanches struck him down, tore off his scalp. His companions recovered his body, carried it on to the fort. There, just outside the walls, he was buried. Rocks were piled on the grave, and among them the little French tailor planted cactus to keep digging wolves away.

Any empire has its price. But not yet was the cost of this one paid in full.

CHAPTER X

TEXIANS

From 1834 to 1838 the diplomatic representative of the United States in Santa Fe was Ceran St. Vrain. There is no indication that he let his official duties strain him; indeed, there was little cause for strain. But after the revolution of 1837–38, matters deteriorated. For reasons unknown, Ceran relinquished the office which he had never filled, and in 1839 Manuel Álvarez became United States consul. Promptly Charles Bent appointed himself as Alvarez's unofficial attaché for northern New Mexico and began crisply to instruct the man in his duties.[1]

The officiousness was hardly necessary. Manuel Álvarez knew his way around the West. A native of Spain, he had come to Mexico in 1819. About 1824 he entered the Santa Fe trade and soon attained proprietorship of a large store in the capital city. He was an industrious, courageous man, fluent in English and loyal to his job with the United States Government. Soon realizing this, Charles Bent climbed off his high horse, and out of mutual respect and common business concerns there grew an abiding friendship. During the next troubled years the two men would work hand in glove to protect American interests in the increasingly hostile atmosphere of New Mexico.

They had to deal with a pair of thorny opponents. One was the governor, Manuel Armijo; the other was Padre Antonio José Martinez, parish priest of Taos. But it was Armijo who precipitated the first crises.

The man had a genius for trickery. Born dirt-poor near Albuquerque to parents of dubious reputation, Manuel Armijo had made his first money, so sneered American traders in Santa Fe, by stealing huge numbers of sheep from the neighboring Chavez family—and then selling the animals back to Chavez![2] Shrewd gambling increased his gains to the point where he could launch himself and his three brothers in the Santa Fe trade, which by now included as many Mexican as American proprietors. Power was a lust in the man—the power of politics as well as of money. He achieved both. The trade made him rich; demagoguery and treachery put him in the Governor's Palace during the revolution of 1837–38. Though Americans mocked Armijo as an arrant physical coward, he was a commanding figure in that land of short-statured people—six feet tall and, until good living turned him fat, handsomely built. His nose and eyes were strikingly arrogant; his lips full and sensuous. A consummate showman, he was given to superb sorrel horses and sky-blue uniforms emblazoned in gold and silver.

In 1839 he enraged the merchants by imposing an arbitrary duty of five hundred dollars flat on each wagon, regardless of contents. This disregard of *ad valorem* taxation obviously worked a hardship on the small dealer in cheap merchandise and led to more smuggling. Some traders increased the size of their wagons. Others, including Bent, St. Vrain, hauled goods to the border in their normal vehicles, then piled tottering loads on a few of the wagons and dragged these on to the customhouse behind doubled teams.

Next the governor exempted native citizens from taxes on their storehouses and shops, a move that put almost the entire revenue burden on Americans and naturalized residents. Informers were encouraged to report violators, and occasional surprise raids were made for suspected contraband. In January 1841 such a raid turned the Taos stores of Charles Bent and Carlos Beaubien upside down; and though this was probably done without the direct knowledge of Armijo, the move did little to endear the government in the heart of either man. Throughout New Mexico, American merchants were convinced, and Álvarez so charged in an angry letter to Daniel Webster, United States Secretary of State, that the harassments were motivated by Armijo's desire to ruin his American competitors.

Protest brought no remedies, but frustration soon found an outlet in the affair of a man named Daley. For some reason Daley had gone to the placer mines south of Santa Fe. Generally Americans were not interested in the mining. There were restrictions against foreigners, and the pathetic methods of the native workers, called *gambucinos,* yielded only the most meager returns. The gambucinos carried their baskets of gravel out of the pits by climbing dizzy zigzags of notched poles ten to fifteen feet long. Lack of water confined operations mostly to winter, when snow could be melted with hot stones. A few cents' worth of metal was then washed out in wooden bowls, gourds, even the horns of mountain sheep. Those who could afford mercury for amalgamating placed their amalgam in the center of a potato, bound the halves together, and baked it. The tiny gold button was then dug out of the potato and the mercury recovered by squeezing. Most of the take eventually reached the Americans via trade, anyhow, but perhaps Daley was interested in a more direct approach. He went to the placers and there he was murdered.

His killers were captured—and released. Here was an issue, and the Americans in Santa Fe made the most of it. Led by William Dryden and a soon-to-be professional scalp hunter named James Kirker, they tumultuously forced the rearrest of the criminals and presented Armijo with a memorial demanding full legal expiation. Correctly interpreting the high-handed procedure as a challenge, the governor called out his ragamuffin militia. The foreigners set up defenses, and a pitched battle impended until Armijo, backing water, promised that the murderers would be dealt with.[3]

To what extent Charles Bent may have been involved in the Daley affair is not known. But it was certainly in his mind when he took up the issue of law and order in New Mexico. On December 10, 1839, he dispatched to Armijo, through Álvarez, still another memorial, this time about a killing in Taos: "It is the request of the foreigners residing heare, that you will present the accompanying petition to the Geovinor and impress upon him the nessaty of having William Langford tried for the murder of Semon Nash imeadiately." A year later it was "the murder of an American citizen near de Mora . . . This is the fourth murder that has been comitted on American citizens within the last fue years, and as yet neather of the murderers have been punished." Did the New Mexican Government consider it poor economics to hang two or more natives merely for killing one foreign heretic? "I say if thare be twenty conserned in the murder of one of us let us insist upon the whole being punished, and with nothing short of death."

Inevitably Charles soon found that his self-assumed diplomatic responsibilities cut two ways. Occasions arose when New Mexico needed assistance on American soil, and the Bents were quick to offer it. There were reasons. Their fort on the Arkansas was under suspicion. In 1840 Armijo wrote Mexico City, "Many years' experience has shown me that the dangers from which this Department suffers result from the various fortresses which North Americans have placed near this Department, the nearest of which is that of Charles Bent. . . . If the President does not remedy this, New Mexico must go to total ruin. . . . These forts are the protection of contraband trade. . . . They are the very ones who supply arms and ammunition to most of the barbarous tribes. They protect robbers . . . in order that they may profit from the spoils."

Part of this outburst was pure calumny. Armijo, uneasy over dissatisfaction at home and threats from Texas, was trying to wring more money and troops out of Mexico City. Nonetheless, it behooved Bent, St. Vrain & Company to be conciliatory. Unfortunately, Mexican suspicion was such that many of Charles's efforts boomeranged.

Take for instance, the charges of protecting robbers. In the spring of 1840 the prefect of Taos, Juan Andrés Archuleta, asked the company's assistance in capturing three horse thieves who had fled with the herd of one Marteau toward the Platte River. Charles alerted Fort St. Vrain. When his warning arrived, however, most of the company men were away, hauling the season's robes to the Arkansas, and it was certain free trappers and Shawnee Indians who, without authorization, took after the thieves. The trio were captured, one being killed in the process. The bourgeois in charge of Fort St. Vrain then demanded the return of the animals. The Shawnees refused, claiming the stolen horses as recompense for their troubles. The bourgeois, fearing nearby Shawnees more than distant Mexicans, compromised by collecting two of the horses for debts owed the company by the Indians. The other animals he let go. He also let the prisoners escape.

The Shawnees went off to visit an Arapaho village. Getting wind of their whereabouts, Marteau, the owner of the ani-

mals, came storming into Bent's Fort with Prefect Archuleta.
Though Charles gave Marteau the two recovered horses,
which represented hard cash owed the firm by the Shawnees,
the man was not satisfied. Angrily he demanded that Charles
compel the Shawnees to surrender the rest of the herd. Charles
declined. If he did that, assuming he could, the Shawnees
would retaliate by raiding the fort's horses. Instead he advised
Marteau to give the principal Shawnees a few barrels of whiskey. That way Marteau would recover at least some of his
animals.

Marteau demurred—said he couldn't afford the liquor. Disgusted, Charles offered to give the man one barrel. Archuleta
offered another and recommended that the horse-seeker buy
two more on his own. Not Marteau. "He said," Charles wrote
Álvarez, "he had no mules to pack it on, the amount of it was
this he was too damd stingy." Back in Taos, Marteau next
threatened suit against the company on grounds that after his
departure Bent and St. Vrain had bought the horses from the
Shawnees. Padre Martinez, it was rumored, would make representations on Marteau's behalf to Armijo. Charles exploded.
A fine return for what had started out as willing co-operation
with the authorities! Sue and be damned! Charles offered to
bring in a flock of witnesses of his own from the Arkansas,
provided Marteau agreed that the losing litigant pay full costs
of the court action. Apparently that checkmated the man; at
least nothing more is heard of the matter.[4]

And Indians. Undoubtedly the company did sell them arms,
but not with the deliberate intent of causing trouble for New
Mexico. Rather, Charles did his best to avoid clashes. When
Arapaho chiefs, in January 1841, asked for his help in securing
the return of certain of their people whom Ute raiders had
sold as slaves to Mexicans around Taos, Charles promised to
do what he could. A visit to the Taos justice, however,
achieved nothing, and now the Arapaho threatened war on
New Mexico. Through Álvarez, Charles sent a warning to
Armijo: "Those Indians are formidable. . . . They are numeri-
ias and well-armed. The Chyeans will join them, there is no
doubt, and you know theas have always had the reputation
of being the most formidable warriors of the North, they are
the Terrir of all surrounding nations." Unless the prisoners were

returned, let the outlying *ranchos* beware; let the caravan that
was "on the eave of leaving Santafe for Missouri . . . be verry
cautious."

Armijo pooh-poohed the warning and added a gratuitous
slur. Bent was just trying to please his customers. On hearing
that, Charles's temper flared again. War, he told Armijo, was
what would really benefit Bent, St. Vrain. The company would
pick up robes which previously had gone to Mexican traders;
there would be good traffic in stolen horses; and if the outbound caravan was successfully raided "of 80,000 or 100,000
Dollars, I have no doubt I could get the whole amount for
15 or 20 thousand Dollars worth of goodes. . . . If I was so
much interested for myself, I should be exerting myself to de-
tain the prisoners . . . I gave the information . . . because I
felt it was my duty . . . [but] from this forward I shall be
verry carefull how I intrude myself."

Still seething, he rode to the fort, where eighteen wagons
were loading for Missouri. Gloomily he noted that a party of
Arapaho camped at Purgatory Creek had "8 Spanish Scelpes,
10 horses, 2 guns, etc." In endeavoring to help the Mexicans,
he had alienated the Indians: they "will listen to us no longer
. . . they say we have deceived them." With that, he washed
his hands of the situation and pointed the company wagons
eastward.

The threatened war never came to full head, and by the
time Charles returned in the fall of 1841, its rumblings had
been forgotten in the face of a far greater dread. A reputed
army of Texians, as residents of the new republic were then
called, was marching against the New Mexican frontier.

Conspirators from New Mexico had gone to Texas during
the previous summer of 1840. They weren't very many, and
apparently they had the active backing of only a few of the
American traders in Taos and Santa Fe. Feeble though the
plotters were, however, they nonetheless found a willing lis-
tener in bumbling Mirabeau Lamar, second president of the
Lone Star Republic. Texas affairs were in parlous shape. Public indebtedness had soared sevenfold; money was worth about
twenty cents on the dollar. Mexico, still refusing to admit
Texan independence, continued to threaten and to incite Indian depredations.

To convince Lamar that a Texan attack on Armijo would have support within New Mexico, the conspirators trotted out the old Pueblo Indian legend of Quetzalcoatl, god of the air, who was supposed to return someday from the east and liberate his people—perhaps even in the form of a Texian. They reminded Lamar of the Lone Star claim, formally legislated December 19, 1836, of owning as far as the banks of the Rio Grande. But what most interested the president were the glittering figures of the Santa Fe trade. Why not divert it through Texas? The year before, in 1839, Josiah Gregg had blazed a crossing from Van Buren, Arkansas, and there seemed, at least in the mellow glow of the conference room in Texas, no reason why a trail even farther south couldn't be inaugurated. Though Sam Houston (out of the presidency because of a constitutional clause prohibiting direct succession) warned that talk of annexing New Mexico was asinine, Lamar refused to listen. It would all be dovelike; New Mexico would fall like a plum —he thought. In September 1840 he sent to Santa Fe as his commissioner William Dryden, one of the leaders in the recent agitation over the murder of gold-miner Daley. Only if the New Mexicans themselves desired union with Texas, so said Dryden's pacific instructions, would the wheels start rolling.

Appointed as Dryden's fellow commissioners were John Rowland and William Workman, naturalized residents of Taos and pioneers in the New Mexican trade. Whether they were chosen purely at Dryden's suggestion or with their own compliance is not known. Nor is it known to what extent Charles Bent was involved. Armijo certainly suspected him—and every other American. Nearly all foreigners in New Mexico were placed under surveillance.

During the uneasy months of early 1841, a certain Juan Vigil, who was involved in a lawsuit against Charles, went to Armijo with what are described only as "false representations" against Bent and William Workman. Echoes of the Texas conspiracy may or may not have been included. At any rate, as soon as the two men heard of Vigil's accusation, they strode through the cold, sparkling noon of February 19 to the home of their traducer. There, Charles wrote to Álvarez, "Workman struck him [Vigil] with his whip, after whiping him a while with this he droped it and beate him with his fists until I thought he had given him enough, whereupon I pulled him off. He run for his life"—straight to the alcalde, or mayor.

Charles, haled into court, was ordered to jail. He declined to go. The nonplused justice then told him to confine himself at Beaubien's house. Charles refused, but finally agreed to remain in his own home until Vigil's threatened suit for assault and battery was formally presented. Workman, too, confined himself at home. After forty-eight hours no warrants had yet been issued, and the two men defiantly emerged.

There was no use being heedlessly intransigent, however. By one of Beaubien's men Charles sent to Governor Armijo the ten pounds of coffee and keg of gunpowder "I promised him"—the promise having been made, to be sure, before the Vigil altercation. By the same messenger Bent dispatched to Álvarez "7 vollums of the Frentch voiages," selected by Beaubien from among the books at the fort. And to John Scolly, whose Santa Fe store had the only plank floor in New Mexico, went "one Vial Elexer of love. Tell the old gentleman not to interfear with the arrangements of your-self and other young men, for no doubt he will be able by the use of this to raise himself very high in the estimation of the ladys."

Meanwhile Vigil, Charles was told, had "armed himself with a Bowie knife and a pair of Horsemans pistols intending, as he sayed, of sending me, one herotic, to the devil. I met him twice but he was as meake as a lamb." For the threatened suit Charles felt only contempt: "I had rather have the satisfaction of whiping a man that has wronged me than to have him punished ten times by the law. . . . [Only] cowards and women take this satisfaction."

Presumably, therefore, it was mere coincidence that during the following week four disguised men approached Vigil's home in the night. Dogs barked a warning, and Vigil fled "nearly naked and crossed the prairie to Del Norte [the Rio Grande] and laid there all day. . . . I think Juan Vigil will be heartely tired of the valley of Taos if he is scarte once or twice more." So Charles dryly reported the attack to Álvarez, with no indication that he himself was in any way involved.

During the height of the Vigil affair, Commissioner William Dryden wrote the president of Texas that two thirds of the

Mexicans and all of the Pueblo Indians were looking forward to deliverers from the East. That was enough for Mirabeau Lamar. Without the sanction of his Congress he ordered half a million paper dollars from a New Orleans printer and sent Major George Howard into Louisiana to buy equipment. There Howard met the editor-owner of the New Orleans *Picayune,* thirty-two-year-old George Wilkins Kendall. Two years before, Kendall had sent out Matt Field to write of the West, including Bent's Fort, and now the editor decided to have a look at the country for himself. He signed up with Howard but took the precaution of obtaining an American passport. If things got too hot in New Mexico he could disassociate himself from the filibuster—or so he reasoned. Actually, if ever a man caught a bear by the tail, it was George Wilkins Kendall.

Expansionism was in the air that spring. In May 1841, as Bent, St. Vrain & Company's eighteen robe-laden wagons crept eastward, the Spanish "Scelpes" in the Arapaho camp on the Purgatory still rankling, Charles met an old friend, one of the heroic figures of a dying era, Ashley's swart, shaggy expert of winter travel—Moses "Black" Harris. Old conflicts with the Hudson's Bay Company had soured Harris on all Britishers, and now Charles found him in a boil because Hudson's Bay had appropriated Fort Hall in present Idaho. That country, Harris fumed, should be American. What's more, men like Charles Bent and himself were the ones to make it American.

In Independence on June 4, 1841, Harris wrote a letter to Thornton Grimsley, state senator from St. Louis: An army of "seven hundred . . . will be with you if you can get the Government of the United States to authorize the occupancy of the Oregon Country." This letter Charles Bent delivered in person to Grimsley, along with certain oral details inadvisable to freeze into writing. Charles, however, refused Grimsley's invitation to join the project. Perhaps he anticipated the government's rejection of the war-pregnant proposal; and moreover, his roots were too deep in the Southwest for him to turn toward Oregon at this late date.[5]

(Another magic name was beginning to sound now along the Missouri frontier. California! John Marsh's letters from the golden coast were being eagerly circulated,[6] and in the summer of 1840 Antoine Robidoux appeared with tales that made

all Platte County yearn. Climate! Why, fevers were so rare out
yonder that when one man did chance to catch the ague neighbors came from miles around to watch him shake. That winter five hundred bemused Midwesterners signed up in "the
Western Emigration Society" for a California trek. But the
ridicule of merchants fearful of losing trade and unfavorable
letters from Thomas Jefferson Farnham caused a cooling off.
When departure time arrived in the spring of 1841 only fifty-
odd men and five women, including nineteen-year-old Mrs.
Benjamin Kelsey and her baby in arms, straggled into the rendezvous. There they formed what history calls the Bartleson-
Bidwell party. They were talking of going to the Pacific via
Santa Fe when Tom Fitzpatrick appeared, guiding Father de
Smet's Catholic missionaries toward Oregon. This tipped the
scales toward South Pass, and away the combined groups
went. Too late Albert Toomes, Isaac Givens, and some others
came galloping up with a mule train. Fearful of following the
Bartleson-Bidwell emigrants across the prairies with their small
party, the late-comers joined a Santa Fe caravan.)

   That same June the New Mexico-bound Texians, well advertised in the expansionist press of the United States, started
westward on one of the most cockeyed ventures in American
history. Reputedly it was a trading caravan—fifty merchants
with grievously overloaded wagons. Escorting them were various adventurers, including Kendall, and 270 soldiers equipped
with one brass howitzer—more men than were needed to fend
off Indians, but too few to attack a foreign nation. Since Texas
possessed no army that year (the legislatures having neglected
to provide funds), these troops were extralegal "volunteers."
Their purpose, apologists vow, was as pure as Rocky Mountain snow. Should New Mexicans prefer to remain New Mexicans, the merchants would content themselves with ordinary
trade and the soldiers would withdraw.

   Withdraw an enemy army that sweetly? Armijo snorted to
himself and called out his militia.

   The Texians left too late for grass and water. They had no
idea where they were; in traveling something less than six hundred airline miles, they wandered through a killing thirteen-
hundred-mile loop. They toiled like Sisyphus, digging wheel
ways, chopping trees, and in places putting twenty yoke of

oxen and fifty rope-hauling men on a single wagon to heave it across a stream—only to have to repeat it all at the next creek. Their cursing, Kendall says, developed "unequalled originality and deep wickedness." They choked with thirst, grew gaunt with hunger. Indians massacred stragglers. As despair deepened, three men named Howland, Baker, and Rosenberg were sent ahead to appeal for help to the supposedly welcoming New Mexicans. Behind them a prairie fire destroyed some of the main column's wagons, and among the chasms and pinnacles of the Panhandle country the expedition realized it was hopelessly lost. Foolishly, then, the command split it in two, letting eighty-seven soldiers and twelve merchants hurry ahead on the best horses.

In New Mexico anyone who bothered to read an American newspaper knew that the expedition was on the way. Although the general populace remained lethargic, Armijo's cries of alarm finally produced funds and a promise of troops from the central government. Buoyed by this, the governor ringed the northern and eastern edges of the province with scouts. But only silence came. Had the plains swallowed the invaders?

Somehow, perhaps brought by a Comanche, word reached Bent's Fort that the Texians expected to be in Santa Fe by September. Ceran St. Vrain repeated the rumor in a letter, and Armijo's scouts got hold of the missive. His suspicions of the fort in no wise lessened by this, the governor ordered redoubled vigilance. And then, early in September, Howland, Baker, and Rosenberg rode their gaunt horses into an outlying settlement. Their desperate appeal for relief was answered with arrest and imprisonment in Santa Fe. The jail was a farce. They escaped but were overtaken in the mountains outside the capital. Resisting, Rosenberg was killed, Howland sorely wounded. With the uninjured Baker, Howland was taken to the hamlet of San Miguel and again imprisoned.

Meanwhile Comanches, no friends of any Texian, arrived with word that the advance column of invaders had worked its way out of the labyrinthine Palo Duro country and was approaching the settlements. Armijo threw troops forward to meet them and set his priests to preaching frightful stories of impending pillage, burning, and rape. Aroused at last, the terrified populace milled through the streets in febrile excitement.

When arrested, Howland had in his possession a letter to William Dryden. Promptly Dryden was incarcerated and so, too, for a time was Tom Rowland, brother of Dryden's fellow "commissioner," John Rowland.[7] As anti-foreign demonstrations in Taos mounted, John Rowland, William Workman, and other nervous American residents decided it would be wise to skin out for California. To raise cash, Rowland and Workman sold their flour mill to Ceran St. Vrain. A secret rendezvous was appointed at Abiquiu. There a few Mexican families joined them, as did Albert Toomes, Isaac Givens, and other emigrants who the previous spring had been too late to go west with the Bartleson-Bidwell party. Charles Bent, recently returned from Missouri via the fort, was sounded out by Workman. But Charles had no intention of running anywhere.

(Northward, the Bartleson-Bidwell group had reached Soda Springs, just inside the future Idaho border. There Tom Fitzpatrick turned northward with De Smet's missionaries. That way was known. The trail to California was not. Suddenly terrified by the dry immensities, the more timorous of the group decided to stay with the missionaries. But thirty-two men and Nancy Kelsey clung to California. Under the molten sun they crawled across Utah's white-baked salt flats. Oxen faltered, failed. Finally, about the time Workman was sending his sheep toward the rendezvous at Abiquiu, the Bartleson-Bidwell party was forced to abandon its wagons.)

Twenty-five frightened people, some of them women, assembled with Workman's family at Abiquiu. Loading their household goods on mules and driving their sheep ahead of them, they followed the Old Spanish Trail—actually only ten years old in 1841—on its looping curve through southern Utah into California. They had no trouble; their mobile larders supplied them well. Early in November they reached a mud hamlet called Los Angeles.

(Northward, the Bartleson-Bidwell party dragged itself across Nevada, over the Sierra. Coyote entrails were one of their feasts. Often Nancy Kelsey's skeleton horse was so weak she had to dismount and lead it, barefooted, her baby whimpering in her arms. Shortly before Workman reached Los Angeles, the northerners limped into John Marsh's ranch not far from San Francisco Bay. Not trappers, either of these parties, nor merchants. They were home-bearers, with all the hopes of home. Though no one knew it yet, least of all the Indians or Mexicans, the United States now stretched inevitably from coast to coast.)

Workman's flight was scarcely noticed. All New Mexico stared toward the town of San Miguel. There a second advance party of five more Texians, including Editor Kendall, had been tossed into prison—all, that is, save a turncoat named W. P. Lewis. In Santa Fe mobs howled through the streets. Alarmed, Álvarez went to Armijo with a demand that American persons and property be protected. The governor promised, but ordered that no foreigner in New Mexico leave his habitation. In his sky-blue uniform Armijo then marched a thousand troops eastward. Straightway two army officers led a gang of citizens against Álvarez's house, where several traders had barricaded themselves. The assault, Álvarez thought, was designed to bring other Americans running to the rescue, and the mob would then have a pretext for massacring and pillaging all foreigners. Fortunately the provincial Secretary of State, Don Guadalupe Miranda, close friend of Carlos Beaubien and Charles Bent, broke up the melee. Álvarez emerged with nothing worse than a painful face wound, and quiet of sorts returned to the city.

In San Miguel, while Kendall and his fellow prisoners watched, Baker of the original trio was pushed to his knees with his head against a house wall. The guard squad shot him through the back. Wounded only, he writhed in agony until a corporal fired a pistol into his heart from so close a range that his shirt caught fire and smoldered until extinguished by his own blood. The wounded Howland was next executed beside him in the same manner. Kendall and his companions, minus W. P. Lewis, were then returned in some trepidation to the hovel which served them as a prison.

Lewis had sold out. With Armijo's nephew he went to Anton Chico, where the first column of Texians had now arrived. He told his enfeebled, ragged erstwhile companions that Armijo was advancing with four thousand soldiers and promised, in the governor's name, that if the Texians surrendered their arms they would be permitted to trade for eight days and depart in peace. The invaders complied—then found themselves shackled together for transfer on foot to prison in Mexico. Though their long march probably was not as brutal as Kendall reports out of his bitter prejudice, it was grueling enough.

Meanwhile, in Taos, Charles Bent had been arrested and brought under guard to Santa Fe. Álvarez hurried to his aid. What transpired we do not know, except that Charles was released with the apology that the Taos officials had misunderstood their orders. The excuse sounds lame even from this distance. The truth may be that Armijo was, at this point, reluctant to bring a hundred armed mountain men swarming down on him from the mud castle on the Arkansas.

Horrified by the treatment of the captured Texians, Charles now consulted with Álvarez as to what could be done. There was nothing. The United States was a third party; beyond voicing a correct diplomatic protest, the consul was powerless.

Among the Texians, however, there was one United States citizen traveling under a United States passport—George Kendall. Through trader James Magoffin, who had influence with the governor, Charles, Álvarez, and Magoffin offered three thousand dollars for Kendall's release. Armijo was in no mood to listen. The whole ill-fated expedition was now his. The remnants of it had come staggering out of the wastelands in early October, so weak from living on snakes, lizards, and an occasional skunk that most of the emaciated men had thrown away their guns. They surrendered meekly. Actually, victory belonged to the plains, but Manuel Armijo knew how to shine up his own prowess in the dispatches he sent to Mexico City. Triumph over Texas—few Mexican generals could boast of that! Compared to it, three thousand dollars was nothing. Although Armijo permitted James Magoffin's brother Sam to send the editor some coffee and tobacco, George Kendall was forced to join the nightmare walk to Mexico.[8] In outrage Álvarez and Bent protested that Armijo was offering an insult to the United States. The governor snapped his fingers in scorn. His own songs of self-praise were beginning to convince him that his province really was invulnerable. Let the North Americans roar. He was Armijo, secure behind an impenetrable boundary.

The last forlorn detachment of prisoners marched south-ward on October 17. A day or two later Charles returned to Taos. Now that the countryside had quieted down, there were business dealings with Beaubien that needed attention.

CHAPTER XI

KIT CARSON'S BROTHER-IN-LAW

During the beginning rumbles of the Texian affray, Mexican officials took an unhappy look at the naked northern boundaries of New Mexico. To bolster the frontier with a fringe of protective settlements and also to stimulate the development of the backward province, the government decided to introduce a policy already familiar in Texas and California —the granting of enormous tracts of land to individuals who seemed able to establish colonies and promote agriculture. Applications were invited, but few native New Mexicans were willing to risk, even for almost unimaginable acreage, the isolation and the Indians. The foreigners were more ambitious. There was at least one of them included in almost every grant issued between 1841 and 1844—though, to be sure, each of these foreigners met the letter of Mexican law by being a naturalized citizen.

First to apply was Canadian-born Carlos Beaubien, in partnership with the province's Secretary of State, Guadalupe Miranda.[1] What they modestly asked for was practically the entire northeastern part of New Mexico, a sprawling wilderness approximately twice the size of the state of Rhode Island, embracing the headwater streams of the Cimarron and the north fork of the Canadian, or Red, River.[2] Since Charles Bent was not a citizen, no mention was made of the fact that he was a sub rosa partner in the grant. Nonetheless, news leaked out, and immediately his old enemy, Padre Martinez, began to fulminate.

Antonio José Martinez, native of Abiquiu, had fallen into the priesthood through disappointment. When he was nineteen his young wife had died. Disconsolate, he went to Durango, took orders, and in 1826 returned to northern New Mexico. In Taos he established the town's first school, admitting, opponents charged, only the sons of the wealthy, and for a brief period in 1835 he published the province's first newspaper. His tremendous vitality was evident in the big egg-shaped head set solidly on a thick neck, in bull-like shoulders and powerful torso. Part of his energy found release in open concubinage. Celibacy, Martinez argued, was so contrary to nature that the Church could not reasonably insist on it for a man such as he, and, furthermore, how could a priest understand true repentance and forgiveness without sinning himself? In spite of these derelictions, Martinez, musical of voice and persuasive in eloquence, held a firm grip over his parishioners, especially the Indians of the Taos Pueblo, whose side he had taken in the revolution of 1837–38.

Charles Bent despised him, called him the Calf, and ridiculed him with a virulence so bitter that it suggests the priest had power to sting.[3] The enmity was reciprocal. Martinez joined Armijo in accusing Bent's Fort of illegal activities and roared clear to Mexico City his opposition to the Beaubien-Miranda grant. Goaded by him, the head chief of the Taos Pueblo joined the protest, saying that the territory in question was the communal grazing and hunting ground of the Pueblo Indians and should not be alienated. Martinez trumpeted that no unnaturalized resident had a right to a single inch of Mexican soil. Then, forgetting legitimate arguments in his passion, he admitted openly that his opposition to the grant was based on one fact only—Charles Bent.[4] Though Miranda's influence was powerful, though Charles and Beaubien brought all the pressure they could to bear on Armijo, the priest won. His objections held matters in abeyance during the summer of 1841, and then the suspicions leveled at Charles during the Texian invasion tipped the scales entirely in Martinez's favor. In spite of everything Charles could do, the grant was withdrawn.

Meanwhile, there were family problems to think about. Sometime during the winter of 1841–42, Kit Carson rode in from the fort. He was down in the dumps. Squaw trouble. After his abbreviated romance with Félicité St. Vrain he had married the belle of the southern Cheyennes, Making Out

Road. The girl was spoiled. She had put most of the Cheyenne bachelors and half the white men at the fort in a slow
burn, and they had showered her with gifts. Now that she
was married she expected Kit to keep her in expensive foofaraw. She ignored her household chores and neglected little
Adaline, the daughter of Kit's dead Arapaho wife. After his and
Making Out Road's only baby perished shortly after birth,
quarrels became increasingly bitter. Finally, in a fury, Making
Out Road chucked Kit, Adaline, and all their possessions from
the lodge. Divorce, Indian-style. Perhaps among the Indian
women at the fort or in one of the neighboring villages Kit
found someone who would take temporary care of Adaline. He
did not sorrow over the broken marriage. But what on earth
was he going to do with the child, to whom he was devoted?

In Taos he met Maria Josefa Jaramillo, sister of Charles's
wife, and fell utterly in love. It was real this time, and well
it might be. Though she was only fourteen and taller than Kit,
Josefa had, in the words of awe-struck Lewis Garrard, who
saw her five years later, an exquisite loveliness "such as would
lead a man with the glance of an eye to risk his life for one
smile."

Opposition immediately developed in the Jaramillo household. Part of it centered on Kit's religion (and it is strange
there is no record of similar opposition to Charles Bent's Prot-
estantism). Carson's answer was to embrace the Catholic faith.
On January 28, 1842, he was baptized by Padre Antonio Martinez. Ignacia Jaramillo Bent perhaps attended the services;
Charles did not.

There was another, harder problem. Haughty old Don Francisco Jaramillo was as cold as the St. Vrains had been toward
the half-breed child of an Arapaho squaw. No such foster-
mothering for Josefa. Remembering how he had lost Félicité,
and in despair lest he lose Josefa for the same cause, Kit sought
advice from Charles Bent, friend, employer, and prospective
brother-in-law. What should he do with the child? If Charles
was unguarded enough to suggest that Adaline's Arapaho relatives might assume responsibility, the proposal was violently
rejected. Adaline was Kit's daughter, and he would not forsake
her. Out of the discussion, in which we may assume Ignacia
Bent's voice was heard, came a compromise: Why not take

Adaline to Missouri and put her in a convent school? There
she could be brought up as a white girl and a Catholic; when
she was older and the Indian stain was washed away, she
could return.

Kit agreed. Perhaps the decision was fortified by Lucien
Maxwell's marriage in March to Maria de la Luz Beaubien,
Carlos's oldest daughter. In burly Lucien's joy Kit saw promise
of his own happiness. The sooner he could provide for Adaline,
the sooner he could claim Josefa—and right now on the Arkansas a Bent, St. Vrain caravan was making ready to roll toward
Missouri. In late March or early April, Kit and Charles Bent
crossed Raton Pass toward the adobe fort. With them, wryly
grinning at their jokes about his truncated honeymoon, rode
Lucien Maxwell. At the fort Kit picked up Adaline from whatever caretaker had been looking after her. Did he feel a brief
pang for her mother, Waa-nibe, Singing Wind, when he saw
William Bent and Owl Woman? No stern relatives frowned on
William's daughter or on his fat new boy, born a few months
before and named Robert in memory of the Bent who had
been killed by Comanches during the previous fall.

The fort hummed. Trade had been prodigious during the
winter. Eleven hundred huge bales of buffalo robes, upward of
fifty tons total weight, and another ton or more of glossy beaver
pelts were loaded into the wagons. In the corrals scores of
horses and wild and foolish mules were being starved to tractability, many of them from California; Peg-leg Smith had been
raiding on the coast in 1840 and again in 1841. Herded with
them outside the walls were two or three hundred coarse-
wooled Mexican sheep. There were cattle, also—extra oxen for
replacing any that gave out along the trail, plus surplus from
the herds grazing along the Arkansas. (Already the company
was utilizing for stock-raising the nutritive grasses which Colorado ranchers would "discover" with fanfare twenty years
later.) Sprinkled among the cattle were ponderous young buffalo that had been captured as calves and domesticated; these
would net a good price from Missouri farmers hopeful of passing them on to eastern zoos and curiosity-seeking English noblemen.[5]

Departure of the caravan was practically a convulsion. Saddle animals pranced and reared in a lather. Teamsters howled

at oxen that seemed to have "forgotten there were such words
as 'wo-ha' and 'gee.'" Cattle were ready to stampede at the
rattle of a yoke chain; mules hitched to light carts bolted full-
flight across the flats. Sheep blatted; the horse herd plunged
and neighed. Out of the pluming dust came creaks, bangs,
frantic oaths in half a dozen languages, and exuberant rifle-
shots from the whooping, civilization-bound mountain men.

Soon the ungainly procession settled down to trail routine.
Before dawn the men were up. Breakfast was a hurried snack
of coffee and bread that had been cooked the evening before.
As the stars paled, night herders swept in the oxen, horses, and
mules that would be used during the day. Generally the start
was over easy country. Camp was always made on the far
side of a stream, lest spring rains lift the water or muddy the
steep banks during the night. Oxen did not pull well in "cold
collars," and if a heavy grade lay at hand at the break of
camp, the wagoners warmed the beasts to harness by driving
in a circle before tackling the pitch.

The night herders crawled into the wagons to sleep during
the day's drive. Kit gave Adaline a hug and ranged out to
search for game with Maxwell and their Shawnee or Delaware
hunters. If meat was killed near the trail, it was dumped where
the wagons could pick it up; otherwise it was packed on horseback to the nooning grounds. During the cool morning hours
the wagons pressed steadily forward, except where there were
pauses to dig down a bank or to bridge spring quagmires with
a mat of willows and long grass covered with dry earth. As
the sun began to heat toward ten or eleven o'clock, camp was
made. Another light breakfast followed, and then the men
napped in the shade of the wagons for two or three hours.
Roused in midafternoon by the wagon master, who was absolute boss of the train even though various of the owners were
along, all hands gorged on the day's one big meal. From then
until dark or later, the wheels rolled again. Indian attacks were
rare but always guarded against. Prairie fires were another
threat; on one undated occasion a Bent, St. Vrain caravan was
saved from disaster when heroic Mexican teamsters dragged a
load of gunpowder from a flaming wagon.

Not all of the company's robes started for Missouri by
wagon. Rippling past Fort St. Vrain was the meretricious

promise of the South Platte. This same spring of 1842, as men at the other Platte forts had done before, company employees under Baptiste Charbonneau built shallow-draft boats, perhaps of pine timber sawed in a pit or perhaps of buffalo hides shrunk tight over willow frames and waterproofed with tallow. The trip was unmitigated hell—the very name Platte means shallow water. Stranded almost hourly on sand bars, Charbonneau's dry-land sailors, mostly Mexicans, floundered into the muck and tried to wrestle the boats ahead. Brute force failing, they unpacked the cargo and lugged it by hand downstream to the next navigable water. They made forty-five miles. Then the shrinking stream stranded them entirely.

Philosophically Charbonneau made camp on a wooded island, named his exile St. Helena, and settled down to wait for whatever came next. He was an interesting man, this Charbonneau. His father, Toussaint Charbonneau, had helped guide Lewis and Clark across the Rockies; his mother, Sacagawea, had lugged him as a nursing infant to the Pacific and back with the expedition. William Clark called the child "Pomp," grew fond of him, and had him educated in St. Louis. Later, Prince Paul of Württemberg took the boy to Europe. After his return Baptiste worked several years for Bent, St. Vrain & Company, not all his assignments being so idyllic as sitting under a tree on an island. He was still sitting there in July, when Frémont came through on his first expedition, and he treated the lieutenant to mint julep, boiled buffalo tongue, and coffee with the luxury of sugar. How or when Charbonneau finally extricated himself and his cargo is not known. Probably wagons were sent after him.

Long before this, the caravan from Bent's Fort had reached the Missouri frontier. There the equipment would have to stay until the return journey in August. Pasturage during the layover presented a problem. Much of the land was owned by transplanted Shawnee and Delaware Indians. White settlers flowing out a dozen miles beyond Independence had already established a straggle of log cabins and wagon shops known as Westport. Down on the river, six miles away, where François Chouteau long ago had built warehouses near a natural rock levee, was a townsite owned by Bill Sublette and various others. They called their place Kansas—later it would add the

word "City." Although ringed by bluffs and forests, Kansas
Landing, sometimes called Westport Landing, lay a day's haul
closer to New Mexico than did Independence, and the Kansas
Landing trail avoided the ford over Big Blue Creek, often impassable during spring floods. As better roads were cut down
through the ravine-split bluffs, more and more Santa Fe merchants, principally Mexican proprietors at first, began unloading at Kansas Landing. Then they drove their teams back
around Westport to graze. For the amusement of the teamsters
there was, a short distance beyond Westport, a tavern called
Last Chance, well fortified with rotgut whiskey and what William Bent's son George termed "low-down women."

Catch-as-catch-can competition for grass among thousands
of draft animals and settlers' livestock led to trouble. In 1842,
Bent, St. Vrain & Company decided to protect itself with a
fenced ranch of its own.[6] Even before this time the company
had occasionally used Kansas Landing for loading its pelts on
St. Louis-bound steamers; and after the acquisition of the
ranch the transshipping of both its inbound and outbound car-
goes was gradually transferred away from Independence—no
small element in lifting infant Kansas City from a collection of
squatters' huts into a lusty young town.

The site chosen for the ranch lay half a dozen miles southwest of Westport. Here sheds were built for storing and repairing wagons; fields were planted to fodder crops; wild
horses from the mountains were polished for sale; cattle—and
buffalo—were raised. To run the farm Charles and William
Bent selected a young nephew, twenty-two-year-old Angus
Boggs, dead Juliannah Bent's second son by Lilburn Boggs.
After Juliannah's death, Lilburn had married old Daniel
Boone's granddaughter, Panthea. By 1842 Juliannah's two
boys, Henry and Angus, had ten half brothers and sisters.
Though not blood relatives, they all called Charles and William
"uncle." Indeed, the oldest of Panthea's boys, Tom Boggs, had
already gone west with a Santa Fe caravan. Meeting Bent
traders on the Cimarron, Tom threw in with them and started
for the fort. Along the way the men lost their horses and had
to hoof the remaining distance with their saddles on their own
backs. "Uncle" William put the lad to work. Tom was only
eighteen or so, but he had his great-grandfather's aptitude for

the wilderness; soon he was one of the company's best hands.

About the time the Bent caravan reached Missouri, the Boggs tribe was thrown into white-lipped fury. On the evening of May 6, 1842, a would-be assassin crept up to Lilburn's house in Independence and pumped bullets through the window into his neck and head. The Boggses, and probably the Bents as well, suspected a Mormon. The sect hated Lilburn— with reason. In 1836 Boggs had defeated William Ashley for the governorship of Missouri; and though Lilburn fathered many excellent projects (among them the building of the state capitol and the establishment of the state university), his term was remembered mainly for the anti-Mormon riots which, with night floggings, burnings, and murder on both sides, swept the western counties in 1838. When the situation seemed ready to explode beyond control, Lilburn unleashed six thousand state militia with the infamous "Extermination Order" of October: "The Mormons . . . must be exterminated or driven from the state if necessary for the public peace." They were driven, to Nauvoo in Illinois; and the only reason Joseph Smith and other church leaders weren't exterminated was that militia commander Alexander Doniphan refused to countenance their execution. Their followers remembered. Four years later one of them, presumably O. P. Rockwell, sought revenge by murder. Lilburn, however, proved hard to kill. Though doctors despaired of him, by fall he had recovered enough to be elected to the state Senate.

Business had to go on. While Lilburn's children hovered about their semiconscious father, Charles and perhaps William started down-river, reaching St. Louis with the first consignment of peltries on May 19. Kit meanwhile had ridden ahead to Howard County, to see if one of his numerous relatives would take care of Adaline until the child was old enough for school. A niece agreed. That terrible load off his mind, Kit told Adaline good-by and went on to St. Louis. He hadn't seen a high-class white man's diggings since 1826, and he wondered what it would be like. In ten days he had enough. The city dwarfed him as the towering peaks of the Rockies never did. His head spun; his feet hurt. He wanted to go back.

Adaptable Charles Bent, however, relished his summer visits to St. Louis. Though Ceran St. Vrain usually put up at the

elegant Planters House (where Charles Dickens had been lav-
ishly entertained in April 1842), the Bents visited their
brothers and sisters, now part and parcel of the old aristocracy
of the town. Brother John was a successful lawyer and noted
bon vivant[7]; Sister Dorcas, wife of distinguished Judge William Chiles Carr, was a famous hostess. Though summer days
might be stickily hot in the banks and odorous warehouses
where Charles conducted the firm's business, evening brought
cool relaxation on the white-pillared verandas set deep among
trim lawns and formal gardens. Parties were frequent and
sumptuous—saddles of venison around pyramids of spun sugar,
candied oranges, nougat. Between dances chicken bouillon was
passed about by liveried slaves. Leisurely Sunday dinners fea-
tured a magnificent, slow-simmered Creole gumbo and snowy
rice—far cry from roast buffalo intestines and unbolted Taos
bread. (Did Ignacia Bent ever go to St. Louis with her husband? Did Owl Woman? There is nothing to indicate it.)

When Charles arrived that spring, either with William or
alone, a social whirl centered about the Brant mansion. Senator Benton's teen-age daughter Jessie had recently acquired a
husband, a dark, handsome army lieutenant named John
Charles Frémont. Though Jessie had remained in Washington
with her father, Frémont came west with full social acceptance as he set about preparing for the first of his soon-to-be-
famous expeditions. He stayed with the Brants, and his hosts
knew he was seeking information from every mountain man he
could meet. It is not unlikely that the Brants invited Charles
and, if he was along, William Bent to dinner one evening, or
that Cyprian Chouteau, Frémont's expediter in St. Louis, asked
the brothers to his office. While talking to the young explorer,
the pair would have told him what he needed to know of the
South Platte route and would graciously have offered him free
use of Fort St. Vrain, where he later stopped.

In St. Louis, Frémont hired Lucien Maxwell as a hunter for
the expedition. And when the lieutenant boarded a steamer
for Kansas (Westport) Landing, there was Kit Carson—quite
by chance, Frémont says. But was it chance? Surely Kit knew
that Lucien was being well paid for going back to the sparkling
freshness of the mountains, the freedom of the plains for which

Carson was so homesick. Was it by sheer coincidence, then, that Kit bought passage on that particular boat?

As the paddle wheels thrashed the yellow current, he fell into talk with the impetuous, nervously excitable lieutenant. Quietly he told Frémont of the far places of the West, places few men knew any better. And did he make no mention of names as respected in St. Louis as Bent and St. Vrain? Indeed, Frémont may already have heard from them about this cool-eyed, bandy-legged little trapper. At least William's son George years later said it was his father who recommended Kit as the expedition's guide, though Frémont himself makes no such statement. Be that as it may, Frémont hired Kit. The wage he offered was one hundred dollars a month—three times the amount Kit had been making as a hunter at the fort. Wait until the Jaramillos heard of this!

His plans jumping ahead, Kit sent two Delaware Indians from Kansas Landing to Taos. They carried word for Sol Silver, Oliver Wiggins, and others of Kit's old crew of rollicking free trappers to meet him near South Pass. When Frémont's expedition turned homeward in the fall, Kit would leave it and trap south with his men through the high meadows of the Colorado Rockies. Beaver prices were a bit higher again, and he had no intention of going to his new Bent and Jaramillo connections as a dirt-poor man.

In the panting days of late August or early September, about the time Kit was leading his crew toward the green coolness of the peaks, Charles returned to the fort and a brand-new problem. Up at the mouth of Fountain Creek, near the site of William's first stockade, a new trading post was being built by George Simpson, J. B. Doyle, and Alexander Barclay, the last of whom had been factor at Bent's Fort during the previous four years. They named their place Pueblo. It had eight-foot, picket-topped walls, squat bastions, and a handful of tiny rooms—"a wretched species of fort," says Francis Parkman, who stopped by and ate off the floor in 1846, "miserably cracked and dilapidated."

Jim Beckwourth was one of Pueblo's early associates. In his recollections, dictated fifteen years later, Jim said he founded the post, but historians regard this no more seriously than they do his claim of having established Fort Cass on the Yellowstone. From Pueblo, Jim packed a load of pumpkins and whis-key out to a band of Cheyennes with whom William Bent couldn't do a thing—so Beckwourth says—and coaxed hundreds of robes out of them. As he returned triumphantly past Bent's Fort, William cried out (Jim still reminiscing), "Beckwourth, how you manage Indians as you do beats my understanding."

There is another story about Jim's managing, however. Old Bill Williams was at Pueblo when Beckwourth got some In-dians rolling drunk and began cheating them blind—one quart of Taos poison for three buffalo robes and two beaver pelts. Old Bill's hands were hardly lily-white, but this was too much. In his high, querulous whine he sneered, "No one but a low-down half-breed nigger Frenchman would stick an Indian that way." Jim would not have minded being called a half-breed Indian, but references to his Negro blood brought him up fighting. He charged Old Bill. And Williams, so the tale goes, beat him unconscious, a matter Jim does not mention in his recollections.

Perhaps neither yarn is literally true. But like most legends, each is true in what it typifies. Located just across the river from Mexican territory, Pueblo was a collecting spot for the scum of the mountains. Mexico had no jurisdiction, and United States law enforcement was hundreds of miles away. Taos whiskey was, of course, no novelty to the plains; but if Pueblo became a central spigot, debauching Indians with im-punity, the post's competition might prove even more dan-gerous to Bent and St. Vrain than had the now-crushed rivals on the South Platte.

Riding back to Taos in mid-September, Charles mulled over the problem. Since there was no way of haling miscreants to justice in Missouri, why not bring law to the Rockies? A military post would do it. And the best place for the post would be the mouth of Fountain Creek, smack-dab beside Pueblo and within finger's reach of the other Mexican-trapper colonies growing up between there and the foothills. On Sep-tember 19, 1842, Charles sat down and wrote a long letter to Missouri's U. S. Senator L. F. Linn, militant advocate, with Benton, of western expansion.

Naturally the protection of one company's trade would not justify government action. But, Charles argued, the fort he proposed would serve national policy; from its central location on the Arkansas, cavalry squads could be dispatched east or north to protect both the Santa Fe and Oregon trails. All the western Indians would be awed, including those wicked wards of New Mexico, the Utes and Apaches. (And here Charles could not resist a private complaint: raiding parties of Utes and Apaches on the plains "almost invariably comit depredations on us; I have had ocation to complain to the authorities of New Mexico" without avail.) Next he glanced at the uneasy relations with the neighboring nation: "The Mexicans pass over the boundary in large partys . . . some times as high as three hundred men . . . and many of them doe not scruple to excite the indians." Charles admitted he had no knowledge of official connivance in such plottings, "but many of the Cheafs have had sent to them by the authorities, Collars and Staffs." These were analogous to the medals distributed by the United States Government and constituted an illegal tampering with the loyalties of American Indians. In case of a war, Charles concluded, the fort he recommended would be a "greate advantage in preventing the Mexicans" from rousing the Indians against "our frontears."

As yet he had refrained from direct mention of the unlicensed, illegal Pueblo post. That came on January 1, 1843, in an angry letter to D. D. Mitchell, former American Fur Company trader and now Superintendent of Indian Affairs: "There are several renegate Americans, who have built houses on the Arkansas river . . . This [Pueblo] is also a harbor for all Mexican traders . . . The only mode to put a stop to the liquor trade from Mexico, is to establish a military post."[8]

Cry wolf. Charles repeated his complaints and warnings on May 4. Manuel Álvarez made representations to the American Secretary of State. But, though government agents that winter raided the liquor-dispensing posts on the North Platte, nothing was done about Pueblo, and no military post was built in the vicinity.

Further agitation boiled up during the early fall of 1842 in the form of still another lawsuit—Charles seems to have been a magnet for legal uproars. This one was with Antoine Robidoux, who had come to New Mexico with Beaubien in the early 1820s and by now was almost the original old man of the mountains, operating at least two rag-tag posts west of the Continental Divide. When the case reached Armijo, the governor inclined to favor Robidoux. In characteristic outburst, Bent roared to Álvarez, "I shall have my pay eather by fair or foul meanes." And he had his pay. On October 7, Robidoux capitulated and gave him 650 pounds of beaver to secure a debt to the company of $1788.

The fall had its joys also. On November 15 the birth of a daughter, Teresina, softened the grief over babies George and Virginia, who had died in infancy; and little Alfredo, almost six now, was full of excitement over his new sister.

Then, in December, Charles was delighted with a famous visitor—Dr. Marcus Whitman, noted Oregon missionary. Whitman was in the middle of a heroic journey. Some months before, his church had threatened to close his mission. Hoping to have the order rescinded, he headed east through the dead of winter, his only companions a guide and a newcomer named A. L. Lovejoy. Lovejoy had reached Oregon that same summer with Lansford Hastings's caravan—and had almost lost his scalp along the way. While he and some others were carving their names on Independence Rock in Wyoming, a hundred Sioux had seized and stripped them. Only the prompt action of the caravan's guide, Tom Fitzpatrick, saved their scalps; and undoubtedly memory of the episode returned to Lovejoy when he reached Fort Hall with Whitman and learned the Sioux were on the warpath.

To avoid the Sioux the travelers swung south.[9] As far as the Continental Divide in central Colorado they had no particular trouble. But crossing the Divide into San Luis Valley and then veering down the Rio Grande to Taos was an ordeal of deep snow, lost circlings, backtrackings, bitter cold, and semi-starvation. Even so, Whitman would not rest in Taos. The missionary's indomitable spirit impressed Charles Bent. "I believe him to be a man not to be stoped by trifles," he wrote Álvarez, helped Whitman refurbish his equipment, and then found a guide who would take the wayfarers to the fort, where they could join a party of mountain men preparing to travel to the States.

Whitman left Taos on December 22. For two weeks his tiny party bucked the snow. As they neared the Arkansas, they met George Bent riding toward Taos. George told them that the States-bound mountain men were on the point of leaving. Alarmed, Whitman decided to hurry ahead of the exhausted Lovejoy and the guide, even though it was Sunday and he had an ironclad rule against Sabbath travel. He vanished. When Lovejoy reached the fort, there was no word of Whitman. And the mountain men had already departed. Frantically Lovejoy dispatched a runner, begging the Missouri-bound party to wait, and then set out with searchers furnished, and perhaps guided by, William. On January 6 they found the doctor, "despondent and fatigued, convinced he had gotten lost because he had traveled on Sunday."

Still refusing to rest, Whitman hurried after the mountain men. Lovejoy, however, was done in. He collapsed at the fort and stayed there until summer, when he rode north to the Oregon Trail to join the so-called Great Migration of '43. Accompanying the disjointed caravan of nearly a thousand people, giving them counsel and medical help, was Marcus Whitman, his mission saved, though on a stringently limited basis.

Christmas in Taos was quiet. But when Kit appeared, flush from selling a good catch of furs at the fort, festivities picked up. Women's foofaraw engulfed them; Ignacia Bent was in a Spanish swirl of animation over her sister's marriage. Truce was declared with Martinez, and on February 6, 1843, the priest married the couple, George Bent signing the register as one of the witnesses.

At home afterward, Charles opened the family's leather-bound Spanish Bible. On its flyleaf he wrote, "Kit Carson & Maria Josefa Jaramillo md 2/6/43. Charles Bent." Kit's men put on a stem-winding celebration. Sol Silver got so drunk he fell from his horse and was laid up for three days. The gentry's feasts and fandangos were, presumably, more genteel.

Romance was in the air. Sometime during this period Ceran St. Vrain married another of Carlos Beaubien's daughters and so became the brother-in-law of his "nephew," Lucien Maxwell.[10] More feasts, more fandangos—a happy time. But it could not last. Texians were on the prowl again.

CHAPTER XII

LAND BEYOND IMAGINING

In the merriment attendant on Kit's and Ceran's weddings, Charles gave little heed to George's report that a Texian colonel had been at the fort during January, trying to recruit men for another filibuster against New Mexico. The adventurer's name was Charles A. Warfield. The Bents knew him, for Warfield had been around the mountains and in Santa Fe before. He had then gone to Texas and in the intense fury that followed word of the treatment accorded the Texas-Santa Fe captives, he heard opportunity knocking at his door.

Sam Houston was again president of a republic so short of cash it could not supply the executive mansion with firewood. But Texas was not short of big ideas. Its first expedition against New Mexico having been defeated, the legislature promptly passed a resolution doing by paper what could not be done by arms: annexing that province, Upper and Lower California, and all or parts of six other northern Mexican states. Although Houston returned the resolution with a remark that times were inauspicious for a legislative jest, the lawmakers overrode his veto and adjourned. Then came word that Mexican raiders, retaliating for the march on Santa Fe, had successfully attacked San Antonio.

Fishing in these troubled waters, Warfield easily convinced touchy patriots that the Santa Fe expedition had been defeated by ill luck and Lewis's treachery rather than by Armijo, and that the bulk of the province was still ready to welcome determined raiders. The effort need not cost the government a cent. Warfield would recruit the men, who would equip themselves in return for half the booty they seized. The other half of the plunder would go to the republic.

On August 16, 1842, Warfield was made a colonel with full freedom of action. Hurrying to Missouri, he commissioned one John McDaniel as a captain with powers to recruit such frontier riffraff as he could. Warfield, meanwhile, was to carry his own recruiting to the mountains, and on May 15 his "army" would meet McDaniel's forces at Point of Rocks on the Santa Fe Trail in eastern New Mexico.

New filibusters were simultaneously shaping up in Texas. Mexicans had again raided San Antonio, and the Lone Star militia set off in chaotic pursuit. Well knowing the bankrupt republic could not support a major war, Houston called off the chase when the enemy raiders retreated across the border. Three hundred hotheads, however, continued fighting on their own and were overwhelmed by the Mexicans. On the march to Mexico City they tried to escape, were recaptured, and outrageously abused. Texas seethed for revenge, and the harassed Houston gave in to demands for attacks against Mexican caravans on the Santa Fe Trail. On February 16, 1843, he authorized one of his staff, Jacob Snively, to raise three hundred men and capture the spring trains, being careful to stay off United States soil during the process. Snively's men, like Warfield's, were to equip themselves and receive half the booty.[1]

Before Snively received his papers, Warfield had reached Bent's Fort, where the usual congregation of trappers were sitting out the snowy weather. Though he promised rich plunder and dramatically waved a bullet-torn flag which had been carried in the early days of the Texas revolution, he did not enlist as many recruits as he had hoped for. Disappointed, he took his promises and flag to the forts along the South Platte. There he lined up a few more hands, and in February twenty-four ragged, whiskery, ill-equipped, buckskin-clad mountain men assembled in a miserable bivouac near Bent's Fort. One of them was Rufus Sage, a youth of better than average education who had come west a few years before to trade with Lancaster Lupton.

Exaggerated rumors of the enemy quickly reached New Mexico. Americans in Santa Fe were haled before Armijo for cross-examination, and once again mobs howled around the home of Consul Álvarez. In Taos the anti-American sentiment soon engulfed Charles Bent. The pretext for attacking him, so Álvarez wrote to Daniel Webster, was deliberately manufactured: "The Prefect of the First District [Juan Andrés Archuleta] and second in authority only to the Governor, in the name of an insignificant individual, caused a suit to be prosecuted, most outrageous and unjust, against Bent."

The name of the insignificant individual was Montero. Exactly what the quarrel was about does not appear, but Charles, an old hand at litigation, was not concerned. On February 18, less than two weeks after Kit's marriage, he wrote Álvarez indifferently, "My suite will comence tomorrow at the Rancho"—a hamlet not far from San Fernandez. He then switched to other topics, including the cheerful news from the fort that "our people are makeing a grate many robes."

The cheerfulness soon evaporated. No sooner had he reached the Rancho than demonstrators began yelling threats around the house where he was staying. Smugly, on February 18, Archuleta wrote Armijo, "the majority of the people in my district, tired of evils originated by Bent, clamor for vengeance against him. . . . There is no doubt they are trying to defraud Montero from his personal work, and it is also true that the latter can prove the accusations against Bent. The only thing lacking is a judge with knowledge and *conscience.* . . ."

The judge soon produced the sort of conscience Archuleta desired. He found Charles guilty and, in Álvarez's words, "forced him on the most frivolous pretext to pay $800 without the shadow of justice." Denied appeal to the superior courts, Charles was ordered confined until the judgment was paid. Ugly mobs gathered in front of the jail.

Eight hundred dollars in cash were hard to come by in New Mexico. Friends sent some. Legend has it that Ignacia dug up more from a cache of gold pieces buried under the floor of their home. Steve Lee hurried the money to the prisoner, and in addition Charles drew on Álvarez. He had to act swiftly. Archuleta's police might at any moment give free rein to the mobs outside. Freed at last, Charles slipped outside through the darkness to a horse his friends had provided and fled to the Arkansas.[2]

On reaching the fort early in March he learned that the agitations were not likely to end soon. Warfield's freebooters were traveling busily. The colonel and fourteen men had marched down the Arkansas to meet the recruits supposedly coming from Texas with Snively and from Missouri with John McDaniel. Ten more men, including Rufus Sage, had set out toward New Mexico "to perform the duties of a corps of observation." Not wishing to be observed themselves, the raiders avoided the main trail along the Timpas and thereby snarled themselves so badly in the canyon of the middle Purgatory that at times they had to use ropes for hauling their horses up the almost perpendicular five-hundred-foot banks. Running out of food, they ate a wolf, boiled some buffalo hide into a glue that almost cemented their teeth, and roasted cactus, which produced agonizing cramps. Completely debilitated, they rested three or four weeks in the beautiful meadows of the upper Purgatory. Then dispatches from Warfield summoned them to a rendezvous at the Rabbit Ears, 170 sterile miles eastward, and the ten men marched temporarily out of the Bents' ken.

Armijo ordered four hundred cavalry to track Warfield down. The governor was distraught. Through his spies he knew that Snively's men were ready to march, but he did not know their destination. If this new expedition was aimed at the province, as the invasion of 1841 had been, he would need all available troops to meet it. But suppose Snively joined Warfield and fell on the spring caravan, in which Armijo was a principal owner? He must rush soldiers to the wagons. But where could he find additional troops?

Taos was the only place, and Taos was unfriendly to Armijo. It was one thing to stir up a riot against Charles Bent, but another to impress troops for protecting the wagons of the ricos. Yet this was an emergency. Armijo's high-handed officers, led by Ventura Lobata, a relative of Beaubien's wife, went to the Pueblo and dragged out several dozen reluctant Indian warriors.

When Manuel Álvarez and Kit reached the fort to go to Missouri with the company train,[3] they brought word that Armijo was planning to start down the Cimarron trail on May 3 with six hundred soldiers. About the same time information arrived of a flagrant crime committed on American soil by the dozen or so men whom "Captain" John McDaniel had recruited in Missouri during the winter. While riding westward to join Warfield, McDaniel's freebooters had fallen on a small eastbound caravan belonging to a prominent New Mexican named Chavez. After robbing it of several thousand dollars in coin and gold dust, they murdered Chavez so bru-

tally and needlessly that even the pro-Texan, anti-Mexican
frontier towns were revolted.[4] Men whom McDaniel and
Warfield had approached earlier in the year began to talk,
and now the United States Government learned officially
what many persons knew unofficially—Texans were planning
to raid the Santa Fe Trail. A strong protest was lodged with
the republic about Warfield's illegal recruiting on American
soil. In order to make sure that no attacks occurred within
United States boundaries, Captain Philip St. George Cooke
and three hundred dragoons were ordered to escort the Mexican caravan as far as the Crossing of the Arkansas.

As Charles and Ceran made their own plans for the eastern
journey, they well knew that they might run afoul of whatever
developed. Many of the men at the fort were still outraged
over Charles's treatment, and among the more than one hundred retainers and hangers-on were the usual lawless opportunists who might try to batten on trouble. Utterly isolated
there on the border between America and Mexico, with
heaven knew how many Texians on the prowl, the company
could not risk bringing the ill will of any of the three nations
down on its head. Both George and William, who were to
remain at the fort, and Charles and Ceran, traveling with the
caravan, would have to keep a tight rein on their independent,
self-sufficient hands.

It was a poor time for experimenting. Ceran, however, came
up with a notion. The unusually wet spring would make the
trails sticky. And the river was high. Why not save wear and
tear on draft stock by boating part of the robes more than
halfway to Westport—as far as Great Bend, where the trail
left the river? He prevailed to the extent of having carpenters
build enough shallow-draft boats to transport the equivalent
of five wagonloads of robes. Charles's roustabouts meanwhile
packed fourteen wagons in the standard way and rounded up
the mules and cattle for the Westport farm.

About the second week of May the double-barreled caravan
set out. As usual, several trappers bound for a spree in Missouri went along. The land travelers would not often see
Ceran's flotilla, for the trail frequently cut well back from the
stream to avoid promontories and bluffs.

Before Charles's wagons had gone many miles a messenger

from William overhauled them with word that the spring-long threats of trouble had at last turned into conflict. Warfield's two dozen men were responsible. In April his and Sage's groups had reassembled near the Rabbit Ears, between the Cimarron and the Arkansas. Ignorant still of Snively's whereabouts and of McDaniel's defection, and fearful of the Comanches in the neighborhood, the raiders had decided to march right back into New Mexico. As the men neared the settlements, however, some of them, wearied of the aimless beatings back and forth, began grumbling. Pompously Warfield ordered his patriots into a line.

"Texas," he proclaimed, as Sage remembered the oration, "wants no *cowards* to fight her battles. None but brave men and true are worthy of that honor! . . . If any timorous spirit —and pusillanimous heart—and *despicable poltroon* wishes his discharge, I stand ready to give it; let him step one pace in advance from the ranks and acknowledge himself a *coward*."

Three despicable poltroons acknowledged themselves and were allowed to depart. The remaining twenty-one cautiously felt their way toward Mora. Four or five miles below the settlement, scouts spotted an ill-guarded camp of sixty of Armijo's cavalrymen. Under cover of darkness the raiders killed five Mexicans, wounded four, captured eighteen. They also seized the camp's entire equipment, including seventy-two horses and mules. The captive soldiers they let go—to show magnanimity, Sage says, but perhaps it was because they did not know what else to do with prisoners almost as numerous as they.

Now Warfield grew careless in turn. As his men sat boasting around their campfires, a Mexican counterattack swept away all but three of their horses. Texas could hardly want even brave men and true to fight her battles afoot in hostile country. The twenty-one fled back across Raton to the Arkansas. A messenger sent to Bent's Fort to learn of McDaniel's whereabouts received neither information nor help from George and William. Discouraged, the group broke up. Sage and a few others returned to Fort Lupton; Warfield and the rest marched down the Arkansas to learn if there were any Texians about.

There were. At about the same time that Charles learned

of the battle at Mora, Snively and 180 filibusterers reached the Arkansas and went into camp some forty miles from the Crossing.

News of the Mora attack had created intense excitement around the fort and in the caravan. Many of the hard-bitten company hunters, sympathizing with Warfield and eager to get into the fun, began prowling around to see what they could see. Near the Crossing they bumped into some of Snively's scouts and passed on the information that Álvarez and Kit had brought from New Mexico—Armijo was leading several hundred troops eastward to meet the westbound caravan. The Texians had better strike before the governor arrived.

To Snively this was a valuable warning. He put Warfield in charge of a strong detachment and sent him along the Cimarron trail to hold Armijo back. In an effort to secure more help, he then offered a share of the plunder to as many mountain men as the Bent, St. Vrain hunters could inveigle into joining the raid. Optimistically totaling up the excited hands and free men accompanying the wagons and Ceran's boats, the hunters on June 2 told the Texians that they could furnish forty men immediately and could soon bring down another forty from the fort. They promised prematurely, however. Charles got word of what was afoot. Visiting the various mess fires, he talked to his own men and to the free trappers like a Dutch uncle. Enthusiasm collapsed and the disconsolate plotters sent word to Snively that the deal was off.

An express now arrived from Ceran. His boats had grated to a standstill on the sand bars and he needed wagons. Charles sent the vehicles to him with word of what had happened. Though Bent had temporarily checked the plot, he did not want to sit around in the rain waiting for his partner, lest disaffection break out again. Accordingly, he told Ceran that he would go ahead until he met the United States dragoons who were rumored to be escorting the westbound caravan. There, under the troops' restraining influence, he would wait.

The days were gray and wet, the little creeks bankfull. As the soaked, muddy men fought the wagons forward, three horsemen joined them. It was not unusual for riders to appear out of nowhere. Charles may not have known that the trio were Texian spies. If he did know, he decided not to incur retaliations by betraying them. He said nothing about the trio when he reached Cooke's encampment near Walnut Creek on June 14, and the spies returned to Snively unchallenged.[5]

The dragoons had got ahead of the caravan they were escorting, and the merchant wagons were now stranded some miles in the rear by the flooded creeks. The weather stayed foul. A violent thunderstorm flattened the soldiers' tents and sent the Bent, St. Vrain men huddling in the mud under their wagons. Charles was so sure that the creek would flood the bottomlands that he moved his camp to elevated ground two miles away. A miserable week dragged by.

On the twenty-second St. Vrain appeared, tremendously agitated. Warfield's detachment, marching along the Cimarron, had soundly whipped Armijo's advance guard under Captain Ventura Lobata, killing twenty or more of the impressed Pueblo Indians from Taos, wounding thirty or so, and capturing most of the rest. Ceran was sure that when word of the defeat reached the main body of troops under Armijo, the governor would retreat. Even if he did not, the westbound caravan would land in trouble the moment it crossed the river onto Mexican soil. Snively himself had come into Ceran's camp, boasting that he intended to stay in the region, Armijo or no, cut off whatever wagons strayed for an instant behind the escort, then cache his booty and attack the settlements. This news Ceran imparted to Cooke under promise of strict secrecy; if Snively's men learned there had been a leak, they would strike back against the company.

The next day, having extricated itself from the floodwaters, the westbound caravan arrived—twenty-four American wagons, thirty-two Mexican vehicles, and about 140 armed men. Ceran's information got to them somehow, and in spite of their strength, the merchants were terrified. They entreated Cooke to escort them as far as Bent's Fort. He refused, having had orders to go only as far as the Crossing. They then asked him to wait at the Crossing until they could summon fresh reinforcements from New Mexico. Again Cooke demurred, saying that he lacked provisions for a wait. Well, then, would he go to Missouri for new orders and supplies while the traders forted up and waited for him to return? Gentlemen, no. He would follow instructions by continuing to the Crossing. More than that he could not do. If Armijo could not furnish protection beyond the boundary, it was not the fault of the United States.

In despair the traders offered Kit Carson three hundred dollars if he would rush an appeal for more troops to New Mexico. To Kit it looked like a heaven-sent opportunity. The long, rain-caused delays had spoiled his hopes of meeting Frémont's second expedition somewhere near Westport Landing. Besides, three hundred dollars was the equivalent of three months' salary with the explorer. Riding two mules in relays, he loped two hundred and fifty miles up the river to the fort. By the time he reached the adobe castle the mules were played out, but not Kit. He borrowed William's best race horse and by crossing the mountains at night avoided the Utes, who, William had warned him, were on the warpath.

When he reached Taos, he found the town in an uproar. Warfield's attack on Mora had already inflamed the district, and now word arrived of Lobata's defeat. Relatives of the slain and wounded men turned against the authorities. Secret meetings were held in Padre Martinez's house in an attempt to devise some way of overthrowing Armijo. But anger at the governor did not include love for foreigners, whom the common people suspected of complicity with the Texians. Threats were screamed at their houses; Carlos Beaubien's store was attacked and looted; Carlos and most of the other foreigners fled from the valley. The justice of the town, Padre Martinez's brother Pasqual, made no attempt to check the rioting and did not even visit Beaubien's store to ascertain the damage.[6] Worried about Josefa and her sister, Charles's wife, Kit hired another man to take the traders' dispatches to Santa Fe, then made arrangements for the protection of his and Bent's families.

Four days later dispatches for the caravan returned from Santa Fe, stating that reinforcements were marching double-time down the Cimarron. Taos was quieter now. Picking up Sol Silver, Kit hurried back toward the Crossing. Somewhere in the mountains Utes surrounded the pair. Standing back to back with cocked rifles, the two held the attackers at bay until the Indians lost patience and withdrew.

A little farther on, probably in the vicinity of Sangre de

Cristo Pass, they met Lucien Maxwell, and from him Kit learned news of Frémont's second expedition. In Kansas the government exploring party had divided. Fitzpatrick had taken part of the men and the baggage along the usual Oregon Trail past Fort Laramie. Frémont and a smaller group had pushed across country to Fort St. Vrain, which they had reached on July 4. Short of supplies, Frémont had hoped to procure more at the fort, but Marcellin was down to a little salt and unbolted Mexican flour. Accordingly, Frémont had sent Maxwell to Taos to buy ten or twelve mules loaded with provisions from Beaubien and return with them to Pueblo, where the lieutenant would meet him on July 14.

Provisions from Beaubien? Not a chance, Kit said, and told Lucien about the riots. Alarmed for his family, Lucien disdained Kit's added warnings about the Utes and hurried on.[7]

Kit raced on to the Arkansas fort. There William told him that his dispatches for the caravan were no longer necessary. As Cooke's dragoons had crept on toward the Crossing with the caravan, firing their cannon at buffalo along the way for artillery practice, an advance guard had spotted Snively's Texians. Arbitrarily Cooke decided that the raiders had crossed the 100th meridian and were on American soil. Forcing them to surrender, he confiscated most of their guns and offered to protect those who desired to accompany him back to Missouri. Later the courts would decide that the impetuous captain had exceeded his authority and the government would pay for the confiscated weapons, but at the time it was a handy solution to the difficulties. Cooke returned home with an easy conscience. Part of the freebooters went with him; the rest beat their way empty-handed back to Texas. Enormously relieved, the caravan crossed over toward the Cimarron, met the Mexican escort, and, William said, would undoubtedly reach Santa Fe without incident.

Freed of his responsibilities and eager to tie in with Frémont again, Kit congratulated William on the birth of a new son, named George, and turned back up the Arkansas to Pueblo. Frémont was there, fretting about Lucien. Mountain men at the adobe post were certain that if the Utes did not kill Maxwell the Taos rioters would. And Frémont had to have supplies. Kit said he could get them from William, was hired, and once again rode pell-mell down to the fort. William provided ten loaded mules, and Kit cut across country to rejoin the expedition at Fort St. Vrain. In spite of the extra miles and packing, he was there before Frémont arrived on the twenty-third—fast traveling in a week's time. A year would pass, punctuated by an arduous midwinter crossing of the California Sierra, before Carson next saw home.

William was not the only member of the firm who furnished supplies to the government that summer. On August 26, in St. Louis, Charles and Ceran signed a contract to haul rations for Cooke's second escort across the plains. The westbound fall caravan which the dragoons were to guard this time was triple the size of the spring train; and its proprietors, mostly Mexican, were by no means convinced that the disarming of Snively's men had removed all Texians from the plains. The United States Government, embarrassed by the thought that outlaws supposed they could operate with impunity in American territory, determined on a sweeping gesture of apology; Cooke was told to accompany the wagons all the way to Santa Fe if the Mexicans so desired. If he did go that far, he would not be able to return to Missouri but would have to withdraw northward and winter on the Arkansas near Bent's Fort.

Bent, St. Vrain & Company agreed to furnish the provisions the dragoons would need en route. The amount of edibles was indeterminate, for if the captain learned that a Mexican escort was coming to meet the caravan, he could at any time cancel the order. Yet the partners had to take along enough foodstuffs to provision, if necessary, several hundred soldiers the entire distance to Santa Fe. Charles and Ceran, in short, were gambling small profits against long odds. The minute they signed the contract they began to get nervous about it.

The trip west was almost as rainy as the eastward journey had been. In one seventeen-day period the wagons succeeded in going only nineteen miles. Again the dragoons forged ahead of the caravan and then had to sit in the mud until the streams lowered enough for the merchants to cross. By now Cooke was sick of the plains. His keenest hope was to be relieved of the escort so that he could get back to the settlements before winter set in. With dismay he learned from a passing

Missouri-bound train, on September 17, that no Mexican escort had yet left Santa Fe. But there were no reports of Texian raiders, either, and Cooke clung to the hope that he might not have to go as far as New Mexico. In his temporizing he kept Charles and Ceran on tenterhooks as to the fate of their contract.

The partners were doubly anxious now for a decision. From the inbound caravan they had learned that Mexican President Santa Ana, enraged by the spring filibusters, had on August 7 issued a decree closing the customhouses in Taos, El Paso, and Chihuahua. Unless Ceran's status as a naturalized citizen, plus the usual bribery, relaxed matters, the company would not be able to take its wagonloads of trade goods across the border. More than ever it was important not to have government supplies added to the loss.

The rains paused and the wagons caught up with the dragoons. Apprehensively the partners badgered the captain for a decision. How far was he going? How many supplies would he need? Cooke consulted with the Mexican traders. In Charles's presence they replied that they wanted the dragoons to keep on. Then they complicated the problem with secret advice that they could soon dispense with the troops, "provided," in Cooke's words, "Bent and his people were kept in complete ignorance [of the plan of the troops to return to Missouri] . . . fearing it would be communicated to . . . the haunts of semi-trappers and semi-brigands who harbor not very far from B.'s [Bent's Fort]."

Now Cooke was in a quandary. For two days, while Charles and Ceran fumed, he balanced desire to return against duty to continue. At last the partners forced a showdown. They pointed out the lateness of the season and said that if the dragoons marched to New Mexico they would certainly have to winter somewhere along the Arkansas. During the layover they would need supplies, which could be procured only in Santa Fe. If Cooke delayed much longer in ordering them, Raton Pass would be blocked with snow and it would be impossible to get the goods across. There could no longer be any stalling.

Reluctantly Cooke resigned himself to a winter on the plains and sent Ceran ahead at forced marches to buy in Santa

Fe sixty-five hundred dollars' worth of flour, onions, beef, and other non-perishable items and store them at the fort.

A week or so later, as the muddy caravan creaked on toward the Caches, it met a belated Mexican escort. It was all very well for America to protect New Mexicans from Texians, but who would defend New Mexico from the Americans? Armijo wanted no United States dragoons in the province. He also wanted to convince President Santa Ana, who was beginning to frown on him, that he could take care of himself. Out went his militia, back went Cooke. Bent, St. Vrain & Company was left holding not only the unused foodstuffs in Charles's wagons but also the sixty-five hundred dollars' worth of supplies which Ceran even then was purchasing in Santa Fe.

The partners had gambled on the possibility of a cancellation of the contract for the supplies they had brought from Missouri. It would not be a total loss, for they could use the material at the fort. But the Santa Fe rations were a complete superfluity. The food had, moreover, been expressly ordered by Cooke and laboriously provided. Surely the government was honor-bound to pay for that much. But the quartermaster protested the charge, and four years dragged by before the firm collected. The experience left Ceran soured on making contracts with officers in the field and in time would cause difficulty between him and William Bent.

The ill wind brought benefits, however. The same mistrust of Americans that had led Armijo to send out the dilatory escort also prompted him to review the question of strengthening his northern defenses by means of land grants to men who would colonize the territory. Petitions were again invited, and at once Carlos Beaubien and Guadalupe Miranda renewed the application which Martinez had blocked for two years.

Though the renewal of the application theoretically precluded Beaubien from asking for still more land, subterfuge was easy under Mexican law. His son Narciso, barely in his teens, joined Steve Lee, whose wife was a sister of Beaubien's wife, in another request "for lands for cultivation," and promised, according to ritual, "to do all that is required for its settlement and for the raising of horned and woollen cattle." On December 30, Lee and Narciso were given the Sangre de

Cristo grant of 1,038,195 acres. Lying due north of Taos, the territory straddled the present Colorado-New Mexico border, absorbed scores of miles along the Rio Grande, and embraced the lower part of Colorado's San Luis Valley. Carlos Beaubien held sub rosa interest in the tract; together with other grants soon to be allotted, it would bring him ownership of more land than any other man in America.

At about the same time that Lee and young Beaubien won the Sangre de Cristo grant, Ceran St. Vrain and Cornelio Vigil, an uncle of Ignacia Bent, applied for a huge tract to the east. The northern boundary of the Vigil-St. Vrain grant would be the Arkansas River; its southern limits would lie approximately along the present Colorado-New Mexico border. There would never be certainty as to exactly how much land it covered. The valleys of the Greenhorn, Huerfano, Apishapa, Chuchara, and Purgatory were included, so that in effect most of southeastern Colorado was embraced—at a rough estimate, about four million acres. On January 2, 1844, the Taos justice of the peace reported to Armijo that he had toured the perimeter of the tract with St. Vrain and Vigil, had erected mounds of dirt at the corners, and, having "closed here the boundaries of this grant and having recorded the same, I took them by the hand and walked with them and caused them to throw earth and pull up weeds, and make other demonstrations of possession." Legal fiction, of course. Horsemen could not have circled the territory in a week.[8] It was all wilderness, and worth exactly as much as the possessors could make it worth in the face of the Indians, who blithely continued to assume that the country was theirs, anyhow.

Foreigner Charles Bent could not, of course, legally share in the grant, but on March 11, 1844, St. Vrain and Vigil quietly conveyed to him by parole agreement a one-sixth interest.[9] This transfer seems to have escaped Padre Martinez's notice, or otherwise the priest would have caused trouble. He was already doing damage enough with his "An Exposition of Things in New Mexico," a long memorial addressed to President Santa Ana. On the previous November 28, 1843, author Martinez had printed several copies of this on his Taos press and then had distributed them throughout New Mexico. It was, in the main, an honest and patriotic document, astutely analyzing the many ills from which the department suffered; and in the course of it Martinez again found opportunity to belabor the American traders who had built forts "since the year 1832 near the shores of the Rio del Napeste [Arkansas], del Rio Chato [Platte]," and other places. These traders were, he insisted, to blame for the dearth of the buffalo meat which played so large a part in the larders of the common people, for they "bring with them a great quantity of all sorts of articles to exchange for buffaloes. . . . It is certain that the buffaloes must greatly diminish in consequence and that this constant slaughter will finally result in the extinction of the species in a very short time . . . and the Indians will be all the more obliged to resort to pillage and robbery. . . . The traders sold the Indians also liquors and ardent spirits, which were prohibited. The result was that these Indian nations became extremely demoralized and were prompted to greater destruction of buffaloes in order to satisfy their appetites for strong drink, which they obtained in exchange. They also made raids in our Department of New Mexico, in order to steal cattle which were bought of them by the proprietors of these forts."[10]

This blanket condemnation was obviously aimed straight at Bent, St. Vrain & Company; yet for some reason Martinez allowed the St. Vrain-Vigil grant to pass unchallenged. Not so the long-delayed, enormous Beaubien-Miranda grant, lying just south of the St. Vrain-Vigil tract and embracing much of northeastern New Mexico. The renewed application was confirmed by Armijo on February 22, 1844. Promptly Martinez renewed his vociferations, insisting that Charles Bent was co-owner. Belatedly Armijo listened again, not through love for the Taos priest but because the governor knew he was out of favor with Santa Ana and he did not wish to leave chinks his enemies could exploit. Late in March he issued another order which once more restrained the grant.

Charles was the stumbling block. For the sake of expediency he withdrew his claims to a share in the land. Beaubien wrote Armijo, declaring that Bent had absolutely no interest in the territory, and the courts then reinstated the grant. Shortly thereafter President Santa Ana removed Armijo from office, and Charles quietly resumed his former share in the tract.[11]

Meanwhile he was preparing to go to the fort and once again take the annual caravan to Missouri. But what goods could he bring back? The New Mexican trade was still closed to foreigners. Not even the New Mexicans liked the embargo, which had shot the price of merchandise sky-high. There were predictions of revolt, American merchants pulled every string possible, and even the United States Government lodged a diplomatic protest. In Mexico City on March 31, 1844, Santa Ana capitulated and ordered the customhouses reopened, though many classes of goods remained contraband and Americans were still forbidden to conduct retail trade in Santa Fe and Taos.

The slow-traveling news from Mexico City had not reached Charles by the time he left Taos for the fort. The caravan departed early this year, perhaps by the middle of April, and William went with it for a rare visit to St. Louis. He was on a special mission. The company's continual written protests against the liquor that was being smuggled across the Arkansas had produced no results. Perhaps direct representation by the Indians to their Superintendent in St. Louis would have more effect. Acting on William's recommendation, the Cheyenne chiefs selected one of their number, called Slim Face by the whites, to go east and personally urge action against this insidious devil which was threatening death to the tribe. William guaranteed to see that Slim Face arrived safely.

George was left in charge of the fort. While his brothers were away, he entertained interesting visitors. On July 1, 1844, he fired the cannon to welcome Frémont's return from California with Kit and famed Joe Walker, the latter of whom the expedition had picked up along the way. Eager to see Josefa, Kit left the party at the fort and hurried with Walker to Taos. A little later another erstwhile Frémont recruit appeared. He was William Gilpin, twenty-two years old, lean, intense, ramrod-straight—a fantastic combination of dreamer and adventurer. Before he was sixteen Gilpin had been a veteran of the Seminole wars in Florida. Returning from the South to Missouri, he had edited a St. Louis newspaper and had been admitted to the Bar. Growing tired of it all at the ripe age of twenty-one, in the spring of 1843 he borrowed one hundred dollars from Charles's good friend Dave Waldo, bought a horse

and gun, and started alone for California. Meeting Frémont at
Elm Grove, he probably saved his scalp by joining the expedition, but by the time he reached Oregon he was tired of exploring too. Dropping out of the party, he helped the handful
of American citizens along the Columbia draw up a memorial
to Congress and then started home, traveling part way with
Peg-leg Smith. While crossing the Rockies with a lone Mexican, he picked up what he thought were samples of gold. At
the fort he became intrigued by the land grants and pestered
George with questions. He never forgot what he learned; in
1862, after a term as Colorado's first territorial governor, Gilpin
would buy part of the Sangre de Cristo grant from Carlos
Beaubien. He was very able, very quixotic, and very overbearing—as William Bent would eventually learn.

The present, however, was troublesome enough for William.
The high water of the previous year had been but a pale forecast of the gigantic floods that swept the plains in the early
summer of 1844. For nearly a month the caravan was stranded
at Pawnee Fork, finally struggled across on May 21, and at
Walnut Creek was bogged for another month amid torturing
swarms of mosquitoes. It was July before William and Slim
Face reached St. Louis. The city dumfounded the savage. People!—he wanted to take back to the tribe some concrete idea
of how many whites there were on earth. So he squatted on a
street corner with a long stick. Each time a paleface walked
by, he cut a tiny notch into the wood. Long before the afternoon wore away, the stick was filled with notches. Hopelessly
Slim Face threw it away. The Cheyennes would never believe
so ridiculous a count.

The long delay on the trail had eaten up William's spare
time, and it was imperative that he return almost immediately
to the fort. With a small party, which may or may not have
included Slim Face, he turned back toward the Arkansas,
traveling fast.[12] Behind him the wagon yards of Independence
and Westport clanged with feverish activity. Word had
reached the frontier that trade with New Mexico could be
resumed, and the merchants were eager to assemble their outfits and roll for Santa Fe before snow blocked the distant,
mountainous end of the trail. It was a frantic race that many
of them did not win.

CHAPTER XIII

RUMBLES OF TROUBLE

Tremendously excited by the bustle in the wagon yards, seventeen-year-old Bill Boggs, Panthea Boggs's second son, ran away from home and wheedled a wheel-greasing job from Sam Owens, the biggest outfitter in Independence. Sam even promised to let Bill go with the caravan clear to the mountains, where his brother Tom was working for Bent, St. Vrain & Company. Then, to keep his own skirts clean, Sam tipped off the boy's father.

Suddenly Lilburn was there in front of Bill. For a moment the ex-governor did not respond to his son's mute appeal. Perhaps during the silence Lilburn remembered the long-ago day when a similar urge to reach the edges of nowhere had led him to take his first bride, Juliannah Bent, west among the Osages. Or it may be that in the back of his mind there stirred a dim awareness that an era was dying, that this might be Bill's last chance to see the wonder which had once been the West.

"Be sure to tell your mother good-by," he said abruptly, and went home to make his peace with Panthea.

Thirty-four wagons, two dearborns, and sixty men assembled at timbered Council Grove, a hundred and fifty miles beyond Independence. Sam Owens was elected captain. Uncle Nick Gentry, who had gone to Santa Fe with Charles Bent in 1829, was wagon master. Profane, lawless, hardheaded, and softhearted, Nick hired Bill Boggs to drive one of his two wagons. It was loaded with contraband tobacco.

Heat, dust, mule brays, firelight, and starglow—the old story, new to Bill. He was proud of Nick, proud of Sam Owens. Except for William Bent's small, fast-traveling outfit (which even now was pulling into the fort), theirs was the first train on the trail. Well behind them were the caravans of Albert Speyer, Connelley and Glasgow, and a pair of Bent, St. Vrain trains, one led by Charles, the other by Ceran.

In spite of Owens's good start, however, the caravan made

poorer time than Bill Boggs realized. Dysentery racked the
men. Swearing and grumbling, old Nick Gentry boiled broth
for the invalids from frogs' legs. Mud Creek mired them, and
at Pawnee Fork they lost two more days drying out the goods
of a wagon that turned turtle in midstream. Time did not
bother Bill, however. He reveled in the excitement of the first
buffalo, and then, one night while he was standing guard over
the grazing mules, his heart leaped at the sound of a great
splashing in the river. Indians, he thought, and scuttled for
Nick Gentry. Nick put his ear to the ground. It was the strang-
est rumbling, neither horses nor buffalo. Investigating, they discovered a vast drove of migrating wolves. All night Bill
watched the ghostly packs plunge into the wide Arkansas and
paddle across—forty thousand of them, he estimated, and was
annoyed the next morning when no one in camp would swallow his figures.

When the caravan reached the ford over the Arkansas, five
men—the Leitensdorfer brothers, a six-foot greenhorn named
James Webb, and a couple of others—started ahead for Santa
Fe, via Bent's Fort, to see what arrangements could be made
at the customhouse.[1] Armijo was rumored to have been replaced by a new governor, and no one knew the least thing
about his successor. Many of Owens's group carried illegal
candlewick, powder, shoes, and what not hidden among their
calicoes and hardware. They feared confiscation. To belittle
their own worries they began chaffering Nick about his un-
disguisable wagonload of contraband tobacco. Nick just
grinned. Armijo had winked at the tobacco because Nick
promptly gambled away his ill-gotten gains and the money
stayed in the province. Why should the new governor prove
any different?

Without incident the caravan crossed the dry jornada to
the Cimarron. Here Sam Owens decided that he too would
ride ahead with an advance party to sound out the new governor. By so doing he missed an uncomfortable experience. As
the wagons were strung out and laboring up a hard pull, a
blizzard struck. Howling like a madman, Nick Gentry managed to whip the collapsing teams into a corral. The place was
bitterly exposed. To save the stock, he drove them to a bluff-
sheltered hollow he knew of two or three miles away. For

three days the storm raged. In relays the men guarded the
openings in the bluffs to contain the restless, starving animals.
The cold bit beyond endurance. Tearing up greasewood, Bill
Boggs and his fellow guard managed to kindle a fire and
squatted with their backs to it while they kept watch on the
swirling murk. Bill's overcoat caught fire and burned out clear
to his collar without his noticing. Owens's best saddle mule
froze to death, as did two or three oxen. Tough enough, Bill
thought—until he heard about the trains of Albert Speyer and
Henry Connelley, caught farther down the Cimarron with no
shelter whatsoever. As the freezing animals began to drop, the
famished living mules tried to eat the ears of the dead. By the
time the skies cleared, both parties had lost almost all their
stock and had to send to Santa Fe for rescue parties.[2]

The drifts soon melted in the dry air. Nick pulled the train
out of the Cimarron and down toward the Red. Here they met
a portion of the first advance party, Jim Webb riding a new
mule he had bought at Bent's Fort from Marcellin St. Vrain.
The group had had its own troubles. To save time they had
avoided Raton Pass and cut across Sangre de Cristo Pass into
the San Luis Valley. Eugene Leitensdorfer grew so sick he had
to be hauled behind his mule on a litter made of rope laced
between two dragging, travois-like poles. In Taos, Carlos Beaubien entertained them well but could give no information as
to what the new governor's policy might be. Completely at a
loss, the couriers decided against going to Santa Fe lest their
probings rouse suspicion. Striking eastward across the mountains, they rejoined the train. From here on matters would
have to rest with luck and Sam Owens.

In Santa Fe, Sam found an ally—Charles Bent. By now
Bent and St. Vrain had a store in Santa Fe as well as Taos;
Charles, too, had ridden in from the fort to see the governor,
and in due time George Bent would follow with the goods
over Raton Pass. Together Charles and Owens visited the
palace. With proper indirection they made the governor a
"valuable present," so says Bill Boggs, and in classic New
Mexican tradition were assured consideration.

Nonetheless, a hitch developed. The inspector, ignoring
Armijo's old practice of accepting invoices only, ordered an
unloading at the customhouse. It was a sop at form; no dili-

gent search for contraband was made. But diligence would not
be necessary to spot a wagonful of tobacco. Nick Gentry began to squirm.

"Come on," he growled at Bill, and strode toward the palace. In his backless overcoat Bill drove the wagon behind Nick,
past a file of parading soldiers. At the door of the palace he met
Charles Bent coming out. They greeted each other warmly.
Charles, forty-five years old now, was beginning to show age.
His once jet-black hair was graying, and in spite of the long
miles on the trail his trim frame had thickened. But his verve
and graciousness remained undiminished. Tom Boggs, he told
Bill, was at the fort, and any time Bill wanted to visit Taos
or the Arkansas, he would be more than welcome. Meanwhile
he gave Nick Gentry an encouraging nod. Nick deposited his
quid and clumped inside the palace. In one hand he carried
an old stocking lumpy with $150 in gold coin.

Governor Mariano Martinez de Lajanza was a native of
Mexico City, and by now he was convinced he had been exiled
to the ends of the earth. Less than two months before, some
Mexicans out chasing Navajos had murderously attacked a
Ute village—though the Utes were momentarily at peace with
New Mexico—and part of the tribe had come to Santa Fe to
demand satisfaction. All night their wild drummings kept the
city on tenterhooks. In the morning three chiefs gained admission to the governor. A quarrel developing, they fell on him
with knives. Martinez warded them off with a chair and yelled
for help. His wife brought him a sword. Martinez ran one
Indian through, and then the palace guard tumbled in. The
remaining two chiefs fought their way outside, howling for
their tribesmen. A sharp battle swept through the plaza. One
soldier was wounded; six or eight Indians were killed. In retaliation the Utes gathered reinforcements and fell on the town
of Albuquerque. Ten or a dozen Mexicans were slain north of
Santa Fe, and in mid-September George Bent, then in Taos,
wrote William at the fort to caution their traders; a general
uprising was feared throughout the northern districts.

And now the gringos. What a strange, uncouth barbarian
this one was! Fortunately Martinez's wife was amused. Be
kindly, Mariano.

Martinez looked at the dirty old sock in Nick's hand. How much?

A hundred and fifty dollars, Nick said, and threw the sock with a clank on the desk. Martinez nodded. Nick made as graceful a bow as he knew how, bolted outside, and sold the tobacco for thirty-five hundred dollars.[3]

The next night Bill Boggs took in a fandango. A fellow teamster grew boisterous and was ejected by the Mexicans. A melee followed, soldiers rushed in, and Bill decided it was time to make himself scarce. Prowling the plaza, he found Nick playing monte with a priest and a gambler from Chihuahua. Two bored women sat with them, smoking shuck cigarettes. A silver pitcher of aguardiente kept going the rounds. Bill lay down on a settee and watched until he fell asleep. Independence, he decided, had never been like this. It was his eighteenth birthday.

Mexican law had its peculiarities. Though foreigners could again bring goods into Santa Fe, they could not retail the merchandise there. Most of the merchants decided to go on south. Owens discharged four or five teamsters he no longer needed and gave each a saddle mule, recommending they ride home via Taos and Bent's Fort. Bill decided to join them. In Taos, Charles put the boy up, gave him a servant to wait on him, and tried to dissuade him from crossing the winter mountains with a green party. But Bill was set on seeing the fort and his brother Tom. Shrugging, Charles provided him with a big Spanish mule, some food, a warm serape, and wished him Godspeed. For a moment Charles contemplated going part way with the boy. George's eight wagons of merchandise were stalled on the upper Purgatory, and he had sent a runner to Taos for fresh oxen and provisions. But Charles was feeling ill and at the last minute dispatched men with the equipment. George knew what to do: leave two or three wagons at Mora to avoid the tax, piling the goods on the remaining vehicles. Álvarez was warned on November 12, 1844, not to mention the caravan's approach "for fear that an escort might be sent out."

At the fort Bill Boggs had an excited reunion with Tom and promptly forgot all about Missouri—luckily, perhaps, because his erstwhile companions were badly frostbitten before reach-

ing the settlements. Wide-eyed, he watched the preparations
for the winter's trade. Kit Carson was there, and jolly, black-
whiskered Ceran St. Vrain. Employees by the score were sort-
ing out equipment. Frisky in the cold air, the horse herd swept
in a wild run to its nightly corrallings. There were roasts of
buffalo hump to gorge on, yarns beyond belief to hear.

And eagles—two live, bald-headed eagles were caged in the
belfry. The Cheyennes were adept at catching the birds. After
the proper rituals, a hunter would dig a hole on a hilltop,
roof it with poles and grass, and crouch inside, waiting. There
was no human odor; the watcher had taken sweat baths and
smeared himself with vermilion mixed, appropriately, in eagle
fat. The floor of his blind was covered with sweet-smelling
sage. His bait, a dead rabbit or raw meat disguised by tufts
of wolfskin, was staked down so the birds could not fly off
with it. When one landed, the watcher reached through a hole
and seized its feet. After a tussle with talons, beak, and bruis-
ing wings, he strangled his prey with a bowstring. If a man's
medicine was right, he might catch as many as twenty in a
single autumn day—a profitable haul, for two dozen feathers
from the wings and tail of each one were worth a horse in
trade. Live eagles were also valuable; their big tail feathers
grew back in for as many as three pluckings.[4]

Eagles, symbol of the soaring freedom of the plains—caged
now. That same fall James Knox Polk was chosen President of
the United States. Hearing the news in Taos, Charles Bent
wrote Álvarez on January 24, 1845, "I am fearfull that this
election will cause difficulty." But what concern was politics
to Bill Boggs, aged eighteen?

He watched and listened and yearned. Finally William Bent
said he could go on a trading trip to the Big Timbers, thirty-
odd miles down the river. Trying not to show his eagerness,
Bill climbed in a cart with leathery William Guerrier, a French
Canadian ancient as the hills. Guerrier wore a hooded white
capote and leggings of white blanket around his trousers. He
was so illiterate he had to use sticks to count, but few men
knew the Cheyennes any better. He had married one, but she
had died after bearing him a son and now he lived with a
Sioux.

It was a rhapsodic winter in a lovely spot. The Big Timbers

was a long belt of gigantic cottonwoods growing where the valley widened and became less austere. Behind shelters of dry sunflower stalks the squaws chattered over their hide scraping, then carried the finished products into the tepee of Chief Cinemo, where the trade goods were stored and where Bill was proudly living. He was even prouder after a dance of savage triumph when White Antelope's war party returned through a snowstorm with eleven Pawnee scalps; White Antelope himself ran a finger across his blackened face and honored Bill Boggs by solemnly smearing a mark on the boy's cheek. The battle brought not only exultation, however. The nephew of Chief Cinemo had not returned. Horrified, Bill saw the mother grieve by thrusting sticks through her breast, tying cords tossed over her shoulder to the sticks, and for hours dragging her son's shield through brush and over logs, blood pouring down her body.

Years before, Yellow Wolf had recommended the Big Timbers as a location for the fort, and William Bent wished now that the firm had followed the advice. He often talked of moving the fort here,[5] but the effort would be prodigious and he substituted two double log cabins which he visited each winter with his wife and three children. This winter, however, the Indians were camped two or three miles from the cabins, and William decided to move into a tepee nearer his customers.

There he fell ill with something which sounds, as Bill Boggs describes it, suspiciously like diphtheria. He could neither swallow nor talk. Worried, Bill went to see him. Owl Woman, "a most estimable good woman of much influence" in the tribe, had forced a hollow quill down her husband's swollen throat and through it was feeding him broth she blew from her own mouth.

Presently a homely, unornamented, laughing Indian appeared, a famous Cheyenne medicine man. He depressed Bent's tongue with the handle of a large spoon and peered into the infected throat. Then he went outside and found a handful of small, sharp-thorned sandburs. He pierced each bur with an awl and tied it to the end of a thread split from a piece of sinew. Next he covered the barbs with marrow fat and with a notched stick rammed a succession of burs down William's throat. As he pulled each one out, it brought up "corrupt mat-

ter . . . as dry as the bark of a tree." At the finish of the operation, William could swallow soup for himself, and in a day or
two he was able to move down to the log cabins. By Christmas
he was up and around and invited Bill to share holiday dinner
with the family.

Through the first part of the new year trade was excellent
—so many buffalo waiting to be killed that William sent runners
to the Arapaho, urging them to join the robe-making.[6] Then,
abruptly, everything went wrong.

The ill luck began with a typical Indian panic. For months
the Cheyennes had been living in dread of the Delawares. The
previous spring a Cheyenne named Plover had taken his wife
and small son a short distance from their village in northwestern Kansas to dig some coyote pups out of a den. As they
worked they were surprised by a party of Delaware Indians
returning from a season's trapping in the mountains. Partly in
fun, perhaps, the Delawares sent some harmless pot shots after
Plover's family as they scampered back to the village. The
Cheyennes, however, did not think it fun. Their warriors took
out after the Delawares, who holed up in a ravine. The eastern
Indians were a strong party, and the matter would probably
have ended in the usual exchange of insults and long-range
shots if an ancient chief named Medicine Water had not
chanced to think up a cunning and deadly stratagem.

Medicine Water many years ago had traded a rusty helmet
and shirt of Spanish mail out of an Arapaho, whose ancestors
in turn had been trading with Mexicans. He now told his son,
Touching Cloud, to don the armor and hide it under a red
blanket. So equipped, Touching Cloud raced his horse along
the line of Delawares, close in and taunting them. His red
blanket made an irresistible target. But the bullets the Delawares volleyed from their old fusees did not penetrate the iron
shirt, and while the enemy were reloading, the Cheyennes
charged. They caught the Delawares with ramrods still in their
guns, butchered the party, and appropriated the booty—many
horses, furs, and dried beaver tails.

A cooling off of their jubilation brought fear. The tough,
well-armed, passionate Delaware tribe would undoubtedly
seek revenge. The Cheyenne village fled south, met Frémont
marching homeward from his second expedition, and begged

him to intercede for them. If he did—and there is no record—
he was unable to calm the Delawares. A party of avengers
started west. Troops from Fort Leavenworth stopped them,
but the Cheyennes did not know this. A whisper of approaching enemy warriors reached Big Timbers and sparked terror.
Refusing to heed William Bent's arguments, the Cheyennes
frantically dismantled their lodges and within an hour the village had dissolved into a dozen fleeing bands.

William knew them well enough to shrug it off. The panic,
he told Bill Boggs, would burn itself out. As soon as the Indians
found a fresh supply of buffalo, they would settle down. Meanwhile the traders might as well cart the robes already acquired
back to the fort, pick up new supplies, and then see if they
could find the Cheyennes again.

A new scare—rumors of many armed Texans on the Arkansas
—caused the already jittery Cheyennes to veer south of their
normal hunting grounds to the Cimarron. Runners informed
William Bent, and he led his party up the Purgatory until its
narrowing brown sandstone canyon pinched them out into Box
Elder Creek and thence across high, cedar-freckled plateaus
to the bluff-girt Cimarron. Tom Boggs, recently returned from
trading for mules in New Mexico with George Bent, was with
them now.

Along the way the party was amused by the antics of William Bransford, a new hand almost as green as young Bill.
Bransford tried to kill a buffalo bull by stepping off his horse
directly in front of the ponderous beast and shooting it three
times in the forehead. No buffalo could be hurt that way. The
bull kept coming; the chagrined Bransford had to scramble out
of its way while the party hoorawed. In time, though, Bransford would prove he had phenomenal skill with animals. Not
long after the party returned to the fort, a huge white dog, as
big as a Newfoundland, appeared one evening with the wolves
that always prowled outside the walls for refuse. The men
lured the dog inside the entry with a bait of raw meat and
slammed the gate shut behind it. Promptly the beast went berserk and chased every person in the fort up on the roofs. From
that vantage point they managed to lasso it, put it in iron
chains, and locked it in the bastion. For two days it stayed
there, howling and leaping bare-fanged at anyone who ap-

proached. Finally Bransford said enough was enough. He walked straight up to the snarling creature and patted its head. From then on it was Bransford's dog. No one else could so much as touch it, and the amazed traders quit joshing about the buffalo episode.

On the Cimarron, William Bent's party found Cheyennes—but no robes. The weather had turned mild, and the buffalo had left the shelter of the trees and bluffs along the creeks. Nor could scouting parties find them on the nearby plains. The only solution, William decided, was to move the village. Under his prodding, the chiefs had the squaws load up the travois and in normal confusion they marched downstream, looking for game. All they found was a great litter of bones—the wolf-gnawed remnants of Albert Speyer's frozen mules. The Cheyennes thought a battle must have occurred, until Bill Boggs told about the wagon train's disaster. For years those skeletons would lie beside the trail; later travelers would amuse themselves by arranging leg bones in geometric patterns, skulls in grinning circles.

And still there were no buffalo. Futilely searching, the village and traders swung north toward the Arkansas, through the bleak sand hills along the present southern edge of the Colorado-Kansas border. Their only water was a brackish liquid obtained by digging into seep holes. Food was gone, but the Indians stayed Indian. Spotting some wild mustangs, they forgot their empty parfleche larders and took off on a horse hunt, chasing erratically hither and yon, their lariat loops held open by reeds. Ill luck plagued that spasm too. They caught only one horse and deemed the bony creature far too valuable to eat.

For two days now there had been no food in the lodge occupied by William Bent and the Boggs brothers. William and Tom were used to pulling in their belts, but young Bill began to look as gaunt as he felt. When he noticed how eagerly the mules nickered when the squaws brought them cottonwood bark, he tried chewing that. It didn't help much. Then he heard a frenzied yelping, investigated, and watched two squaws choke an old dog to death with a piece of rope half hitched around its neck. They threw the corpse onto a brush-wood fire, where it stank and bloated horribly, and scraped off the singed hair with sticks and butcher knives. Bill took his queasy stomach elsewhere.

Tom found him sitting disconsolately on a log. "We've got a stew up in the lodge."

"Dog stew?" Bill asked suspiciously.

"It's good meat."

"Not for me," Bill said, and went hungry to bed. When he woke the next morning, there was a scattering of bones on the floor. Regretfully Bill helped himself to some more cottonwood bark.

The village moved on toward the Arkansas. Along the way they encountered one ancient bull. In a twinkling it was dead and skinned, the warriors gulping the raw liver, blood dribbling down their chins. But one tough bull wasn't enough to feed the village for long. The next morning William Bent rode off on his white mule with some warriors to look for deer. As the village trailed along, a courier dashed back with news that the hunters had trapped a band of Pawnees on an island in the Arkansas.

Hunger forgotten, Bill and Tom Boggs dashed ahead to see the fun. They passed one Pawnee corpse pincushioned with arrows, saw Bent across the river on his white mule, and splashed over to join him. Nearby, Chief Whirlwind sat on the ground, holding his jaw. A bullet had passed through both cheeks and knocked out half his teeth. The brothers were all for piling into the battle, but William called them back. It was a standing rule of the company that traders keep out of Indian squabbles.

The Cheyennes set fire to the grass on the island, hoping to drive the Pawnees into range. Instead, the smoke covered the enemy as they slipped down to a sandspit and dug foxholes. Showing off, young Cheyennes raced their horses along the bank, bent low and yelling challenges. The Pawnees had rifles. They killed five or six horses and sent the riders tumbling. Disgusted, William told the chiefs to stop the nonsense before someone was killed; the way to get the Pawnees was to starve them out. But that took patience. The battle dwindled off; the Cheyennes picked up their wounded and in milling pandemonium turned up the Arkansas toward the fort.

Trade everywhere had been poor—a mere two hundred bales

to load into the wagons. Still, the ill wind had blown some good. Up on the South Platte, Lancaster Lupton threw in his hand. That competition gone, Marcellin was directed to abandon Fort St. Vrain, for now company wagons from the Arkansas could roam unchallenged between Texas and Wyoming.

In the bottomlands meadowlarks sang, redheaded woodpeckers drummed. Gaudy cactus, primrose, and the candelabra bloom of yucca dotted the sand. Bill Boggs felt spring's brief tenderness touch the scrubby hills and knew contentment. He had seen the elephant: Old Nick Gentry outwitting a blizzard and then corrupting a governor's palace with a bribe in a dirty sock; Indians fighting their little wars for the sheer, pulse-lifting verve of the fight. Men he had lived with had starved and feasted, living how they could—if they could—by whatever lights each one carried inside himself. Sunburned, toughened, and infinitely richer than when he had left home, Bill rode with the lightly loaded caravan back toward Independence. He would never return—and neither would the dying glory he had touched. When the train reached Missouri, Frémont was in St. Louis, recruiting fifty expert riflemen for a "topographic" survey of the Mexican province of California.

Bill Boggs was young. He had not heard, or at least did not note, the warning rumbles. But others heard. In Santa Fe the previous November, while Bill was there, Charles Bent had warned the traders that Colonel Warfield had been at the fort again with threats that Texas freebooters were once more approaching the trail to raid Mexican caravans.[7] It was the appearance of these mysterious invaders (who seem to have found no caravans to attack) that had sent the Cheyennes south to the Cimarron. William Bent's runners had kept St. Vrain apprised at the fort of what information he could pick up, and from the Arkansas St. Vrain relayed the word to Charles in Taos. Charles in turn wrote Álvarez that "thare are people of the single star on the lookout for game on the plains." Warned by Álvarez, most of the Mexican traders decided not to risk the trail that spring.[8]

Peripheral rumblings, these. On March 1, 1845, President Tyler signed into law a joint resolution by Congress admitting Texas into the Union; and, as a corollary, Texas's quarrel with Mexico became the United States's quarrel. Three days later

Tyler relinquished office to James K. Polk, elected on a platform that advocated "reoccupancy" of Oregon and the acquisition of California by purchase or pressure. A smart newspaper editor summed up history in a catch phrase—Manifest Destiny—and Juan Almonte, the Mexican minister, demanded his passport and returned to a nation on fire with resentment. None of these men, quite naturally, was any more conscious than Bill Boggs that they had just turned Bent, St. Vrain & Company upside down. Never again could the plains of the Southwest be a private domain.

At the beginning of Polk's term war was no part of his program. Nonetheless, it was well to be prepared. In mid-June he sent Zachary Taylor to occupy a disputed strip of land in southern Texas, and even before that he had ordered into the West three oh so peaceful expeditions.

Stephen Watts Kearny's 250 dragoons were the first to march. While Captain Philip St. George Cooke grumbled that their route was taking him away from the scene of the "inevitable" war with Mexico, the column marched up the Oregon Trail to South Pass, carefully counting along the way 460 emigrant wagons bearing 850 men, 475 women, and 1000 children. Supposedly the military demonstration was to awe the Indians into leaving emigrant trains alone, but on its homeward journey the command rattled an American saber at Mexico by swinging south to the Arkansas, where Kearny was to reprovision himself with supplies hauled in from Missouri by Charles Bent.[9]

As the fort's little cannon roared a three-round salute, Charles and Ceran rode out to welcome the visitors. Despite Cooke's frequent encounters with the partners during the past sixteen years, this was the first time he had seen their establishment. He was impressed by its "military semblance . . . fine appearance and strength." As far as Mexico was concerned, the military semblance was sharpened when Kearny's scouts pounced on twelve terrified New Mexican traders and questioned them closely before allowing them to proceed with their trading venture among the Cheyennes.

A lavish dinner was spread in the big apartment. Kearny, who had been at Fort Atkinson on the Missouri as early as 1820, was an old acquaintance. Like everyone else from St.

Louis, the partners knew of his stormy romance with Mary
Radford, stepdaughter of William Clark. Meriwether Lewis
Clark, the general's son and Charles Bent's friend, had also
been in love with Mary. The night of her wedding to Kearny,
as myriad candles blazed and a string orchestra played soft
strains behind a screen in Clark's St. Louis home, young Meriwether had bounded up to Mary's room in hot protest. Minutes
dragged. Then the buzzing guests were sent away with an
excuse that the bride-to-be was ill. Kearny won, however, and
the next day wed Mary in a private ceremony at the general's
country place. St. Louis society clacked for years, until the
rivals spoiled the fun by becoming firm friends.

Conversation in the fort that night was more martial. Over
the coffee cups Charles told Kearny what he knew of New
Mexico's strength and weakness. For Charles Bent it was a
significant interview; within the year Kearny would have occasion to remember the talk and the talker.

When the dragoons marched on, their guide, taciturn,
white-haired Tom Fitzpatrick, stayed behind to wait for the
next groups. Early in August the fort's telescope picked up,
far down the Arkansas, the dust of a double-headed expedition: Frémont, leading his largest force yet to "survey" California, and Lieutenant J. W. Abert, bound southward to look
over the country along the Canadian and Washita rivers.
Abert's survey was based on a sophistry. Both New Mexico
and Texas claimed the present Panhandle country of Oklahoma and Texas. After annexing Texas, the United States,
without so much as a gesture toward adjudication of the
claims, decided to examine the disputed land. It was mere
scientific curiosity, of course, as the diminutive size of Abert's
thirty-three-man party plainly showed. But who could tell
when the army might need the maps he brought back?

The fort's routine had already been disrupted by army hauling and army bivouacking, and now Frémont upset plans still
more by asking for Kit Carson. Kit and Dick Owens were south
on the Little Cimarron in New Mexico, planting crops and
building a house, for Kit was at long last anxious to settle
down. The company was anxious that he should settle. On
the strength of Charles's part ownership of the Beaubien-
Miranda grant, Bent, St. Vrain & Company had started de-

veloping ranches along the pretty streams that finger eastward out of the mountains of northern New Mexico. The year before, Maxwell had made a settlement of sorts on Rayado Creek, and in the spring Tom Boggs and John Hatcher had gone to Ponil Creek. Both projects collapsed. Though Boggs and Hatcher had built a hut and planted corn, they soon grew tired of lying on scaffolds and shooting marauding grizzly bears away from the crops and cattle. They had quit the place and were at the fort now. Even earlier Maxwell had gone east with a caravan and there had signed up with Frémont. Now only Carson and Owens were at work. Small matter. Frémont sent runners to the Little Cimarron, and all the ranches came to a standstill.

While the expedition waited for Kit and Owens, William Bent eyed Frémont's twelve tough Delaware hunters. Here was an opportunity to settle that tribe's threatened war against the Cheyennes. He persuaded Yellow Wolf and a Cheyenne delegation to sit down with the Delawares inside the fort's placita, had old Bill Guerrier act as a three-way interpreter, and scolded his red children for their antics. The peace pipe circulated, Yellow Wolf and Old Bark made gladsome speeches, and everything was lovely. The army might be the official bearer of the Pax Americana, but, as in the case of the peace between Cheyennes and Comanches five years before, traders like William Bent were the ones who implemented it.

Although the War Department had ignored Charles's advice about building a post on the Arkansas, it was now finding Bent's Fort a handy substitute. For two weeks Frémont and Abert stayed there, buying beef cattle to drive with them and using the fort's shops to prepare their equipment. In mid-August they split, Frémont moving west along the Arkansas, Abert heading south up the Purgatory. Fitzpatrick was Abert's guide. But Fitzpatrick knew nothing more of this country than what he had seen during his hard-luck 1831 trip along the Santa Fe Trail with Bill Sublette and Jedediah Smith. Abert asked Bent and St. Vrain for help. To show him the way to the Canadian they gave him two top hands, one named Greenwood and the other their grizzly-hating farmer and one of the champion yarn spinners of the West, John Hatcher, from Lord knows where.

Like so many plainsmen, Hatcher was small in size, a dead shot, utterly fearless, and so ugly he was comical-looking. Though generally he was cheerful, his temper sometimes slipped and he bull-whipped his indolent Mexican roustabouts in exasperation. He was a master of the southern plains. When Abert's column reached the Canadian, they met a wrinkled Kiowa squaw who fell weeping for joy on Hatcher's neck. Years ago she had adopted him as her son during his first trading trip to her nation.

Greenwood and Hatcher were to accompany Abert only as far as the Bent, St. Vrain trading houses in what is now Hutchinson County, Texas. Comanches and Kiowas had been waiting there for the company wagons, but the turmoil at the fort had delayed the caravan. Losing patience, the Indians scattered out to hunt. After sizing up the situation, Hatcher and Greenwood gave Abert some final directions and cut across country back to the Arkansas. They traveled by night; two lone men were tempting bait for even the "friendly" Comanches.

Abert moved on eastward. But the very fact of his passage led Ceran St. Vrain and William Bent to follow him shortly with a gang of Mexican adobe makers. Until now the company had conducted its southern trade first from tepees and then from log cabins, because the New Mexican Government would have objected to a private American fortress on its soil. But if the United States now claimed the ground, that deterrent was removed.

Ceran had reason to want more protection than logs. Legend says that on one of his trips to the Canadian, Indians stole every animal he owned. Completely stranded, he ran up a white flag and invited the chiefs inside the log stockade for a council. Slamming the gates shut and breaking out his guns, he informed the tribe that their leaders would be killed unless his stock was returned and his party given safe conduct to Bent's Fort. The treachery—if that is the word—brought him out unscathed, but left him wary of Comanche temper. From now on he and his traders would be secured by a stout fort eighty feet square with walls nine feet high. The name he gave the structure was appropriate, if unimaginative—Fort Adobe.[10]

The marching columns vanished, sand sifted into their

tracks, and uncertainty gripped the Southwest. The complicated weavings of Mexican politics brought Armijo back into power as governor. Charles and he, smoothing out their earlier differences, became cordial if not altogether trusting acquaintances. Just before his inauguration in November, Armijo banqueted United States traders and recklessly said that in event of war there would be little fighting by New Mexico. Nonetheless, tension kept mounting. On February 9, 1846, Álvarez wrote the State Department that American lives and property in Santa Fe were in danger. Taos was even more explosive. Rumors swept the town that large bodies of enemy troops were concentrated at Bent's Fort and later at Fort Adobe. Gloomily Charles wrote Álvarez on February 24, "I think it more than likely thare will be an outbreak. . . . Thare may be verry shortly orders heare to expell us, or doe worse, we should be prepaired and on our gard."

Rumors, alarms, hair-trigger tempers—but against exactly what? Not one definite fact trickled across the winter wilderness. Locked behind its miles of isolation, the Southwest clung as best it could to the remnants of the life it had created, and in foreboding waited for the changes spring would certainly bring.

CHAPTER XIV

WAR

In the fall of 1845 a young invalid of influential family background came to Bent's Fort and thereby precipitated himself into a series of public and private wars. He was Francis Preston Blair, Jr., son of a member of Andrew Jackson's kitchen cabinet and one-time publisher of Old Hickory's Washington organ, *The Globe*. Francis, Jr., had graduated from Princeton in 1841, breezed through Transylvania Law School, and then had gone to St. Louis to join the law firm of his elder brother Montgomery, who was also mayor of the city. In St. Louis, intense study coupled to a taste for high living broke Francis's health. Mutual friends put him in touch with the Bents. He went to their fort to recuperate, and within weeks the mysterious alchemy that dissolves divergent backgrounds and alien occupations brought to him and George Bent one of those blood-brother friendships which occasionally grow between young men. Frank, as the Bents called him, was twenty-four, George thirty-one.

At the fort Blair mended fast. He was genial, lively, adaptable. During the long December nights lighted by buffalo-tallow candles, his banjo rang incongruous echoes from the adobe walls. With Indians, Mexicans, and French Canadians he gathered in the employees' big dining room for raucous candy pulls over taffy boiled from New Orleans molasses. On Christmas there was an all-night ball. Here half-breed Rosalie, consort of one of the employees, and black Charlotte, wife of Charles's slave Dick, queened it over Mexican and Indian women who could only stare at the whirling convolutions of the backwoods American dances. By March the once-ailing attorney felt well enough to ride with George Bent across the icy mountains to Taos for a visit with his new friend's wife and children.[1]

Needle-pointed granules of snow shrieked on a fierce wind. The temperature dropped below zero and stayed there. But the invalid stood it better than some of the small party. One man riding humped up beside Blair toppled grotesquely from his saddle—frozen dead when he hit the ground.[2] After thawing out for a time in Taos, George and Frank continued to Santa Fe. Behind them they left, through no doing of their own, a town vibrant with hate.

Charles Bent and Padre Antonio Martinez were at complete loggerheads. Early in February, Ute Indians had stolen from outlying ranches eight thousand sheep and four hundred cattle, including every animal Martinez and his brothers owned. At midnight Taos was drummed awake. Each resident was forced to produce at least one saddle animal for the pursuit. At first Charles was amused by the frantic efforts of Martinez and one of the local justices. There were, he wrote Álvarez, two bloody engagements, one at Lee's stillhouse, where "the vallient Justice . . . fell five or six times," and another at Turley's, where "as before Captain Whiskey gained the batle but not the field, as most of them slept on it that night." The first expedition having failed, Martinez wanted to dispatch a second. "Have these people nothing to do but serve the Calf as herders?" Charles snorted.

His grin faded when Martinez accused Americans of complicity in the attacks and sent agents to the reactivated Bent, St. Vrain ranch on Ponil Creek to determine if the Utes had obtained ammunition there. Angrily Charles denied it. To fortify his position, Martinez next set about having his brother elected the district's superior judge. Promptly Charles, Steve Lee, and Carlos Beaubien formed what the priest called an "unlawful plot" to support the opposition candidate. The election—"verry unfair," according to Charles—went to Martinez, and now everything became an issue.

First an American was attacked just outside Taos by nine Apaches, shot, lanced, and beaten until his face "was one-third broughder than when living." One dead gringo—Taos officialdom was indifferent. Charles took it upon himself to storm until soldiers seized half a dozen Apaches to be held as hostages for the surrender of the murderers. Within a week the hostages had been let go. Sourly Charles wrote Álvarez, "It has turned out as I expected." Next, a trivial lawsuit arose involving Charley Autobees, the hoarse-voiced trader who had gone with William to the Arkansas before there was a fort. Both Charles and Martinez jumped into the affray, and the insignificant case ballooned into the Governor's Palace. See Armijo, Charles urged Álvarez, and "doe all you can to give the Priest a hoist."

Martinez lost the case. Furious, he now resumed his old attacks on the land grants, trying to "imbarris the settling of our ranches." To this attack he added a charge that Charles was illegally trading with Ute Indians at Pueblo and Hardscrabble, another ragtag post farther up the Arkansas. A bald-faced lie, Charles retorted: "At neather of theas places have we any person imployed or in any way connected with us." Angry though he was, however, he did have one good laugh out of Martinez's reckless accusations. The priest somehow got the notion that Charles had dug a hole "from my house to the Church in which I had deposited three kegs Powder for the purpus of blowing them up on good friday. . . . He called on the justice his brother to examin my house . . . but his brother, fool as he is, told the Priest . . . it was too ridiculous to believe."[3]

During the growing tensions spring came, soft sunshine on the retreating snow line of the rounded peaks. In the fields new green shoots were appearing as George and Frank Blair returned to the angry town. Several days later St. Vrain arrived with a friend, Jared Folger, who had come to New Mexico for adventure and who rode a grizzled mule named David, to whose indifferent ears he discoursed loudly and profanely on all subjects. Tom Boggs also rode in and took a long look at a child who all at once was no longer a child—Charles Bent's stepdaughter, Rumalda Luna, just turned fourteen. Though by no means as handsome as her mother, Rumalda looked good to lonely Tom. He married her that spring, and thus the unrelated boy whom Charles called nephew became a sort of son-in-law.

Perhaps there was a post-wedding fandango on Saturday, May 2, or it may have been only a gentlemen's gathering that caused Frank Blair to wake up Sunday morning feeling in need of the hair of the dog that had bitten him. One eye-opener called for another. Soon he was so tanked that George had to help him navigate toward home. As they crossed the plaza, they passed a crowd of loafers, some thirty or so, congregated about Steve Lee's store. Two of Padre Martinez's brothers were nearby, one of them the newly elected justice. So, too, was Justice Martinez's subordinate, José Valdez. But no gringos were about. Charles had ridden a short distance from town on business; St. Vrain and Folger were at Ceran's home, sleeping through the siesta hour.

Blair, in his cups, may have made derogatory remarks or gestures. But Charles always believed that Pasqual Martinez lighted the flame; certainly various Martinez employees were in the gang. With sudden shouts of "Kill! Kill!" the mob surrounded the pair. Justice Valdez glanced uneasily at Justice Martinez, who seemed oblivious of the uproar at his elbow. Uneasily Valdez decided that he too should remain oblivious. Supported by this silent connivance on the part of the officials, the mob went joyfully to work.

Blair was beaten severely, thrown into a mud puddle. George gave a better account of himself, but he too was sorely pummeled before friends arrived and somehow got both bruised and bleeding men behind the adobe walls of George's home.

A messenger raced for Charles. Most of the mob, he was convinced after learning the identity of some of the participants, had also been involved in the 1843 attack on Beaubien. When he sought out Martinez and demanded arrest of the miscreants, the justice spread his hands in a Spanish shrug. It was Sunday. The necessary documents could not be prepared.

Unchallenged, the mob roamed through the town, drunk now and singing triumphantly. At evening they gathered outside George's home, waving torches and shouting threats through the window. Short-circuiting the justice's unco-operative office, Charles prevailed on the captain of the local garrison to station soldiers around his brother's home. Then in a white heat, while a mounted courier waited, he penned an agitated message to Álvarez, demanding that the governor intervene "for his honor as supream authority here is at stake."

Armijo replied with an order to the prefect of the district that the attackers be tried. An indeterminate number of suspects were jailed. Hopefully Charles wrote Álvarez, "Thare is no doubt but the Priest and brothers ware the prime movers in this affair, as yet we have not been able to fix it on them clearly, but . . . may if the delinquents are punished sevearly." Apparently, however, they were not punished, for on June 1 Charles wrote Álvarez, "The prisoners . . . have presented themselves to Justice Martinese, he instead of having them . . . put in jail told them he had nothing to doe with them."

Those words are the last that is heard of the brawl. A few days later Charles, Ceran St. Vrain, and Jared Folger left for the United States and a far bigger conflict. In view of coming events, the ruffled tempers of Taos would soon seem petty enough. Yet the memories of that spring would be very much alive when Charles Bent again visited his home the following January.

Shortly before leaving New Mexico, Charles called on Armijo in Santa Fe. Yes, the governor said, there were still rumors of war, but no confirmation from Mexico City. He added, poker-faced, that he was expecting the arrival, in the fall, of General Urrea, leading from three to five thousand troops. Perhaps the remark was pure bluff. The New Mexican governor was a born gambler, and he knew that Bent would repeat to military authorities in the United States whatever he learned. Ever since the defeat of the Texas-Santa Fe expedition in 1841, Armijo had counted on the plains as a powerful ally. To men broiling in the wastelands, rumor of an enemy army waiting to crush them might be enough in itself to demoralize any attack, secure another triumph. But Charles Bent knew his man. If such thoughts passed through Armijo's mind, the American trader read them accurately.

War or no war, plans to settle the Beaubien and St. Vrain-Vigil grants went rapidly ahead that spring. After several fumbling starts, the company was determined to inaugurate cattle ranching on a large scale. While Charles was in Santa Fe, George and Ceran crossed the mountains and on the Little Cimarron (a different stream entirely from the Cimarron River) selected a site for one ranch. There was another site on Vermejo Creek, and in Taos additional colonists were being recruited to augment the settlement on Ponil Creek. These three ranches lay within the Beaubien boundaries. A fourth project was to occupy a spot on St. Vrain-Vigil land, near the northern base of Raton Pass, just above the upper end of Purgatory Canyon.

On June 2 Charles took the Taos settlers to Ponil Creek. Then, seeking a shorter road from the ranches to the fort, he swung east around Raton Peak to Trinchera Creek. (Raton Pass circled the western flank of the peak, now called Fisher Peak after a Bent trader.) Meanwhile he dispatched Charley Towne and Pedro Luna along another route to see what sort of roadway they could find. So far Charles was in no hurry.

On June 11 he reached the fort. There was, he wrote Álvarez, no news from the United States. Nonetheless, something suddenly galvanized him into action. On the morning of the twelfth he, St. Vrain, Folger, and about twenty others headed east, without wagons, at as fast a pace as their horses could hold. The normal caravan time of from five to six weeks Charles intended to cut to less than two. In order to manage it his party would have to travel upward of forty miles a day, living off the land as they went.

Not far from the fort they encountered Mexican buffalo hunters, who told of seeing several caravans pushing unusually fast up the Cimarron. Was it true war had come? Charles and Ceran did not know, but four days out of the fort, at the Crossing of the Arkansas, they learned. Hostilities had been declared.

Their informant was George Thomas Howard, on a special mission for Secretary of War Marcy. Howard was an old hand at intrigue. One of the leaders of the ill-fated Texas-Santa Fe expedition, he had signed up George Kendall in New Orleans and had been imprisoned with the *Picayune* editor in San Miguel. Now he was New Mexico-bound again. On May 13, the day Congress formally declared that a state of war existed, Marcy dispatched Howard from Washington as a special emissary to race down the Santa Fe Trail, alerting American caravans. This done, Howard was to continue into Santa Fe, secretly apprise American citizens of the declaration before Armijo learned of it, and then try to create a "favorable impression" among friendly New Mexicans. He had lost time, however, in detouring via Fort Leavenworth for dragoons to escort him through the Indian country. Meanwhile various merchants, anticipating the truth, had bought up extra mules and were pounding down the trail at high speed to clear the customs before the gates were closed. Howard broke down his stock trying to overhaul them, and when he learned from Charles how far ahead the caravans were, he abandoned the chase. He did, however, send two men ahead to contact the Americans in Santa Fe. Perhaps remembering Armijo's jail, Howard himself followed with the exhausted stock at a more leisurely pace. He would wait for the couriers at the Bent, St. Vrain ranch on Ponil Creek and there learn what his messengers accomplished. As events turned out, it was nil; his two agents barely escaped Santa Fe alive and were largely responsible for rumors that New Mexico was preparing a formidable resistance.

Near Pawnee Fork, Charles and his party next encountered Tom Fitzpatrick leading Captain Moore's two companies of dragoons on a more militant pursuit of the same caravans, particularly the twenty-five wagons belonging to the firm of Armijo and Speyer. Two of those vehicles were loaded with

munitions, and Moore would not call off the chase even though
Charles assured him it was useless. Rigidly following orders,
the captain continued as far as the Crossing before giving up.
Grumpily Moore then returned to Pawnee Fork, gathering
later caravans, which he herded to an army-designated rendezvous at Bent's Fort.

The rest of Charles's and Ceran's trip was made through a
barrage of questions. One hundred and thirty merchant wagons
were on the trail,[4] and every last proprietor and teamster
wanted a blueprint for the future. Would Armijo fight? Where
would the battle be? Were the customs closed? Why had the
blankety-blank army shut the Cimarron trail? How long . . .
what . . . when . . . Charles shook them off, spurred faster.
On the twenty-second, however, he did pause long enough to
pay his respects to Sam Magoffin and Sam's bride of six
months, Susan Shelby, eighteen years old and obviously pregnant—quite probably the first white woman in such condition
to risk the trail. Husband Sam was making things as comfortable as he could; the couple traveled in a carriage and each
night bivouacked in a tent equipped with carpet, furniture,
and mosquito netting. When Susan learned Charles was east-
bound, she asked if he would take back a letter to mail to her
papa. Affably Charles waited while she hurried into the tent
and composed it.

Did a courier reach him about this time with orders to
report to Stephen Watts Kearny, newly created commander
of the Army of the West? Or did he act on his own initiative?
There is no telling, but at any rate Charles, Ceran, and Folger
left their party at Westport and swung north to the incredible
pandemonium of Fort Leavenworth.

Kearny had performed prodigies. Formal orders had not
reached him until May 26. Fortunately both he and the governor of Missouri had foreseen inevitability. Their machinery
was ready, Kearny's to organize his forces, the governor's to
issue a call for volunteers. Fortunately, too, Kearny knew the
West and had, in his plains-trained First Dragoons and in
officers like Philip St. George Cooke, a solid core around which
to build his army. Otherwise he would have had nightmares.
He was expected to lead, without adequate preparation time,
an ill-equipped force of raw recruits across nearly eight hun-

dred miles of man-killing wastelands. An enemy army, properly generaled, might easily cut in behind him, snap his laboring supply columns, and use the desert to complete the defeat. He could draw some small comfort, however, from his previous summer's talk with Charles Bent at the fort. New Mexico would probably be neither well generaled nor well garrisoned.

Swiftly, while newspaper editorials rang out visions of glory and the assembling recruits boasted of their fighting prowess, the colonel turned to the more prosaic problem of commandeering every supply wagon and teamster he could lay hands on. He would never get enough vehicles, and the green teamsters would prove hopelessly inefficient, but nonetheless he had one hundred wagons and eight hundred beef cattle on the trail by the time Charles Bent's party reached the Missouri frontier. As the supply column's rendezvous with the army, Kearny selected Bent's Fort. News of this unauthorized appropriation Charles and Ceran picked up along the trail. Obviously there was nothing to do but acquiesce.

They reached Fort Leavenworth as the first detachments of undisciplined, overconfident recruits were pouring out for the start of the grueling march. Charles told Kearny what Armijo had said about General Urrea's reinforcing army of three to five thousand men. This was not good news; Kearny had mustered no more than seventeen hundred troops. But, Charles pointed out, Urrea might be sheer bluff. If he did materialize, autocratic Armijo would resent Urrea's interference and the invaders could perhaps play one enemy general off against the other—a bit of wishfulness that Kearny duly relayed to his superiors in Washington. But the best bet, Charles said, was to beat the suppositious Urrea to Santa Fe. Until and unless he arrived, there could be no effective resistance.

Promptly Kearny rushed word to his officers to push the grumbling troops even faster. As he prepared to follow, he asked Charles not to delay in St. Louis but return west as soon as possible. There would be work for him in New Mexico.[5]

In Santa Fe the persistent rumors of war were confirmed on June 26 by the arrival of the first traders. In the plaza uproarious mobs cheered inflammatory speeches urging the plunder and murder of all American residents. To Armijo's credit, so

Álvarez grudgingly admitted to Secretary of State Buchanan, government troops quickly stamped out the embryo pogrom. Nonetheless, demonstrations in Taos were alarming enough that George Bent and Tom Boggs took to the security of the fort their own families, plus Kit's Josefa and Ignacia Bent with her three children, the youngest, Estafina, a child of two or three. John Hatcher accompanying them, they arrived on July 3, just in time for the post's traditional Independence Day celebration. As the men sipped juleps in the big apartment, they predicted that New Mexico would offer no serious opposition if official representatives traveled ahead of the troops with assurances that persons and property would be respected. At once the advice was relayed eastward. Soon afterward, the alarm simmering down, Tom took Josefa, Ignacia, and his own wife back to Taos.

As nearly as he could, William kept business on its routine keel, knowing disruption would come soon enough. Bent traders, like others from Taos and Pueblo, journeyed north to the Oregon Trail, where the increasing flow of emigrants offered markets for provisions and fresh draft animals. Lilburn Boggs may have been one of the purchasers; he and three of his sons, including young Bill and his new bride, moved to California that summer, and on the golden coast the ex-governor would at last find the financial success that so long had eluded him.

Inside the adobe walls the daily dramas went on. From the beginning the firm had made a practice of ransoming captives from the Indians. This summer, down in Durango, Old Mexico, a husband somehow learned that his Comanche-stolen wife was safe in the gringos' faraway post. Eagerly he journeyed the fifteen hundred miles—only to find her living with one of the fort's employees. Rejected, he turned leadenly back. What were rumors of armies to him? And on another occasion a caravan arrived with a terrified white woman named Dale. Pawnees had killed her husband; her seven-year-old son Paul had vanished. Carried away captive by the Indians, the woman had managed to crawl out of camp one night, steal a pony, and ride it without saddle or bridle back to the trail, where a fort-bound train picked her up. William gave her a job in the kitchen, assuring her that if her son was alive his traders would eventually pick up word of it. In time more than word came.

Blackfoot John Smith and some trappers had chanced to hear
the racket of the Pawnee attack and had rescued the boy.
Beaten back by the Indians, they had taken little Paul with
them to Independence, then had brought him back to the fort,
thinking there might be word of the mother there. They arrived hot and thirsty, and Blackfoot John led Paul into the
kitchen for a glass of milk. An unfamiliar white woman bent
over the adobe hearth glanced up from her cooking and
startled the old trader half out of his wits with her sudden
scream.[6]

Toward the last week of July the first troops began to arrive, Fitzpatrick with Moore's dragoons and two companies
commanded by Dave Waldo, whom William had been seeing
off and on along the trail ever since the dangerous days of the
Indian-beleaguered 1829 caravan. The dusty troops strutted
into the placita, staring at the trim ankles of the Indian women
and clamoring to buy the fort's rum at twenty-four dollars a
gallon, tobacco at four dollars a pound. Two drunken dragoons
had a rousing fight. Afterward one of them went swimming
in the river, lay naked under a tree, had a stroke, and died.
His company wrapped him in a blanket, laid him on a bier
made of willows, saddled his horse, inverted his boots in the
stirrups, and marched solemnly to the shallow grave, where
twenty-four muskets fired a parting salute. The next morning
five more roisterers were court-martialed for insubordination,
and each was sentenced to pack forty pounds of sand back
and forth every alternate two hours during the day. War had
come to the Arkansas.

During the closing days of July it arrived in an overwhelming rush. George and William were mercilessly beset. There
were the commanding officers to entertain—Kearny himself;
huge-bodied Alexander Doniphan, whom the volunteers had
elected their colonel; and Major William Gilpin, who had spent
the summer of 1844 at the fort. Lesser officers importuned for
advice on camp sites and grazing grounds; the quartermaster
corps cried for storage space and repair facilities. With no one's
by-your-leave the troops poured through the iron-studded
gates, arrogant, curious, toughened by a hellish march through
appalling heat, rattlesnakes, mosquitoes, thirst, and foot-blis-
tering sand. They felt they had earned the right to purchase

additions to their short-ration diets and were enormously indignant when Holt, the fort's storekeeper, could not supply
demands he had never been prepared for.

Swarms of Indians stood by and gawped. It had been a poor
hunting season and they were hanging around the fort for
handouts, meanwhile exclaiming over and over that they had
never guessed so many people were in the white man's tribe.
They had reason to be amazed. Tents stretched for miles along
the river. The herders of more than twenty thousand horses,
mules, and oxen quarreled over patches of grass. At the mouth
of Purgatory Creek wolves set off a stampede of several hundred mules that turned into a frenzy as the running beasts
lashed themselves with their own dragging picket pins.

Added to it all were the hundreds of traders forced to travel
with the army. Worried about markets, exasperated by delay,
many of them tried to presume on prior acquaintanceship
for favors the Bents could not render. To white-faced Sam
Magoffin, however, William lent a sympathetic ear. Susan was
ill. The heat, the mosquitoes, the confusion were distressing
her terribly. Would it be possible for her to rest in the fort?
Immediately William ordered one of the upper-story rooms
prepared. Since it contained neither chairs nor table and only
a mattress on the earthen floor, Susan's own furniture and cot
were carried up the outside staircase.

While waiting, Susan went into the big apartment. Other
ladies were present, among them the Mexican wives of George
Bent and Eugene Leitensdorfer. Some, she suspected, were not
wives at all. Shyly she sat beside them on one of the cushions
that lined two of the walls. A bucket of water stood on the
table; whenever anyone drank from the common dipper, any
water remaining in it was tossed onto the floor. Susan was even
more revolted when one Mexican señorita, ignoring the presence of Eugene Leitensdorfer and the married women, calmly
combed her long black hair and put on so much grease it
dripped.

Later, in her own room on her nineteenth birthday, July 30,
while the din of blacksmith hammers, braying mules, crying
children, and quarreling soldiers assailed her ears, she felt
"strange sensations in my head, back and hips." Sam rushed
for a French doctor he had earlier located in one of the trader's

caravans. It was no use. On the night of July 31 she suffered a miscarriage, and William had to show Sam a decent place to bury the dead child. At almost the same time a squaw in a lower room gave birth to a healthy papoose, rose within half an hour, and carried it to the river to bathe.

There were other sick to be housed, one of them Lieutenant Abert, babbling with fever. Twenty-one more were down with dysentery and scurvy; soon six of them would die. Other events were more in accord with what the books said war should be like. Three Mexicans arrived, looking altogether too innocent. George and William pounced on them. In their pockets the trio carried letters addressed to Kearny, but the contents were blank—a clumsy dodge to get them past the pickets to spy. Let them take a good look, William decided. He led them past the fluttering guidons, the cannon, the endless wagons and tents, then turned them over to the commander.

July 31, the day of Susan's tragedy, was a busy day for Kearny. First he issued a proclamation to the citizens of New Mexico, saying he came "with the object of seeking union and to ameliorate the condition of the inhabitants," and promising to respect the rights of all who offered no resistance. Giving copies to the spies the Bents had picked up, he sent the trio home to tell their superiors what they had seen. Next he directed Eugene Leitensdorfer and Lieutenant De Courcy to prepare to ride ahead under a truce flag to Taos with twenty dragoons, there to distribute more copies of the proclamation, sound out the populace, and make overtures to the Pueblo Indians.

Almost simultaneously James Magoffin, Susan's brother-in-law, arrived with secret orders from Polk. Magoffin was to attempt subverting Armijo and his officers, and now he wanted an escort of twelve dragoons to accompany him to Santa Fe, again under a flag of truce. Kearny sent an express down-river to fetch Captain Philip St. George Cooke, who arrived grumbling furiously that once again an assignment was depriving him of a chance to win glory on the fields of battle. To Cooke the commander gave a letter dated August 1 and addressed to Armijo, stating that the United States was annexing that part of New Mexico lying east of the Rio Grande. Kearny justified the seizure on the strength of Texas's old claim and warned Armijo not to try to resist the formidable army that was approaching.

William Bent was then summoned to headquarters. The swiftly assembling army, Kearny told him, would start its invasion on August 2. Though all responsible traders predicted scant resistance, there were too many contrary rumors for comfort. It was quite possible that Armijo had been reinforced, and an ambush in the Raton Mountains or beyond might be fatal. Could William form a spy company—today they would be called scouts—reconnoiter the passes, and pick up all the information possible?

In return for the proposed service Kearny named a fee that struck William as an insult. The army had already ruined the company's business, stripped its stores, glutted its repair shops and storage sheds. Dead-tired and on edge from the piling harassments, William snapped that if Kearny wanted still more help he could damn well pay what it was worth. And out he went.

No other available man of dependable intelligence knew the route and the Mexicans so well. Kearny sent a peacemaker after the bristly little trader, and the next day a compromise was reached. In his scouting party of half a dozen or so skilled mountaineers William included his brother George, Frank Blair, and Estes, a Taos tavernkeeper who had often acted as Charles's messenger between that town and the fort. Glumly Marcellin St. Vrain heard that he was to remain in charge of the fort, an assignment whose monotony he would relieve by hunting antelope with Joe Walker, lately arrived from the coast with a drove of California stock to sell the would-be invaders of California.[7]

Preparations delayed the advance parties—Captain Cooke's and Magoffin's, Lieutenant De Courcy's and Leitensdorfer's, and William Bent's. The vanguard of the army marched first, guidons popping in a gale of blowing sand. The fort's flag rose in salute. Perched on the parapets, a solid row of red, brown, and white watchers followed the long columns out of sight.

In the big apartment the advance emissaries toasted each other's success from an ice-tinkling pitcher "covered with the dew of promise." Then James Magoffin climbed into a mule-

drawn carriage beside a companion named José Gonzales.
Cooke's twelve dragoons mounted, and one man picked up the
lead rope of their pack mules. Promptly one animal bucked
off its load of pots and pans, had to be run down and lassoed.
Engulfed by the marching columns, the advance parties failed
to advance. Magoffin used the time philosophically. He had
plenty of claret in the carriage, but no brandy. Each time they
passed a trader's camp he sent his servant Juan out with an
empty bottle, begging. Juan had no luck, and Magoffin
mourned that the haul up Timpas promised to be dry indeed.

It was horribly dry. The wind never died; the thermometer
rose to 120 degrees. The bandannas the marching troops tied
over their noses and mouths brought scant relief from the sifting, powder-fine dust. At the potholes of alkaline water, teamsters leaped from their seats and ran like madmen to get ahead
of the livestock, which would plunge uncontrollably into the
puddles, first muddying the water and then invariably urinat-
ing into it. Captain Angney managed to choke down the liquid
by mixing in it molasses he had bought at the fort for a dollar
a pint. Others merely "shut both eyes and held their breath."
The alkali physicked them violently. But not Magoffin. With
Cooke and a basket of claret he nooned under the shade of a
piñon tree.

At the head of the Timpas, where there was a refreshing but
not army-sized pool known as the Hole in the Rock, the advance parties at last shook themselves loose from the army,
crossed swiftly into the blessed coolness of the upper Purgatory, and then toiled over the pass. Here their ways forked.
While Magoffin's party hurried south toward Santa Fe, Leitensdorfer and De Courcy swung right toward Taos. The latter
group had its own pack-mule troubles. Their beast collapsed.
De Courcy ordered each dragoon to strip off his shirt and
drawers, tie a share of flour in the sleeves and legs, and pack
it behind his saddle, along with distributed portions of bacon
and other supplies.

William's scouts sent back word the pass was clear. Of
enemy, he meant. But natural obstacles caused almost as much
delay among the supply wagons as Mexican soldiery might
have. Susan Magoffin, somewhat recuperated and crossing a
week later, left a glimpse of the ordeal in her diary: "Worse

and worse the road! . . . It takes a dozen men to steady a wagon with all its wheels locked—and for one who is some distance off to hear the crash it makes over the stones is truly alarming. Till I rode ahead and understood the business, I supposed that every wagon was falling over a precipice." (A month later one of Marcellin St. Vrain's wagons did fall and smash fifty-seven hundred pounds of freight against a pine tree.) The day-long toil, Susan added plaintively, advanced them "the great travel of *six* or *eight* hundred yards."

William's scouts seized five Mexicans who had been sent out aboard diminutive donkeys to reconnoiter the American forces. More Mexicans were captured who carried a proclamation from the Taos prefect ordering the drafting of all males between fifteen and fifty. Lieutenant De Courcy returned breathless from his mission with word that five thousand Indians were being readied to harass the columns. Two days later William and Estes brought Kearny four enemy soldiers who said an advance force of six hundred Mexicans was preparing to slow down the invaders at Las Vegas. But William said, darned if he could find any sign of gathering opposition.

An ambiguous message arrived from Armijo. "If you take the country," the governor wrote Kearny, "it will be because you are strongest in battle. I suggest to you to stop at the Sapillo, and I will march to the Vegas. We will meet and negotiate on the plains between them." Exactly what did that mean—defiance or conciliation? And why was there no word yet from Cooke and Magoffin? Sending out flankers, the army marched on into Las Vegas. No one appeared, either to fight or to negotiate. Kearny stationed guards to protect the villagers' corn from the army's horses and went to bed, still a colonel. At midnight three officers racing up from Bent's Fort awoke him to present him his commission as brigadier general.

The next morning he ordered the villagers summoned and at eight o'clock, accompanied by his staff and the local alcalde, climbed a rickety ladder onto a rooftop. There he made a speech absolving the people from allegiance to Mexico and Armijo, denied rumors that their religion would be disturbed or their women branded "on the cheek as you do your mules on the hip," and guaranteed that "not a pepper, nor an onion will be taken by my troops without pay." To this he added

an impossible promise that the Americans would protect the
territory from Apaches and Navajos. "But listen!" he warned.
"He who promises to be quiet, and is found in arms against
me, I will hang!"

On they marched. In each little settlement crowds of bewildered people came to see them, wistfully offering for sale
pats of cheese, goat's milk, eggs, chickens, vegetables. The soldiers leered at the women. A shocking sight, Susan thought
when she passed through: the women "slapping around with
arms and necks bare, perhaps their bosoms exposed (and they
are none of the prettiest or whitest). If they are about to cross
the little creek . . . they pull their dresses, which in the first
place but little more than cover their calves—up above their
knees! . . . Children running about perfectly naked . . . I am
constrained to keep my veil drawn closely over my face at all
times to protect my blushes." . . . And still William Bent
could find no trace of opposition, though rumor grew that
surely Armijo would defend the narrow jaws of Apache
Canyon.

The alarms that troubled Kearny were nothing to those that
racked Santa Fe. Following the same sort of instructions that
Armijo had issued prior to the Texas-Santa Fe invasion, the
priests unleashed dire warnings of pillage, desecration of
churches, debauchery of women. On August 9 the Mexican
spies who had been captured at the fort returned with reports
grown mightily during their journey—five thousand troops
were on the way! People on the outlying ranchos piled goods
into their carretas and fled into Santa Fe; simultaneously,
many residents of the city scampered with their possessions
into the hills.

On August 12 Cooke and James Magoffin arrived under
their flag of truce. After confusion and embarrassment, they
were formally received, Cooke being housed in the palace itself. Magoffin vanished, probably to talk to Colonel Diego
Archuleta, second in command of the army and a more militant, more capable officer than General Manuel Armijo.

Exactly what happened will never be known. This conjecture, however, is probable. When Magoffin left Washington,
the government had apparently been doubtful that Kearny

could reach California, and Magoffin seems to have gained the impression that in return for a bloodless victory Polk was willing to take, temporarily at least, only the eastern half of New Mexico, which Texas had long claimed. In his letter of August 1 from Bent's Fort to Armijo, Kearny had claimed no more. Magoffin, therefore, acting either on his own responsibility or under Polk's secret orders, apparently suggested to Archuleta that Mexico could retain part of the territory. The colonel need only abandon Armijo and then, with the silent consent of the United States, set himself up as governor of the land west of the Rio Grande.

What neither conspirator realized was that Kearny's orders allowed him to continue to California at his own discretion. By the time the army reached Bent's Fort the commander had decided to risk the venture, provided New Mexico proved as easy as the Bents predicted. Even his guide, Fitzpatrick, was aware of the plan and hinted as much in a letter written to Andrew Sublette on July 31. This was the day before Kearny's letter claiming only eastern New Mexico. But evidently Magoffin was not informed of the California hope, perhaps because he did not fully reveal his own orders. Now, in Santa Fe, the emissary was offering Diego Archuleta territory that Kearny's enlarged plans could no longer allow.

Ambitious Archuleta accepted. The fact that he was double-crossing his own superior would in no wise lessen his fury when Kearny, in what looked like another double cross, annexed all New Mexico. Kearny, however, would escape the results of that fury. The Bents would not.

Thus the ground was completely cut from under Armijo's feet. By now he knew there would be no help either from Mexico or from the Pueblo Indians, the latter of whom had hated him ever since the Snively disaster of '43. The plains he had counted on had betrayed him, and his best officer was now saying that a fight was hopeless. Late at night the governor went with Magoffin to Cooke's quarters for a secret conference. Did Armijo use the last of his nuisance value to wring the assuagement of hard cash from his conquerors? No one knows. For the benefit of history he ordered his troops to build token defenses in Apache Canyon. Then he fled south amid

rumors of his assassination. On August 18, Kearny's Army of
the West entered Santa Fe without having fired a shot.[8]

The day before this, on the seventeenth, Charles Bent had
reached the fort after another swift crossing of the plains. (St.
Vrain and Folger had stayed behind to bring in the annual
fall caravan.) At the Arkansas post he learned what he could
of the army's progress and made preparations to follow. It is
quite possible that on the way he heard of the occupation of
Santa Fe and shifted his route to Taos to do a few jobs there
for the conquerors and to pick up Ignacia. She would want to
be with her husband during the stirring days that were to
follow.[9]

In Santa Fe he found Kearny wrestling with the problem of
a civil government for the conquered territory. In the palace
Alexander Doniphan, erstwhile frontier lawyer, was sweating
over a constitution and code of laws. Among his helpers was
Frank Blair. David Waldo, the only real Spanish scholar in
the occupation forces, was making translations. Immediately
Charles was pressed into service as a chief adviser.

While the government-makers worked, Kearny took half his
forces on a hurried swing through the southern towns, placating the priests, attending church services, calling on Indian
delegations. All seemed well, and when he returned to Santa
Fe he learned that Sterling Price was marching down the Cimarron cutoff with reinforcements. Convinced that these troops,
plus the volunteers he would leave behind, could easily awe
the Indians and check what little trouble might develop,
Kearny determined to press on to California with his dragoons.
Before he left he appointed, on September 22, the list of civil
officials who were to try to govern a foreign conquered territory after scarcely a month of military occupation.

Charles Bent was named governor, and in the rest of the
slate Bent's hand is clearly evident. His territorial secretary
and lieutenant governor was Donaciano Vigil, only major hold-
over from the Armijo regime—and a relative of Charles's wife.
Eugene Leitensdorfer became auditor. Twenty-five-year-old
Frank Blair, probably the only civilian available with legal
training, was named attorney general. One of the three judges
of the superior court was Carlos Beaubien; another was Joab

Houghton, who had reached New Mexico only two or three years before and, as Charles's letters to Álvarez show, had quickly become a close friend of the new governor. The list reads almost like pure nepotism, but Charles well knew that the "conquest" was paper-thin. The families of some of the vanquished had been in New Mexico before the Americans had seen Plymouth Rock, and the incoming governor did not expect that kind of allegiance to wash off in a month. To the confusion that would inevitably attend replacing century-old governmental forms Charles could not afford to add open resistance. In keeping the way smooth he had to depend on men whose qualities he knew, whose integrity he could trust. Rule out friendship as a guide in choosing, and what was left?

It was too much to expect that the appointments would be greeted by the conquered with complete approbation (though New Mexico histories, Yankee-written, generally state that they were). Padre Martinez's long fulminations had their effect. One soldier wrote home that many dissatisfied New Mexicans were repeating the priest's old charge that Charles Bent had for years been the instigator of bloody Indian attacks on the northern settlements. Another lieutenant, though not questioning Bent's abilities, mocked the other appointees: "All the judges of the superior court together do not possess the legal knowledge of a justice of the peace in St. Louis." And in private Diego Archuleta nursed a red rage over what he considered his betrayal.

The problems of the conquered territory might well have staggered more politically experienced men than the traders and merchants who were assigned to cope with them. On September 22, the day Kearny announced his appointment, Charles sent an urgent letter to Secretary of State James Buchanan, outlining some of New Mexico's immediate needs. The new government and its courts had no lawbooks of any description, no stationery, none of the necessary forms or blank books for the transaction of public business. Translators must be appointed. A mail service operating at least once a month should be established with the States. Education, "criminally neglected" under the Mexicans, must be provided —at least primary schools supervised by bilingual teachers, for "a rude and ignorant people are about to become citizens of

the U.S." Payment had to be provided for the interim officials
who had administered local affairs between Kearny's occupation and the institution of civil government. Indeed, the payment of all government officials must for a long time be the
responsibility of the conquerors because the territory was "im-
poverished and undeveloped." As Charles considered the net-
tlesome problem of taxation, he undoubtedly recalled that in
1837 Governor Albino Perez had lost his head when he had
tried to alter the inefficient but habitual customs. Accordingly
the new governor warned Buchanan that any precipitate attempt to raise revenue by direct taxes would be "imprudent."

The only hope he saw of making New Mexico even partially
self-sufficient was the development of mining. To this end he
urged laws to stimulate that industry and the appointment of
competent persons to explore for mineral resources—a behest
which, if it had been heeded, might have started the gold rush
to the Rockies a decade earlier than it finally came. Another
necessary commission, he said, was a board of surveyors to end
the chaos about land titles and boundaries. And always there
was the pressing danger from Indians, both the civilized Pueblos, by law now citizens of the United States, and the wild
tribes who for two centuries had raided the territory almost
unchecked. A strong military force would have to be maintained in New Mexico during the next several years. In addition there would have to be an Indian agent and three subagents to handle the problems of the restive tribes.

In hopes of gaining sponsorship in Congress for these measures, Charles repeated them two days later in another letter
to Missouri Senator Thomas Hart Benton. To Benton he suggested appointees: for surveyor general, Charles's close friend,
Meriwether Lewis Clark; as land commissioners, Ceran St.
Vrain, David Waldo, Manuel Álvarez; as subagents to the Indians, Jared Folger, Tom Boggs, John Hatcher; as head Indian
agent, George Bent—a list even more loaded with familiars and
relatives than the officials already in office. Whether or not
Washington was aware of the loading cannot be said. In any
event, the suggestions were not followed, and before any of the
offices was belatedly filled, it no longer mattered to Charles
Bent.

Pressing though the governmental shambles loomed, it was

not allowed to mar the gaiety of the farewell ball which the new officials gave in the Governor's Palace on the night of September 24 for Kearny and his officers, who the next day would march for California. Though all prominent New Mexicans in Santa Fe were invited to the celebration, the death of a leading citizen who was related to half the city is said to have kept many of them away. Gertrudes Barcelo, notoriously known as La Tules, was there, however—Armijo's one-time mistress and operator of a tony gambling sala and bordello located near the palace on the road leading to Tusuque. Some Americans thought La Tules was French and appreciated the way her prewar adoption of American styles had boosted sales of fancy silks, satins, and calicoes. But she was not French. Like her hostess, Ignacia Bent, La Tules was a native of Taos.

What Ignacia thought of the woman's presence is not known. But little Susan Magoffin, decked out in "a scarlet Canton crepe shawl to be in trim with the Natives," was shocked. Why, La Tules was an old woman, the teen-age bride sputtered incorrectly to her diary, "with false hair and teeth," flaunting "that shrewd and fascinating manner necessary to allure the wayward, inexperienced youth to the hall of final ruin." Expediency, however, had reasons that Yankee primness knew not of. The paymaster's wagons had not yet arrived with specie, and New Mexican merchants were reluctant to accept unfamiliar paper vouchers. Nor could supplies be arbitrarily requisitioned from people who were now legal citizens of the United States. In order to raise money for equipping his company, David Mitchell, one-time American Fur Company trader and more lately Commissioner of Indian Affairs, had borrowed one thousand dollars from La Tules. Her price was 2 per cent a month—plus being squired to the ball, strikingly beautiful in her own red hair.[10] Charles, it is to be supposed, explained matters to his wife.

Despite, or perhaps even because of, La Tules, the party was wonderfully gay. The orchestra played with verve; the candlelit palace shimmered with color. Kearny's officers flocked around Susan. Momentarily she forgot the baby buried back at Bent's Fort, and the lilting of her heart and her little feet thawed her reserve to the point where she could even call the native *cuna*, or cradle, a beautiful dance. During it the part-

ners stood face to face, arms circling each other's waist to form
the sides of the cradle—not a bottomless cradle either, one observer commented dryly, "for both parties lean well back as
they swing."

William Bent was not at the ball, though he was an honorary "colonel" now by virtue of his having scouted the way
to Santa Fe. The embellishments of society made him uncomfortable. Even before his brother's inauguration he turned
back toward the Arkansas, worried about the fort and about
the new ranches. The approach of the army in August had
sent the colonists fleeing from Ponil Creek. Government teamsters had then appropriated the ranch, together with the more
primitive farms on the Little Cimarron and Vermejo Creek,
and were using the places as stopovers and grazing grounds
for their draft animals.

Except for sending in herders to keep an eye on company
stock, nothing could be done now. William decided to con-
centrate on the proposed farm on upper Purgatory Creek.
Hatcher was directed to bring in from Taos wagons, oxen, and
fifteen or sixteen Mexican laborers. For several weeks the ex-
trader worked at a two-mile-long irrigation ditch. The site was
lovely, the gently curving stream bordered by willows laced
with grapevines, the rank grass cool under cottonwoods and
locust trees. But Hatcher had seen plenty of lovely meadows
without digging. He was relieved when George Bent appeared
late in the fall and, though the ditch was still incomplete,
took him mule-trading among Utes and Apaches and then,
one account adds, on down into Old Mexico on the heels of
the army. William, meanwhile, sent company stock up to the
ranch to winter. It wasn't long before government teamsters
moved in on them too.

The climax of the mess, however, was at the fort. Kearny
had outmarched bureaucracy. The hidebound Quartermaster
Department, ignorant of the shorter Cimarron trail, was still
sending its wagons to Bent's Fort, and by the time the plains-
hammered farm boys who drove the vehicles reached the shelter they'd had enough. This was where they had been hired
to go, and this, by God, was as far as they would go. While
the troops in Santa Fe grumbled about short rations and in-

adequate clothing, the stranded supplies piled higher and higher. Outraged soldiers were sent to ferry the stuff on over Raton Pass. During the latter part of October they were moving it out at the rate of thirty wagonfuls per week, but on the last day of the month 140 tons of miscellany still littered the fort's placita and corral.

The Indians, too, were beginning to wonder if life had forever changed. Hunting had been poor during the past two years, and the company could not keep on endlessly feeding the improvident southern Cheyennes. William had already talked to the chiefs, to Yellow Wolf especially, about farming. It was no revolutionary idea. Tribal lore still told of the prehorse days when the Cheyennes had raised corn and squash along the Missouri River and in the Black Hills. To be sure, when the company itself had tried to farm the bottomlands along the river, the capricious Indians had destroyed the crops, but now the idea took hold with Yellow Wolf.

An intelligent Indian, he saw the problems involved. The young men would not give up their hunting and horse-stealing forays, and during their absence the immobile farms—tended inevitably by children, old men, and squaws—would be defenseless against enemy raids. The solution Yellow Wolf proposed was for the government to build strongholds, modeled after Bent's Fort, into which the villagers could flee in case of attack.

The government, William suspected, had waged too many wars against Indians to take kindly to a suggestion of fortifying potential enemies. To the hungry tribe, however, Yellow Wolf's idea had the charm of novelty. All winter long the unagricultural Cheyennes talked agriculture. It is barely possible that prompt action then by the Indian Department would have started the tribes of the plains toward self-sufficiency—an inescapable problem which the government failed to solve throughout the latter part of the century. But there was no action, and the Cheyennes had no more consecutiveness of purpose than had any other aborigines. When buffalo returned in the spring, the idea died.

In its own routine way, though, the government at long last had begun to think about the tribes along the foothills of the Rockies. In April 1846 the agency of the Upper Platte and

Arkansas was created and Tom Fitzpatrick had been placed
in charge. But Tom did not learn of the appointment until
his lathered horse pulled up at Bent's Fort on October 14,
1846.[11] It was sheer accident that he appeared even then. He
had been California-bound with the dragoons when Kit Carson met them. An army lieutenant now, Kit was racing eastward to Washington with dispatches from Frémont in California and was eager to establish a transcontinental record.
He was also eager to spend just one night in Taos with Josefa,
whom he had not seen for more than a year. Kearny chopped
it all off. Fitzpatrick did not know the Gila route to California;
Carson had just crossed it. Kearny ordered Kit to give the dispatches to Tom for delivery, turn around, and guide the dragoons to the coast. Incensed, Kit would have gone over the
hill that night if Maxwell had not talked him out of it—easy
enough for Maxwell; he kept on toward his wife Luz in Taos
and, eventually, the fort.

Headquarters of Fitzpatrick's new agency was to be Bent's
Fort. William heard it gloomily. Not because of Broken Hand.
The mountains had produced no better men than Tom Fitzpatrick; if agent there must be, he would fill the job well. But
from the fort's inception until now the government had not
given one solitary hoot about the Cheyennes or Arapaho. They
were Bent, St. Vrain Indians, their lives and the company's
life interlocked in mutual honesty for mutual benefits. Now
. . . who could tell? But one prediction was safe: things would
never be the same again.

Toward the end of October, St. Vrain and Folger arrived
with the caravan. Ceran had with him a teen-age adventurer
like Bill Boggs. This one was Lewis Garrard, in ecstasies already over the dull caravan trip and on fire to swallow the rest
of the West in one wonderful gulp. William liked him and let
him go on a trading trip to the Big Timbers with Blackfoot
John Smith. Garrard reveled. He lived in a tepee with John,
whooped songs with him, was shocked to see Blackfoot discipline his half-breed child by pouring ice water over the
naked boy. He watched the squaws scrape hides; he traded,
learned a few Cheyenne words, and discovered how cold the
winter plains can be. He joined a dance over Pawnee scalps,
and he flirted joyously with old Cinemo's sloe-eyed daughter.

In short, he found Romance with a capital R. But like Bill Boggs, he found it fully only because he would look at nothing else. And all the time, across the river, the government trains and the government couriers were marching on, on, everlastingly on toward the Shining Mountains.

William Bent, riding down to Big Timbers to join Owl Woman and his children in the village, saw the passage clearly enough. He sensed what it meant. Even so, he could hardly have anticipated the violence with which the end would come.

CHAPTER XV

REVOLUTION

A week after Kearny left Santa Fe, he was overhauled by messengers bearing word that the Navajos were raiding. In Las Vegas, Kearny had specifically promised that the Americans would not allow the Navajos to do that sort of thing. Back to Doniphan went orders to wind up the trouble before marching south to join General Wool, supposedly advancing on Chihuahua from Texas. Back to Charles with additional messages went Tom Boggs, who had left Santa Fe as one of Kearny's scouts. And, shortly, back came some of Kearny's own dragoons, for Kit Carson had met the command and had told the general, prematurely it turned out, that so many troops weren't necessary; California was firmly in the grip of Frémont and Stockton.

In barracks-room talk the Navajo campaign sounded simple enough. No trouble had been encountered by the several expeditions Kearny had sent among the Indians during September. This job would merely take a few more men on a little longer march. Additional men soon arrived, Colonel Sterling Price's 2nd Missouri Regiment and the Mormon Battalion.

The battalion was a military oddity. The previous July five hundred grumbling Saints had signed up to fight the war on the side of what they considered an even more prime enemy than Mexico—the Government of the United States. Their volunteering had been dictated by Brigham Young in order that he could draw their pay and thus help finance his people's flight to new homes in the Salt Lake basin. Marching with the battalion were thirty or more wives of the volunteers, who managed the feat by liberally interpreting a War Department regulation that allowed each army company, during peacetime, the services of four laundresses to keep the soldiers clean and happy. Accompanying these wives were assorted children, fathers, grandfathers, and other relatives too decrepit for army service but who nonetheless considered themselves capable of keeping up with their militant comrades.

Reality turned out harsher than anticipated. By the time the battalion reached the Crossing of the Arkansas, many of the hangers-on were ready to quit. A handy miracle made the quitting possible. Down the Arkansas, out of the reaches of nowhere, rode five Mormons who announced that forty-three brethren—twenty-four men, an indeterminate number of women and children, and five Negro slaves—were camped at a place called Pueblo. The previous spring these campers had left Mississippi in nineteen wagons to join the great migration westward and unwittingly had gotten far out on the Oregon Trail ahead of the main body of Saints. Needing a place to winter, they had followed a trader down the front range of the mountains to the adobe post at the mouth of Fountain Creek. Cordially welcomed by the handful of Americans and Mexicans living there, they had set about building cabins. The five men who chanced to meet the battalion were on their way eastward from Pueblo to pick up their families in Mississippi.

Hearing of the camp, seven battalion families and assorted trail-weary relatives determined to march up the Arkansas with a small escort of soldiers and join the winterers. They were not the last. Deciding the Mormons would not be needed in Santa Fe, Kearny ordered Philip St. George Cooke to take them over and find a wagon road to California. Cooke promptly stated that no laundresses were going in *his* command. Although five women managed to evade his directive and stayed with the battalion when it marched out of Santa Fe on October 19, he dispatched twenty others northward across Raton Pass. With them went several sick soldiers, escorted by Captain James Brown and a company of able-bodied, who on November 9 requisitioned sixty days' rations from Quartermaster Enos at Bent's Fort. Later on, other ailing were sent back by Cooke, until finally there were about 275 Mormons camped in a log town near the Pueblo adobe. During the winter nine of them died, one couple married, and seven children were born—probably the first of unmixed white blood to see light of day in what is now Colorado.

Well before this, during late September and early October, Charles had made a hurried trip to Taos, perhaps to return Ignacia to her home and children. He came back to an explosive situation. Doniphan had not yet been able to prepare his forces for the field, and the Indian raids which Kearny had ordered checked went on unabated. Although Major Gilpin had brought in a delegation of Utes from Abiquiu during Charles's absence, the governor had no hope that the savages would keep the peace until, as he wrote Buchanan on October 15, "they have been made to feel the strength of our government." Even as he was dictating the letter, a band of Apaches set up camp near the settlement of Mora, arrogantly killed cattle and appropriated horses, turned their own stock into the residents' fields, and whipped those who tried to drive the animals away, seriously wounding a boy in the process. Angrily Charles notified the beset Doniphan that a detachment must be sent out to deal with the matter.

Almost as worrisome as the Indians were the new garrison troops who had arrived under Colonel Sterling Price on October 3. The conquest was over by then, and Price's raw volunteers had not even the satisfaction of a bloodless victory to bolster morale. As other occupation troops have done in other times and places, they undertook to act like conquerors. Within a week Charles was requesting Doniphan, Price's superior, "to interpose your authority to compel the soldiers to respect the rights of the inhabitants. These outrages are becoming so frequent that I apprehend serious consequences must result sooner or later if measures are not taken to prevent them."

The governor was not jumping at shadows. Plots were afoot. Conspirators were discovered drilling in the hills behind Santa Fe. Couriers came to the capital with word that dissatisfied Mexicans in the south were in communication with an enemy army in Chihuahua and that spies were nosing about the camp that American traders had set up at Valverde, far down the Rio Grande, where they were impatiently waiting for the army to open the trail into Mexico. Promptly Charles suggested to Major E. V. Sumner, in command of the dragoons guarding the Valverde camp, that American merchants be used in El Paso to "intercept correspondence between the enemy and the discontented and rebellious of the territory."

Doniphan was of course alerted, and on the same day, October 20, Charles sent an express to Kearny naming the suspected agitators: Diego Archuleta, Augustin Durán, Priest Gallegos (a protégé of Martinez), the Armijos of Albuquerque, and others. "I have my eye on them," he wrote the general, "and shall certainly give them a high berth if the fact can be proved on them. . . . One example will strike such terror into these people that I doubt whether anyone will have temerity enough to embark on such a perilous enterprise in the future." But sternness to would-be rebels did not obviate fairness to the ordinary citizen. Crisply the governor told Kearny, "There is a great want of discipline and subordination among the troops here. . . . I shall use every means to impress on the commander the necessity of a more rigid care with regard to the treatment of the inhabitants. He must conciliate and not exasperate."

In Santa Fe itself guards were doubled, outposts were set up on all roads leading into the plaza, and Price's complaining volunteers were paraded twice a day through the streets. Artillery was unlimbered in the plaza, and howitzers were hoisted onto the earthen roof of the palace, where they could command any surreptitious activity on the adjacent housetops. Either the conspirators' plans were premature or this show of force was enough to counsel the wisdom of delay. Nothing happened, and by October 26 Doniphan felt justified in turning command of the city over to Price while he himself set into motion a nutcracker squeeze to subjugate the Navajos. Small detachments were sent directly into the western deserts. Major Gilpin and 180 underequipped men moved northward from Abiquiu on a tremendous march that took them into Colorado, across the Continental Divide in deep snow, and then south through icy winds past the Canyon de Chelly to an ap-

pointed rendezvous with his commander near present Gal-
lup. Doniphan himself circled the lower part of the Navajos'
starkly beautiful red-and-white land. On the very day he left
Santa Fe, the unawed Navajos raided Albuquerque, killing several people and running off five thousand sheep.

Back in the capital, Charles heeded his own advice about
conciliating rather than exasperating the inhabitants. Loving
gaiety anyhow, he found pleasure in bringing conquered and
conquerors together at frequent parties in the palace. Under
his auspices a dramatics society of volunteers presented during several November evenings, again in the palace, a production of *Pizarro in Peru,* carefully chosen to salve the wounded
pride of the once-proud Spanish blood. An entr'acte of black-
face minstrels further delighted the New Mexicans in the audience with "Git Along Home, You Spanish Girl" and "The
Blue-Tail Fly."

As Doniphan marched westward on his temporary saber-
rattling expedition, Charles sought in the quiet of his office
for a more permanent solution to the Indian problem. On
November 10 he prepared for Washington a long report concerning the numbers, characteristics, and range of the tribes
within his jurisdiction. Spasmodic punitive expeditions were
not enough to keep them in check. There must be, he wrote,
a permanent military force in the territory, manning permanent forts—one on the Arkansas, another south toward El Paso,
and also smaller stockades judiciously placed throughout New
Mexico. As soon as possible delegations from each tribe should
be sent to Washington, so that the Indians could gain a proper
idea of the power of the United States. "I would also," he
added, "suggest the propriety of sending with this delegation
of uncivilized Indians a delegation from the Pueblos."

The Pueblos. They worried Charles Bent. He had already
written Buchanan, on October 15, that they were in complete
control of their priest—Martinez, though Charles did not
name him—and "it is not to be doubted they would be ready
to join in any revolutionary enterprise to which they might be
instigated by those whose orders they have long been accustomed to obey with blind submission." Now, as he dictated
his report to the Commissioner of Indian Affairs, he may well
have paused, picturing the white roading leading past his Taos

home to the multistoried buildings and irrigated fields three
miles beyond. The Pueblos . . . Long since, their names had
been Hispanicized. Ostensibly converted to Catholicism, they
heard Padre Martinez at Mass each Sunday. But dark whispers
said that in a secret kiva was a monstrous stone idol with turquoise eyes and red mouth, symbol of the serpent Bibiron, to
whom girl babies were sacrificed. Less than ten years before,
they had revolted against an imported governor. . . . Charles
returned to his report. "If excited so to do [the Pueblos] might
cause a great deal of difficulty. A small expenditure by the
Government . . . *now* might be the means of avoiding bloodshed hereafter."

Indians were the dramatic but not the only part of his burden. All through October and November the ordinary affairs
of government stayed bogged down in bilingual impasses, insufficient funds, and snail-slow communications. Finally, as
the weeks dragged by and no answers came from Washington
concerning the letters he had written in September, Charles
on November 30 again wrote Senator Benton, repeating his
recommendations about roads, schools, Indian agents, land
surveys, and assistance to mining. Appropriations were desperately needed. There were no court buildings and not "a single
jail or prison in the whole Territory in which a criminal can
be safely confined." His requests for regular troops to replace
the volunteers became more explicit and pressing. Two hundred dragoons, two full companies of artillery, and eight hundred infantrymen were essential not only to quell the Indians
and guard the southern borders against Mexican bandits, but
also to forestall revolution. Without the troops, outbreaks
would be attempted: "My knowledge of the people for many
years past renders this perfectly certain." On the other hand,
the presence of well-disciplined troops would "incite in the
inhabitants and emigrants a fresh spirit of enterprise; the settlements would be extended; new discoveries of mineral
wealth would be made; the numerous flocks and herds that
the Indians have caused to disappear from the valleys and
tablelands of New Mexico would reappear. The agricultural
products of the country would be greatly increased; and it
would soon become a territory capable of sustaining itself but
[sic] of adding something to the wealth of the Union."

Unfortunately Price's volunteers brought no such stimulation. Ignoring the perfunctory harangues of their officers concerning discipline, they continued with their drunkenness, swaggering, bullying, and petty arrogance to rub raw a New Mexican pride already sore hurt by Armijo's abject flight. The garrisons, moreover, had been depleted by the campaigns in the Indian country. On November 22 Doniphan and Gilpin were far west at Ojo del Oso, signing a treaty with the Navajos —which impressed Charles Bent not at all; he had seen Indian treaties before and, he wrote Buchanan, "I have but little grounds to hope it will be permanent."

Nor were Doniphan's eight hundred men scheduled to return to Santa Fe. Instead, on completion of their Indian parleys, they were to march directly toward Chihuahua, there to meet General Wool, who was supposedly advancing from San Antonio. All New Mexico knew this operation was in the offing. Charles himself was helping Doniphan's quartermasters secure stock for the trip by insuring the local owners for their horses and mules, thus convincing suspicious ranchers that they would get their pay. (He also, incidentally, contracted with Price to pasture "the horses of your regiment . . . at the Ponil and its vicinity.")

Noting how thinly American strength was being spread, Diego Archuleta, Augustin Durán, and Tomás Ortiz kept on with their plotting. They found recruits they might not have found had the dragoons been less overbearing.

How far their machinations actually spread is impossible to say. Certainly most of the provinces of Rio Arriba—that is, the northern counties—saw night riding, whispered conferences, overoptimistic countings of available arms. Taos was involved, and in spite of lack of evidence it is difficult to believe that Padre Martinez was not cognizant of the clandestine rumblings.

The plotters were amateurs at the business. They had to depend on a rank and file that was abysmally ignorant, miserably equipped, and long inured to accepting whatever came down from above. Nonetheless, the plan that evolved was classically direct. On the scheduled day conspirators in Santa Fe would go to the church in groups small enough not to arouse suspicion and remain there in hiding. Under cover of darkness

Archuleta would lead forces from the surrounding countryside to places of concealment on the outskirts of the city. The midnight pealing of the church bells was to synchronize the assault. The men hidden in the church would rush out and seize the artillery in the plaza. Kidnapers would fall on Charles Bent and Sterling Price. The simultaneous attack from the outskirts would catch the defenders between two fires and guarantee paralyzing confusion. Couriers would alert the northern towns. Raiders would strike the undermanned garrisons, cut supply roads, and prevent reinforcements from reaching the capital.

The attack was timed for mid-December, but incompleted details caused a postponement until Christmas. The delay, unwelcomed at first, seemed to play into the conspirators' hands. Doniphan marched toward Chihuahua with eight hundred men. The remaining occupation troops were further depleted by sickness. Supply problems for the Americans remained acute as snow piled up in the mountains and Indians began raiding the caravans on the plains. To cap the good luck, an electrifying rumor said that Doniphan had been defeated in the south.

The plotting, hinged now on achieving concert with the victorious Mexican Army, redoubled—and leaked. A commonly accepted tale says that the mulatto wife of one of the rebels learned a few details and ran for advice to La Tules, the *salon* keeper who had so shocked Susan Magoffin. La Tules decided to support the conquerors and reported to Donaciano Vigil.[1] Charles, of course, was immediately informed and "brought into requisition every means in my power to ascertain who were the movers in this rebellion." Seven "secondary" plotters were seized, but the ringleaders were luckier. Donaciano Vigil met conspirator Augustin Durán underneath the portal of the palace and, moved by some feeling of compunction for his countryman, let Durán know that the government was aware of the underground activities. Durán raced away to Ortiz and Archuleta with the warning.

A squad of soldiers searching Ortiz's home missed him as he lay flat on a balcony. The troops gone, Ortiz dressed himself as a servant girl and eluded the watch stationed in front of his house by being hoisted on ropes over the roof of the cathe-

dral chapel, which adjoined his gardens. In the street on the
other side he climbed pick-a-back onto a friend, Pedro Trujillo.
When one inquisitive soldier made a remark, Trujillo stam-
mered that his sister was too sick to walk. Not anticipating
that a leader of rebellion would ride pick-a-back, the guard
failed to look under his own nose, and the pair reached the
home of Trujillo's mistress. There arrangements were made
for horses and Ortiz escaped, as did Diego Archuleta and
Durán by means less glamorous.

The escapes worried Charles. On Christmas Day he wrote
Colonel Price that he feared "the principal movers . . . may
well not leave . . . the country without a last and desperate
struggle." Accordingly he asked a cancellation of pending orders to send Meriwether Lewis Clark's battalion of artillery
southward after Doniphan, a request seconded by a petition
from the frightened American merchants in Santa Fe. The
mere presence of the artillery, the governor told Price, might
be enough to restrain the plotters and thus do away with the
necessity of putting down a revolution with bloodshed, an
eventuality that could only "breed lasting antipathy" toward
the Americans.

Price acceded. The guns stayed in Santa Fe, their dark
snouts commanding every cranny of the plaza. Reinforced
guards patrolled every street, and throughout the territory suspects were seized for interrogation.

Other, simultaneous difficulties were not so easily overcome,
however. Eastward, Comanches had declared war. Disease had
gotten among them. Blaming the influx of white soldiers for
having blown an evil breath on their children, the Indians were
out for revenge, a motive delightfully fortified by their discovery that the government's green teamsters were easy pick-
ings—a fact that Pawnees were likewise learning. The situation
on the Canadian River, Ceran St. Vrain told Lieutenant
Abert, was so dangerous that his company would not send
traders to Fort Adobe that winter. Santa Fe was snarled in red
tape and short supplies. Abert, eager to return home after
completing a quick topographic examination of New Mexico,
could not requisition equipment or funds for his party's journey; only a loan from Ceran kept the men from being stranded
indefinitely.

Charles let none of the turmoil upset the palace's glittering Christmas entertainment, held on December 26 amid "all the luxuries of eastern tables, delightful champagne in abundance." New Year's brought cause for more celebration—word that Doniphan, far from having been defeated in the south, had instead crushed a Mexican army at El Brazito, near El Paso. Feeling that this news would completely dismay any plotters who had been counting on the enemy army's support, Charles on January 2, 1847, released Clark's artillery for its southward march. Three days later he issued a general proclamation announcing Doniphan's victory and the smothering of the revolt, and urging the populace not to heed the "false and poisonous" doctrines of resistance that were still being spread. "The rebellion," so Sterling Price later wrote his superiors, "appeared to be suppressed."

The confidence in the Governor's Palace and in the barracks was not justified, however. Taos still smoldered. Down to Santa Fe to consult with Charles came the town's uneasy officials: Sheriff Steve Lee, Circuit Attorney James White Leal, and Prefect Cornelio Vigil, Ignacia Bent's uncle and part owner of the St. Vrain-Vigil land grant. After talking to the trio Charles felt that he should try to allay the discontent in Taos by visiting his home. Besides, he was eager to see Ignacia and the children.[2]

Immediately Santa Fe officialdom protested the move. Donaciano Vigil told the governor he would be rashly exposing himself. Other friends tried to prevail on Charles to wait at least until an escort of soldiers could be provided to accompany him to the troopless town. Surely, too, there were reminders of the attack on George and Frank Blair, which had occurred only eight months before. Charles was adamant. He would go—and without an escort. Troops would betray lack of confidence, and in Taos, of all places, he should surely show the confidence he felt.

On the cold morning of January 14 the little party of officials set forth. Two youngsters rode with them—Ignacia's brother, Pablo Jaramillo, and Narciso Beaubien, Carlos's son and partner of Steve Lee in the Sangre de Cristo grant. After spending the past five years at school in Missouri, Narciso had returned in the caravan which St. Vrain and Folger had

brought to the fort the previous fall. Though the elder Beaubien stayed in Santa Fe, Narciso decided to go home with his
friend, young Jaramillo. Deep snow made progress painfully
slow. The pack mules floundered in the drifts that filled arroyo
beds and gorge bottoms. Past the bleak-looking villages of La
Cañada and San Juan, through the narrows of El Embudo the
party plodded. Sullen looks followed their passage. Riding this
way only a few days before, George Ruxton, English adventurer and perhaps an English spy, had found "the most bitter
feeling and most determined hostility" against the conquerors.
The wife of one family with whom Ruxton stayed had exclaimed, on learning his nationality, "*Gracias a Dios,* a Christian will sleep with us tonight, and not an American!"

The fourth day arrived before Charles's party, climbing
through pines and cedars, reached a summit ridge and saw
below them the snowy, mountain-cupped valley dotted with
its villages and farms. Hard travel still lay ahead. Soft snow
balling up on the horses' feet forced the travelers to dismount
and wade afoot through the slush.[3] They were wet, cold, and
cross when they reached the town. There they were met by a
gang of Pueblo Indians.

Perhaps the Indians acted on the spur of the moment, but
more probably they had been apprised of the party's approach
and were primed to do as they did. With great clamor they
surrounded the newcomers and demanded the release of certain friends who had been jailed for theft. Patiently Charles
told them that the matter would have to be handled through
the normal process of law. Uneasily then, with hostile growls
following them, the travelers separated and went to their
homes.

It was good to relax in the warm room where piñon logs
crackled in the corner fireplace. Charles was forty-seven now,
completely gray-haired and grown stout at his desk in Santa
Fe. The job had tired him more than he had realized during its
daily excitements. Whether his three and a half months of
stewardship had been truly productive he could not tell. Legis-
lation had been no part of his previous training or experience.
In so short a time he could not have foreseen that the machinery he set in motion would, by and large, serve New Mexico
until statehood, more than half a century away in the future.

To him it must have seemed that all his efforts at orderly development had been hamstrung by Indian wars, split authority with the army, lack of funds and equipment, and continued threats of revolt. Well, he had done what he could. Now it was good to be home.

In the absence of their husbands, Ignacia's sister and daughter were living with her—Kit's Josefa and Tom Boggs's Rumalda, neither of them yet out of her teens. The women were frightened. In the streets the noise grew—howls, gunfire. Frightened messengers slipped into the courtyard with hurried warnings. The mob was increasing; the family had better flee.

A governor flee? That was Armijo's way, not Charles Bent's. He refused to budge, tried to keep the children from sensing the alarm, and put the family to bed as though it were any coldly peaceful winter night.

In the town conspirators were extemporizing quick plans on the skeleton work first prepared for the abortive December revolt. Did Charles's old enemy, Padre Martinez, share in the night's work? There is no evidence, although Kit Carson and Ceran St. Vrain always believed he did. The active leader was Pablo Montoya, soon to style himself the Santa Ana of the North. His couriers galloped three miles to Tomás Romero at the Pueblo. Bring reinforcements. All night long Indians rode into town to join the Mexicans whom Montoya's lieutenants were rounding up. While demagogues preached that the gringos meant to seize their lands and used liquor to multiply the fury, the two ringleaders made their plans.[4]

In the icy starlight just before the late winter dawn they gave the signal. A lucky pretext existed to impart cohesion and passion to the mob—the men in the jail. Howling and waving torches, the gang surged toward the building. Sheriff Steve Lee was dragged out of bed into the cold. Helpless to resist, he might have yielded the prisoners. But the din had aroused Prefect Cornelio Vigil. He ran up, his thin face taut with the chill anger of the Spanish patrician who brooks no protest from inferiors. Calling the rioters thieves and scoundrels, he ordered them to disperse. With screams of rage they fell on him, hacked him literally to pieces. Lee broke clear and fought his way to a housetop. There he was overhauled and butchered.

Berserk now with blood lust, the mob broke into segments, following coached leaders toward the houses of a proscribed list of Americans and American sympathizers. Fortunately most of the targets were, like George Bent, out of town, but the houses and stores of many were looted. Circuit Attorney James Leal was captured and marched naked through the frozen streets until the fun palled. Then he was shot full of arrows in such a way that the wounds would not be mortal and scalped while still alive. Blinded, he groped through the streets for hours, until finally someone killed him—and left his body lying where hogs ate most of it. Meanwhile Narciso Beaubien and Ignacia's brother, Pablo Jaramillo, heard the attackers coming, fled into a barn, and hid under straw in a manger. They might have escaped had not a woman servant climbed onto the roof and called the insurgents back: "Kill the young ones, and they will never be men to trouble us!" Trapped in the manger, the pair were stabbed and lanced until their bodies were unrecognizable.

It was after seven and growing light when Charles was awakened by the sound of people running outside his house, scaling the walls, and jumping into the courtyard. Hurriedly dressing, he called through the door, "What do you want?" A confused roar answered. All the terrified household was up now, clustered about him in their nightclothes. Ignacia brought his pistols. He shook his head. Violence on his part might lead to the massacre of everyone, women and children alike. He told his wife and the others to escape by digging through the wall into the adjoining house, whose doorway perhaps was not watched. He would try to stall off the attackers.

With a poker and a big spoon the women began frantically prying out adobe bricks in a back room. Charles offered the attackers money. They hooted him down. Ten-year-old Alfredo said stoutly, "Let's fight them, Papa." Gently Charles motioned the boy back toward his mother. Calling through the door, he suggested a council at which grievances could be aired. Redoubled blows on the panel answered, and now he heard the sound of men tearing at the roof above his head. How were the women coming with their work? He could not see. A gun butt broke the window. Striving desperately for time, he offered to go with the mob as its prisoner if they would spare the other Americans in Taos.

A fusillade of musket fire splintered the door. A bullet grazed Charles's chin; another struck his stomach. Ignacia. His children . . . He tried to steady himself. A hole gaped in the roof. A panel of the door crashed inward. Arrows struck his face, his chest. He pulled some of them loose and staggered into the rear of the house. The women had succeeded in making a hole. They had all crawled through, pushing the three children ahead of them, when Charles came dizzily up to the breach.

Helping hands caught him, dragged him on. It was too late. Pueblos running across the rooftop dropped into the courtyard beyond and blocked the doorway. Other Indians broke into the Bents' home and ran to the hole. Held in Rumalda's arms, Charles spoke inarticulately. Realizing dimly that no one had understood him, he fumbled a piece of paper from his pocket, gestured blankly. An Indian leaped up, seized him by the suspenders, and dashed him to the floor. Ululating others crouched over him and, as the Pueblos could, deftly scalped him with a bowstring.

The terrified neighbors got Rumalda into another room and hid her under blankets. Ignacia stayed behind, begging for her children's lives. The Pueblos began mutilating Charles's body. A furious voice cried out that they were fools, that they should have kept the governor alive as a valuable hostage. Abashed suddenly at what they had done, the Pueblos milled uncertainly. At last they told the women to remain in the foodless, ice-cold house as prisoners. Fastening Charles's scalp to a board with brass tacks, they went howling off after fresh prey. All that day and the next, as the American traders' stores were looted and burned by whooping mobs, the women waited in their thin nightclothes, Charles's body beside them in a pool of drying blood. Then friendly Mexicans came, took Charles away and buried him secretly where the Indians could not find the body. Others led the mourning family to shelter. For them the revolution was over.[5]

CHAPTER XVI

RETRIBUTION

Quickly the leaders of the revolt moved to exploit their advantage. Horsemen galloped east, north, and south—toward the Bent, St. Vrain ranches, across the snowy passes to Mora, into the little villages along the Rio Grande. The blow had been struck. Rise and kill!

Despite precautions by the rebels, shadowy figures slipped out of Taos. Charley Towne raced for Santa Fe, stumbled into the hotel which Jim Beckwourth had been running since his return from California, and gasped out his story. Jim hurried to Colonel Price.[1] Meantime hoarse-voiced Charley Autobeas rode twelve miles from Taos to Arroyo Hondo, where several Americans lived in the settlement that had grown up around Turley's distillery. Without dismounting, Autobeas shouted out word of the massacre, warned that a mob was approaching the Arroyo, and spurred up the trail leading to Bent's Fort.

Like Charles Bent, Simeon Turley had difficulty believing the Mexicans would attack him. He had lived among them since 1830, had built up a prosperous establishment where many Mexicans and Indians found better employment than most of the district offered. Reluctantly he closed the gate in the stockade surrounding his mill, granary, stillhouse, and barns. He moved none too quickly. Soon five hundred rebels were pouring arrows and musket balls at the eight or ten defenders. For two days the besieged held out. Then the attackers gained the corrals, fiercely speared and shot quantities of pigs and sheep, and at last succeeded in setting fire to the main buildings. Some of Turley's men were dead now. Ammunition was almost gone. Under cover of darkness the survivors tried to break away into the cedar-covered hills.

Three made it. One was John Albert. Coatless, hatless, clinging to his knife and gun, he alternately walked and trotted northward through the subfreezing mountains. He avoided the settlements. It was well. In a town on Rio Colorado[2] a pair of Americans carrying furs from Pueblo to Taos were surrounded, disarmed, and shot through the back.

To reach succor, Albert had to travel 140 miles. Half frozen, starving, he finally killed a deer. When he gulped its raw liver, his cramped stomach revolted and he vomited. With a fire he cooked some meat, which he managed to hold down, then made a rough coat from the fresh deer hide and trudged on. He risked a brief rest at the Mexican settlement on Greenhorn Creek in southern Colorado, where he kept his mouth carefully shut, and then continued to Pueblo. In the darkness he missed the Pueblo fort. Dogs barked as he tottered into the Mormon camp. Men peered out, heard his fainting call, and carried him in to warmth.

When Albert's information reached the mountaineers in the Pueblo fort, fury swept them. The fifteen or so Mexicans working around the place were incarcerated in a single room. A messenger was sent down the Arkansas to find William Bent. Dick Wootton led a handful of trappers back toward Taos. They knew they could not suppress a revolution, but if they hung around the hills above the town they might find some way to help avenge Turley and Charles Bent.

Meanwhile revolutionists had fallen on a caravan at Mora and had killed eight Americans, among them L. L. Waldo, younger brother of William and David Waldo. Here reaction was swift. Troops from the garrison at Las Vegas smashed into the Mora houses, where Mexicans were firing through the windows, shot or bayoneted twenty-five to death and captured seventeen. The survivors fell back into an old fort and from there drove off the Americans. Not until artillery was brought up and Mora practically demolished did the insurgents yield.

On the evening of January 24, guerrillas attacked the Ponil and Vermejo ranches of Bent, St. Vrain & Company. In addition to company stock, there were at these ranches a thousand head of government beef cattle, several hundred draft oxen, four hundred or more horses and mules. The first dash of the rebels caught soldiers, teamsters, and the company's Mexican herders flat-footed. In a twinkling the raiders swept off every horse and mule, two hundred cattle. Terrified, the troops and herders fled to the upper Purgatory ranch, where Frank De Lisle was camped with several company wagons and considerable livestock.

Panic bred more panic. Surely a rebel force would follow to

exploit the victory. Hoping to save what could be saved, De Lisle ordered the wagons hitched up and started toward the fort. The officer in charge of a nearby government party was bolder. He put his vehicles in a square on top of a hill above the creek, dug ditches, threw up breastworks. He ordered the soldiers fleeing with the Bent men to stay with him and had his herders take the government stock back into out-of-the-way meadows.

De Lisle's wagons moved so slowly that Louis Simonds was sent ahead to the Arkansas with word of the attack. It was anticlimax. When he arrived at the fort, Autobeas was already there with the grimmer news that Charles was dead.

The placita was a turmoil of uncertainty. Maxwell, whose brother-in-law Narciso had been slain, paced back and forth, frantic with worry over the rest of his family. No one would accompany him to the fallen town. Rumors flew that Price, too, had been defeated at Santa Fe. Captain Jackson, stationed at the fort with one company of able-bodied men and a score or more soldiers too sick for service, refused to dispatch his men on an unreasoned charge against heaven knew what. If a counterattack developed from the revolt, Bent's Fort was Mexico's next logical objective. Turning a deaf ear to Maxwell's importunities, Jackson sent an express upriver to Captain Brown, in charge of the Mormon soldiers at Pueblo. In case of need, how much help could be counted on from that quarter?

Autobeas was dead-beat from his long crossing over the storm-swept mountains. To Louis Simonds fell the task of riding to Big Timbers after William Bent. He reached the belt of cottonwoods late in the afternoon and found that the Cheyenne village had moved to the south bank of the river. Crossing over the ice, he wound his way among the tepees to the log shanty that Blackfoot John Smith and young Lewis Garrard had recently built. Smith and Garrard were inside, leisurely replenishing their larder by swapping beads for meat. Until a squaw called to them, they did not notice Simonds's approach.

It had been a cold winter, as Garrard had discovered during his moves with Smith from camp to camp. Travelers on the trail suffered terribly. In January, Tom Boggs, carrying dispatches from Santa Fe, had somehow lost most of his mules, and he knew that the fort had no more to lend him. Abandoning his surplus baggage, he distributed essentials on the remaining animals and with his little party set out to walk until he found replacements. The only help Smith and Garrard could give him at their camp was a little dried meat, but Tom kept hoofing for two weeks down the Arkansas, until he found mules in an Osage village. Harder luck awaited Lieutenant Abert, traveling a few days behind him. Storms and wolves killed four of Abert's mules; Indians ran off the others. The troopers tied a long rope to the tongue of their lone wagon and, with the aid of a single broken-down yoke of oxen they found beside the trail, desperately hand-hauled their vehicle toward civilization. On February 17 a few traders overtook them and Abert learned that Charles Bent was dead. In the midst of his own troubles—storms, hunger, sickness, and exhaustion—the lieutenant wrote sorrowfully in his diary, "I esteemed and admired him greatly, and everyone in that country looked on Charles Bent as one in a thousand."

At the Big Timbers, Louis Simonds climbed stiffly from his horse. A messenger hurried to William's lodge. As Simonds wolfed the food set before him, he told what he knew. "Scalped *him!*" The listeners clutched their knives. "Scalped Charles!" Yes, and Steve Lee and Narciso Beaubien and Charles's young brother-in-law, Pablo Jaramillo. And now the rebels were marching on Santa Fe. Woefully Louis wagged his head. "I'm afraid the 'Mericans will go under." The traders were depressed and alarmed. Surely the fort would be next.

William's shadow fell across the door and he called Simonds outside. The other men stared at the ground. "We pitied William," Garrard wrote later. "His murdered brother, being much older than himself and George, was loved and respected as a father."

News of the murder reached the Cheyenne chiefs. Criers stalked through the village, haranguing the people. At solemn council it was decided to send the tribe against New Mexico. William refused. This was the white man's problem. The army had created it and soldiers living at the fort would carry against the enemy whatever war was necessary.

The next morning, under clouded and sullen skies, William

rode to the fort with only young Garrard for company. During
the entire forty miles he spoke scarcely a word. Along the way
the two encountered a Mexican employed by William Tharpe,
a small-time trader who used alcohol to compete with the company in the Big Timbers. William unlimbered his rifle, so grim-
faced that Garrard thought he meant to shoot the man on the
spot. Under the pointed muzzle he cross-examined the quak-
ing Mexican closely, learned nothing, and told the fellow to
"*vamose pronto!*"

At the fort he found Captain Jackson unwilling to lend him
even a reconnoitering party, although an express had just arrived from Pueblo with word that the Mormons were drilling
daily and available as reinforcements whenever needed. William called his own men together. There were twenty-three
of them there, a hopelessly inadequate number for launching
an attack against Taos. But they might be able to scout out
the situation on the ranches, salvage some of the stock, and
then edge across the mountains toward the town, improvising
as they went. If they managed to burn a few enemy ranchos
and lift some Mexican hair along the way, so much the better.
How many of them were willing to take the chance?

A few days ago they had been in panic. But now every man
volunteered. It was William's intention to go with them. But
then Frank De Lisle arrived with the company wagons from
the Purgatory. Frank was convinced that a Mexican army was
right behind him, and out of the resultant confusion and Captain Jackson's belief that all hell was about to break over his
head, one fact emerged starkly clear: If the fort was attacked,
a responsible company man had better be there with the defenders. Reluctantly William decided he could not afford the
luxury of vengeance now and put Bill Bransford in charge of
the company's seventeen roustabouts. The others were, like
Bransford, head traders or so-called "free men," entitled to de-
tach themselves from the group whenever they chose. All had
families in Taos: Lucien Maxwell, Manuel Le Fevre, François
Lajeunesse, and a fourth identified simply as Tom.[3] Young
Garrard went along for the excitement.

Only the five free men had horses, for the normal requirements of the trading parties in the field and requisitions by
government expresses moving along the trail had stripped the

corrals. The party's provisions and bedding were loaded into a single wagon, and the roustabouts, mostly French Canadians, set cheerfully out to walk as far as the Purgatory ranch. Here they hoped to find mounts—if a Mexican army had not reached there first.

The group had scarcely departed when word arrived that John Albert was at Pueblo. The thought that Albert might have firsthand news of how Charles had died was irresistible. Swiftly William rode the seventy miles to Fountain Creek. When he reached the adobe fort, the fifteen imprisoned Mexicans were herded out in front of him. If he had so much as nodded, the mountain men would have gladly killed all fifteen. But obviously Mexicans working on the Arkansas could have taken no hand in the Taos slaughter. William and Albert said to turn the captives loose. Though Albert repeated the grisly details of the fight at Turley's, he could add nothing definite concerning Charles. Disappointed, William returned to the fort.

Meanwhile Bransford's party was toiling up the Timpas. A snowstorm immobilized them one day. What little water they found by chopping through ice was so impregnated with alkali that even coffee made from it was almost unpalatable. For two nights they had no firewood. To keep warm Garrard slept with Bransford, but before he could go to bed Bransford had to convince his huge white dog that a guest was tolerable. At Hole in the Rock the dog's furious barking sent the men dodging through the trees, fearful of an attack that never came.

The moccasin-shod Canadians slipped and fell repeatedly on the icy hillsides. But they never lost their amiability. As they floundered along, they kept popping away with their muskets at rabbits, coyotes, or just marks in the brush, always mutually congratulatory about the shooting: "*Votre fusil très bon, wagh!* One Mexican, he go ondare. *Pauvre* Mexican!"

At the Purgatory ranch they found the government teamsters forted up and nervous but living well on fifty wagonloads of stranded provisions. Mingled with the U.S. stock were company animals, which the Bent, St. Vrain men reappropriated after a vociferous dispute. Now all were mounted and their provisions switched to pack mules. With Maxwell scouting the way they crossed Raton. On the pass's far side they pounced tumultuously on a lone horseman who turned out to be one of George Bent's Indians on his way to the fort from Taos. From him they learned the latest news.

The word of the Taos uprising which Charley Towne had brought to Beckwourth on January 20 was quickly confirmed by the arrest of rebel emissaries carrying appeals for Santa Fe to join the uprising. Fifteen hundred troops, the messages said, were advancing under General Tafoya against the capital. Fifteen hundred! Colonel Price had less than three hundred effectives in Santa Fe.

He summoned Ceran St. Vrain. Could St. Vrain recruit a company of volunteers among the mountain men and merchants in the city? For avenging Charles? Ceran most certainly could. Commissioned a captain by Price, with a trapper named Metcalf as his lieutenant, he quickly rounded up sixty-five volunteers. Among them was Carlos Beaubien, grimly determined to repay the murder of his son. Jim Beckwourth signed on. So, too, did several New Mexicans who had loved and admired the dead governor; one named Chavez declined a proffered commission lest Americans in the company be irritated.

The advancing rebels were gaining recruits every day. Price determined on a long chance: hit the enemy fast, even though it meant leaving Santa Fe undefended against an internal uprising until reinforcements could be rushed up from the garrison at Albuquerque. After jailing all suspected conspirators and clamping down a semblance of martial law, he marched northward on January 23. His total muster, including St. Vrain's volunteers, was 353 men. Only the volunteers were mounted.

The next day at La Cañada (present Santa Cruz), twenty miles north of Santa Fe, Price met the advancing enemy. For once in the Mexican War the numbers of the opposition had not been exaggerated. At least fifteen hundred Pueblo Indians and Mexicans held the hills above the town or were fortified in the adobe houses. But they were a disorganized, untrained ragtag mob, not an army. Banking on this, Price told St. Vrain to guard the baggage train and straightway attacked.

The mountaineers were infuriated by what they considered

the ignominy of their assignment. Soon, however, Price's wisdom became apparent. As the regulars stormed the town, a detachment of Mexicans tried to cut in behind them and capture the ammunition wagons. With whoops of joy Ceran's mountain men sent them reeling, forgot the baggage train, and chased them into the hills. Seeing that the sweep had carried them onto an unguarded flank of the rebel forces, Ceran ordered an attack on the Mexican rear. Demoralized, the rabble retreated up the canyon. Behind them they left forty-five prisoners and thirty-six dead, including General Tafoya. Price lost two killed, seven wounded.

Tremendously inspirited, the troops pressed on through deep snow and bitter cold. As the canyons narrowed, they were delayed by having to cut a road through trees and boulders for the baggage. On the twenty-eighth reinforcements overtook them: Captain Burgwin with a company of cavalry and Lieutenant Wilson, who added a six-pounder to Price's little howitzers. Thus they numbered 480 men when they met the regrouped rebels at El Embudo, the narrowest part of the trail.

The enemy forces in the canyon bottom were strongly flanked by detachments on both hillsides. Price ordered a three-way attack. One company of soldiers charged the east hill. Burgwin led three companies against the center. Dismounting his volunteers, Ceran led a sweep up the western hillside. All parts of the rebel line buckled at once. For two hours St. Vrain's men pursued the vanquished through the drifted snow of the high mountains. As a result, most of the casualties to the Americans came from crippling frostbite.

This second defeat broke the spirit of the Mexican insurgents, and the bulk of them vanished. Deserted but still defiant, the Pueblos fell back to their village without again offering contact. Unopposed, Price entered Taos at midday on February 3. His men were exhausted by their two battles and the twelve-day slog through the snow. Nonetheless, on hearing that the Pueblos were concentrated in their settlement three miles away, the colonel decided on immediate attack.

The place was stronger than he bargained for. Surrounding it was a stockade of timbers and adobe, built many years before as a protection against raiding Utes, Apaches, and Comanches. In one corner of the stockade towered a tall, thick-walled

church. The two walls of the church which faced the outside
approaches were devoid of windows, but now new, ugly little
loopholes spotted the once blank adobe. The rest of the village
consisted of a pair of five-storied dwelling houses, each story
recessed on the one below, so that the general effect was of
irregular, truncated pyramids. No outside entries led into the
dwellings. The residents climbed ladders which could be pulled
up behind them, and then dropped into their rooms through
holes in the roof. Counting a few loyal Mexicans, six or seven
hundred fighting men and their families were now congregated
there. In spite of their numbers, however, reducing the stronghold by starvation would have been painfully slow. The bee-
hive of apartments was well stored with grain and provisions,
and a creek running between the two buildings provided ample
water.

Price entertained no notion of a siege. His small howitzers
and Lieutenant Wilson's six-pounder, he thought, would soon
create breaches big enough for storming parties. But for two
hours the mud walls absorbed the bombardment, and at the
approach of darkness, while the Pueblos jeered triumphantly,
Price pulled his troops back into Taos. Begging for food and
fire, the famished soldiers deserted their own messes for the
houses of friendly Mexicans—and those who expediently pretended friendliness. Dick Wootton and the men who had come
from Pueblo slipped down from the hills above town and
joined St. Vrain's company.

At nine the next morning the attack resumed. St. Vrain's
mounted volunteers were sent to the rear of the pueblo to cut
off any retreat into the mountains. A small howitzer poured
grape against the dwellings. The other cannon hammered at
the church, where most of the defenders were stationed.

By eleven o'clock it was plain that artillery alone could not
effect a breach. Captain Burgwin's dismounted dragoons were
ordered to charge through galling fire from the loopholes and
secure lodgment against the west wall of the church, Francis
Aubrey's company against the north wall. They made it. Duck-
ing in underneath the defenders' range, part of Burgwin's men
put up ladders and set fire to the wooden roof. The rest swung
around the corner and attacked the south door with battering-
rams. They were repulsed, Burgwin fatally wounded. As the

roof began to smolder, sappers attacked the west wall with axes. They managed to make small holes and by hand tossed in shells that created havoc in the crowded building.

Amid the smoke and crashing explosions the Pueblos fought back furiously. Raging in the fore was a gigantic Delaware Indian called Big Nigger, who had married a Pueblo woman and now did herculean service on the side of her people. So spirited was the defense he led that the holes could not be enlarged by hand. The soldiers fell back; the six-pounder was hauled up to point-blank range. At 3:30 P.M. it began firing, and after ten rounds one of the ax holes was smashed wide enough for a storming party. Leaping unauthorized in its vanguard went Dick Green, Charles Bent's jet-black slave. Inside, the church was dense with smoke from the shells and the collapsing roof. Bodies lay everywhere, the screams of the wounded mingling with the yells of the charging Americans.

From the church and from the western section of the village a portion of the defenders began a panicked flight toward the mountains. St. Vrain's men swept in to cut them off. It was a grim and bloody vengeance. Training school for the mountaineers had been Indian battles where quarter was never granted, and now many of the volunteers had private scores to settle. Mercilessly clubbing and shooting, they rode the fugitives down.

In isolated knots in the snowy fields some of the Pueblos gathered to fight back. Individual battles raged, Ceran in the thick of them. Luck sat on his shoulder. Once while he was afoot, aiming at two Indians riding down on him, a third jumped from behind a cedar and grappled for his rifle. Chavez, the Mexican who had refused a commission from Ceran, split the Pueblo's head with a blow from his rifle, and the two then turned on the mounted attackers. Later, riding across the fields with Dick Wootton, Ceran saw lying on the ground an Indian who he knew had been a leader in the revolt. Dismounting, he stooped over the prostrate form. The fellow was shamming. He seized Ceran's throat, swung St. Vrain between himself and Wootton, and tried to stab Ceran with a steel-pointed arrow. Fortunately Wootton managed to get behind the Pueblo and close matters with a tomahawk.

In spite of the mountaineers, a few of the fugitives broke

clear. Among them was Big Nigger, who fled into the Colorado mountains, gathered three other Delawares about him, and lived unmolested with a large bounty on his head; no one had nerve enough to try collecting it.[4] Others, seeing escape cut off, returned to the town. Evening closed down before Price could exploit his capture of the church, and he decided to wait until morning before advancing against the dwellings.

During the night the wailing village counted its losses—at least 150 dead, including fifty-one killed by St. Vrain's men. Wounds had further reduced the defenders by at least half. Unable to resist longer, at dawn the chiefs sent out women with white flags, children with crosses. They came weeping on their hands and knees, begging for mercy. Price accepted surrender on condition that the ringleaders be surrendered. He had lost seven men killed and forty-five wounded, several of whom later died. Learning of the success back in Washington on April 20, President Polk wrote in his diary, "The number of troops engaged was comparatively small, but I consider this victory one of the most signal which has been gained during the war."[5]

Leaders Tomás Romero and Pablo Montoya were imprisoned in the one-window jail on the north edge of Taos. A drumhead court was scheduled to try them within the next three days, but Romero never faced his accusers. A recruit named Fitzgerald, whose brother had been captured and killed during the Texas-Santa Fe expedition, walked up to the rebel and shot him down. Captured, Fitzgerald was imprisoned in a small adobe hut to await trial but cut a hole through the roof and escaped.[6] Montoya died more legally. After a quick court-martial (held, it is said, in the home of Padre Martinez) he was led in front of the army and executed. So much for the military's concern. Now civil authorities moved in to try those rebels suspected of direct participation in the various murders.

As Frank Blair set the territory's untested judicial machinery clanking into motion, St. Vrain learned of the guerrilla attacks on the ranches and sent five men across the mountain to count the losses. Before they arrived, Bransford's party from the fort reached Vermejo Creek.

Steep, timbered hills bordered Vermejo's mile-wide valley,

where bright-spotted cattle grazed on grama grass. Humble enough the place was, to be the precursor of the gigantic outfits that would "pioneer" the land thirty years later. The rancho building was a mere lean-to of poles covered with hides, sheltering beds of piñon boughs. A fire blazed in front. To one side of the hearth a branch was driven into the ground; on the stub end of its twigs tin cups were hung. For months on end the wild Mexican herdsmen lived on atole and meat. Expert riders and ropers, they protected themselves with bows and arrows, were paid from four to eight dollars a month, and were content.

At Vermejo, the party from the fort divided. Maxwell and the "free men" rode to Taos. Bransford left ten or eleven of the French Canadians to round up what cattle they could locate along the creek and then continued with Garrard and two others to Ponil. Here they found the Bent, St. Vrain majordomo, an intelligent Mexican in leather pants, blue blanket, and peaked sombrero covered with oilcloth. St. Vrain's five scouts from Taos were camped nearby. For the rest of February and March the men zigzagged back and forth along the creeks, built corrals, and kept count of the animals they recovered by marking the tally in a journal book with a bullet hammered into a point in lieu of a pencil. Many a later cowboy would live the same way, on skimpy food in March's wind, sleet, and thin sunshine. Many would echo the remark Bransford made as he raised pale red whiskers and weepy eyes from a smoking cook fire and groaned to Garrard, "Don't you wish you were in the Planters House?"

John Hatcher rode in from Taos. He had recently returned from his mule-trading trip with George Bent, and now he was bearing to William an account of the trial preparations and word that Charles's body, disinterred from its secret grave, had been taken to Santa Fe for reburial. He borrowed Garrard's saddle mule in exchange for a promise to bring back three clean shirts, and trotted on. After his departure the men at the ranch varied their diet by tying wild cows to wagon wheels and milking the animals between their hind legs into tin cups and kettles. Then they parched and ground coffee beans and dumped the powder into boiling milk. For excitement they fruitlessly pursued unknown raiders, either Mexican or Indian, who one night ran off thirty horses and mules.

The meadows were greening when Hatcher returned with three soldiers from the fort. William was not with them. In the blunt directness of his nature there was no room for the secondhand satisfaction of watching society exact its retributions. But curiosity pulled Garrard and Louis Simonds with Hatcher over the hills to the village. "Waugh!" yelled John. "This hoss is for Touse tonight—*comme la va, señorita!*"—bowing to an imaginary Mexican lady—"Wish to dance?" and with a genuine war cry he started for his mule.

The trials were under way, ostensibly in accord with Anglo-Saxon concepts of justice. A grand jury brought in indictments. A duly appointed judge presided while three different petit juries listened to the witnesses.

But . . .

One of the judges was Joab Houghton, close friend of the slain governor. The other was Carlos Beaubien, whose son had been murdered and who had helped club down the fleeing rebels behind the pueblo. Foreman of the grand jury was George Bent, and one of his veniremen was Elliott Lee, a relative of the slain sheriff. Foreman of one of the petit juries was Robert Fisher, company trader. On Fisher's jury sat Lucien Maxwell, brother-in-law of Narciso Beaubien. Other jurymen included Asa Estes, Antoine LeRoux, Charley Towne, Charles Autobeas—Bent men all. Ceran St. Vrain acted as interpreter, and the prosecuting attorney was Frank Blair. Extenuation? Well, in Taos there was no such thing as impartiality. If associates and relatives of the murdered did not sit on the juries, then associates and relatives of the murderers would have—and many Spanish names do appear on the jury rolls, though what their allegiance was cannot be determined. And if the judiciary disqualified itself, who else was there in the territory to serve? Still . . .

The courtroom was a small oblong, divided by a thin rail. The principal witnesses—Ignacia Bent, Josefa Carson, and Rumalda Boggs—sat on a bench against one wall. Their dress and manner, Garrard says, indicated higher than usual refinement. When Ignacia gave her testimony, the accused impassively watched her drawn, beautiful face. As soon as the jury retired, one French Canadian on the panel cried, "Hang 'em, *sacrés enfants de grâce,* dey damn grand rascale, dey kill Monsieur Charles, dey take *son* topknot . . . Hang 'em, hang 'em, *sa-acré-é!*" A few moments of such debate produced a verdict of guilty. Carlos Beaubien pronounced the sentence, "*Muerto, muerto, muerto.*" There was a moment's silence. A bystander sobbed. Then the convicted drew their serapes around them and went out with the guards.

Court was in session fifteen working days. Fifteen men were sentenced to death, one for high treason. Despair settled over the village. Through Manuel Álvarez, Padre Martinez sent a letter to Price saying that "the judge of crimes, Don Carlos Beaubien and his associates, are endeavoring to kill all the people of Taos." Because the jail was crowded, it was deemed expedient to hang the first six of the convicted before the trials of the others were completed.

April 9 was set for the execution. Acting Sheriff Metcalf, recently lieutenant of St. Vrain's volunteers, borrowed rawhide riatas from Garrard, Hatcher, and Simonds and some hempen picket cords from a teamster. In a room beside Estes's bar the Bent men tugged at the hangman's knots. The ropes were stiff, and Metcalf charged the United States with twelve and a half cents' worth of soft soap for greasing them. Openly dangling the loops, the quartet walked through town to the jail, where a brass howitzer stood with its muzzle four feet from the door.

Soldiers formed three sides of a square. Armed mountain men formed the fourth side. In the hollow were the prisoners, arms tied behind them. On the backs of their dark heads perched the white cotton caps that soon would be pulled over their faces. Another howitzer on the roof of the jail covered the gallows—two upright posts and a crossbeam placed 150 yards away in the fields. Two hundred and fifty soldiers paraded out and stood at attention. Lieutenant Colonel Willock mounted his horse. The flat roofs of the white and tawny houses were crowded with silent spectators.

Two mules were hitched to a government wagon that stood beneath the crossbeam. Across the wagon's rear rested a single plank. The condemned ranged along it, moving carefully not to upset its balance. The victims spoke a few words for their families; the wagon driver whipped the mules. As the bodies dangled, the mountain men took up a collection and sent word to Estes's tavern that they would want a bowl of eggnog.

"With the execution of those for murder no fault should be found," Garrard reflected as he helped cut the bodies down, but for a man to rise in defense of his native country and then be hanged for treason "is most damnable."[7]

There would be more trials and on April 30 another multiple execution, but the curiosity of Hatcher's party was satisfied. They returned to Vermejo. Orders arrived from William Bent to separate a hundred head of company cattle from the government stock and bring the herd to the upper Purgatory ranch. Along the way the crew met Jim Beckwourth, driving a band of horses and mules. He struck Garrard as able and genial, but Hatcher suspected that Jim was stealing livestock. Without a by-your-leave he searched the herd, found an animal belonging to Ceran, and appropriated it. Jim made no objections.[8]

William and three other men were at the Purgatory, working on the two-mile-long, four-foot-wide ditch which Hatcher had left incomplete the previous fall. Lives might end, but work did not. After time out for hunting bear and talking to Kit Carson and Lieutenant Beale, who rode through with dispatches from California, they all pitched in to build the intake dam. As the tide poured through the first irrigating ditch of any consequence in the American West, William's face relaxed a little. Taking the men down to the grassy meadow, he set them to building cabins and barns of cottonwood logs, had them till the field with iron plows which the company had recently introduced, and planted sixty or more acres to corn.

Young Lewis Garrard did not wait for these developments. In late April he returned to the fort and there joined a quartermaster's train bound for the States. Cajoled by John Smith and hoping to get into an Indian fight, he stopped off to help build Fort Mann, a miserable little post which the government was constructing near the Big Bend of the Arkansas. It had been an interesting winter, he thought.

CHAPTER XVII

DESTRUCTION

From all directions the Indians struck. They knew the whites were at war with Mexico, and the mere existence of hostilities inflamed their own ingrained love of raiding—as did the prospect of rich booty in the ill-guarded quartermaster caravans. But they had real grievances also. Personnel of the increasingly frequent emigrant and army trains slaughtered the buffalo or else by their mere passage drove the herds away from accustomed grazing grounds. Wantonly the whites heaped onto their oversized campfires the scanty cottonwoods which were the Indians' principal source of fuel, shelter, shade, and bark for winter forage. When for any of these causes the red men struck back, some were killed. Now the women wailed for revenge, and the aroused warriors stalked the next party that appeared. Chain reactions became inevitable, and some white men took to shooting on sight—an old American custom born during colonial days on the Atlantic seaboard.

Under the pressure of expansionism these killings could do nothing else than grind on toward a war of total extermination. Caught squarely between the millstones lay Bent, St. Vrain & Company. For fifteen years it had maintained its precarious position by preaching peace to the people of the plains. And now there was no peace.

The wars, the weather, and the tardy arrival of the trading parties from the Platte delayed until May 4, 1847, the departure of the company's Missouri-bound caravan. Landmarks of years left with the train: Ed, the little French carpenter, brokenhearted because gay Rosalie had forsaken him for another company employee; and Dick Green, Charles's slave, who had been given his freedom by George and William because of his bravery during the storming of the Taos Pueblo. With Dick went his wife Charlotte, whose cooking had been a magnet for travelers and mountain men of the entire West. At Big Timbers, competitor William Tharpe joined the train for its protection, and at shabby little Fort Mann the caravan picked up Blackfoot John Smith. Some weeks earlier John had let himself be talked into helping build the post, but constant Pawnee alarms had made him fearful of losing his seven head of horses. Missouri sounded safer, and along he went. As things turned out, neither Tharpe nor Smith gained what he was after. Comanches hit the train at Walnut Creek. Tharpe and a man named McGuire, out hunting buffalo, were surrounded, killed, and hideously mutilated. Forty yoke of oxen, sixty horses and mules were lost—including John's seven and two belonging to young Lewis Garrard, who had sent them from Fort Mann with Blackfoot for safekeeping.

Traveling a few days behind the train came Ceran St. Vrain and a small, fast party—one wagon and twenty-five choice horses and mules under charge of Blas, expert roper and best of the company's herders. With Ceran was Asa Estes, the Taos tavernkeeper; Dragoon Fitzgerald, who had shot insurgent Tomás Romero in Taos; and Frank Blair, who would shortly resign his office as New Mexico's district attorney, marry in St. Louis in September, and never again return to the mountains.

Ceran's group was luckier than the caravan and escaped trouble, but Tom Fitzpatrick, whom they just missed near Westport, did not. Fitzpatrick was bound for his new agency post at Bent's Fort and left Leavenworth on June 8 with Lieutenant John Love's dragoons, who were escorting $350,000 in specie to pay the troops at Santa Fe. At Pawnee Creek, Comanches killed five soldiers, wounded six, and made off with 150 head of stock. Broken-Hand Tom Fitzpatrick, survivor of some of the bloodiest trapper battles in the early days of the Rockies, was hard to frighten. But this year he dared not leave Love's dragoons at the Crossing and take his small agency caravan alone up the Arkansas to the fort. Instead, he went hundreds of miles out of his way, clinging to the government train along the Cimarron route to Santa Fe and then, after a pause in the New Mexican capital, looping clear back over Raton Pass.

He had reason to be cautious. During that summer Comanches, Kiowas, and Pawnees killed 47 Americans, destroyed 330 wagons, stole 6500 animals—and there is no count concerning

Navajo and Apache raids in New Mexico or Ute wars in southern Colorado. The Arapaho were belligerent, and even the
southern Cheyennes came within an ace of joining the attacks.
Comanches and Kiowas invited them to do so, boasting that
whites were easier to kill than buffalo and far more profitable.
Additional motive came from the death of old Chief Cinemo,
who peacefully approached a government train to beg for
tobacco and was shot down by a teamster. The furious tribe
wanted to declare war, but in his last breath Cinemo told them
to maintain the peace which, under William Bent's influence,
the southern Cheyennes had never broken with the whites.
William added his own entreaties, promising that the new
agent would soon arrive with presents to reward their good
behavior.

The Cheyennes were but a drop in the bucket. Back in
Washington, worried army officials decided that a punitive expedition must be sent into the Southwest. In July a call for
five companies of volunteers was issued in Missouri, and the
years-long debate over the most effective way to police the
plains was reawakened. Many experienced traders favored
building forts at strategic locations, similar to those which
Charles Bent had recommended for years. Other traders were
opposed. As long ago as 1831 Joshua Pilcher had pin-pointed
the objection: forts would be hard to supply and the continual
hunting parties would enrage the Indians. The army was
similarly divided in opinion. Kearny, who had marched across
the plains in 1845 to awe the Indians, was known to favor
Pilcher's belief that the best pacifier would be annual demonstrations by strong cavalry squads riding through whatever
parts of the Indian territory were restive at the time. But other
officers argued so vigorously for forts that already two had
been started: Fort Mann near the Big Bend of the Arkansas
and a log post on the Missouri River near present Nebraska
City. They were compromise affairs, however, and neither was
strong enough to be effective.

Ceran St. Vrain, known to many military men as one of the
shrewdest of the plains traders, was drawn into the argument
shortly after his arrival in St. Louis on June 12. As he talked
with the officers about forts and possible locations for forts,
some of his own half-considered problems began to crystallize.

The company situation was uncertain. As yet there had been no decision about the disposal of Charles's interests in the Taos and Santa Fe stores, in the Beaubien and Vigil-St. Vrain land grants, and in the Arkansas fort.

Because of the chaotic condition of the tribes, the Indian trade did not look good to Ceran. Besides, he was losing his taste for the hardships of a trader's life. He was forty-five now and had covered his share of dangerous miles. His gregariousness, grace, and what one friend described as his "peculiarly winning manner" gravitated him more and more toward the leisurely social intercourse of the towns. Moreover, commercial prospects in New Mexico were bright. The troops quartered in Santa Fe, the building of Fort Marcy above the city, and an increasing influx of settlers had already stimulated business a hundredfold. Undoubtedly more settlers would keep arriving, and more posts would be built in the territory. The Indian trade held out no such promise, and as Ceran considered matters it occurred to him that the government's interest in forts might offer a way to solve the entire problem.

Consulting with George and William would take months. In the meantime the army might suddenly decide to build a post at Pueblo or in the Big Timbers, sites that had been recommended as long ago as 1835 by Colonel Dodge. To forestall the possibility and acting impulsively, as he often did, Ceran on July 21, 1847, sat down in his room at the Planters House and dictated a letter to Lieutenant Colonel Mackay of the quartermaster's office in St. Louis:

"Having heard it intimated that the U. S. Government have taken into consideration the project of erecting Forts at the most suitable points on the road from Ft. Leavenworth to Santa fe, with the view to afford protection against hostile Indians, to Government stores, teams &c and to Citizen Traders, I deem it proper to offer to sell the Government, on such terms as may be considered just, the establishment known as Bents' Fort." He described it at some length, declared its facilities were "easily convertible into quarters, warehouses, and Hospital uses," and stated with some exaggeration that "firewood and timber for building purposes have been and always can be procured within a convenient distance." The objection that the fort was not on the direct trail to Santa Fe he met with an argument that the upper Arkansas route was preferable "on account of the better quality of wood, water, and grass."

He knew, of course, that Mackay would refer the offer to the quartermaster general in Washington and that some time must elapse before he received a reply—all the more reason for his acting promptly. Surely there was no harm in finding out the government's price. If the Bents objected—well, that was a problem that could be faced when it arose.[1]

Back on the Arkansas Owl Woman bore William a fourth child—and died. Perhaps her death occurred at the fort; more probably it happened in one of the nomadic villages. William probably did not reach her until after her body, clothed in the finery she loved best, had been placed according to Cheyenne custom on a rude scaffold in the branches of a cottonwood tree.

As soon as he could William visited the lodge and picked up the child. Another boy. And this one had cost Owl Woman her life. As he held it he remembered his dead brother. Charles, he said. That would be its name. And he looked at his dead wife's younger sister, Yellow Woman, who had spent so much time in the lodge with the family. It was Indian custom for a bereaved husband to marry, if possible, a younger sister of the deceased mate—if indeed he had not already married her while the elder still lived. That step William had not taken. But the children needed a mother, and they were used to Yellow Woman. Perhaps without William's spoken words she continued living in the lodge and so, as the months slipped by, became through the slow transition of habit his second wife. Probably there was no other ceremony.[2]

Meanwhile Indians were justifying Ceran's fears. They stole Hatcher's mules and horses, ordered him off the upper Purgatory ranch. When he persisted in staying, they killed all but three of the cattle around the meadow, then told him that the country was theirs and no one could settle on it. John decided they meant business and prepared to leave. Lacking enough oxen to draw his wagon, he cut the vehicle in half, built a cart on its fore wheels, hitched up the single yoke of oxen the Indians had spared, and pulled out. Many years would pass before another attempt was made to settle on the Purgatory's course.

Late in August, Fitzpatrick's agency train reached the fort. With it came Blackfoot John Smith, his Cheyenne wife, and their son Jack. Missouri had soon palled on John. Joining a government caravan, he had returned to Santa Fe, and there Fitzpatrick had hired him as interpreter at a salary of twenty-five dollars a month. Fitzpatrick needed someone who could talk convincingly. Prickling the flats around the fort were a multitude of tepees where the Cheyennes, still angry over the shooting of Chief Cinemo, waited for the gifts that had been promised them.

Tom had no gifts. His requisitions had been sidetracked in Santa Fe and distributed among New Mexican Indians. In scorn the Cheyennes mocked the new agent: tribes who plundered the Americans were rewarded with presents, while they who had been good received nothing. His ruddy face worried under its thatch of white hair, Fitzpatrick consulted William. On credit William gave him coffee and bread, delicacies which the Indians rarely encountered and relished highly. Summoning the chiefs to a feast, Fitzpatrick scolded them for drinking liquor smuggled across the Arkansas, dropped a warning that he was learning which tribes were raiding the Santa Fe Trail so that only the guilty would be punished, and suggested agriculture. Yellow Wolf answered for the tribe; they would be very interested in farming if they could get equipment and instruction. (As usual, they didn't.)

For the time being, Fitzpatrick's promises of gifts next year sufficed. To show satisfaction, the villagers swarmed into the fort and put on a dance. In the middle of it an old woman, drenched with the blood of self-inflicted wounds, entered the circle and exhorted the warriors to remember that Arapaho had killed her son the previous spring. In great excitement a war party rushed off to a nearby Arapaho village—apparently the long alliance between the tribes had worn temporarily thin —killed two braves, captured a squaw, and so had reason for another dance. Fitzpatrick was discouraged. He had just been extolling peace, and now this happened. Gloomily he wrote his superiors that he doubted if agriculture would ever make the Indians settle down. The only law they understood was the

law of retaliation, the only persuasion was their fear of punishment.

William, too, was discouraged. All indications, he told Tom,
pointed to a general uprising throughout the Southwest. Probably it would come with warm weather next spring, and restraining the Cheyennes and Arapaho might prove difficult.
The whites had better hope that the new Indian Battalion arrived soon and put on the brakes by handing the greatest
troublemakers, Comanches and Kiowas, a thorough drubbing.

George came in from Taos. He too was discouraged. With
the southern tribes raising hell all along the Canadian, it would
be folly for the company to go ahead with its plans of reopening Fort Adobe. As compensation, they would have to risk
American Fur Company objections and shift operations northward clear to the North Platte. Learning of the decision, Fitzpatrick said he would go along with George and winter among
the Sioux somewhere near Fort Laramie.

As preparations were under way, George came down sick.
Drawn and feverish, he finally took to his bed. As he grew
weaker, he remembered that Frank Blair had agreed to look
after George's son Elfego when the lad went east to school.
Elfego had already left, and now George asked that if anything happen to him Frank be appointed guardian of his children.

The mere fact that George made the request alarmed William more than anything else. He didn't know what was the
matter or what to do. He called the disease consumption,
which it may have been, and pottered fruitlessly with the
medicine chest which each year was filled for him by a Westport apothecary. Calomel, rhubarb, camphor, Seidlitz powder,
assorted pills—nothing helped. The only other remedies he
knew were the rough-and-ready ones of the frontier. A man
who was shot or cut would wash the wound in cold water,
clap on a pad of buffalo wool, beaver fur, or even chewing
tobacco, and bind himself up with a strip of blanket. Rattlesnake bites were sometimes treated by flashing gunpowder in
the fang marks, and there were those who claimed that rubbing rattlesnake oil on stiff joints would cure rheumatism. Irritated stomachs and dyspepsia were relieved by drinking
buffalo gall mixed with water, and in the spring the Indians

purified their blood by brewing tea from wild-cherry bark. Nearly a hundred different plants and roots were used in various ways by the Cheyennes—for food, dyes, poultices, and internal remedies, always with appropriate magic—and undoubtedly some of them had therapeutic value.

Nothing William tried had any effect. Sometime in October, thirty-three years of age, George Bent died.[3] He was buried outside the walls, next to Robert's grave, and later the bones of both were taken to St. Louis for reburial. When the word reached Santa Fe, the city's recently established newspaper mourned George as "highly esteemed and respected and possessed of almost unbounded influence with the various Indian tribes . . . one of the few to whom the mountains and plains were familiar." The same issue carried an advertisement for two new stores which St. Vrain and Bent had just opened in the capital, one on the plaza, the other at No. 1 Main Street: DRY GOODS, muslins, marinos, alpaccas, cassimeres; ladies' and gentlemen's boots and shoes; CLOTHING excelling in quantity and quality any ever opened in Santa Fe; glassware, tinware, queensware; GROCERIES, coffee, tea, jellies, oysters, sardines, sperm candles, saleratus, cigars, etc; SPIRITOUS LIQUORS, BOTTLE CHAMPAGNE. "People from the country, and those connected with the Army will do well to call and examine."

Lassitude settled on William, and he canceled the trading party bound for the North Platte. Yet work had to go on in spite of him. In mid-November, William Gilpin, a lieutenant colonel now, arrived with the Indian Battalion's two companies of dragoons. Its three companies of infantry he had left in Kansas to repair and enlarge Fort Mann, which had been abandoned under threat of Pawnee attack.

Even two companies were hard to supply, though Bent & St. Vrain had more than a thousand head of cattle wintering along the Arkansas or running wild near the abandoned Purgatory ranch. William was willing to furnish Gilpin with beef and the few other foodstuffs which he had available, but St. Vrain, returning from St. Louis and remembering the difficulties encountered in collecting for the provisions furnished Cooke in '43, said no. Unless contracts came through the quartermaster's office in advance, there were quibbles and delays.

Supplying the soldiers regularly stationed at the fort was trouble—and profit—enough. Forget these requisitions by officers in the field.

William did not insist, but the quarrel left a coolness between the two men.[4] Probably there was iciness over Ceran's unauthorized proposal to sell the fort to the army. If so, it simmered down in the spring when the partners learned that the government had rejected the offer on the advice of Major Swords and Captain A. W. Enos, the latter of whom was frequently at the fort and objected on the grounds that "wood . . . is at present supplied by hauling from 5 to 8 miles and the scarcity is yearly increasing. Grazing also . . . is not good." If the government contemplated a post in the vicinity, Enos said, the Big Timbers was a far better location.

Gilpin's dragoons moved on up the river toward Pueblo and went into winter camp in tents. Their commander was not well. He had just endured a strenuous year and a half: the march with Kearny across the broiling prairies, the cold campaign against the Navajos, the battle-punctuated swing with Doniphan across northern Mexico. He had scarcely returned to Missouri when he was assailed with requests that he take command of the new Indian Battalion. Worn out when he agreed, he now saw the troubles which beset him through a sick man's eyes.

Never a modest person, he asserted that the presence of his dragoons pacified the Cheyennes and Arapaho—though William and Tom Fitzpatrick had not been exactly idle before the troops arrived—blamed the officers back at Fort Leavenworth for treating him with "the most unrelenting malice," and settled down to a winter-long quarrel with Fitzpatrick. The agent retaliated by rejecting Gilpin's brainstorm of settling the Cheyennes and Arapaho on a reservation along the Arkansas as an enforced buffer against their allies, the Comanches, and then needled the commander with charges of waging a sit-down war. Gilpin got even by refusing to grant Fitzpatrick ten dragoons to escort him to the South Platte, where Tom wanted to confiscate some illegal liquor and arrest a fugitive who had murdered a man at Pueblo. Each of them, it is a safe guess, growled continually to William Bent about the other, and by spring he must have been heartily sick of the whole mess.

In March the dragoons crossed Raton to Mora and equipped themselves for a punitive tour down the Cimarron and Canadian rivers. Behind them, the Utes and Apaches promptly went on the warpath. Among other misdeeds, the Indians caught Lucien Maxwell and a party of fourteen in Raton and killed three men, including the Bents' good friend Charley Towne. Elliott Lee and Maxwell were severely wounded. Luckily Dick Wootton somehow learned of the battle through friendly Arapaho, formed a rescue party, and picked up the survivors. But they had lost all their equipment and nearly a hundred head of horses.

Troops in New Mexico were delegated to punish the Utes. Trader Robert Fisher and Old Bill Williams were among the scouts. It was a culminating bit of treachery on Old Bill's part. He had married a Ute—a succession of Utes, probably—and had been living with the tribe during the past few years. The previous winter some of the Indians had given him several packs of furs to trade in Taos. Pocketing the proceeds, Old Bill went on a howling drunk, during which he amused himself by buying bolts of calico, gathering all the peon women he could find, and unrolling the cloth in the street just to watch them fight over it. Since he did not dare return empty-handed to the tribe, he decided he might as well fight them. In the process he got his arm shattered by a bullet and, talking to himself in his querulous whine, shambled down to Pueblo to recuperate. What grew out of the episode would cost John Charles Frémont—and Old Bill himself—one of the West's horrible tragedies.

Fitzpatrick meanwhile had made his way north to the Platte with a party of traders. After holding talks with the Sioux, he swung down the Oregon Trail toward St. Louis and Washington. In his report he accused Gilpin of having accomplished nothing. This is only partly true, and Gilpin's failure did not result from lack of trying. Ranging far and wide along the Canadian, Cimarron, and middle Arkansas, the battalion killed 250 Pawnees, Comanches, Prairie Apaches, and Osages. Surely it was a "strong demonstration" after the pattern advocated by those theorists who believed in a mobile policing of the plains. But Gilpin emerged from the campaign convinced that the mere passage of troops and the fighting of random battles could not of themselves impose peace. As indeed they could not.

Shortly after Gilpin left the Canadian, a gang of Comanches, Prairie Apaches, and rebel Mexicans felt cocky enough to jump no less than two hundred American soldiers under Major Edmondson. The troops beat the attackers off, but travel remained almost paralyzed. Even such an old hand as Kit Carson, on another dispatch-carrying mission from California (and aware perhaps of Marshall's discovery of gold), avoided the southern trails and from Taos circled around by the Platte. In short, the Indians had learned to roll with the punch, and as soon as the troops passed on they happily resumed their raids. Realizing this, Gilpin wrote his adjutant general on August 1, 1848, "Since neither . . . fortified points nor troops *now* exist to control this numerous cloud of savages, it is clear that all the atrocities of a very severe Indian war may be momentarily looked for, and are certain to break forth in the early spring" of 1849. Thoroughly converted to the theory of forts, he proposed a string of posts along the Arkansas and "I further recommend the purchase of Bent's Fort."

And so that problem, which William thought had been solved by the War Department's earlier rejection, was now open again.

The Bent, St. Vrain 1848 caravan underwent its own attack by Comanches, fought them off, and made some capital of the event by giving the Cheyennes a Comanche scalp to dance over. Apparently both partners went with the wagons,[5] and in St. Louis they heard strange talk. For several years visionaries had been proposing a transcontinental railway. Now St. Louis businessmen—Robert Campbell, Thornton Grimsley, perhaps Senator Benton, and others—were dispatching a party up the Arkansas and across the Continental Divide in search of a practicable route. Its leader was to be Frémont, and he planned to cross the mountains in midwinter to determine whether snow would prove an insuperable obstacle to steamcars. Probably Ceran or William, or both, talked to Frémont and his backers—Campbell and Grimsley were old friends—and if so, they surely pointed out the enormity of the risk. Frémont would not listen. He had recently been court-martialed for insubordination to Kearny in California, and although President Polk watered

down the sentence and would have permitted his rejoining the
service, Frémont angrily resigned. Now he was determined to
show the world what he could do. Even Kit Carson's refusal
to join the reckless project could not sway him.

William returned to the fort. In early October, St. Vrain
followed, Fitzpatrick traveling with him. At Big Timbers a
huge encampment of Cheyennes, Arapaho, Kiowas, Comanches, and Prairie Apaches was waiting for the agent—six hundred lodges, or about thirty-five hundred people.[6] Close behind came Frémont's party of thirty-three men, their supplies
on pack mules. The explorers stopped by to watch the present
distribution, feasting, speechmaking. Dr. Benjamin Kern, one
of three brothers in Frémont's party, found syphilitic ophthal-
mia prevalent among the Arapaho, gathered several around
his fire, and treated them, "one of whom hug'd me to the
great danger of my becoming lousy."

Between the Timbers and the fort a fall of snow delayed
the party for a day, and when they reached the post Frémont
was warned that he was courting disaster. Hatcher refused to
guide him; Dick Wootton went along for a way, saw the increasing whiteness of the mountains, and backed out. Stubbornly Frémont continued to Pueblo, described by Richard
Kern as "a compound of Spaniards, horses mules dogs chickens
and bad stench." If Old Bill Williams had not been there recovering from his wounded arm . . . But he was, sixty-one
years old now, bleary-eyed and irascible, his lank body full of
the miseries of a harsh and misspent life. Yet who knew the
mountains any better? Sure, he'd take the party across. But, he
warned Frémont, it would not be easy.

Fitzpatrick, meanwhile, was having fine luck with the Indians. His talks and presents, fortified perhaps by memories
of Gilpin's punitive expedition, filled the tribes so full of good
will that a dazzling project occurred to the agent. Why not
hold a mammoth council to which the entire Indian population of the plains would come—Crows, Blackfeet, and Shoshoni
from the north; Sioux and Cheyennes from the middle plains;
Comanches and Kiowas from the south? At this all-embracing
gathering the hereditary enemies would make peace with each
other and with the United States, their respective territories

would be demarked, and the government would bind itself to furnish food in place of the diminishing buffalo herds.

It was a utopian scheme to come from so knowing a man. But Fitzpatrick took his duties seriously. In the dismal roll of America's corrupt and blundering Indian agents, his name is one of few that leave no sour taste. He labored endlessly against petty frustrations, and he had vision enough to see that piecemeal policies and isolated gift-givings would not succeed much longer. Perhaps a plains-wide integration could not succeed either. William Bent did not think so. An Indian promised anything when surrounded with presents, then forgot the promises the moment he saw a chance for a profitable raid.[7] But William agreed that conditions were so miserable something had to be tried.

In spite of his doubts about the efficacy of peace talks, William now decided to test the results of the Big Timbers powwow and try reopening Fort Adobe on the Canadian River. Kit led the party. He had recently returned from Washington, tired out by his constant courier trips back and forth across the continent. He wanted to settle down and build a home; and partly for the sake of the wages involved he agreed to risk the Comanches. With him he took as potent a group as the plains afforded—Lucien Maxwell, Blackfoot John Smith, Robert Fisher, "Goddamn" Murray, and two Mexicans for cooking and herding.

Peace talk on the Arkansas and peace performance on the Canadian were different things. Kit's party acquired a large herd of horses and mules, only to have Jicarilla Apaches kill the herder and run off every animal, save for a couple of mules tied inside the post. Staying there without horses was impossible. Burying their trade goods and the buffalo robes they had gathered, the men packed their ammunition and camp gear on the two remaining mules and under cover of darkness started the long walk back to Bent's Fort. Stone bruises and cactus thorns so inflamed their moccasin-clad feet that they ran fevers. Then one dawn Kiowas spotted them and charged. Bunching the two mules in the center of a little circle, the whites fired in careful rotation, dropped several horses, and killed three Indians. The booty on two mules was not worth such losses. Sullenly the Kiowas withdrew.

But those were Kiowas. Protesting innocence, a few Comanches came to the fort, said they had missed the opportunity to trade, and asked that goods be sent them. Business was poor on the Arkansas, and William decided this might be an opportunity not only to bolster it but also to recover the goods which Carson's party had been forced to abandon. Kit and Maxwell, however, had gone on to Taos. So William asked for volunteers, and Dick Wootton offered to take out a dozen men and two wagons. The group found the Indians so arrogant and quarrelsome that they dared not visit the villages, but required the Comanches to come to the fort and even then would admit only two or three at a time. Finally matters grew so bad that the whites locked themselves in, cut a hole in the wall "about as big as a ticket window in a railroad station," and traded through that. Annoyed at the arrangement, the Comanches took to shooting at the wicket. Finally an old chief calmed things down, and the whites left with a good supply of robes and deerskins. But, Wootton says, "it was the most hazardous trading expedition I ever had anything to do with."

Completely disgusted, William decided to give Fort Adobe one last try himself. In the spring he went down with some ox-drawn wagons—and promptly Indians killed part of the stock. Enough was enough. But he would not leave the fort intact for Indians or Mexican Comancheros to appropriate. With gunpowder he blew up the interior and returned to the Arkansas.[8]

Everything was collapsing. At Bent's Fort, Marcellin got into a wrestling match with an Indian and killed him, accidentally, it is said—little Marcellin, five feet six, weighing one hundred and fifteen pounds. In other years the trouble could have been smoothed over by presents and a feast. But not this year. In ugly clamor the savages surrounded the once inviolate walls and yelled for satisfaction. So long as Marcellin stayed inside he was safe, but some fine day the vengeance seekers would catch him on the trail. William and Ceran advised him to get out of the country, go back to Missouri.

(And, Marcellin demanded, what of his family? He had two wives, the Sioux Red, whom he had married at Fort St. Vrain and who had borne him two sons and a daughter. Later there was another—an incongruous match, a rawboned Pawnee six feet tall, noted chiefly for her ability to tan buckskin. She was the mother of two boys, but when Marcellin fled she was apparently left to shift for herself and drifted up to Pueblo, where she perhaps married one of the hangers-on and then, either single or wed, scratched out a garden of corn, pumpkins, and melons. But Red was something else. At Marcellin's insistence that she be cared for, Ceran agreed to take her to Mora, where he had just moved from Taos to set up a gristmill and another store. Oh, Marcellin assured Red, he would be back. But in Missouri he met Elizabeth Jane Murphey, and on June 26, 1849, they were married. When Marcellin returned west in 1851 or so, it was to pick up Red's sons and take them away. As she had been doing before, Red kept climbing a hill alone each day and from it looked for hours toward the east. For years she maintained the vigil, then finally yielded to Bill Bransford's entreaties and married him. It was a happy ending. She became a Catholic, bore Bill seven children, and died at the little town of Trinidad sometime in 1885 or 1886.)

Marcellin's departure was a bitter pill for the company to swallow.[9] The day had been when this empire and this empire's men would have yielded to no one. And now a St. Vrain was running like any scared greenhorn from a bunch of yammering Indians!

Perhaps Ceran would not have acquiesced so readily in Marcellin's flight if he himself had not decided to leave the firm. He and William could not agree. Charles was the one who had held the widely varied company projects together. Had George lived, his wife in Taos and his love for the plains might have furnished a motive for keeping the gap bridged. But no common bond was left now. There is not one record that William Bent ever went to New Mexico for any purpose other than necessary business. Though his brothers and Ceran had married Mexican women, his wife was a Cheyenne. The Indians and the rolling immensity of the plains—those were the fibers out of which he had woven his life. The robe trade might collapse as completely as Ceran feared, the prospects in New Mexico might be as dazzling as St. Vrain argued. No matter. William could not bring himself to leave the Arkansas, nor Ceran to stay.

When the dissolution was completed is not known. Perhaps

it was in early February 1849, when Ceran rode through from
Taos on his way to the United States. He had news of still
another disaster. A few days before, he had dined at Kit's
home with Frémont and had seen what was left of the expedition. On top of the Continental Divide snow had swallowed
the party. By the time the remnants of it floundered back to
Taos, eleven men—one third of the total—were dead, all mules
and equipment lost. And still Frémont was determined to continue to California. He tried to persuade Kit to go with him.
But Kit and Lucien were planning to try ranching again on the
Little Cimarron. After all these years Josefa, childless still and
taking care of Charles Bent's daughter Teresina, had a right to
expect some kind of permanent home. In '45 Frémont had interrupted Carson's first ranching attempt, but this time Kit was
adamant. No more California for him.

Hearing that Ceran was bound for Missouri, Frémont gave
him, to mail to his wife Jessie, a long letter describing the
disaster and placing the blame on Old Bill Williams. For years
trappers' fires and traders' posts would hear bitter controversy
over whether Old Bill or Frémont or just plain bad luck had
brought about the ghastly debacle whose toll was not yet
over.[10] No doubt Ceran and William had their opinions, but
when first the men at the fort heard the news, it may well
have struck them as one more black mark against the blackest
year they yet had known. Was there a curse on the land? Could
nothing go right?

In those dark days Bent, St. Vrain & Company ceased to
exist. Details cannot be resurrected. Probably no more cash
changed hands than was necessary to balance off Ceran's interest in the fort against William's share of the New Mexico
stores. The claims of Charles's and George's families of course
had to be met. Like William, they all retained their interest
in the St. Vrain-Vigil land grant, although Bent realized that
the touchy temper of the Indians would hold development in
abeyance for some time to come.

A last julep, a handshake, and Ceran rode on down the trail.
William turned back through the iron-studded gate. Conceived largely as a result of his first venture among the Cheyennes, the sprawling castle was now entirely his. But ghosts
walked with him across the placita, up the stairway to the

big apartment. Three brothers, his wife . . . It was all his now. And he was alone.

The army would have bought it from him. Proponents of western forts had partially won their battle. To protect the Oregon Trail, Fort Kearny was built near Grand Island on the Platte, and Fort Laramie in Wyoming was purchased from the American Fur Company for four thousand dollars. As part of the over-all plan, the War Department approached William about Bent's Fort. Unauthenticated rumors vary the offer from twelve to fifty thousand dollars. Whatever the amount, William thought it a poor return after the use the army had made of the post since the days of Dodge's visit and finally, during the Mexican War, all but ruining the company's business. The quartermaster, naturally, was figuring price brick by brick, not weighing the bristly sentimentality of the owner who not so long ago had watched ten times twelve thousand dollars' worth of business flow through the gates in a single season. Contemptuously William refused.

When spring 1849 arrived an incredible surge of whites swept over the plains. Gold in California! The first argonauts hurried through Fort Laramie in May. Not long afterward a mail carrier counted ten thousand wagons straining westward. The size of the flood dumfounded the Indians and perhaps helped stay the uprising Gilpin had predicted. Though the Oregon Trail bore the brunt of the frenzied rush, southern routes shared in the travel. Troops protected three thousand emigrants who went from Fort Smith, Arkansas, up the Canadian to Santa Fe. Other hundreds flowed past Bent's Fort to Pueblo, then frayed north or south around the mountains by various routes.

Gold! The magic word did not excite William Bent. The possibility that it lay nearer at hand than California must have crossed his mind before. Undoubtedly he had heard the Arapaho legend of the golden bullets. Years before, the story said, Chief Whirlwind and a war party which possessed only three guns had run out of ammunition, had discovered on the ground small pieces of yellow metal soft enough to be worked, and had molded them into balls. Later the Arapaho defeated a party of Pawnees, every yellow bullet killing an enemy—obviously great magic. Many traders in New Mexico believed the Pueblos knew of secret gold deposits other than the placers below Santa Fe. Wandering the mountains in the early 1840s, Rufus Sage speculated on their mineral possibilities, as did William Gilpin during his return from Oregon in 1844. Old Bill Williams and a trapper named Du Chet were reputed to have picked up nuggets. During the years other nuggets or reports of nuggets had come into Fort St. Vrain and probably into Bent's Fort also; and there is a legend that in 1848 William himself picked up specimens when he and his family were returning from a visit at Jim Bridger's and Louis Vasquez's fort in southwestern Wyoming. All very interesting, but not worth going out and digging for. Certainly California was too far away to appeal to William Bent.[11]

So far as the plains were concerned, the main thing brought by the rush was a new horror—cholera. The disease was not unknown along the eastern end of the Oregon Trail (Whitman had fought it there in 1835, three years after it had ravaged New Orleans), but this year its virulence surpassed prior experience. In St. Louis, at the height of the epidemic, the death wagons were carting off sixty to eighty persons a day. Barrels of tar, sulphur, and other reputed disinfectants were burned on the street corners in hopes that the dense, stinking clouds of smoke would "dissipate the foul air." A hundred-dollar fine was imposed for bringing fresh vegetables or meats into the city from the country, and emigrants were quarantined in a special compound. From St. Louis the disease moved upriver to Independence and Westport, then rode westward with the California-bound caravans. Hundreds of graves began dotting the Oregon Trail.

Far out on the plains the epidemic began to burn itself out, but not before a Cheyenne village had visited a camp of emigrants who were drying meat beside the Platte. As the Cheyennes moved on southward, mysterious cramps began to seize men and women. They fell from their horses, went into convulsions, died. The survivors had no idea what was the matter. In terror they fled toward the Arkansas, and when the deaths stopped they supposed they had outrun the invisible enemy. Recovering confidence, they crossed the river to a conclave of prairie tribes gathered to celebrate a new peace between the Osages and Kiowas.

So lucrative a trade spot might have attracted William, but he had gone to Westport with the caravan and had taken his eldest boy, eight-year-old Robert, with him. Perhaps he had a notion of continuing to St. Louis, but the plague drove him away from the settlements. Meanwhile Yellow Woman had gone to the tribal conclave with her aged mother and her step-children—Mary, George, and the baby Charles. It was a fine gathering—lots of feasting and trade. Yellow Woman picked up an iron kettle she needed, and then everyone gathered to watch the Kiowas' farewell dance.

In the middle of the drumming a big Kiowa warrior keeled over, writhing and clutching at his belly. The medicine men carried him into a lodge, where he expired. A curious Osage elbowed through the crowd to take a look, groaned suddenly, and collapsed. Now White Face Bull, one of the Cheyenne chiefs, recognized the mysterious slayer which had followed the party from the Platte.

"The Big Cramps!" he yelled. "Everybody run!"

Panic swept the encampment. Shrieking Indians scattered in every direction. Some did not tarry long enough to take down their lodges. In mortal terror Yellow Woman assembled her family. Eleven-year-old Mary was big enough to ride, but George and baby Charles were piled into a mule-drawn travois with a keg of water, some dried meat, and bread. As fast as the horses could go, the Cheyennes streamed toward the Cimarron, the travois bumping and the children screaming with fright until exhaustion put them to sleep.

All along the way people died, but darkness finally forced the unreasoned flight to pause. While they were making camp, more perished. One warrior donned full war dress, mounted his best horse, and rode through the village, calling for the cowardly enemy to come into the open and fight. There was no answer. As he stepped from his horse, convulsions seized him and he died in his wife's arms.

During the night the children's grandmother, old Gray Thunder's widow, died in agony. Yellow Woman persuaded some friends to help her hastily put the body in a tree scaffold, and at dawn the wild flight began again. Completely bewildered, afraid of each other, afraid even of the dry wind that whispered across the sand, the group split into smaller and smaller segments. Finally Yellow Woman slipped away from everyone else and took the children to the fort.

She arrived completely worn out, too exhausted even for emotion. William was there, or arrived shortly. As she told her tale leadenly, as he checked reports from other sources, he learned that within weeks the epidemic had wiped out half his people, half of the southern Cheyennes.

The knowledge that the big fort's allies were crippled perhaps emboldened the other Indians who drifted back and forth along the river that summer. Or perhaps it was just the general restlessness of the Southwest, swelling after spring's brief quiet to such ugliness that Ceran told James Calhoun, the new agent at Santa Fe, "a worse state of things has not existed in this country." Whatever the cause, Utes and Apaches, Comanches and even Arapaho became increasingly impudent. They openly insulted the traders, defied suggestion, circled the walls with taunts and threats of attack.

There was no real danger. William could shut the gate and fight off every Indian on the plains.

But the fort had not been built primarily for warring against these people.

Suddenly William Bent stood up. The rooms, the ghosts that walked the rooms—he could no longer endure them. Not here.

On August 21 he ordered his employees to strip the place of every article of value. The resultant pile filled twenty wagons, each pulled by six yoke of oxen. He put the children and Yellow Woman on their horses or in the travois. Silently, as the employees stared in perplexity at each other, he led the train to a creek five miles down the river. He told them to camp there.

Then he rode back alone.

A strange, defiant pride was in him. He could have collected many thousands of dollars from the government for this adobe fortress. But the army should not have it, nor its memories, nor its ghosts. Nor would the Indians be able to move into it, hold their dances, mock his passing, fight his white nation.

He rolled kegs of powder into the storage and trading rooms

along the eastern wall. Making a torch, he moved from apartment to apartment and into the northeast tower, setting fire to the wooden roofs and to the piles of junk accumulated through the years of living. As greasy smoke spiraled into the sunset light, he reined out through the gaping gates and eastward along the river.

Behind him, the death boom of the prairie's greatest feudal empire split the evening sky.

CHAPTER XVIII

TURN BACK THE CLOCK

The distant boom reached the ears of Leon Palladay, a Bent trader camped on Timpas Creek with a States-bound government train. As the caravan crept on the next day, Leon's unbelieving eyes saw fumes curling upward from the shattered eastern wall. For two more days the sour-smelling rubble smoked, and in the blackened remains the stunned men could find nothing but a few saddles that had been overlooked in the southwest bastion. The possibility of willful destruction never entered their minds. All they could think was that somehow Indians had done the impossible and seized the place.[1]

Then they found wagon and cattle tracks leading down the river to the Big Timbers. There William had gone into camp, and Palladay's bafflement must have increased. Why had William obliterated the post? What was he going to do next? The spectacular ending suggested a terrible finality, a closing of the books on the past, and, as a corollary, a brand-new plan for the future.

That is exactly what did not develop.

Under the shelter of a stone bluff in the Big Timbers, William built three log cabins joined in the shape of a square-bottomed U, their open side, facing the river, defended by a picket stockade. It was no castle. But in that humbler environment William Bent settled down to exactly what he had been doing in more luxurious surroundings for the past seventeen years—trading with the Indians.

Why, then, the impetuous destruction? What, basically, was the character of the man?

His life had been dangerous and austere, compounded of patience and quick flares of anger; of deep loyalties and touchy individualism, of courage and gruff sentimentality. But he also possessed a shrewd commercial sense which had long realized that the Big Timbers furnished a better site for trade than had the old location; and now no partners remained to preach caution to his boldness by pointing out how much had been invested in the former fort. Up it went in smoke, partly to keep anyone else from utilizing it. It was a dramatic gesture. But the man who made that gesture was no mere sentimentalist.[2]

Business was good in the Big Timbers that fall. The arrival of Fitzpatrick made it better. Tom had carried his dream for a prairie-wide council of Indians clear to Washington and had won support, but the lateness of the season led David Mitchell, in office again as Superintendent of Indian Affairs, to advise postponement of the gathering until 1850. For keeping the red men happy in the interim, Fitzpatrick was allotted five thousand dollars' worth of presents.

Comanches and Kiowas joined the Cheyennes and Arapaho to enjoy the gifts. Buffalo were thicker along the river than they had been for several years, and hundreds of squaws walked down among the trees or over the ice, carrying robes on their own backs or on ponies. There were other causes for celebration. Yellow Woman bore William Bent his second daughter and fifth child, Julia. Then in mid-November Irish Tom Fitzpatrick, fifty-one years old, took to himself as wife the teen-age daughter of trader John Poisal and an Arapaho, sister of Chief Left Hand. By way of a honeymoon the newlyweds rode in the agency wagon to Fort Laramie, where Fitzpatrick visited the Sioux and northern Cheyennes. He returned to the Big Timbers in January with word that the Indians he had seen were excited about the proposed treaty. Peace talk floated everywhere—except in New Mexico, where Kit Carson, Robert Fisher, and Bill New tangled on Kit's ranch with Jicarilla Apaches; and in the United States Congress, where the House of Representatives declined to pass the Senate bill that would have authorized the prairie council.

In the spring the rush to California picked up again, and the traders of the plains flocked toward the Platte, "as keen," one observer wrote, "as any Yankee wooden nutmeg or clock peddler." They sold sugar at twenty-five cents a pound, flour at eighteen dollars a hundredweight, brandy at eighteen a gallon. And draft animals. William and Kit went up with a drove of horses and mules, stayed until late June. Back at the ranch on Little Cimarron Creek, meanwhile, Josefa bore her first child after seven years of marriage. When the delighted Kit reached home, he named the boy Charles after his dead friend. Charles Bent's two daughters, staying on the ranch with their aunt Josefa, were happy at having a new cousin to play with. Three years later there would be another, named William.

It soon became evident that there was small profit in taking groceries to the Fort Laramie side of the Oregon Trail. The emigrants left Missouri well provisioned, and on the overgrazed trail fresh draft animals were their first requirement. During the next years Bent traders did not carry even their own groceries northward. They swapped food with the pilgrims, sold animals, purchased the caravan's worn-out oxen for a song, fattened the beasts along the South Platte, and resold them at fancy markups to later trains. After 1850 the trade became double-pronged as argonauts began returning to the States, many of them carrying California-minted, octagonal fifty-dollar gold slugs. Until excessive competition diluted the trade, Hatcher, Goodale, and other Bent men returned to the Big Timbers with their saddlebags clinking from the heavy coins.

Although the southern Cheyennes had been severely reduced by the cholera of 1849, the northern branch had suffered little. They, the Arapaho, and the Sioux gravitated around the tributaries of the Platte. This, coupled to the proximity of the Oregon Trail, led William to repair temporarily Fort St. Vrain. Considerable work was necessary. As long ago as 1846, according to Francis Parkman, "the walls of unbaked brick were cracked from top to bottom . . . the heavy gates torn from their hinges and flung down. The area within was overgrown with weeds, and the long ranges of apartments once occupied by the motley concourse of traders, Canadians, and squaws, were now miserably dilapidated."

Mexican labor was still cheap. Soon the motley concourse reoccupied the apartments, the Indians danced again in the placita, and the benign Little White Man once more gratified them with presents of looking glasses, combs, beads, and brass rings.[3]

For a year Congress held up Fitzpatrick's treaty, but by the early spring of 1851 arrangements were completed. In May the agent's wagons moved up the Arkansas, stagnant and drought-shrunken this year, to a new fort called Atkinson, built near the ruins of short-lived Fort Mann. William either traveled with Tom or met him in the vicinity. Various military personnel were about, including the wives of some of the officers. Colonel E. V. Sumner marched in with a command bound for New Mexico—"Bull-Head" Sumner he was called, because a musket ball had once bounced off his cranium without doing appreciable damage.

Fitzpatrick sent out runners to gather the Arkansas Indians. Soon a swarm of Cheyennes, Arapaho, Comanches, Apaches, and Kiowas gathered to eat the agent's bread, coffee, and pork, receive his gifts, and hear his announcement that the delayed council would be held in the summer near Fort Laramie. The Cheyennes and Arapaho amiably agreed to attend, but the others were sullen. Too many enemies. If they went up there they would lose every horse they owned. None of Fitzpatrick's assurances could sway them.

The tepees, feathered warriors, and buckskin-clad women were a great curiosity to the green troops. And of course an Indian was always insatiably inquisitive. The two races began fraternizing with a freedom that neither William nor Fitzpatrick approved. "Such free and unrestrained intercourse," Tom wrote, "carried on between officers, privates, squaws, and Indians . . . was certainly a new thing to me." He warned the commander, but the word came too late and an incident occurred that threatened to destroy all hope of a peaceful council.

A young Cheyenne chief, very popular in the tribe, saw a ring on an officer's wife and took it from her finger to look at it, a liberty he would not have essayed had the whites maintained the dignity which traders long ago had learned was necessary. The woman screamed for her husband, who appeared with a buggy whip and lashed the Cheyenne across the face. In Indian eyes no greater insult could have been inflicted. Fury boiled throughout the Cheyenne village. A great medicine man named Bear donned his bear robe, put two bear's ears on his head, painted his face with white chalk and green powder, and rode among the lodges, haranguing the tribe to prepare for war.

Sumner ordered his dragoons into battle array. Fitzpatrick and William rounded up some cooler chiefs, blocked off Bear and his furious followers. Loaded rifles on one side, drawn bows on the other—a nervous finger could have precipitated horror. But luck was right that day. The whites cooed softly, and finally the hotheads relaxed.[4]

The various parties went their ways, but the Cheyennes had not forgotten. As was so bitterly usual in white-Indian affairs, persons unrelated to the original trouble paid the tab—or in this case nearly paid. Along came Kit Carson with wagons belonging to Lucien Maxwell, who was now in a merchandising partnership with his father-in-law, Carlos Beaubien. In the train was Kit's thirteen-year-old half-Indian daughter, Adaline, returning from school in Missouri, for Kit hoped that Josefa's own child would forestall jealousy. Cheyennes dogged the caravan, spoiling for trouble because of the recent whipping. Kit gained time by an adroit mixture of bluff and mild talk and that night sent a runner slipping away after troops. The next morning the Cheyennes saw the messenger's tracks and were persuaded to behave themselves. Another man than Carson might have let the incident balloon into the first southern Cheyenne attack on whites since the day William Bent reached the country and lined his Indians up on the side of peace. What then would have happened to Fitzpatrick's treaty is anybody's guess.

Though the conference was not scheduled to begin until September 1, Cheyennes, Arapaho, Oglala and Brûlé Sioux began gathering near Fort Laramie by the end of July. One hundred and ninety-five dragoons were on hand to give the Great White Father an adequate show of might. Fitzpatrick's father-in-law, John Poisal, and Blackfoot John Smith served as official interpreters. Dozens of plainsmen, William among them, rolled in their wagons to batten on the unprecedented trade opportunities. Many had their Indian families along and shared in the feasts and ceremonies.[5]

The hot days of August drifted by and then more dragoons appeared, escorting fancy carriages loaded with David Mitchell and other big chiefs of the whites. Thoroughly embarrassed, Mitchell had to report that the army had fouled things up at Westport Landing and the wagonloads of presents would not arrive at the conference for several days. Sighing, Fitzpatrick went out to explain to the Indians.

So far the assembled red men were all allies. But now word arrived that the Shoshoni, gathered by Jim Bridger, were approaching under their magnificent chief, Washakie. A roaming party of Cheyennes violated the truce by killing and scalping two Shoshoni outriders. Bridger, Bent, Fitzpatrick, and everyone else talked fast, the Cheyenne headmen promised reparations, and rage simmered down. One noon representatives of the enemy tribe appeared, sixty or more warriors marshaled in front, their women, children, and baggage cluttered in the rear. A bugle's sharp trill threw the dragoons into parade line. Then a crazy Sioux whose father had been killed by the Shoshoni let out a war whoop and singlehanded charged the approaching army. Washakie jerked up his gun; friends of the Sioux reached for their quivers. But a racing interpreter overhauled the Sioux and threw him from his horse before he could precipitate carnage. Now Washakie raised his hand. Down swept the Shoshoni warriors in thunderous splendor, wheeling right and left in full gallop, clockwork precision that left the white cavalrymen agog. With good reason Jim Bridger strutted proudly about, boasting of "his" Indians.

Ten thousand savages were there. All had extra horses for trading and for display. The fantastic herds roamed for miles. Grass began to disappear, the camps to stink beyond endurance. And still the wagon train of presents and provisions did not arrive. Fort Laramie was stripped of every edible it possessed, and at last the commissioners decided the villages would have to move. In choking dust the travois, the carriages, the howling dogs and curvetting horsemen marched in indescribable pandemonium eastward to Horse Creek. There Mitchell put up a huge conference tent, lodgepole pines were lashed together into a flagpole, and to the booming of a cannon the talks began, punctuated by wild, gun-firing cavalry displays by the various tribes. New delegations kept arriving: a solid column of Crows, some Assiniboins, Arikaras, Minnetarees. With the last named came missionary Father de Smet for a field day of baptisms in a painted buckskin lodge—305 Arapaho children, 253 Cheyennes, 280 Sioux, and 60 or more half-bloods, including Fitzpatrick's year-old Andrew Jackson. Protestant William Bent's brood probably stayed away, unless the mass excitement set Yellow Woman to thinking that such magic might be worth trying on some of her little ones.

After interminable discussion by the men who knew the country best, tribal boundaries were drawn up. To the Cheyennes, Arapaho and portions of the Sioux went a massive 122,500 square miles between the Arkansas and North Platte —roughly all Colorado east of the mountains, a big slice of western Kansas, and the adjacent southern corners of Nebraska and Wyoming. Emigrants were awarded transit rights and the government won permission to build forts. Annuities were guaranteed to the tribes, and a delegation of chiefs was selected to visit President Fillmore in Washington. Blackfoot John went along as one of the interpreters. He'd have big tales to spin when he returned the following spring.

And still no wagons came. As food ran out, the Indians slaughtered innumerable dogs to keep the feasts going. The fetor of the new campgrounds grew so overpowering that the troops moved two miles off for relief. Then at last, on September 20, the caravan appeared. Chiefs and subchiefs, grotesquely decked out in parts of army officers' uniforms, supervised the chaos of the distribution of presents, and on the twenty-second the gathering began to dissolve.

Peace in our time. And for a little while there was. The next July, to be sure, William had a tiff near Fort Atkinson on the Arkansas, where Kiowas and Comanches were awaiting the presents they had grown to expect. Bent was leading a small caravan westward—five wagons and two "traveling carriages," a new style twist for his family. (Evidently Yellow Woman frequently visited the Westport farm, something her elder sister seems to have done but rarely.) A little behind his party came the nine-wagon caravan of a man named King.

William was just unyoking at the fort when a courier galloped
up with word that the Indians were trying to stampede King's
loose stock by screeching around the wagons and waving buffalo robes. Pretty soon someone would shoot and all hell would
break loose.

Returning at a dead run, "howling Indian, French, English
and Spanish," William and his men broke through the cordon
and formed a guard around the caravan. As the wagons gingerly advanced, the Comanches threatened with mock charges
that stopped just short of actual collision. William defied
them with bawdy gestures and Indian-style boasting, and at
length, aided by a friendly Arapaho chieftain, ensconced King
in the fort. The small garrison was so taut with alarm as to be
almost useless. Knocking out the head of a sugar keg, William
put the hostile chiefs in a line and fed them sweets out of an
iron spoon. This kept them pacified until two companies of
riflemen, summoned by the worried commander at Atkinson,
came marching up at double time. Fearing retribution for
their antics, the Indians tore down their lodges and splashed
away across the river.

In spite of the brief friction, William the next autumn followed the Comanches south to the Canadian for trade. The
old pattern was tugging at him. Fort St. Vrain did not satisfy,
nor did dickering with grass-green wayfarers on the Oregon
Trail. Always the Arkansas had been the pivot of his life, and
the three log cabins in the Big Timbers were a pale substitute
for the days that had been. He knew Fitzpatrick planned to
come out in the spring and add the Comanches and Kiowas to
the signatories of the great peace treaty of 1851. Perhaps sta-
bility would last. Perhaps William could turn back the clock
and rebuild the empire that once had embraced the middle
plains from Texas into Wyoming, from the mountains to the
middle of Kansas.

In the winter of 1852–53, after returning to the Big Timbers from the Canadian, he put ten men to hewing stone out
of one of the bluffs on the north side of the river, then hurried
to Westport for supplies. There he also landed a contract for
hauling freight to Santa Fe. This filled most of his wagons,
but he left room for materials such as the old fort had never
dreamed of—building hardware, ready-made doors, window

frames, glass. He hired stonemasons and carpenters, and in
June 1853 lined his wagons up the Arkansas.[6]

He himself had to go to Santa Fe with the freight. At Aubrey's Crossing the train split. Driving one wagon loaded with
the children and household goods, Yellow Woman went with
the workers to Big Timbers. William kept on into New Mexico. Quite likely he saw Ceran, who was engaged in furnishing
materials for the hideous new territorial capitol and was still
neck-deep in politics despite an unsuccessful 1850 campaign
for the territory's lieutenant governorship. Ceran heard of
William's new plans, but if any twinge of envy woke old memories, there is no record. William turned back over Raton,
down Timpas, past the moldering ruins of the old fort. What
he thought as he looked at those bleak remnants is unguessable. He must have passed them before, but this time he was
re-creating another post in their image.

The stone walls of the new fort were rising when he reached
Big Timbers, thirty-eight miles away. Standing on elevated
ground above the river in such position that it could be approached from one direction only, the structure was somewhat smaller than its predecessor.[7] It was extensive enough,
however. There were twelve rooms around a central court,
each room ten feet high and ranging in size from two apartments fourteen by fifteen and a half feet to a warehouse fifty-
five feet long. There were parapets, but evidently no bastions,
and the little cannon were placed on corners of the roof. From
the top of the walls, sixteen feet high, one could see on a
crystal day a dim line that was the mountains.

While construction was under way William lived with his
family in a lodge shaded by one of the region's huge cottonwoods. The Bent children romped with the Indian children,
swam daily in the river, practiced hunting with blunt arrows.
George was ten now, could ride bareback at breakneck speed
through gullies and among trees, and was already dreaming
of his first buffalo kill—an exhilaration his twelve-year-old
brother Robert had already experienced. Six-year-old Charles
rolled in the dirt, climbed on the gentler horses, pretended to
hitch packs to dogs. Julia was still small enough to play with
dolls made of buckskin stuffed with hair and ornamented with
bead noses, eyes, and mouths. They were lean, supple,

bronzed, long-haired—and savage. The eldest, Mary, was a particular worry. She was fifteen now, and love flutes of courting
swains sounded outside the tepee on the soft summer nights.

Perhaps Mary and Robert had already experienced brief
exposure to school at Westport during a few winter weeks, but
occasional indoctrination was no longer enough. Unless the
children left their present environment, they would become
complete Indians. Certainly they deserved as much opportunity as Charles's Alfredo or George's Elfego, both of whom
were in St. Louis, or as Teresina and Estafina, who had left
Kit's ranch to be educated at the convent of the Sisters of
Loretto in Santa Fe. Were not William's children equally
bright—and equally Bents?

Early in the fall he took his three eldest with him when he
went east to pick up the annuity goods which henceforth
would be distributed at the new fort. In Westport he sought
out Albert Boone, Daniel's grandson and a brother of Panthea
Boone Boggs. Boone was a business associate as well as William's close friend; with W. M. Bernard he ran a huge outfitting concern that bought and sold quantities of Bent's goods.
At William's behest, Boone agreed to assume guardianship of
the three children until they were able to go on to a more
advanced school in St. Louis, where William's sister, Dorcas
Bent Carr, would look after them.

The Westport pause, William felt, was a necessary transition. The Carrs were part of the social aristocracy of St. Louis;
during the 1850s their blooded race horses were consistent
winners at the big October meet on the fairgrounds; and one
of the tantalizing vacuums of the Bent story is the impression
which the liveried slaves, glittering candelabra, and snowy
linen of their aunt's mansion later made on these young half-
red relatives from the wilds. To judge from future developments, it was not profound.

Westport would not be so completely strange. Roustabouts
from the plains congregated in its taverns, many Indians still
tied their shaggy ponies to its picket fences, and several trappers had homes on its outskirts. Adjacent to the Bent farm,
where the children would spend much of their time, were the
farms of Louis Vasquez and Jim Bridger. Though Vasquez's
children were white, Old Gabe's, by first a Flathead and then

a Ute and currently a Shoshoni, were as wild as the Bents. They made familiar playmates.[8]

Satisfied that the children were provided for, William returned to the fort with the agency goods and worked out the method of distribution which would be followed for the next several years. Runners summoned the tribes. Hundreds of lodges dotted both sides of the river above and below the stone fort. Drumming, singing, and the exchanging of gifts went on for nights. The different soldier bands danced barbarically in the placita, and William repaid the compliment by feasting the chiefs in the main dining room. When distribution time came, the boxes of goods were unloaded on the prairie. Men, women, and children sat in dense circles around the piles. Since Indians did not understand boxes, William's employees opened the crates. Then the head Indians took over and appointed soldiers to sort the food, clothing, and ammunition and see that everyone received his fair share.

The affair was joyful, noisy, very Indian—and indicative of tragedy. The tribes could no longer support themselves. More and more they would depend on white man's charity, turn into beggars, become degenerate. Fitzpatrick saw it as he made his last swing through the agency in 1853. Sadly he wrote in his final report, "They are in abject want of food half the year. . . . The travel upon the road drives [the buffalo] off or else confines them to a narrow path during the period of emigration, and the different tribes are forced to contend with hostile nations in seeking support for their villages. Their women are pinched with want and their children constantly crying with hunger. . . . Already, under pressure of such hardships they are beginning to gather around the few licensed hunters . . . acting as herdsmen, runners, and interpreters, living on their bounty; while others accept most immoral methods with their families to eke out an existence."

There were other signs that the white man's tracks would soon be large upon the land. California had filled with a heterogeneous population not yet stable enough to feed itself. In New Mexico, Carson, Maxwell, Wootton, Hatcher, and other ranchers threw together huge herds of small, coarse-wooled sheep and drove the animals across mountains and deserts to astounding financial rewards on the coast. California needed more than sheep, however, and the cry for a transcontinental railroad grew so vociferous that Congress at last authorized the surveying of northern, central, and southern routes.

Frémont, advocate of a line along the thirty-eighth parallel, expected to lead one of the expeditions but was passed over in favor of Captain John Gunnison, whom William met and advised shortly after the surveyors left Westport in the early summer. Aggrieved, Frémont formed his own party and once again, in the words of his father-in-law, Senator Benton, "chose the dead of winter . . . that he might see the worst"—and also remove some of the stain of the 1848 debacle. He stopped at the new fort in the fall of '53 and from William obtained fresh animals, a small buffalo-skin lodge for himself, another that was large enough to house twenty-five men, quantities of dried meat, sugar, coffee, tobacco, stockings, gloves, moccasins, and overshoes. There was much less snow this winter than there had been in 1848, and by following the route Gunnison had already surveyed over gentle Cochetopa Pass, the Pathfinder got through, though not without considerable discomfort and the loss of one man. At that he was luckier than the government party, for Captain Gunnison and six of his men were slain by Indians in Utah.

In the East, the railroad talk led several companies to take out grandiose charters. The excitement reached to New Mexico and Ceran St. Vrain, who dashed off a note to Carson, "There seems to be a new stir in regard to a Rail Road through New Mexico if you will sign this letter it May adjust the Matter Some." But no railroad came. Neither the North nor South, fast approaching irreconcilability, would let the other strengthen itself by tapping the West.

Yet somehow the mountains of freight had to be moved more expeditiously. In 1855 Congress appropriated $100,000 for surveying better wagon roads, one to go from Fort Riley on the Platte to Bridger's Pass in Wyoming, the other from the same starting point southwestward to Bent's New Fort on the Arkansas. At the Big Timbers, William told Lieutenant Bryan that a shorter way down the Arkansas could be found by striking cross-country to Walnut Creek. These white man's tracks, however, were too large for the Cheyennes and Arapaho to stomach; they refused to act as guides and objected so strenuously to the proposal that the short cut was abandoned.

By now the Santa Fe Trail was rutted so deep that the trace would be visible a century later. Wagons grew monstrous in size, the three-hundred-pound hind wheels towering higher than a man's head. Even so, the rough road prevented loading more than five or six thousand pounds on a single vehicle. Often trailers were attached and tremendous lines of yoked oxen were necessary to drag the vehicles at snail's pace through the dust. The loquacious, singing French-Canadian drover of earlier days began to give way to a hirsute, profane, dirt-encrusted bullwhacker who walked beside the cattle armed with a three-foot handle to which was attached a twenty-foot lash of braided rawhide. The whip was heavy. From the handle, the lash swelled gradually until it reached a circumference of ten inches, then tapered to a foot-long, ribbon-shaped thong. A dexterous teamster could knock a coin off the top of a stake, or with a cruel, pistol-like pop draw a mist of blood from the hip of a lagging ox. One famed bullwhacker bet a comrade a pint of whiskey he could cut the seat of the other's pants without marking the skin. The friend agreed and bent over. There was a loud crack, followed by an anguished yell and the longest jump on record. "Thunder!" said the whip wielder sadly. "I lost the whiskey."

In such a train William Bent each spring hauled increasing loads of Indian annuities to the fort at an average rate of seven and a half cents a pound, or a payload of about four hundred dollars a wagon. His teamsters were paid twenty-five dollars a month and found, and his return trips were more profitable than those of most Santa Fe haulers because he could load on buffalo robes which his traders had collected during the winter. As soon as the annuities were distributed, he returned east for his own trade goods. There are no figures concerning his net profit, but he did tell his son George that out of each government trip he cleared enough to pay for the next winter's trade items. He also took back to emigrant outfitting points, such as St. Mary's Mission, herds of half-broken horses and mules.

There were moments when the old ways lived again, when the world wore a morning freshness and aboriginal gods smiled

on an aboriginal people. One time, for some reason of trade
or distribution, William drove his teams beyond the Big Timbers toward the site of the old fort. Six hundred lodges of
Cheyennes followed. They were running out of food when
inspiration came to White Face Bull. This, his medicine said,
was a propitious time for an antelope surround.

Train and village halted. White Face Bull made two antelope arrows, each consisting of a ten-inch hoop tied near the
end of a three-foot pole in such wise that the pole was the
hoop's diameter. The symbols were painted black and decorated by dangling raven feathers. With the arrows White Face
Bull rode out onto the plains, the camp following. When his
magic told him he had reached the proper spot, he dismounted, sat on the ground, and beckoned for two unmarried
girls to sit beside him—fat girls so the antelope would be fat.
Holding the arrows at arm's length, he drew them toward him,
just as the antelope were to be drawn. Then he gave the arrows
to two other girls, who ran with them until overtaken by young
men on horseback. In diverging single-file lines, with White
Face Bull as the junction point, the warriors galloped out of
sight.

The elder men, the women and children, hundreds of them,
all holding blankets or robes, formed in a long, shallow crescent, its center on Bull and its horns pointing in the direction
taken by the horsemen. William and his men joined the line.
The thing was impossible, of course. Unless a runner had
tipped the medicine man off, he could not know whether there
were antelope within miles; if there were, this hocus-pocus
would serve only to make them bolt.

The minutes dragged; the waiting Indians jabbered and jos-
tled. Then they saw a dust—a huge herd of leaping antelope
running straight toward the crescent. Mounted warriors raced
on either side and behind the herd. The leading horsemen
galloped up to White Face Bull and gave him the magic symbols. The crescent swung inward, forming with its blankets
and robes a circular human fence. But bows or guns could not
be used for fear of endangering the people. So White Face
Bull and his son, Porcupine Bull, advanced into the circle.
With his wands the elder made circular motions. A curious
frenzy seized the antelope. They milled in circles, broke their

legs, exhausted themselves. Though a few broke away, most subdued themselves with their own panic and lay helpless. Now the people ran forward and killed them. Every woman in the village had at least one antelope, and William's train was supplied with all the choice tongues it could use.[9]

As always, the Cheyennes came to William for help in forestalling dangers that passed their ken. In the spring of 1854 one of them brought smallpox from a Kiowa camp to his small village near the stone fort. Ten lodges were infected and panic threatened. Knowing that flight might spread the scourge across the plains, William calmed the people down, persuaded them to stay where they were, set up a strict quarantine, and doctored the sick. When the disease had run its course, he burned every suspect article. Only one Cheyenne died.

While winter's cold held white travel to a minimum, the Indians could maintain illusion, killing their buffalo and tanning their robes in the old way. But each summer brought increasing numbers of caravans, and restlessness grew, first among the mountain Utes, who had signed no treaty. They harried the settlements which Beaubien was establishing on the Sangre de Cristo grant, attacked dragoons near Taos, and Christmas Day, 1854, they wiped out the redolent old adobe post at Pueblo. Twenty miles from Pueblo, where Dick Wootton and Charley Autobeas had established ranches at the mouth of Huerfano Creek, nine Cherokee teamsters were massacred and their wagons burned. Autobeas's stock was run off and one of his men was slain. Completely beset, Governor Meriwether of New Mexico called up six companies of volunteers and commissioned Ceran St. Vrain their lieutenant colonel. Guided by Kit, St. Vrain's men marched with Colonel Fauntleroy's regulars through the San Luis Valley, whipped part of the Utes at Poncha Pass, chased others eastward to the Purgatory, and at the moment of victory were called off. Kit was furious: "If the volunteers had continued in service three [more] months and had been under the command and sole direction of Colonel St. Vrain, there would never again have been need of troops in this country."

Now the trouble spread to the plains. In hindsight, its appalling aspect is the triviality of the incidents that started it. In the summer of 1854 a Sioux killed one footsore cow lost by

a Mormon emigrant. The Sioux chiefs offered ten dollars in-
demnity; the Mormon demanded twenty-five. After a long
quarrel, hotheaded Lieutenant Grattan marched out of Fort
Laramie with thirty-two men and two howitzers, melodramati-
cally proclaiming that he would "conquer or die."

He died. So did every one of his men.

The standard punitive expedition was then sent out under
Colonel William Harney. Never mind who was responsible for
the earlier wrongs. Just shoot anybody. Inevitably those least
able to run away were shot first. At Ash Hollow on the North
Platte, Harney fell on a Sioux village that fled without offering
resistance. The soldiers killed eighty-six Indians, many of
them women and children. (As slight justification, it should
be noted that at a distance Indian males and females were
indistinguishable.) Another seventy women and children were
seized as hostages; piles of equipment were captured. Completely terrified, the Sioux agreed to give up the man who had
killed the cow.

The northern Cheyennes had their initial trouble over a
horse. At the Upper Platte Bridge an officer demanded from
a passing band four horses which he said belonged to white
men. The Indians handed over three animals but argued that
the fourth was theirs. Losing patience, the officer arrested
three of the Cheyennes. Frightened, they tried to break away.
One escaped, one was killed. The third, who had had nothing
whatsoever to do with any of the horses, was recaptured and
imprisoned at Fort Laramie, where he died a year later from
the effects of the confinement.

The arrests sent the band fleeing, with the disputed horse,
into the Black Hills. There they vented their annoyance by
killing a trapper totally unacquainted with the matter. A few
weeks later another band approached a mail wagon to beg for
tobacco. The driver had heard that trouble was afoot. Nervous,
he shot one of the Indians and in turn was wounded in the
arm. Troops aroused by his panicked flight galloped out from
Fort Kearny, killed six Indians, wounded eight or ten more,
and captured—or stole, depending on the viewpoint—twenty-
two horses and two mules. The Indians retaliated by attacking
two innocent emigrant trains, killing a total of four men, two
women, and two children. A third woman was "passed on the

prairie"—raped to death in relays, an act of revenge not uncommon among the prairie tribes. Another incident at Fort Kearny resulted in the unprovoked wounding of a chief named Big Head, and the feeling grew among the northern Cheyennes that the white men were deliberately seeking war.

In the fall William called all the Cheyennes together to receive their annuities. He was despondent. The stone fort had been a mistake, and he knew now that the things he had hoped to recapture were forever gone. Archaic, the post was also expensive; what Indian trade was left should be conducted from a smaller, easily maintained stockade. During the summer he had tried to sell the fort, but for some reason the deal collapsed.[10] Reluctantly he stayed on. He still had his investment to protect. He still had his duties to his people.

When they gathered, sullen and angry, he tried to preach patience. The northern Cheyennes would not listen and took the southern branch with them to winter on the Solomon River in western Kansas. At a series of indignant councils, relatives of the slain men pleaded for revenge. Times seemed propitious for a fight. Eastward, the whites were falling out among themselves. Kansas bled as Free Soilers and Slavers fought for supremacy under the doctrine of squatter's sovereignty. Troops were recalled from the plains because of the sacking of Lawrence and subsequent guerrilla savageries by John Brown and his ilk. At the Indian camp two powerful medicine men, White Bull and Dark, argued that now the Cheyennes could take advantage of the whites' troubles.

It was wishful thinking. In May 1857 eight companies of cavalry left Leavenworth to teach the tribe a lesson. Four of the companies under Major John Sedgwick marched up the Arkansas, guided by a powerful 190-pound Delaware named Fall Leaf, who had been with Frémont in 1853. White-haired, trumpet-voiced Colonel E. V. Sumner, old Bull-Head, led the rest of the troops up the North Platte to Fort Laramie and then swung south to rendezvous with Sedgwick. So far the Cheyennes had avoided both columns, but now Sumner heard that the entire tribe was congregated on the Republican River in western Kansas. The report was only partly true. The southern Cheyennes, reconsidering the winter's war talk, had gone to the Big Timbers to consult with William Bent. Sumner, however, thought he had an opportunity to crush them all at a single blow. Leaving his baggage wagons behind, packing his equipment on mules, and driving beef cattle with him, he made a lightning march toward the Republican.

William knew in general of the movements, probably through visiting Indians. So, unfortunately, did the unusual number of Mexican traders who had congregated along the river that spring. These men, William learned, were trying to make capital of the situation by prompting nearby Cheyennes and Arapaho to seize the fort. The arrival of the annuity goods did nothing to relieve the situation. With the train came a new agent, Robert C. Miller, a thirty-year-old ex-sailor with blond hair hanging to his shoulders and ships tattooed on his arms. Miller refused to distribute any goods until he had consulted with Sumner, who might order the Cheyennes' share withheld as punishment. Pending Sumner's arrival, Miller wanted to store the annuities in the fort.

William refused. By every indication he could learn, Sumner would not parley with the Indians but would provoke a fight. The northern Cheyennes would most likely oblige him and probably would be whipped. The defeat would inflame their southern brethren and allies. Heeding the Mexican troublemakers, they might well fall on the unprotected fort to get the annuity goods, which they felt were rightfully theirs anyhow—particularly since arms and ammunition were included in the shipment. Not for a thing like that would William Bent risk a battle with people against whom he had never raised a hand in anger.

Miller now ordered him to receive the goods as contracted. William's men, picking up the rumbles from the Indian camp, said they would not stay in the fort if the annuities were put there. On July 19, after a long conference with Miller, William washed his hands of the mess by offering to rent the fort to the government until such time as the goods were disposed of. The agent agreed, and the next day William loaded up all his transportable equipment. On the twenty-first, driving his cattle ahead of him, he abandoned his home for the second time.

By one of the West's weirdest coincidences, the attack he feared did not develop. Medicine Men White Bull and Dark had convinced the northern Cheyennes that if the warriors dipped their hands in a certain lake the white man's bullets could not harm them. In supreme confidence, chanting their war songs, three hundred clean-handed braves drew up to await Sumner's cavalry. For some incredible reason the colonel did not fire. Instead he ordered a saber charge. The Indians were prepared to resist guns and might have met an orthodox attack with bravery. But the flashing steel dismayed them. Convinced that their magic had been circumvented and that all was lost, they broke and fled.

They were well mounted. The pursuing cavalry succeeded in killing only four, according to Cheyenne count, nine according to Sumner, who lost two men killed, eight wounded. Not defeat, then, but terror swept the Indians in complete rout across the prairies. They abandoned most of their tepees. Sumner found the deserted village, burned 171 lodges and destroyed eight or ten tons of dried meat.

Unable to overtake the fleeing segments of the band, he swung around to Bent's Fort, confiscated the annuities, threw powder, lead, and flint into the river, and gave the Cheyennes' share of the goods to the "friendly" Indians gathered there. Still burning for blood, he would have pursued the tribe farther, but the outbreak of the so-called Mormon War led to his being ordered into Utah. Though the northern Cheyennes tried to restore face by a few inoffective raids along the Platte, the failure of their magic and the sight of the huge supply columns moving toward Brigham Young's intransigent Mormons took the heart from them, and the winter passed in comparative quiet.

The fort was soon turned back to William, but he did not reoccupy it immediately. After leaving the Big Timbers in July, he took his wagons and cattle about twenty-five miles westward and crossed the Arkansas to the rich bottomlands at the mouth of the Purgatory. There, close to the spot where he and his brothers had first talked to Yellow Wolf about moving permanently into the vicinity, he built a temporary stockade.[11] This was no squatter's right. He could, and did, claim title to the ground through his interest in the St. Vrain-Vigil land grant, just as his niece, Charles's daughter Estafina, was also claiming title to another 5118 acres on Greenhorn Creek, seventy-five miles farther west.[12]

During that fall and winter of 1857 on the Purgatory, William undoubtedly heard that in the summer Blackfoot John Smith had taken some Mexicans to the South Platte and there, about two and a half miles from the present state capitol building, had dug out a quantity of gold dust. Quite possibly, also, he learned that Major Sedgwick's Delawares, burly Fall Leaf and Little Beaver, had met some Missourians prospecting along the Front Range and from them had obtained a goose quill containing a few golden grains.

As yet none of those stories had reached Kansas. Oddly enough, however, talk of Rocky Mountain gold filled the air. It was born of despair. Depression crushed the land. In the little towns along the Missouri River bankrupt farmers and unemployed artisans remembered the California rush of '49, "when a poor man had a chance." Those placers were exhausted now, and the more recent Fraser River stampede seemed abortive. But surely not all the gold was as far away as the Pacific.

One man, William Green Russell, was certain of it. He had learned mining around his native home of Dahlonega, Georgia, and in California. In 1857, back east again, he had moved from Georgia into Kansas to farm. There word somehow reached him through relatives of his Cherokee wife that in 1850 a California-bound party of Cherokee Indians had panned a show of color somewhere along the South Platte. Seven-year-old gossip—but it couldn't be any worse than Kansas farming was that year. He talked to his brothers and friends, wrote to some Cherokees in Indian territory, and during the winter drummed up a party.

On June 12, 1858, Russell's group of seventy whites and Cherokees reached the stone fort in the Big Timbers. Though only three employees were there, the post's beautiful appearance and "spacious" apartments impressed the wayfarers—as did a few barrels of liquor, "of which we partook at a cost of a dollar a pint." Not all of the visitors were gold seekers. Among them were three mysterious women: a Mrs. Kirk and her two children, white; a Mrs. Kelley and her sister, Cherokees. According to the chronicles, Kirk and Kelley were taking their women with them only as far as the fort. No reason is given, and the women vanish from the scene. They did not reach Cherry Creek with the argonauts, and they were not at the fort when a second party hurried up on June 28.

The newcomers were the Lawrence party, formed almost overnight after their leader, John Easter, saw Fall Leaf's goose quill of gold. Included in the forty-four members were prim Mrs. Middleton and twenty-year-old Julia Archibald Holmes, most definitely not prim. Julia, whose husband had been one of John Brown's fiery followers, was a feminist. She wore what she called the "American Costume"—a calico dress that reached scarcely below her knees. Beneath it, most shamelessly, were pants, or bloomers. To this outfit Julia added Indian moccasins and a man's hat, walked along the trail with the men while Mrs. Middleton rode in a wagon, and was annoyed at not being allowed to stand guard duty at night. At Bent's Fort the employees gaped openly, but a "gentlemanly man" recovered enough to do "the honors in Mr. Bent's absence." Several males in the party celebrated by getting roaring drunk.[13]

William was en route east and certainly passed the Lawrence party along the way. On July 15 the Kansas City *Journal of Commerce* noted his arrival in that town with the remark that he had "probably transported more goods over the Great Western Plains than any one man living." In his own way he was becoming a legend. To be sure, Jim Beckwourth had received more notoriety with his book of bloody bombast dictated in California to a man named Bonner and published in 1856; and in 1858 Kit Carson was glorified in a biography by army surgeon DeWitt Peters. If he so chose, William could have read mentions of himself in either book, but no amanuensis had tried to pin him down for his own story—or, trying, had been bluntly rejected. Still, his name was known. An October 1857 article in *Harper's Magazine*, describing his rescue of King's caravan at Fort Atkinson, had led off with no more identification than that "the name of Bent is too well known to require a card of introduction to the public." When information was wanted about the plains, he was the one sought.

Strangely, no one seems to have asked him about gold that

July. But when he returned from St. Louis in September, after
a visit with those of his children then living with Dorcas, he
was engulfed by a frenzy of excitement:

GOLD! GOLD!! GOLD!!! GOLD!!!!
HARD TO GET AND HEAVY TO HOLD
Come to Kansas
California and Frasers River "No whar!"
CHERRY CREEK AND PIKE'S PEAK AHEAD!!!

The headline was typical.[14] "The excitement," reported
the Missouri *Democrat's* Kansas City correspondent, "is vastly
on the increase. . . . Old men, young men, women, and
children may be seen in groups, discoursing the merits and
demerits of the wondrous discoveries of gold 'almost in our
midst.' If there is not an abatement of this feeling before
spring our city will be depopulated."

The word "demerits" might have been emphasized. Months
before this, the bulk of William Green Russell's Cherokees
had quit Colorado in disgust and turned homeward, leaving
only thirteen of the original party to explore the creeks draining out of the foothills. But the frontier did not know this. A
dribble of fact had ballooned rumor into extraordinary pro-
portions. A few more people had seen Fall Leaf's dab of gold.
George Simpson, an army teamster (and before that one of
the founders of the noisome Pueblo fort), had visited the little
towns with yellow dust he had panned from Cherry Creek in
May. Then along had come a man named Cantrell with a sack
of dirt he had obtained from the Russell party. An old California miner panned Cantrell's dirt in the main street of Westport and revealed a few shiny grains. Promptly the sack of dirt
became a sack filled with pure, unalloyed gold.

The moment William reached Kansas City to load his annual caravan with goods, wild talk began to circulate about
what he was going to do and what he knew. The *Missouri
Democrat*, September 8: "Col. Bent, of Bent's Fort, is loading
his teams in this place now for exporting goods to the mines.
He expects to establish a trading post there." The Kansas City
Journal of Commerce, September 7, reported that six men
from Jefferson City had written to make arrangements for
traveling west with Bent and estimated that a total of twenty

or twenty-five gold seekers would accompany him to the fort, "forty or fifty miles distant from the discoveries on Cherry Creek"—a distance shrinkage William would never have been guilty of; air-line from the fort to Cherry Creek was about 165 miles; by the usual trail via Pueblo, about 220 miles. In addition, said another article in the same issue of the *Journal*, "Some forty-odd Frenchmen arrived here Sunday morning . . . to go out with Col. Wm. Bent to his fort upon the Arkansas, near the new gold regions, where they are to be employed by the colonel, about his fort, trains, trading post, and the mines."

Most of this was rampant speculation which may have come from some of William's men but hardly from him. So on September 15 the *Journal of Commerce* sent a reporter to the docks for a direct interview. What William told him was not specific, but not discouraging either:

> Col. William Bent has been trading in the vicinity of the country for many years. He says the existence of gold has been known to the Indians ever since his residence among them. He made many inquiries after the discovery of Gold in California and ever since has been satisfied of its existence. The Indians, however, have always remonstrated against the knowledge being made known to the whites. . . . As one old chief told Bent, if the white men ever found the gold they would take from them their "best and last home."

Shortly after talking to the reporter, William started toward the fort. Perhaps a few gold hunters went with him; undoubtedly French roustabouts helped goad the oxen. Despite the newspaper talk, however, he did not employ a single Frenchman at any mine; he did not establish a trading post near the diggings. There is no indication that he ever seriously considered doing so. His whole plan was to continue as best he could the life he had long ago created for himself and for his people of the plains. As the interview shows, he knew— and the Cheyennes would soon know—that these discoveries would accelerate the death of that life. Even then he was probably groping for some means to ease the passing.

CHAPTER XIX

THE WHITE TIDE

William had scarcely reached the fort when the issue that would rack the plains for the next decade became clear cut. Whose country was this? In October gold hunters from Lecompton came through the Big Timbers bearing commissions from Governor Denver of Kansas Territory as officials of "Arapaho County." In 1855 the Kansas legislature had drawn a paper county reaching to the mountains but had never organized the district for want of population. Matters now were different. The white men flooding up the golden trail were to govern themselves as white men should—in the Kansas image. Governor Denver told his commissioners to set up Arapaho County as a functioning entity. What William Bent told them is not of record. But he knew that the land north of the Arkansas was, by Fitzpatrick's treaty of 1851, expressly reserved to the Sioux, Arapaho and Cheyennes. Neither Kansas nor any of the squatters congregating along Cherry Creek could legally claim one square inch of it. Nor, for that matter, could William, except for such building permits as accrued to him through virtue of his license as an authorized trader.

A county. And in the county, towns. Close behind the Lecompton party came another, which numbered in its members a tall, arrogant ex-general of the Pennsylvania militia, dressed in a long blue overcoat. He was William Larimer, devoted to the cause of temperance and less interested in gold than in town-company speculation. With Larimer was his adult son. In their four-yoke ox wagon the future city builders carried six pine planks, some nails, window glass, tools, and a year's supply of provisions. Though the cabin they planned to erect and the town company they hoped to form must of necessity stand on Indian land, they seem to have dismissed the matter as scarcely worth consideration.

At the fort General Larimer purchased from William twelve apples for a dollar, a buffalo robe for four dollars. He also wrote a letter to his wife which contains one of the most

puzzling remarks in the often puzzling story of the Bents:
"Mr. Bent has a white wife; I did not see her, but some of the
boys did. She wears hoops and I guess makes annual visits to
St. Louis with the Colonel. They live in the most retired spot
of earth. . . ." It is difficult to imagine Yellow Woman in
hoops, or even a white woman so clad at the Big Timbers. The
general's informants perhaps saw the Mrs. Kirk who had journeyed to the fort with the Russell party the previous spring
and then vanished from the chronicles. There is no reason to
believe that William ever married a white woman, and sup-
position that he brought a mistress to "the most retired spot
of earth" strains credulity. Someone must have been pulling
the boys' legs.

Others besides the general were interested in town companies and would spend the winter jockeying for supremacy
along the banks of Cherry Creek before the Lecompton
party's and Larimer's Denver finally emerged triumphant over
would-be Montana City, St. Charles, and Auraria. Meanwhile
a village of inquisitive Arapaho settled nearby. After all, it
was one of the tribe's ancient camping grounds. Vague notions
that the Indians might try asserting their rights began trou-
bling some of the promoters. About that time Blackfoot John
Smith, trading this season for Elbridge Gerry, drifted down
from his station near the ruins of Fort St. Vrain with another
trader called Jack Jones—real name William McGaa, an Eng-
lishman of reputedly noble birth. Both men had their Indian
wives with them, and Smith's half-Cheyenne son Jack was also
on hand, digging intermittently near the placers his father
had opened the year before. Thinking the two traders might
have influence over the Arapaho, certain promoters gave them
stock in their town company and for the sake of John's squaw,
pregnant again, helped Blackfoot put up his half of the town's
first cabin. Actually John avoided most of the work. It was
an enjoyable winter for him. When his company displeased
him, he blandly switched to another.

Despite the nearness of snowy weather, more emigrants
kept arriving. Some seventy-five cabins and two stores were
built along Cherry Creek that fall. Smaller settlements appeared near the sites of Fort Collins, Boulder, Colorado
Springs, and Pueblo. It would be strange if William did not

yield to curiosity and visit some of the towns. And if he did not see them with his own eyes, he soon heard of them from the Indians.

Late in November a delegation of Cheyennes and Arapaho visited him at the fort. Restless and bewildered, they begged him to write the Great White Father and stop these invaders from cutting down their trees, pre-empting their favorite haunts.

William realized that the stampede could not be stemmed now, yet he knew that some compromise would have to be worked out that would protect the Indians. On December 1, 1858, he wrote on the chiefs' behalf to A. M. Robinson, Superintendent of Indian Affairs in St. Louis. Urgently he advised the sending of commissioners west to conclude a treaty that would clearly define the Indians' rights before "they cause a great deal of trouble." Now more than ever the savages would need to be tutored in agriculture. "They are anxious to get at it. If you will only give them a start they will go ahead."

This letter from a man whose judgment he respected worried Superintendent Robinson. At best Congress acted slowly. There was little likelihood that a treaty would be authorized in the immediate future. Yet William said prompt action was necessary. The only solution, as Robinson saw it, was to appoint an agent who could control the tribes while the government made up its mind what to do. A good agent, unfortunately, was something the plains had not been blessed with since the days of Tom Fitzpatrick. There were, to be sure, hordes of applicants for the job; dishonest men had long ago learned that fortunes could be made with goods deliverable to illiterate savages who had no notion of bookkeeping and who signed with their marks any voucher they were told to sign. No such man could possibly meet this situation. But who could?

Robinson thought he knew. Acting on his own responsibility, he wrote Washington, recommending that William Bent be appointed. On April 27, 1859, the commission was signed by President Buchanan. Shortly before this date William arrived in St. Louis. Counting on the fact that agency selections were almost automatic on his say-so, Robinson presented the news of the appointment to William as a *fait accompli.*

Agent! There was nothing about the red-tape-snarled job that William wanted. The salary would be no compensation for the interference with his business. He needed to oversee personally his caravans, the fort, the traders. He—

And meanwhile what would happen to the Cheyennes?

It was the beginning of agonizing problems that would consume most of the rest of his days. Early in May he reluctantly accepted the position and began buying the materials he needed.[1] They did not include farming implements. Such items were not in the department's budget.

With him in St. Louis was his oldest son, Robert. Though only seventeen, the boy was mature and level-headed, eager to get started on his own. William decided to lend the youngster some wagons and let Robert take out a contract for hauling the annuity goods to this year's distribution point on the South Platte. William would be traveling with the train and could make sure that Robert garnered valuable experience without too many headaches.

When father and son reached the junction of Beaver Creek and the South Platte in mid-July, the main body of Indians was hunting in western Kansas. Only forty-five lodges of Cheyennes were waiting for him. William sent runners after the others, then conscientiously sat down before a box in his tent. Though no report was yet due from him, he laboriously wrote Robinson of what he had done and what he planned to do. The Indians peered over his shoulder at the strange magic and demanded to know what he was telling the Great Father. It was not the panacea that they implicitly believed he could bring about. But from it—and it is one of the few documents we have in William's own hand—much of the man's character shines forth.

> The Cheyans and Arrapahos [he wrote] have took my advice to them last Winter and this last Spring. I am proud to say they have behaved themselves exceedingly well. . . . Theair will be no troble settling them down and start farming. They tell me they . . . have passed theair laws amongst themselves that they will do anything

I may advize. It is a pitty that the Department can't send
Some farming implements and other necessarys this fall
Sow as they could commence farming this Coming
Spring. . . .

After I deliver the Indians theair goods I intend . . . to
have a conversation with the Kioways and Commanches.
I suppose that [they] will be purtay saucy—but as I have
bin appointed agent I feel it my dutay to see all of the
Indians under my Agency—if they sculp me.

I am compelled to visit St. Louis abought the last of
August as I left some of my business unsettled which
must be settled this fall. I received Commissioner Mixes
letter ordering me to remain with the Indians but my
business unsettled in the States Amounts to more than
three times the Amt of my Salary. I dont think the Department will blame me for going to St. Louis and Staying 8 or 10 days and return this fall to the uppur Arkinsas.
I have mutch more to say but the Indians bother me so
that I shall have to close you Must excuse my bad Spelling as I have bin so long in the Wild Waste I have almost
forgotten how to Spell.

Not until the middle of August did the hunting parties
return. The delay hurt Robert, for the worried boy had to pay
and feed his idle men during the wait. ("He is now nearly out
of Provishions," William wrote Robinson, "and it is costing
him about 75 dolls per day"—a parental exaggeration?—"to remain here. I am afraid this tripp will ruin him.") And all this
time emigrant wagons, freight caravans, horsemen, and private
expresses were flooding past. Though the Cherry Creek diggings had proved a delusion, new strikes farther back in the
mountains once again sent excitement to fever pitch. Unend-
ing lines of hopeful argonauts—sixty thousand of them, William would estimate in his annual report—poured up the Arkansas, along the Platte, and, more seriously, through the
Indians' favorite buffalo country on the Smoky Hill route between the two main rivers.

The old Cheyennes were alarmed, the young men ready to
fight. Earnestly William entreated them to stay patient a little
longer and promised to see that a fair treaty was forthcoming.

Then he started for the Arkansas, his belated business trip to St. Louis subordinate now to the larger considerations of obtaining speedy action on behalf of the Indians.

Though the caravan may have cut directly south to the Big Timbers, William veered westward to the raw, lawless town that was the source of his troubles. There he quite likely saw Dick Wootton and Ceran St. Vrain. The former, a leading citizen of the community now, had brought in several wagonloads of goods the previous Christmas and had quickly made himself "Uncle Dick" to all Denver by broaching a keg of Taos Lightning, hanging a tin cup beside it, and inviting everyone to partake. In the spring he had built a store on whose canvas-roofed second floor W. N. Byers established Colorado's first newspaper. About this same time Ceran had sent in a train of "the greatest stock of goods yet seen on the market," and that August followed in person with another caravan of whiskey, bacon, coffee, tobacco, tools, women's and men's shoes, and flour milled from his own San Luis Valley wheat—$40 for a 196-pound barrel.[2] Also, as William would shortly learn in Westport, his neighbor, Louis Vasquez, with Jim Beckwourth as clerk, was likewise about to invade Denver with a load of nails, window glass, crockery, groceries, dry goods, dried fruit, catawba wines, and champagne. William, however, had no desire to forsake his old trade to join this new merchandising rush. Always the Indians and the needs of the Indians were his primary concern.

He wasted no time in Denver. Early in September he started east from the Big Timbers. On the fifteenth he met the sullen Comanches and Kiowas at Walnut Creek, got nowhere talking to them, and hurried on. By October he was in St. Louis. There, while he attended to his own business with only part of his attention, he hired a secretary to put a final polish on his report to Washington. But it was from no secretary's heart that the urgent eloquence came:

"A smothered passion for revenge agitates these Indians, perpetually fomented by the failure of food, the encircling encroachments of the white population, and the exasperating sense of decay and impending extinction with which they are surrounded. . . . A desperate war of starvation and extinction is imminent and inevitable, unless prompt measure shall prevent it."

The first measure, he said, must be a new treaty. Illegal though the towns along the foothills were, the Cheyennes and Arapaho had no choice now but to cede those lands, as well as strips of territory along the main routes of travel. In return, they must be given adequate annuities and an ironclad guarantee that the territory remaining to them would this time be inviolate. Since the Kiowas and Comanches, expelled now from Texas, were crowding northward and competing for the last buffalo, it was imperative that instruction in farming be started immediately.

William knew that opponents of Indian agriculture would scoff, as they had for years, at any dream of settling the prairie tribes on farms. He knew the belief of the young braves that soil tilling was a squaw's work, their proclivity for war, and the temptations offered by the endless caravans. Both red men and white would have to be protected from themselves, by force if necessary. Abandoned forts along the Arkansas, like Atkinson, would have to be replaced and a new one built at— here he hesitated, thinking of the ruinous effect on his trade but also of the stone post he no longer wanted—at the Big Timbers.

More than this he could not do. The rest was up to the government. After the briefest of visits with young George and Charles, he hurried back up the Arkansas, where the Kiowas were preparing to go to war with the United States. The other Indians, enraged by this breach of the peace which they had promised William to keep, offered to punish the Kiowas if Bent said the word. Such an internecine struggle he refused to countenance, though on November 28, 1859, he wrote privately to Robinson that "it would be the cheapest plan to get rid of the Kioways." In the East, meanwhile, a punitive expedition was being slowly prepared under Major John Sedgwick, who had been with Sumner in the angry days of '57.

In February, William returned to St. Louis. The government was acting with unwonted swiftness. As a result of his report Fort Larned was already being built near Pawnee Fork, and he was asked his price for his stone building in the Big

Timbers. Twelve thousand dollars, he said, and refused to be budged by the quartermaster's clucks of outrage. He learned, too, that an appropriations bill to implement his proposed treaty would shortly be introduced in Congress, and Robinson was sure it would pass. William thought that now he could resign from the agency job he had never desired. The superintendent, however, was too delighted with what he had accomplished to let him escape, and prevailed on him to return to the plains as agent, distribute the summer annuities again, and keep an eye on the other tribes during the Kiowa war.

Meanwhile there were personal troubles. A message came from Albert Boone in Westport that Mary, William's eldest daughter, was in love with a saloonkeeper named R. M. Moore.

A saloonkeeper! Half Indian Mary might be, but she was also a Bent. William went to Westport with fire in his eye. Moore calmly faced him down, and when William began investigating, his temper cooled. The twenty-seven-year-old Ohioan had sent himself through Cleveland Commercial College by clerking in a store, then had gone to St. Paul and out of youthful inexperience had let himself be fleeced in ill-judged land speculations. Saloonkeeping had been just a way to keep alive when he had drifted penniless into Westport. Businessmen around town liked him, and William decided that perhaps poverty wasn't a degradation after all. Besides, the young people were stubborn.

Realizing that nothing he could say would change their minds, the reconciled father on April 3, 1860, gave Mary away at a lavish wedding on the farm—a jubilant occasion to which he invited every available trader and trapper he had known in the mountains. A little furry-tongued afterward but benign with reminiscences of life before the blight of gold, he lent his new son-in-law money enough to start in the mercantile business and then returned through a blistering drought to the Arkansas.

In July three thousand Cheyennes, Arapaho, and Apaches gathered at the stone fort to receive their annuities. The Kiowas and Comanches were not with them. Sedgwick's troops had pounced on Chief Satanta's village, and although Satanta escaped, his wife and children were seized. Sedgwick gave

them to William for safekeeping as hostages and then returned to Fort Larned. In early August the captives escaped—
or William let them escape; he had little sympathy with hostage holding. Still, formalities had to be observed. Dutifully
he sent Mark Ralfe, a young Frenchman, down the Arkansas
to Sedgwick with a report of the flight. Twenty-five miles or
so below the fort, Kiowas shot Ralfe three times, stabbed him
when he still twitched, and with a dull knife took off all his
scalp save tufts of hair above each ear. He should have died.
But Cheyennes found him breathing and took him back to
the fort, where he recovered.

Sedgwick received word of Ralfe's experiences at about the
same time that orders came from the War Department for
him to return to the Big Timbers and start erecting a new
cantonment, to be known as Fort Wise after the governor of
Virginia. Promptly Sedgwick forgot Satanta's escaped family.
Exasperated by the assignment, he complained by letter to
the assistant adjutant general about embarking on such a project so late in the season and then suggested utilizing Bent's
Fort as part of the proposed layout. "I would strongly urge
that it be purchased,—both for the convenience and the economy. It is offered for sale for twelve thousand dollars, and I
do not think the government can put up such a work for that
money." But, he added in a later letter, "we could build one
that would answer the purpose for much less. . . . Whether
some consideration is not due to Colonel Bent for locating
the Fort near him and injuring his trade with the Indians is
not for me to say."

Faced with the problem of settling his affairs for the winter,
William had no intention of sitting around the Big Timbers
while the army made up its mind. Sedgwick, meantime,
needed a place for storing his equipment. After considerable
dickering, William got together with the regimental quartermaster, Lieutenant James B. McIntyre, and on September 9,
1860, executed what he supposed would be a temporary lease
of the stone building to the army for sixty-five dollars a month.
It was an ill-judged hope. For the next seven years the simple
three-clause agreement would cause him trouble.[3]

Failure of the Indians to assemble in September caused a
postponement of the projected treaty. The chiefs, however,

promised to gather their people during the winter. Feeling his job as agent was done, William resigned on September 19 and suggested the appointment of Albert Boone as his successor. In February, Boone reached the stone fort with his medals and goods, ready to wind up the treaty. William was not there. If he had been, some of Boone's mistakes might have been avoided. For one thing, the new agent violated Cheyenne and Arapaho custom by arbitrarily appointing the six chiefs with whom he would deal rather than let an Indian council select the men. Also, he acted before the tribes were fully assembled and thus left the door open for a repudiation of the treaty by those who were not present or who, in times of future disgruntlement, would say they had not been on hand. As a result, the paper he finally got signed was never worth the cost of mailing it back to the Senate for confirmation. So much for William's months-long sacrifice and patient preparation. He should have been on hand to help Boone, even though he thought his old friend far more capable than the man actually turned out to be.

He was not there at the time of the council because he was busy enlarging the temporary stockade he had built three years before at the mouth of Purgatory Creek. Though no fort, the resultant structure was a powerful square, each side at least a hundred feet long. Log pickets fifteen feet high and a foot or more in diameter were set solidly in the earth. Along their tops ran heavy, square-hewn beams fastened to the pickets by wooden pins driven through augur holes. The rooms which ranged around the central court averaged approximately sixteen by twenty feet. William's own living quarters lined the northern wall. On the west and south were warehouses and employees' rooms. To the east were stables and a blacksmith shop. A gate large enough to admit the huge freight wagons opened in the southern wall. Just outside of the northern and western pickets were ditches five feet deep from which earth had been dug to cover the roofs of the buildings. These ditches extended well beyond the corners of the stockade and were maintained as trenches, to be used in case of attack.

Robert helped his father with the building; Mary Bent Moore soon came out with her new husband and William's first grandchild. All around stretched rich farmlands waiting to be developed. Here the whole family could build homes, be together. Eagerly William looked forward to the time when George and Charles would be finished with their school and could join him. But that dream ended with the thunderclap of the Civil War. In Westport on summer vacation, George, not quite eighteen, enlisted in the Confederate Army. A little later, lying about his age, Charles followed him.

Southern sentiment was strong on the Missouri frontier. Only seventy-two of Kansas City's more than five thousand residents had voted for Lincoln; and one reason that the entire state did not swing to the South was the prompt action of Nathaniel Lyon and Frank Blair in securing the St. Louis arsenal and forcing the surrender of Camp Jackson's rebel-inclined state militia.[4] The sympathies of the St. Louis Bents, many of them slaveowners, as Charles and William had been, leaned toward the South. When the war broke out, William's youngest and only surviving brother, Silas, resigned his navy commission, though he did not actively fight on the side of the Confederacy.[5]

William remained loyal to the government and hauled enormous quantities of army freight to New Mexico. Here the only far-western battles of the war soon would be fought. Faced with an invasion from Texas, the territorial governor appointed Ceran St. Vrain commander of the New Mexican volunteers. Ceran, however, was nearly sixty, fat and apoplectic. On September 30, 1861, he resigned in favor of his lieutenant colonel, Christopher Carson. The next spring, aided substantially by Colorado volunteers under an enormous Methodist elder named J. M. Chivington, Union forces drove the Texans back home. Thereafter Kit's services were limited to the extraordinary, almost bloodless campaigns that outmaneuvered and forced the surrender of the Mescalero Apaches and Navajos—"the greatest feat of Indian warfare," it is said, "ever accomplished by an American soldier."

Except for William Bent, there might have been need of similar campaigns in Colorado. At the outset of the war the Confederates began wooing the western Indians. Commissioner in charge was Albert Pike, the Arkansas lawyer and poet who had first learned the West on the way to Taos with Charles Bent in 1831. Though Pike always insisted that his

Indian alliance was intended only to keep the savages from falling into the hands of the North, some southern strategists, abetted by sympathizers in Colorado and New Mexico, wanted to use the red auxiliaries in an attempt to disrupt the Santa Fe Trail, isolate New Mexico, and perhaps even cut off California. Principal targets were Fort Larned and Fort Lyon, the latter the cantonment which had been built around William's stone post in the Big Timbers. (The name Wise, for the governor of Virginia, had been dropped when that state seceded, and Lyon substituted in commemoration of Nathaniel Lyon's death at the battle of Wilson Creek, Missouri.)

Runners came from Pike's allied tribes to solicit the support of the Kiowas and Comanches, the Cheyennes and Arapaho. The first two tribes, long enemies of Texas, were reluctant to ally themselves with their former foes. The Cheyennes and Arapaho wavered, torn by promises of booty and angry over the continued usurpation of their homelands by the gold diggers. Finally the chiefs went to the Purgatory stockade and asked William's advice. A nod of his head could have created havoc. But he told the tribes to stay out of the white man's fight, and when Sibley's Texans invaded New Mexico they received none of the support from the plains tribes which they might otherwise have counted on.

Eastward, against Pike's protest, Indian auxiliaries were called on to support General Van Dorn's troops at the battle of Pea Ridge in the Ozark Hills of Missouri. Facing a charge was no part of the red men's concept of war. They broke, wandered as they listed, and committed atrocities which aroused furies of resentment in the North. Young George Bent fought in that battle, though not with the Indians. After the defeat he stayed in the army during the dreary campaign through Arkansas and into Mississippi. At Corinth, in October 1862, the war ended for him. He was captured and sent with two hundred other Confederate soldiers northward toward a prison camp in Missouri.

As the bedraggled column passed through St. Louis, a schoolmate of George recognized him. The unnamed boy ran to Robert Bent, who chanced to be in town on business for his father. Robert hurried to military headquarters, where many a high-ranking officer knew William Bent from days on

the plains, and secured George's release on the promise that
he would go west and fight no more.

Early in 1863 George reached the Purgatory stockade. The
arrival brought fresh worries to William. Charles had returned
some months earlier, perhaps discharged because of his age.
The younger boy had been sullen, knife edges of hate sharp
in his black eyes. After hanging around the stockade for a
time, he rode off with some Indians. To be sure, they were his
mother's people. But Charles had had no more than random
encounters with them for half a dozen years. His environment
had been pure white. Too pure, perhaps: high-born relatives
in great houses, an indefinable sense that he was suffered for
his father's sake. A half-breed, an inferior. And as compensation in his own mind he dreamed of the wind and the drums.
Thunder of stampeding buffalo, neigh of stolen horses. And
bloody scalps bobbing on the ends of willow wands.

It had not touched Robert or Mary. They were living and
working happily at the stockade. The same blood. Half red,
half white—must it be irreconcilable?

Fear tainted white nerves. In the fall of 1862 a northern
branch of the Sioux had perpetrated hideous massacres in
Minnesota. The word flashed westward, and Coloradans
thought with a shiver of the Sioux along the Platte, Sioux in
alliance with Cheyennes and Arapaho. The Civil War had
stripped the western forts. On the Arkansas there were thirty-
three soldiers at Larned, thirty-nine at Lyon; on the Platte,
125 at Kearny, ninety at Laramie—287 troops to police 200,000
square miles of territory. Confederates meanwhile were renewing their solicitation of the Indians. Cheyenne and Arapaho
chiefs who had been to Washington in 1862 refused to listen,
and the Osages actually turned against the Confederates. Defenseless Colorado did not know this, however, and alarm
boiled up toward terror.

Nonetheless, the whites kept coming, not all of them miners.
Farms sprang up along the foothills, a large cluster near
Pueblo. Young John Prowers brought in a hundred head of
cattle to range the Arkansas eastward from the mouth of Purgatory Creek. Hard-driving and ambitious, Prowers had gone
to work for Bent in 1857 when only eighteen. He married
Amache Ochinee—he called her Amy—daughter of a chief

named One-Eye; and as he drove Bent wagons to Fort Union in New Mexico and Laramie in Wyoming, he looked at the rolling miles of grass and in them saw a future that held no place for buffalo. There would be others like him, among them Tom Boggs. After a five-year stay in California with his father, Tom had returned to New Mexico and a responsible job with Lucien Maxwell. In the fall of 1863 Tom would bring several hundred head of Maxwell cattle to the Purgatory.

White man's ways. But young Charles had ridden off. Julia already had, or soon would, marry Ed Guerrier, half-breed son of old Bill Guerrier, and would go with her husband to live in the Indian camps. William tried to hold George. He bought him a five-hundred-dollar horse in Denver, gave him a pair of fine field glasses. The boy was nearly twenty now, husky, intelligent, and better educated than many of the whites flowing each day up the trail. There was a place for him in the stockade, with the caravans, at the trading camps, and on the farm which William hoped to break out of the tangled bottomlands as soon as he had more time, more help.

George would not listen. That summer he too went to visit the Indians, camped then in western Kansas. There he learned anew the excitement of the buffalo chase, watched Sioux and Cheyenne braves pierce their chests with skewers and stoically swing from the medicine poles. Adjusting himself quickly to the ways his father had tried to educate out of him, he joined a soldier society. That fall there came an atavistic surge of triumph when his war party scalped two Delaware hunters and returned rich in booty to dance with blackened faces in the center of the circle of the lodges. His mother's son. Could white men offer this?

In the spring of 1864 William started his caravan toward Missouri. Among his own private irritations was the stone fort in the Big Timbers, which the troops at Fort Lyon were now using as a commissary and storehouse. For nearly two years after leasing the building he had received not a dime's rent. In July 1862, completely exasperated, he had again offered the fort for sale at twelve thousand dollars, adding, "for the above amount I will binde myself to give the U.S. a Quit-Claim Deede, for a hundrede ande sixty acres of Lande, upon which said Forte is built." This had aroused the War Department to ask for a title search, and the General Land Office replied that the Indians owned the real estate: "The title of Colonel Bent is only that of a trespasser." A trespasser! To complete the irony, southwestward across the river lay unmapped millions of acres to which he held part claim through the squiggle of a Mexican governor's pen. What, indeed, was the entire occupation of the West, Spanish and American alike, but trespass? Yet at this 160 acres the now righteous government boggled.

The army had next asserted its own title to the plot by establishing a military reservation around the cantonment. The War Department paid William his rent up to September 1862 and again forgot about him. After more years of dickering the quartermaster general on February 5, 1864, finally recommended to Secretary of War Stanton that the stone fort be purchased. On March 31, however, that hope collapsed with word from Stanton that "the question of the change of location [of Fort Lyon] is now under consideration and no decision relative to the purchase of the building will be made." Nothing was said or done about back rent—or would be for more years.

As William moved down the Arkansas from Lyon he met, near Fort Larned, troops under Lieutenant George Eayre. Proudly Eayre announced that he had just had a fight with the Cheyennes on Ash Creek and had killed seventeen. Why? Eayre shrugged. He had been sent out from Denver to punish the Cheyennes for stealing 170 cattle from a government contractor's camp, though the Indians denied the thefts. Running out of supplies and transport after shooting a few Cheyennes and burning some lodges, Eayre had returned to Denver and commandeered fifteen wagons right off the streets. Meanwhile there had been other battles along the Platte, and when Eayre marched again it was under orders, according to one of his men, "to kill Cheyennes whenever and wherever found." Far east of his jurisdiction, at Ash Creek in Kansas, he had at last found a large village. The way he told the story to William, he had won a signal victory.

A different version came from an angry Indian messenger who overhauled William shortly after Eayre hurried on toward Larned. The Cheyennes, so the messenger gasped, did not know why the white lieutenant had attacked them. Although their five or six hundred warriors could easily have over-whelmed Eayre's straggling eighty-four dragoons, the red men had tried to avoid conflict and had sent out a friendly delegation to meet the soldiers. Leading the peacemakers was Lean Bear, one of the chiefs who had been to Washington in 1862. To his breast Lean Bear pinned the medal which had been given him in the East, and in his hand he carried papers officially proclaiming him to be a good Indian, ally of the Great Father. Some distance from the troops he had ordered his companions to halt while he advanced alone, hand up in the gesture of peace. Without warning the troops had shot him down.

His friends had attacked the whites then, and as fast as warriors in the village could catch their horses, they plunged toward the battle. Eayre's cannon, loaded with grape, had killed many, but the troops were falling back when Black Kettle rode among the Cheyennes, yelling for them to stop the fight. Finally he had quieted them, and Eayre had retreated toward Fort Larned, passing William along the way.

Furious, the young men of the Cheyennes the next day had raided some ranches near Walnut Creek, and many medicine men were preaching general war. But Black Kettle and other elders, hoping that matters might still be settled, had sent an express to William. What should be done?

William took a deep breath. Were Charles and George in the Ash Creek village?

No, they were back on the Smoky Hill. Runners had gone to that camp with word of the fight.

If the conflict became general . . .

Half red, half white. Must they ever be irreconcilable? William told the messenger to have the chiefs restrain the young men, gather together as many of the tribe as possible, and meet him in twenty days at Coon Creek, not far from Fort Larned. Meanwhile he would talk to the white officers.

Sending his wagons on, he rode back to Fort Lyon. There he found Colonel Chivington, commander of the Colorado volunteers and hero of the Civil War battles in New Mexico. William informed the one-time Methodist elder of what he had learned from the express and said that he was sure the Cheyennes could be persuaded toward peace.

The colonel towered above the trader. Chivington was well over six feet tall and broad in proportion. He had political ambitions. Always his opponents in Colorado would accuse him of deliberately stirring up Indian battles in order to make a reputation and attract votes. Now he contemptuously told William that he had no authority to make peace and, in fact, was on the warpath.

That kind of talk, William retorted, was asking for trouble. To date the tribes had never risen in concert. If they should, there were not enough troops in the country, despite recent reinforcements, to protect government and citizen trains. Settlers in Kansas and Colorado would inevitably bear the brunt of the suffering.

The settlers, Chivington replied, would just have to figure out some way of protecting themselves.[6]

Completely frustrated and not knowing what to tell the Indians, William rode to the Purgatory stockade. There was no use going to the current agent, S. E. Colley, for help. Utterly dishonest, Colley had hit on the profitable practice of "accepting" presents of horses and robes from the Indians before delivering their annuities. His son acted as a trader and within two or three years had accumulated, according to William's estimate, twenty-five or thirty thousand dollars. The goods young Colley used were identical with the annuity goods supposedly consigned to the Indians. What was worse, this precious pair had prevailed on Blackfoot John Smith to help them in their dealings with the tribes.

It was this agent who quite unwittingly offered hope that Chivington might be circumvented. He summoned William back to Fort Lyon. A proclamation had just arrived there from Governor Evans of Colorado Territory. Worried by the growing restiveness of the Indians and hoping to split their solid front, Evans called on all friendly Kiowas and Comanches to go to Fort Larned, all southern Cheyennes and Arapaho to Fort Lyon, all others to certain northern points. At the forts, where obviously they would be under the eyes of the army, the Indians would be fed and could avoid any danger of conflict with soldiers soon to be scouring the plains for hostile tribes. Colley had been directed to see that the wandering bands received copies of this proclamation. He did not go himself, however.

Northward from the river he sent John Smith and Chief One-Eye. William was asked to deliver copies eastward along the Arkansas.

It was a dangerous 240-mile road, but he refused an escort of troops lest the uniforms draw rather than prevent attack. No civilian would go with him; and well known though he was to the tribes, a lone white man was a powerful temptation for glory-hunting young men to shoot first and look afterward. Nonetheless, he set out with renewed heart. Half red, half white—but perhaps peace could be salvaged even yet.

CHAPTER XX

THE LAST AGONIES

When the Cheyennes came south in answer to William's summons, young Charles and George Bent were with them. On reaching the Arkansas, they learned that the Arapaho, Kiowas, and Comanches were camped on Medicine Lodge Creek above Fort Larned. Crossing the river, they joined the other tribes, and there William found them.

Endlessly he rode back and forth between Larned and the tense, sprawling, odorous villages, consulted white officers and red chiefs, translated Governor Evans's proclamation to the Cheyennes, and urged acceptance of its terms. Captain Permeter, the drunken commander in charge at Larned, treated the first delegation of chiefs which William brought in with an arrogance that threatened to upset everything. Satanta's Kiowas, William noticed, were particularly touchy. Later, however, Major Anthony appeared, and with him a more amicable council was arranged. At it the Cheyenne and Arapaho headmen promised to urge their people to report at the various forts as soon as the summer medicine dances had been held.

All seemed well. After warning the officers at Larned to keep an eye on Satanta's Kiowas, William sought out his sons. Charles refused to return with him to the Purgatory, but at last George agreed. The two had scarcely started homeward, however, when the incident William feared shattered all his work.

Because of his warning, the sentries at Larned were ordered to keep the Kiowas at a distance. Unfortunately no one notified the Kiowas that they could no longer approach the fort as freely as ever. When Satanta tried, a guard threw up a rifle and the tempestuous chief promptly shot the man through the arm with an arrow.[1] In an effort to remedy the resultant ill feeling, the whites called a council at the fort. The Kiowas acceded merely as a cover for treachery. Some squaws came with the chiefs and put on a dance. While the soldiers gawked, young Kiowa warriors ran off the post's entire horse herd.

The Cheyenne-Arapaho alliance, mindful of its promises to William, was dismayed. Chief Left Hand of the Arapaho led a delegation of twenty-five Indians under a white flag toward the fort. He was intending to offer help in recovering the stolen stock, but he got no chance to speak. Nervous soldiers touched off a cannon. The first shot went wide, and before range could be adjusted, the Indian emissaries fled without injury.

Rage swept the villages. The white man spoke with crooked tongue. He wanted no peace. Very well, he should have war. In confusion and anger the Cheyennes and Arapaho poured northward to a great conclave on the Solomon River with their northern relatives and with the Sioux.

There George Bent rejoined them. The taste of excitement had been too fresh on his tongue for the quiet of the Purgatory ranch to hold him, and on the Solomon he found the turmoil he wanted. The northern tribes had again begun raiding the Platte caravans. Each village echoed to the shrieks of the scalp dance. Almost daily war parties arrived with plunder from the merchandise trains. Indian braves strutted in ladies' bonnets. Colored silks were sewn into garish dresses for the squaws and shirts for the young men—George had half a dozen made. An estimated two hundred travelers and settlers were killed; scores of lonely ranches burned to the ground. A few women captives survived; one of them, Mrs. Eubanks, probably testifies for all: "An old chief . . . forced me, by the most terrible threats and menaces, to yield my person to him." When the chief was through with her, he passed her on to others.

Stark terror filled the Colorado towns. For more than a

month not one wheel rolled between the mountains and the eastern cities. Although William clung tenaciously to the Purgatory stockade and bluffed off Satanta's Kiowas on August 7, less powerfully defended farmers fled from their homes to blockhouses in the settlements. Food in Denver became so scarce that the price of flour doubled and redoubled until it reached twenty-five dollars for a hundred-pound sack.[2] Outrages and reports of outrages piled on one another. One will suffice. Jack Smith, Blackfoot's half-breed son, reputedly led a band of Cheyennes that wiped out three government wagons and some soldiers. Among the whites were a husband, wife, and two children. Before the mother's eyes the husband was "mutilated in a way shocking to relate" and the children were brained. Jack then passed the woman on the prairie to his followers. Unfortunately surviving this, the next night she managed to hang herself from a lodgepole. The story may or may not be completely true, but all Colorado believed its truth. The furies engendered by it and similar tales of atrocities had much to do with what followed.

William made one last effort. Unable to reach the main Cheyenne camp himself, he sent a letter by an Indian messenger. George and Julia's husband, Ed Guerrier, were in the villages. Either one could read the letter to the chiefs.

The message led the elder chiefs to call a council at which the objections of the fiery Dog Soldiers were overridden. George and Ed Guerrier were instructed to write identical answers, one addressed to Agent Colley, the other to Major E. W. Wynkoop, commanding officer at Fort Lyon:

> *Cheyenne Village, August 29, 1864*
> We received a letter from Bent wishing us to make peace. We held a council in regard to it. All come to the conclusion to make peace with you, providing you make peace with the Kiowas, Comanches, Arapahos, Apaches and Sioux. . . . We hear that you have some Indian prisoners in Denver. We have some prisoners of yours which we are willing to give up, providing you give up yours. . . . We want true news from you in return.

On the receipt of this letter, Wynkoop led 130 men and a battery toward Smoky Hill to recover the white prisoners. The

Dog Soldiers would have battled him, but the elders intervened. Four children were handed over, and the Indians promised to return the other captives, held in different villages, as soon as possible. A delegation of chiefs then accompanied Wynkoop to Denver for talks with Governor Evans, Colonel Chivington, and other prominent Coloradans.

The rest is controversy. A century of argument has not settled who promised what, who ordered what, who did what. But this much seems certain. Black Kettle's influence over the tribe was by no means complete, and in spite of the statement in the letter about "all" the tribe wanting peace, a large portion of both the Cheyennes and Arapaho remained hostile. Among the white citizens and the military the desire for war was even more rampant. The Indians, it was felt, deserved punishment, and General Curtis, commander of the district, wrote Chivington, "I want no peace until the Indians have suffered more." Major Wynkoop was replaced at Fort Lyon by Major Anthony, apparently because it was thought that Wynkoop would temporize with the savages.

At the Denver council Evans scolded the chiefs for not having gone into the forts in accord with his proclamation. Rightly or wrongly, the Indians—and William Bent—interpreted this as meaning that if they now reported to the forts they would be fed and protected in spite of their warfare during the summer. Six hundred and fifty-two Arapaho moved into the Big Timbers. Cynics scoffed that they were peaceful because they could not fight during the winter. Major Anthony, who had been ordered not to make peace, fed them for ten days, then returned the arms they had surrendered and ordered them to hunt buffalo to support themselves. All but Left Hand and a few followers drifted eastward.

Left Hand and his handful of people joined a village of Cheyennes which had moved onto Sand Creek, about forty miles north of Fort Lyon. The fact that the women in the village outnumbered the men five hundred to two hundred indicates that most of the younger warriors were still not ready to submit. Black Kettle and a delegation, however, rode into Fort Lyon and told Anthony they wanted to come to terms. The major replied that he had no authority to treat and advised the Indians to return to their village, promising to notify them if he received instructions to negotiate. When he wrote district headquarters he did not ask for such instructions. Instead, he gave the location of the village and said he would attack it if he had more troops. One thing that restrained him was his knowledge that a much larger village was camped about seventy miles farther on at Smoky Hill.

Chivington received Anthony's word in his snowbound camp on Bijou Creek at about the time when his hundred-day volunteers, recruited during the August raids, were nearing the end of their enlistment period. They wanted a fight and so did the colonel. More controversy, bootless here, rages over the exact nature of Chivington's instructions and his understanding of his duties. Whatever his motives, however, he meant to hit by complete surprise the Sand Creek camp which was awaiting word about peace. His guide was Jim Beckwourth, old now and little able to endure the cold.

Chivington was an inspirational leader. Though his 750 cavalrymen did not know their destination, were lightly clad, poorly armed, and wretchedly mounted, they cheerfully wallowed through two feet of snow to the Arkansas. After tending their horses they crawled into icy beds each night after ten and roused each morning to a bitter-cold reveille at four.

To keep his surprise from leaking, Chivington stopped all travel on the Arkansas and threw a guard around every farmhouse.

At the Purgatory stockade everything seemed quiet. After writing the letter for the chiefs, George had come home and appeared content. When he heard that Black Kettle's village was on Sand Creek and that Charles and Julia were with them, he decided to pay a visit. William did not object. The Indians were waiting to make peace. Blackfoot John Smith had even calmed down his son Jack and had gone up to the camp to trade.

Three days after George left, twenty dragoons splashed across the Arkansas, unlimbered their rifles, and announced that no one was to leave the stockade. Across the river William saw the long blue column and snub-nosed cannon snaking eastward. No one would tell him why or where they were marching. But in his heart he guessed. Three of his children there on Sand Creek . . .

Soon there was a fourth. Robert was at Lyon, and when the dragoons reached the fort, old Jim Beckwourth collapsed, so stiff he had to be lifted from his horse. Chivington ordered Robert Bent to lead the soldiers to the village.

At eight o'clock in the evening, with the winter stars frosty overhead, the riders started northward in ranks of four. There was not much snow here and they marched fast—walk, trot, gallop, dismount and lead, then repeat. Toward midnight they splashed through a shallow lake, and the men thought their guide was hoping that the water would reach and spoil their ammunition. As the dipper wheeled toward dawn, something roused Chivington's suspicions. He swung over beside Robert and slapped his revolver.

"I haven't had an Indian to eat for a long time. If you fool with me and don't lead me to that camp, I'll have you for breakfast."

In the first dim light they saw five or six hundred Indian ponies grazing on the prairies. A detachment wheeled out to cut off the animals from the village. The rest of the soldiers swung into line on the low bluff above the skin lodges. The cannon were unlimbered and aimed.

A few early-rising squaws cried alarm. Some ran to Black Kettle, who raised an American flag and beneath it a white one. As the village woke in panic, he called for the people to remain calm: nothing would happen; they were under government protection. Other women ran to John Smith and told him to talk to the white men. He started toward the troops, but then the withering fire opened. Black Kettle now shouted for the people to flee. Old White Antelope, who had been among the first visitors at William's original stockade on the Arkansas, would not budge. Arms folded, he stood in front of his lodge, singing the death song of the prairie tribes:

> "Nothing lives long,
> Except the earth and the mountains."

A bullet cut him down. Another struck Yellow Wolf, more than eighty years old now. Chief One-Eye died, and Left Hand, and—no one knows how many. Such Indians as could gather their arms fought savagely. Major Anthony, no friend of the Cheyennes, wrote later, "I never saw more bravery dis-

played by any set of people on the face of the earth than by
these Indians. They would charge on the whole company
singly, determined to kill someone before being killed themselves."

It was hopeless from the beginning. The grape from the cannon, followed by the charge of the cavalry, split the village
before the defenders could group. Some of the dazed warriors
tried to protect their lodges, some raced for the pony herds,
some tried to flee with the women and children up the stream
bed. When troops overhauled the fugitives they dug pits into
the sandbanks and fought until they were out of bullets and
arrows. At one such set of pits two miles or so above the village
a ball shattered George Bent's hip.

Charles Bent and Jack Smith were captured at the outset.
Jack, reputedly confessing to the earlier ambush and rape, was
shot down in cold blood. Pistols were aimed at Charles's head,
but Charley Autobees's half-Mexican sons, serving as scouts
with the volunteers, managed to save him. It would have been
better if they had not.

In the afternoon Chivington called off the pursuit. Writing
headquarters from the field of battle, he announced proudly,
"I at daylight this morning attacked a Cheyenne village of
. . . from nine hundred to a thousand warriors. [Not so: even
counting women, there were not that many people in the
camp.] We killed . . . between four and five hundred. [Not
so: Chivington's implication is that warriors were killed.
George Bent estimated 163 deaths, 110 of them women and
children, and no figures exist as to the number wounded.
Chivington's losses were nine killed, thirty-eight wounded.]
All," said Chivington, "did nobly."

But Robert Bent said:

> I saw five squaws under a bank. When troops came up
> to them they ran out and showed their persons to let the
> soldiers know they were squaws and begged for mercy
> but the soldiers shot them all. I saw one squaw lying on
> a bank whose leg had been broken by a shell. A soldier
> came up to her with drawn sabre. She raised her arm to
> protect herself when he struck, breaking her arm; she
> rolled over and raised her other arm when he struck,

breaking it; then he left without killing her. . . . Some
thirty or forty squaws, collected in a hole for protection
. . . sent out a little girl about six years old with a white
flag on a stick. She was shot and killed. . . . All the
squaws in that hole were killed. . . . I saw one squaw
cut open with an unborn child lying by her side. I saw
the body of White Antelope with the privates cut off, and
I heard a soldier say he was going to make a tobacco
pouch out of them. I saw one squaw whose privates had
been cut out. . . . I saw a little girl who had been hid
in the sand. Two soldiers drew their pistols and shot her,
and then pulled her out of the sand by the arm. I
saw quite a number of infants in arms killed with their
mothers. . . .

A cheap victory. The brave Chivington did not follow it up,
in spite of previous rodomontade that he would: "I think I
shall catch some more of them about eighty miles north on
the Smoky Hill." But survivors had fled that way, and the
Smoky Hill camp could not be caught by surprise. Chivington
turned back toward the Arkansas to search for a camp of
Arapaho. Alarmed in time, they fled. Giving up the chase,
Chivington marched back to a conqueror's welcome at Denver.
Along the way he dropped Charles Bent off at Fort Lyon. Six
other prisoners, three women and three children, were turned
over to William for safekeeping. Three more children were
taken to Denver and exhibited in a carnival from which the
government later ransomed them.

Afoot, more than half of them severely injured, George
Bent's small party of survivors started toward the Smoky Hill.
George could scarcely drag himself along. Then some of the
men caught a few stray horses and put the wounded on them.
The night was bitter. Most of the Indians had been driven
from the camp half clad, and when the cold became unendura-
ble those who could move crawled about, pulling up tufts of
dry grass for tiny fires—they could find no wood. All night
they kept shouting to attract other survivors wandering on the
desolate plains. The next day Indians summoned from the
Smoky Hill camp rode out to help them.

For a month George stayed in the wailing, drum-beating

village. His wound would not heal properly, and finally with Ed Guerrier he rode south to the Arkansas. Near Fort Lyon they saw soldiers. Afraid they would be overtaken and shot, Ed surrendered, but George slipped on by and reached the Purgatory stockade.

Half red, half—no. Their world was split and a man could no longer straddle. William had read the choice on Charles's lean, embittered face. Now he saw it on George's. Heartbroken, he did not argue when George, his hip mended, returned to the Indian camp, taking with him the prisoners William had been keeping.

Furiously the Indians struck back and horror flamed along the Platte, George and Charles in the thick of it. The Sioux joined, and now the Indians came as near achieving unity as they ever would. Twice the little town of Julesburg in northeastern Colorado was frightfully sacked. In Kansas and Nebraska caravans were attacked, stage stations and ranches burned, telegraph lines destroyed, women seized. Troops could not catch up with the mobile bands, though great prairie fires were set in an effort to starve the Indians out. Bad as the situation was, however, the winter leanness of the pony herds kept it from being far worse. The tribes met in great councils to lay war plans for the spring when the grass grew green and the horses fat. To subsist in the meantime the people needed to find buffalo and decided on a hunt near the Powder River in Wyoming. As they withdrew northward, General Connor set after them with eight hundred men. As scouts and auxiliaries Connor took with him seventy-five Pawnees, ancient foes of the Cheyennes and Sioux.

The fury with which the whites had reacted to the depredations of the previous August did not greet these winter raids. Remorse pricked. At first Chivington, largely on the basis of his own reports, had been treated as a hero, but as details of the Sand Creek slaughter became known, revulsion set in.[3] Congress determined to investigate not only the massacre but the conditions that had led to the attack. In August 1865 testimony was taken at Fort Lyon before Congressmen Doolittle, Foster, and Ross. William was there. Kit Carson, a brigadier general now, was also summoned from the dreary camp he had been ordered to establish on the Cimarron trail to pro-

tect Santa Fe travelers. Not that Kit had been anywhere near
Sand Creek. But government bigwigs supposed him to know
more about Indians than any other man alive. The claim had
justice to it, but Kit himself said there was a man who knew
more—William Bent.

What the government wanted of the two was not recrimi-
nation over the past but recommendations for the future. The
future . . . Was everything William had worked for to be lost
now in blood and horror? He refused to believe it. Passion-
ately he declared to the congressmen:

"If the matter were left to me, I guarantee with my life that
in three months I could have all the Indians along the Arkansas
at peace without the expense of war."

And what, the congressmen asked, did General Carson think
of Colonel Bent's statement? Quietly Kit said, "His suggestions
and opinions . . . coincide perfectly with my own. . . . I have
much more confidence in [his] influence with the Indians than
in my own. . . . I believe that if Colonel Bent and myself
were authorized, we could make a solid, lasting peace."

*"I guarantee with my life that in three months I could have
all the Indians along the Arkansas at peace . . ."* Almost while
William was speaking those words, some of Connor's Pawnee
scouts, chasing a fleeing group of Cheyennes near the Powder
River, overhauled five laggards and killed them. Triumphantly
they brought the scalps back to camp, to dance and sing
around the fire. One of the dripping topknots was Yellow
Woman's.

"I guarantee with my life . . ." He was instructed to help
call the Indians together in mid-October for a council on Bluff
Creek, about forty miles south of present Wichita. There Kit
and he served on the government's panel of commissioners. But
when the Indians began to assemble, William realized that
only pacifists like Black Kettle's band and opportunists in search
of presents were showing up. There was only one grain of
hope: if the terms offered these Indians were fair, the others
might be persuaded.

The government humbled itself, confessed that Chivington's
attack had been most damnably wrong, and gave reparations
in money and land to those who had lost relatives. Increased

annuity allotments were promised, new reservation boundaries discussed. It was the same hidebound pattern that had not worked before and would not work again. Implicit in it was the whites' old assumption of the servility of the Indians, who should be grateful for the Great Father's largess. There were no provisions for farms or schools or help in adjusting to a new way of life—none of the things that Kit and William wanted, none of the things that would enable the Indians to live as a free and self-sufficient people. And they would live in no other way. Their hopeless, magnificent fight would go on until overwhelming forces crushed them into apathy and a remorseful government, decades too late, recognized what it should have done years before.

Among the whites at the futile council were a few who recognized its tragedy. As the meeting broke up, Samuel Kingman wrote in his diary of Bent's and Carson's efforts, "Their fate as commissioners will be that they died of too large views."

"*I guarantee with my life . . .*" Less than a month after the council, young Charles Bent led a band of Dog Soldiers against Downer's stage station on the Smoky Hill road. By treachery he lured the eight whites out from a sheltering cave for a "conference," then fell on them without warning. One man was killed, two were captured. The other five, most of them wounded, managed to fort up in a buffalo wallow on the top of the bluffs. As they watched, the station was pillaged and razed. Then Charles and his Indians staked one of their naked captives spread-eagled on the plain. They cut out his tongue and "substituted another portion of his body in its place," built a fire on his stomach, and howled like ecstatic demons while he died in agony. It was the beginning of a terrible career of betrayal, cruelty, and ravishment which would make Charles Bent, namesake of William's beloved brother, the worst desperado the plains have ever known.

George split with young Charles—and there is no question of the frightful power these two white-trained warriors might have caused if they had stayed together. As the Union Pacific crept westward under continual Indian harassment, Granville Dodge wrote in alarm to General Sherman, "If the Bent brothers are with the Cheyennes, they will play hell with the road." But fair fight was one thing, treachery another. After leaving Charles, George in 1867 helped gather the tribes for another treaty that would soon prove as hollow as its predecessor. Occasionally he came home to visit his father and Robert and Mary. Meanwhile Charles's savageries grew so dreadful that a price was put on his head and William disowned him. After that the youngest son came to the ranch to kill his father, but fortunately William was away.[4] In 1868 Charles was severely wounded in a fight with Pawnees, caught malaria, and died in an Indian camp.

In New Mexico, where the Indians had been crushed earlier, Lucien Maxwell was busy establishing full control over the Beaubien-Miranda grant. He had bought out the heirs of the original grantees, and now only Charles Bent's two daughters and son Alfred (the name now Anglicized) stood in his way.

As early as 1859, acting on the advice of Ceran St. Vrain and Kit Carson, the children had brought suit against Maxwell for a one-third interest in the grant. Only an oral agreement had validated Charles's title. Maxwell—fleshy, brave, debonair, and utterly unscrupulous—roared that he would law the Bents until hell froze over and then law them a day or two on the ice. After Alfred was murdered in Taos on December 9, 1865, by a Mexican called Greek George, William stepped into the lawing on behalf of Alfred's three small children. The courts went against Maxwell and on May 3, 1866, he bought out the two girls and Alfred's children for $18,000. He got a bargain. Four years later he sold the massive grant for $650,000 to a company which almost immediately resold it to an English syndicate for twice that amount.[5]

The old ties between him and William were too strong to be broken by a lawsuit. The Indian trade was gone now—almost never did Cheyennes or Arapaho visit the Arkansas—and William turned his wagons to freighting government goods to Fort Union and Santa Fe. Often he stopped over at the great ranch on Little Cimarron Creek, not far from the foot of Raton Pass. A bustling village of workers' homes surrounded the huge stone gristmill and Lucien's two-story adobe house. In every direction grain fields shimmered; thousands of cattle and tens of thousand of sheep grazed the valleys. There could have been mines. Maxwell knew gold existed on the grant; he even kept nuggets in a buckskin bag for his children to play with. But he wanted none of its heartbreaks and would have ignored the glittering metal entirely had not a flood of squatters poured onto his lands and forced him to try setting up some sort of control—seed ground of quarrels whose bitterness eventually led him to sell the place.

Not only William, but Ceran and other friends stopped by to reminisce on the sprawling veranda. Newcomers appeared, among them spade-bearded Charles Goodnight, famed Texas trail driver, edging his herds to new range in the north. On Raton itself there was another prognostication of the future. There Maxwell had deeded twenty-five hundred acres to Dick Wootton, and in 1867—about the time a puny corporation named the Atchison, Topeka and Santa Fe Railroad Company was trying to sell bonds and win land allotments from Congress —Uncle Dick began to chip out a toll road. Soon Santa Fe locating engineers would come in with their transits and compasses, not knowing how long ago the way had been found.

The departure of the Indians from the Arkansas brought settlers into the lush bottomlands along the Purgatory. At first it was almost a family corporation, with titles drawn through Charles's and William's interest in the St. Vrain-Vigil land grant. First Robert Bent and Tom Boggs broke out a mile-long irrigating ditch to fields above William's stockade, now a thriving ranch. John Prowers bought acreage from William and joined them. Young Charles Ritz (or Ritc or Rite; the name appears variously) married Tom Boggs's daughter Rumalda and joined the settlement. Outsiders began buying plots and the town of Boggsville slowly took shape—later it would become the modern city of Las Animas.

In 1867 Kit resigned from the army and bought two pieces of property from Ceran, one near William's ranch and one several miles farther up the Purgatory. Josefa had six children now, and Kit was still dreaming of the permanent home that he had never quite succeeded in obtaining. He was not well and thought that the continual pains in his chest were the result of a horseback accident suffered several years before. If he could just take it easy—but no, the government sent him back to Washington with a delegation of Utes.

Shortly before this, William, too, for purposes unknown, had also gone to Washington on what was probably his first venture east of St. Louis. While there he tried to collect the five years' back rent still owed him on the stone fort. He also hoped to obtain the return of the building, for the War Department had finally decided to relocate Fort Lyon closer to the mouth of the Purgatory—a shift which considerably stimulated the growth of Boggsville (although it did not stop Ute and Apache raids along the Purgatory in the late summer of 1868). But the new fort had not been completed when William was in Washington during the winter of 1866–67, and the quartermaster said the building in the Big Timbers was still needed for storage. Again William was reminded his title was only that of a trespasser, and in disgust he returned to Westport —sans rent.

There, in the spring of 1867, he married Adalina Harvey, daughter of a Blackfoot squaw and rambunctious Alexander Harvey, one of the roaringest river men of the early fur-trade days on the Missouri. William took her to the Purgatory that summer—and she is never mentioned again. From the silence one might surmise, perhaps without justification, that the marriage failed and that Adalina soon left.

The next spring Kit returned to Boggsville. Two weeks later Josefa bore her seventh child and within half a month was dead. Grief-stricken, Kit lost all desire to live. His chest was a torment. He could scarcely get around, though on sunny days he liked to sit outside the house and gossip with Tom Boggs, whom he had appointed guardian of his children. Once George Bent came up to buy a horse and listen to stories about old days with William. But Kit was failing fast. On May 14 he was taken to Fort Lyon to be under the care of the army surgeon there. The change did him no good. When William came back from Missouri with his caravan, he learned that his oldest friend had died on May 23.

On the plains the grim wars went on—Hancock's smashing of a Cheyenne village on Pawnee Fork, the Beecher Island fight, and then, almost exactly four years after Sand Creek, Custer's ruthless crushing of the Cheyenne camp on the

Washita River. The people of the plains were broken now, though a few years later some of the Cheyennes would find revenge fighting with the Sioux who wiped out Custer on the Little Bighorn. William's people—he would never see them again. Cowed, helpless, they would be driven to a reservation along the alkaline streams and in the parched red dust of what is now Oklahoma.

In May 1869, not long after the Washita fight and just days before his sixtieth birthday, William started a caravan eastward from New Mexico. Over Raton he went, down the Timpas—the old trail. Through the raw weather that sometimes comes to the piedmont plains in May he saw the walls of the old fort ahead. Repaired and whitewashed, they had been turned into a stage station.[6] Now the battlements seemed to dance in front of his eyes. He was sick, feverish. When he reached the Purgatory ranch some miles beyond, Mary put him to bed and called the doctor from new Fort Lyon. The man shook his head. Pneumonia.

On May 19 William Bent died. A few days later, in a city where a creek once called Fontaine-que-bouille runs into the Arkansas, the Pueblo *Chieftain* paid its respects with a proper obituary and estimated that he left a fortune of between $150,000 and $200,000. Concerning the other things he had left to the plains and the mountains, things that had made such cities and such newspapers possible, the account had little to say.[7]

A NOTE ON THE NOTES

In a book of this sort, nearly every statement made necessarily rests on earlier authority. Anyone seriously interested may obtain chapter and verse of each source by communicating with me, but to cite them here would take a disproportionate amount of space. The following Notes, therefore, have been confined largely to three types of material: an explanation of why certain assumptions have been made though no direct data exists to document the guesses; the reasons for my conclusions where my interpretations differ from those of other published accounts; and the presentation of additional information whose inclusion in the text itself would interrupt the flow of the narrative.

Sources are given for most of the material that appears in the Notes. To prevent duplication, authors and titles are condensed. Full data can be found in the Bibliography.

It should hardly be necessary to add that much remains to-be done before history fully traces out the influence which the Bents, the St. Vrains, and their forts exerted on the fur trade, the Indian trade, and western expansion in general. Although this is the first full-length study of a long-neglected field, I am painfully aware of the gaps it still contains. An examination of the Mexican archives may shed additional light, as may further searches through the overwhelmingly vast batteries of the National Archives in Washington. And it is always to be hoped that somewhere, somehow, forgotten journals, account books, letters, and other records will turn up to give voice to the silence left by the Bents and St. Vrains themselves.

NOTES

Chapter I

THE TOWN ON THE RIVER

1. The Bent name appears in Hampshire, in the south of England, as early as 1519. Apparently it derives from the tough, wiry bent grass that covered some of the moors. (Allen Bent, *The Bent Family in America*, 7, 9.) By coincidence, there is also a bent grass that grows on the prairies of western America, where later Bents took root.

2. Silas Bent, brother of Charles and William and grandson of the Revolutionary Silas, gives the Tea Party story in a letter of November 7, 1866, to his old teacher, Elihu H. Shepard. (Letter loaned to me by courtesy of Mr. Silas Bent McKinley of St. Louis.)

3. The unadorned name Charleston, (West) Virginia, in Bent genealogical records, passports, etc., naturally suggests the capital city of that name. However, Rufus Putnam's map of Ohio in 1804 (see Hulbert, *Historic Highways of America*, IX) shows a Charleston some miles north of Wheeling. This is in Brooke County. And in 1802 Silas Bent was appointed postmaster of Brooke Court House. That he ever resided in the more famous Charleston seems to me unlikely.

4. On September 28, 1826, twenty-one-year-old Lucy Bent became the second wife of Joseph Russell. Her third child she named Charles Silas, after her father and eldest brother. Charles Silas Russell became the father, on March 19, 1865, of Charles Marion Russell, famed western artist. There is appropriateness in the fact that one of the West's best-loved painters was related to and a namesake of one of the West's great pioneers.

5. Statements in New Mexico histories that Charles Bent graduated from West Point are in error. His name does not appear in the *List of Cadets Admitted into the United States Military Academy From Its Origin Until Sept. 1, 1901* (Washington, 1902). His presence at Jefferson is attested to by his friend, the Reverend Barrows, in a letter to William Ritch (Ritch papers,

1713, Huntington Library); John's presence, by W. V. N. Bay (*Reminiscences*, 248).

While on the subject of the Bents' education, this may be the place to correct statements in *The Bent Family in America* and the *Dictionary of American Biography* that Silas Bent, Charles's brother, was among the first Missouri appointees to the Naval Academy at Annapolis. Silas entered the navy, not the Academy, as a midshipman in 1836. The fact that he became an eminent hydrographer indicates sound practical training and alert intelligence; but, as he tells his old teacher, Elihu Shepard (Note 2), "I received most of my education from your own flagellating hands."

6. Following Juliannah's death, Lilburn Boggs located at Independence. During a trading venture on the Santa Fe Trail his life was saved by Hamilton Carson, one of Kit's numerous brothers. In 1823 Lilburn married Panthea Grant Boone, a granddaughter of old Daniel. This remarriage brought no weakening of his ties with the Bents, as future chapters will show.

7. George Bent, one of William's sons, says that his uncle Charles was on the river as early as 1816–17. (Hyde, ghost-writing the first-person Life of George Bent.) George Bent's dates, however, are unreliable. W. Barrows to W. Ritch (June 14, 1877, Ritch papers, Huntington Library) says that Charles was with the Missouri Fur Company "as early as 1823." Chittenden (*History of the American Fur Trade*, rev. ed., 927) says that Charles was among the well-known traders with the company in 1822. Since Charles needed time to acquire a reputation, an assumption that he worked for the Missouri Fur Company as early as 1819 is not unwarranted, although the earliest record I have found that names him specifically is Kennerly's diary, May 3, 1824.

Chapter II
THOSE BLOODY WATERS

1. This information from Mr. Dale L. Morgan, who unearthed it in the course of his studies on William Ashley, the results of which will appear in his projected volume of Ashley papers. My entire second chapter and much of Chapter IV lean heavily on Mr. Morgan's meticulous research, both as it is evident in his recent, definitive *Jedediah Smith* and through private correspondence between us, during which he most generously made available information not yet published. Such experiences considerably brighten the often dreary chore of historical spadework.

2. One of the pair who returned to Fort Atkinson with Fitzpatrick was a man named Branch—Francis Z. Branch, as Dale L. Morgan guesses. (*Jedediah Smith*, 405.) Or perhaps, as I guess, he

was Alexander K. Branch. The other man who returned with Fitzpatrick to Atkinson was named Stone. Men identified only as Stone and Branch a year or two later were active in the Southwest. (See Peg-leg Smith's reminiscences, *Hutchings' Illustrated California Magazine*, January and February 1861, V, 320, 324.) Records show that an Alexander Branch trapped with St. Vrain in New Mexico and Colorado, 1826–28, as my text will indicate. Was he Fitzpatrick's companion in 1823–24? Another Branch—or the same Branch—was a merchandising partner of Stephen Lee in Taos in the late 1830s. (Charles Bent to Manuel Álvarez, January 16, 1841; March 22, 1841, etc.) Ceran St. Vrain's second wife was Luisa Branch. How all these Branches were related I cannot determine, but undoubtedly there was some connection.

3. A hitherto unsuspected transaction unearthed by Dale L. Morgan, who adds that this shows that Fitzpatrick was "a completely independent free trapper even then."

4. House Doc. 118 (Serial 136), 19th Congress, 1st Sess.

5. According to Beckwourth (*Life, 54–57*) Pilcher, whom Beckwourth calls Pitcher, gave Ashley at Fort Kiowa a live grizzly bear as a "plaything." There may or may not have been secret symbolism in Pilcher's mind. Anyhow, the bear bothered Ashley no more than the Missouri Fur Company's short-lived competition had. Beckwourth got rid of the animal for Ashley, so Beckwourth says, by chaining it to an apple tree in the front yard of Major Biddle's St. Louis home—all this assuming, of course, that there was a bear. Dale L. Morgan doubts both the grizzly and the meeting of Ashley and Pilcher at Fort Kiowa. But whether the meeting was there or, possibly, farther down the river or even not at all, Pilcher and Charles Bent certainly learned very soon and with envy of their one-time rival's success.

6. The date of William's first venture on the river is unknown. Hyde (Life of George Bent, Chap. III, p. 1.) suggests 1823–24. This seems too early, for William would have been only fourteen or fifteen. George Bent insists, however (to Hyde, June 17, 1914): "My father was very young when he went up the Missouri with his brother."

Various authorities (*Dictionary of American Biography*, Grinnell, etc.) say William was employed on the Missouri by the American Fur Company. There is in the American Fur Company Ledger, Retail Store, Western Department, July 7, 1828, under account of P. N. LeClere 334, this reference: "To Cash paid William Bent on your order on [Alexander] Laforce Papin 2. . . ." Such a record amounts practically to the final settlement of IOUs passed around almost anywhere at any time and doesn't necessarily mean William was connected with the American Fur Company. Indeed, considering William's youth and close ties with Charles, it seems far more likely that he followed his brother into the reorganized Missouri Fur Company.

7. The American Fur Company ledger entry of July 7, 1828, cited in the note above, does not necessarily mean that William received the money on that date, but that the wandering order was finally charged against LeClere's account on July 7; the cash could have been paid to William months before.

George Bent says (to Hyde, May 11, 1917), "I know my father . . . met Arapaho on the North Platte River long before coming to the Arkansas River." William came to the Arkansas in 1829; considering his age, he couldn't have seen the North Platte "long" before this, and indeed Pilcher & Company's 1827–28 venture seems the only time William could have been on the North Platte. And finally, as Chapter V will indicate, by 1829 William knew how to handle himself in an Indian fracas. The scuffles Pilcher & Company had on this trip may well have been his training ground.

8. Reasons for assuming the meeting, in addition to similarities in time and place, will develop in Chapter IV.

Chapter III
THE TRAPPER FROM TAOS

1. Legend says that Charles de Lassus helped persuade Amos Stoddard, the American representative at the transfer, to allow the French tricolor to remain aloft for twenty-four hours so that St. Louis's French population, many of whom had never lived under their own flag, might have one brief illusion of home. On a day so charged with emotion, Jacques St. Vrain and his wife may well have gone with his aging father and their children to watch the ceremonies at Government House. If so, and assuming the legend is true, Ceran must have been told the story many times. Scion of French nobility, nephew of the last foreign lieutenant governor of the vast territory—there was honest background for the courtliness which later contemporaries at times noticed in Ceran St. Vrain on the cruel and indifferent plains of the Southwest. But it is not likely that any of them ever saw the armorial bearings he was entitled to use: *"D'azur à un roitlet d'or, volant vers un soleil du même, mouvant du canton dextre du chef, coupé d'argent à une aigle de profil de sable, le vol levé."* (References concerning the St. Vrain background from Paul St. Vrain's *Genealogy of the Family of DeLassus St. Vrain*, 1943; J. F. McDermott, "Diary of Charles de Hault de Lassus from New Orleans to St. Louis," *Louisiana Historical Quarterly*, April 1947; Jougla de Morenas, *Grand Armorial de France*—with generous assistance from Frances Biese, Missouri Historical Society, and J. Tandeau de Marsac, Paris.)

2. The close association between Mme. St. Vrain and the former
   lieutenant governor is implied in a letter of August 24, 1824,
   which Felix St. Vrain wrote in French to his uncle Charles D.
   Delassus (sic) from Kaskaskia, Illinois (where Felix was in the
   merchandising business with Gregory Pratte and had just
   bought a two-story house, finished except for chimneys and plas-
   tering, for—shades of inflation—$336): "When I write you I al-
   ways write mother." The farm is indicated by letters of April
   1825 and September 14, 1830, from Ceran in New Mexico to
   Bernard Pratte, instructing that certain stock be taken to his
   mother's farm.

3. These three groups included five Missourians led by William
   Becknell, who, in spite of their dangerously few numbers, had
   gone out to trap and trade with the Comanches; a much larger
   group of trappers under Hugh Glenn working up the Arkansas
   River toward the Colorado Rockies; and eleven men under
   Thomas James and John McKnight. Only the last-named group
   apparently intended actually to penetrate Mexican territory,
   their object, in addition to trade, being to secure the release
   from prison of John's brother, Robert McKnight. (For Becknell,
   see *Missouri Historical Review,* July 1906 and January 1910. For
   Glenn, Jacob Fowler's *Journal,* ed. by Elliott Coues. For Thomas
   James, his own *Three Years among the Indians and Mexicans,*
   ed. by Walter B. Douglas.)

4. Profit was not the only motive of Baird's return. He felt that the
   United States had not acted energetically enough on his behalf
   when he was in prison, nor afterward to help him obtain redress.
   Equally disgusted was his erstwhile leader, Robert McKnight,
   who declared, "I will go back to Mexico . . . and become a
   citizen. I have resided the prescribed term of years [in jail!] and
   there is a better chance for obtaining justice from the Mexicans,
   scoundrels though they are, than from my own government."
   (James, op. cit., 155.) Go he did, making a fortune in the Santa
   Rita copper mines, where in 1828–29 young Kit Carson worked
   briefly for him as a teamster. James Baird also became a Mexican citizen, and in 1826 protested vigorously against the trapping activities of "foreigners" in Mexico.

5. Smith's flamboyant later career has obscured the equally robust
   days before he became peg-legged. That he first went to Mexico
   with the famous Storrs-Marmaduke party, though accounts of
   the party seldom mention him, is indicated by his own garrulous
   talk to reporters in California many years later. "The Story of an
   Old Trapper," San Francisco *Evening Bulletin,* October 26,
   1866: "At the conclusion of his spree he engaged with St. Vrain
   . . . who was on the eve of a trip to Santa Fe for the purpose of
   purchasing gold dust and furs." This was the Becknell-Storrs-
   Marmaduke party, for Smith names Le Grande as its captain,
   as does Marmaduke in his journel. Further corroboration comes

from "Peg-Leg Smith—A Short Sketch of His Life," *Daily Alta California,* March 8, 1858: "In 1824 he started for the unknown west . . . in company with Legrande [sic]"; and from *Hutchings' Illustrated California Magazine,* July 1860, in which the size of the Le Grande caravan is considerably exaggerated.

Smith, who died in San Francisco in 1866, became notorious in gold-rush California partly because of his "discovery" of the fabled lost Peg-leg gold mine, for which people still search. Though his reminiscences to popeyed reporters were well colored, they were basically truthful, as can be determined by checking with other accounts. However, he was probably in error when imputing to St. Vrain leadership of an 1824 expedition to New Mexico to buy gold and furs. The confusion about St. Vrain's role may arise from the fact that in his old age Peg-leg remembered Ceran as the one who had hired him and from the fact that later on in the mountains he did work directly for St. Vrain.

6. Shortly after Sylvestre Pratte's party left Cabanné's post, four opportunists took its trail, led by a man whose name—Sylvester Pattie—is confusingly similar to that of young Pratte's. One-time captain of a company of Missouri frontiersmen in the War of 1812 and later a pioneer in wild Gasconade County, Pattie had decided, after the death of his wife, to try a trading trip up the Missouri. With his son, James Ohio Pattie, and two older men, he wandered into Pilcher's fort in July 1824, secured a handful of goods, and started for the Indian country, only to be turned back at Fort Atkinson because of lack of proper licenses. Fortunately Sylvester Pattie knew of Sylvestre Pratte's plans, and, wheeling southwest, took after him. The years of extraordinary adventure and ill fortune which followed finally found fruit in the most famous and exasperating book on the early days of the Southwest, James Ohio Pattie's *Personal Narrative.* (See Note 13, this chapter.)

7. Ceran St. Vrain to Bernard Pratte, April 27, 1825. Ceran, who probably had not written many letters since the New Year, absent-mindedly dated the missive 1824. However, a clerk's notation on the outside shows that it was sent April 27, 1825, and received June 10 of the same year.

8. Smith (*Hutchings' Illustrated California Magazine,* loc. cit.) says St. Vrain outfitted him and nine other men. St. Vrain's letter to his mother, July 1825, says, without naming Smith, that he had "equipt" seven men, as nearly as I can make out from the difficult penmanship.

I am assuming, incidentally, that both men are referring to the same event. This may not be the case. The dates concerning Smith's early ventures are confusing, but a reasonable compromise makes the spring of 1825 probable; and St. Vrain's statement is then highly suggestive, if not conclusive.

9. Everything about New Mexico annoyed George Sibley. The following summer, when his men roughed up a Mexican who apparently was trying to steal one of their horses, he refused (and
the attitude was typical of most of the Americans in New Mexico) to heed the alcalde's command that he testify about the
matter: "I am very busily engaged and cannot attend your summons." And again, concerning an official communication sent
him through a mere deputy alcalde: "You *ought* to know that
whatever official intercourse I may have in this country must be
with the Superior authorities and not with you." As a blunt hint,
in case the deputy decided to interfere anyhow, he added, "I
shall commence my operations tomorrow . . . with an escort of
armed men." (Both letters in the Ritch collection, Huntington
Library. For Sibley's account of the survey itself, see his diaries
and papers in Kate Gregg's *The Road to Santa Fe*.)

Sibley, incidentally, had been a partner of both Paul Baillo
and Lilburn Boggs, Juliannah Bent's husband, in the Indian
trade at Fort Osage—one more curious interlocking in the western wanderings.

10. The *Missouri Intelligencer*, April 14, 1826, reported from Franklin that "a company of nearly one hundred persons (including
all those lately returned) will start from this place and vicinity
in a few weeks for New Mexico. It is the intention of some of
this party to penetrate to some of the more remote provinces and
to be absent for several years." The joint presence of St. Vrain
and Young on the trip is the conclusion of T. M. Marshall. ("St.
Vrain's Expedition to the Gila in 1826," *Southwest Historical
Quarterly*, January 1916.) Marshall also shows that Inman's
statement, in *The Old Santa Fe Trail*, that St. Vrain went to
Santa Fe during the fall of 1826 with young Kit Carson in his
caravan is erroneous. Kit went out in the autumn of '26, all right,
but with someone else. By autumn Ceran was trapping deep in
the Southwest.

11. The diary is printed in Senate Doc. 90, 22nd Congress, 1st Sess.
Wetmore offered it as part of his testimony to the Secretary of
War, October 11, 1831.

12. Although Baird speaks of the Americans as introducing themselves in a body, and although the dishonest passports were obtained suggestively close together, the hunt was probably not a
unified expedition in the sense that orders emanated from one
command or that profits flowed into a single till. Rather it was a
case of one fire showering several sparks. The tributaries of the
northern Rio Grande and San Juan had been fairly well scoured
when news came that Pattie's and Pratte's men had found rich
ground—and deadly Indians—in the south. The result was something like the mining stampedes of a later date, and the various
parties operated independently.

13. The main details of the Robidoux-Young wanderings come from Pattie's inflated *Personal Narrative*. Pattie gives few names. His dates are incorrect, his "personal" exploits are suspect, he lets blood flow too freely for even that gory era. Yet the book tells us most of what we know about one of the great adventures of the early Southwest. Later scholars have added a few names to Pattie's account of the 1826–27 wanderings; even so, the picture remains fragmentary. (See Hill, "Ewing Young in the Fur Trade of the Far Southwest"; T. M. Marshall, "St. Vrain's Expedition to the Gila," in which St. Vrain's personal activities are not described despite the title; and, for a highly readable abstract of the confusing threads, Cleland, *This Reckless Breed of Men.*)

14. Whether Ceran was with Pattie's and Young's far-ranging group cannot be said. Probably not. In any event, he was back in Taos that spring, for on June 3, 1827, he was witness at a wedding. (Marriage Book 39, p. 9, Taos Parish.)

Chapter IV
MOUNTAIN WINTER

1. Oddly enough, a year elapsed before St. Vrain reported Sylvestre's death in a letter to Messrs. B. Pratte & Company, September 28, 1828: "All the assistance I could give him was no youse his Pickup lasted but very few days, I have never yet experienced such feelings as I did at that moment, but it is useless for me to Dwel to long on that unfortunate subject, it was the will of God." Two minor discrepancies concerning the death may be noted. The San Francisco *Evening Bulletin*, "Story of An Old Trapper" (Peg-leg Smith), October 26, 1866, says that "Joe Pratt" was killed, presumably by Indians. And James Pattie, who had found Pratte sick in Santa Fe in 1825, speaks of Sylvestre dying of a lingering illness "in this place," which seems to refer to the town of San Tepec but may mean New Mexico generally.

2. The accounts of the amputation, even as told to reporters by Smith himself, vary in many details. My reconstruction is not authoritative, merely an effort to piece together what might have happened. It is somewhat surprising that, although Smith was one of the notorious "characters" of the mountains, tales of his extraordinary surgery are to be found only in obscure sources. Later writers who met him seem to have accepted his stump leg without much question, which allowed various people to claim a part in the operation. (For example, a certain Jim Cockrell, not mentioned in the list of Pratte's engagés, is said in Coutant's *History of Wyoming*, 201, to have done the cutting. And Hubert H. Bancroft (*Life of William Gilpin* 25) says Smith lost the leg after it had been run over on the plains by one of the wagons of a Bent caravan.

Milton Sublette's presence on the trip perhaps accounts for Wyoming legends that Milton, too, amputated his own leg. Milton did lose a leg a few years later, but it was the result of an infection (osteomyelitis, Bernard De Voto surmises, *Across the Wide Missouri*, 186). Although surgeons in Missouri performed the operation, it was probably, the times considered, not much less brutal than Smith's. From then on Milton was grounded to a mule cart, until 1836, when, having endured successive whittlings on his malignant stump, he died at Fort Laramie. All in all, Milton was well experienced with knives. Some four years after the Smith episode he was stabbed by a Bannock chief who apparently disapproved of Sublette's intentions concerning his daughter.

3. It is barely possible that Charles and William Bent, knowing of the waterlogged goods on the Sweetwater and hoping to recoup by trapping streams less crowded than those around Bear Lake, may have traveled part way toward Taos with St. Vrain's group. Reaching the Arkansas, they may have stopped and built a crude stockade for protection while they hunted and traded. This would be one way of accounting for a persistent tradition that the Bents reached the Rockies with St. Vrain by at least 1826 and constructed a primitive fort somewhere between the present Colorado communities of Pueblo and Canon City. For the following reasons, however, I doubt the tradition:

Charles Bowman ("History of Bent County" in the *History of the Arkansas Valley*, 827) seems to be the first to tell the story and date the stockade in 1826. Bowman, a newspaper editor who came to the town of Las Animas on the Arkansas in 1873, undoubtedly knew William Bent's daughter Mary, perhaps other Bent children, and also men who had worked for the Bents in the early days, though few, if any, who had arrived before the 1830s. This would lend authenticity to his statement—except for the fact that "old-timers" are notoriously unreliable respecting dates.

From Bowman's account the 1826 date passed into Hall's *History of Colorado*. Through Hall it passed into Allen Bent (*The Bent Family in America*, 121): "About the year 1826 four of the Bent brothers, Charles, William, George, and Robert, together with Ceran St. Vrain, went from the upper Missouri or Sioux County [sic] (whither they had gone, some of them, as early as 1823, in the service of the American Fur Company) to what is now Colorado, where they immediately built a wooden fort." The remark about service with the American Fur Company is apparently in error, at least as far as Charles is concerned; and since in 1826 George would have been twelve and Robert ten, their presence on the supposed trip is unlikely. However, as eminent an historian as Elliott Coues accepts the fact that three of the brothers were on the Arkansas in 1826. (*Journal of Jacob Fowler*, 47n.)

The *Dictionary of American Biography* advances to 1824 the arrival of Charles and William in the mountains (at which time William would have been fifteen). Authority seems to be Grinnell's "Bent's Old Fort and Its Builders," *Kansas Historical Collections*, Vol. XV, the best short study of the subject despite several small errors. One error apparently arises from Grinnell's arithmetic. He says, "Testifying before the joint committee of Congress which inquired into Indian affairs in the plains in 1865, William Bent stated that he had first come to the Upper Arkansas in 1824." What William actually said (*Condition of the Indian Tribes*, 83) was, "Having been living near the mouth of the Purgatoire on the Arkansas River . . . for the last thirty-six years . . ." This testimony, given in 1865, would fix 1829, not 1824, as the date for settling near the Purgatoire.

"Settling" does not, of course, preclude the possibility of trading or trapping trips before 1829. Charles, however, apparently corroborates William's date in a proclamation which the elder brother issued as governor of New Mexico on January 8, 1847: "In the year 1829 I came for the first time to this country." Charles, of course, may have been speaking of New Mexico, not of the Arkansas. But the 1829 date receives still further substantiation from the Reverend W. Barrows of Boston, a friend of Charles, who collected information from "his [Bent's] friends and mine" and on June 14, 1877, wrote to William C. Ritch, territorial secretary of New Mexico, that "as early as 1823 he [Charles] traded on the Missouri . . . in connection with the Missouri Fur Company. In 1828 he commenced trading for furs about Sweet Water Lake and Bear River. Thence he gradually extended his trade south to the Plains of the Platte and Arkansas Rivers." (Ritch papers, 1697, 1712, 1715, Huntington Library. In early annals Bear Lake was sometimes called Sweet Lake.)

In accepting dates earlier than 1829 for the Bents' first penetration of the Colorado mountains, both Grinnell and George Hyde (Life of George Bent) rely on letters written to them by William's half-Indian son George, who took up the story almost forty years after his father's death. George Bent's dates, however, are often confused. Referring to the Bents' first stockade in the mountains, he dates it variously as 1826, 1827, 1828, 1829 in letters to Hyde on February 20, 1914; April 14, 1908; June 11, 1914; March 6, 1905; and April 10, 1906. After examining hundreds of George Bent's letters, I am inclined to think that he read white men's dates in various histories and then tried to adapt them to the dateless family and Indian traditions with which he was familiar. Rejection of his dates, however, by no means also entails rejection of his stories; most of the things he tells quite probably happened at some time or another.

It is impossible to prove flatly that no Bent saw the Arkansas prior to 1829, for there simply isn't enough documentation to pin-point the brothers' every move during the years 1820–29. The mere possibility that they could have gone to Colorado during that period is negative evidence, however. It is my own opinion that they did not and that the first stockade was built by William alone in the fall of 1829, as Chapter VI will indicate.

4. There was considerable variation in the amounts received by St. Vrain's engagés. Milton Sublette was paid $919.07½; A. K. Branch, $360.63¾ (however the fraction was arrived at!); Bill Williams a mere $29.67½. Tom Smith apparently got nothing, though he did sign the deposition of the engagés. The varying amounts probably indicate varying degrees of prior indebtedness owed the company by the employees.

5. This hazily known trip followed by several months Jedediah Smith's first journey to the coast from the Great Salt Lake but probably preceded Smith's second venture and Pattie's fall crossing. (For the best summary of the various expeditions, see Cleland, *This Reckless Breed of Men*.) In time Campbell would turn his attention to the primitive placer mines south of Santa Fe, where he seems not to have thrived. (Abert, *Notes of a Military Reconnaissance*, 451–53.)

(The David Waldo, Ricardo Campbell, Ceran Sambrano passports of September 30, 1828, are among the Ritch papers, 108, Huntington Library.)

6. J. P. Cabanné on October 14, 1828, to his brother-in-law, Pierre Chouteau, in a microscopic hand that makes the idiomatic French exceedingly difficult to translate. After discussing the troubles involved in buying out the vacillating Joe Robidoux, the progress of McKenzie's keelboat, and local gossip (Papin wanted to go down the river because he was tormented by a growth on his neck), Cabanné continues:

"Pilcher and Co. have dissolved. The first has remained in the mountains, and [illegible] Vanderburgh and perhaps Charles Bent would like to return there. They have talked to me about it, but what can I do? They haven't much of anything. If we had been able to give them a hand, there would have been two less people to fight next year. . . . The end of young Pratte moves me to tears, and I behold with greatest sorrow the profound affliction of a family to whom we are all attached. . . . PS. There is enclosed herewith an order on Mr. Charles Bent that you will please cash and if it has already been paid you will please place it to Bent's credit."

Chapter V
DEATH ON THE TRAIL

1. William Waldo ("Recollections of a Septuagenarian") says that William Sublette, Milton's brother, was also present on the tragic trip. Perhaps. But William Sublette was carrying furs from the rendezvous for his company, and it seems unlikely that he circled back via Taos.

2. A curious problem is presented by Alphonso Wetmore in his diary, July 16, 1828: ". . . reached the upper Semiron spring, at the base of an abrupt rocky hill, on the summit of which is a cross standing over the bones of two white men, who were slain while asleep by the *gallant, high-minded, persecuted,* gentlemen Indians." (Sarcastic italics by Wetmore.) This certainly seems to refer to McNees and Munroe—yet authorities agree they were slain in August. It looks as though Mr. Wetmore, grinding an ax, may have doctored his July 16 entry before submitting the diary to Congress as testimony concerning the Mexican trade.

   Wetmore, incidentally, memorialized the traders' slaying of the Indians with doggerel too wonderfully macabre not to be sampled in part. In the verse a traveler is depicted as passing the death site a little time after the killing. Wolves were
Gorging and growling o'er carcass and limb,
They were too busy to bark at him.
From a Pani's scull they had stripped the flesh,
As ye peel the fig when the fruit is fresh;
And their white tusks cranched o'er the whiter scull
As it slipped through the jaws when the edge grew dull,
As they lazily mumbled the bones of the dead
When they scarce could rise from the spot where they fed.
And so on.

3. It is possible that one of the younger Bent brothers was also along, for with their father dead and the boys restless, a summer trip, even with danger threatening, would be one way to take care of them. William's son George says that his uncle Robert accompanied the caravan. (G. Bent to Hyde, May 2, 1917.) Robert, however, was only thirteen in 1829; his brother George, who was fifteen, might have been a more logical choice. Youngsters often went West with well-guarded caravans; Frémont, for example, took on his first expedition his young brother-in-law, Randolph Benton, age twelve. However, since no contemporary record of the 1829 trip mentions a third Bent, I have omitted one from this reconstruction.

4. In March 1829 Milton Sublette went to the mountains with his brother William. The next year Milton, Tom Fitzpatrick, Jim Bridger, Henry Fraeb, and Jean Baptiste Gervais, calling them-

selves the Rocky Mountain Fur Company, bought out William Sublette, Jedediah Smith, and David Jackson. Smith, Jackson, and Bill Sublette then entered the Santa Fe trade, following Milton's footsteps to the Southwest while he followed theirs to the North.

5. ". . . few of us but have purchased our goods on a credit in which our relations and friends are involved." (Waldo, Bent, and Collins to Major Bennet Riley, from twenty miles west of the Arkansas River, July 13, 1829—quoted in full in Otis E. Young's *The First Military Escort on the Santa Fe Trail*, 184–89.)

6. It has been argued by Grinnell and others that Charles's election presupposes prior acquaintance with the trail. But, as previously noted (Note 3, Chapter IV), Bent himself stated in a proclamation to the people of New Mexico, January 8, 1847, "In the year 1829 I came for the first time to this country."

7. No record names St. Vrain as arriving with the rescuers. (Waldo names Carson as being with Young's men.) However, if Ceran was in Taos at the time, as seems likely (he was witness there at a marriage on July 2, 1829—Marriage Book 39, p. 45, Taos Parish), he would hardly have ignored Young's call for volunteers to aid beleaguered countrymen.

It is probable that the rescue marked the first meeting of Carson and the Bents. Certainly there is no documentation to support, and plenty that militates against, the widely accepted myth that Kit's first trip west in a Santa Fe caravan during the fall of 1826 was under the aegis of Charles Bent. In the fall of 1826 Charles was on the Missouri.

Chapter VI
THE PEOPLE OF THE PLAINS

1. The presence of the refugees complicates an appraisal of the caravan's profits. According to *Niles' Weekly Register*, December 5, 1829, quoting a dispatch from Fayette, Missouri: "From 15 to 20 of our citizens . . . have just reached their homes . . . having realized an average profit of about 100%. . . . The aggregate amount of their returns is computed at $240,000." This agrees with Gregg, but not with figures produced by eastern opponents to the use of taxpayers' money for protecting private commercial ventures on the Santa Fe Trail. Trying to depreciate the value of the trade, these objectors offered statistics which state that $133,000 of the party's $240,000 and 900 of its 1200 mules were the property of the Spanish refugees and that the bulk of the furs belonged to independent trappers. Chittenden (II, 509) sets the value of the caravan's return cargo at $34,000, which is certainly too low. As usual, the truth probably lies somewhere in between.

2. Another discrepancy bobs up here. As nearly as can be deci-
phered from the torn pages of the New Mexican passport records
(Ritch papers, 108, passport 28, Huntington Library), Charles
Bent was issued a passport for Chihuahua and Sonora on October 10, 1829. This was the day before the caravan reached the
Arkansas, several hundred miles from Santa Fe. The passport,
of course, doesn't necessarily mean that Charles went to Chihuahua; he may have had one of his men take out the document
in his name and go south with the goods for him. Another indication that Charles himself didn't go south lies in a letter of
José Chavez, written to Riley, September 17, 1829, in which
Chavez states that he has offered Bent his small resources for
the return to the Arkansas. This certainly implies that Charles
was planning to go with the caravan. William Waldo, writing
half a century later, is explicit about Charles's presence. However, neither Riley nor Cooke mentions him. My own presumption is that Charles went to Missouri with the caravan in the fall
and returned to New Mexico the following summer. At all
events, he was in Santa Fe the next August or September 1830.

3. My source for the traditions concerning William's early ventures
in southeastern Colorado are letters written by George Bent
after he was sixty years old. George was familiar with the early
material only through tales told him by his father and by the
Indians. Though there is no reason to doubt the events, there is
reason to question their sequence; for, as indicated in previous
notes, George Bent's often self-contradictory dates cannot always be reconciled with other contemporary data. My re-
arrangement of his chronology is presented not as authoritative
—except in a few instances, the scanty amount of material available makes authority impossible—but as what seems most logical
in view of other known facts.

My text, incidentally, ignores the possibility that during his
first trip to the Arkansas in 1829–30 William may have had
dealings with two interesting traders called by the Indians
Crane and Bald Head. (George Bent to Hyde, May 13, 1914;
May 2, 1917; May 8, 1918.) Crane and Bald Head may have
been Jefferson Blackwell and John Gantt. (Grinnell, "Bent's Old
Fort and Its Builders.") John Gantt was the same Captain John
Gantt who was at Leavenworth's 1823 Missouri River battle
with the Arikaras. Charles Bent had known Gantt at Fort Atkinson before the captain was finally dismissed from the army in
1829. William's pre-fort contact with Gantt, if any, could have
occurred only in 1830, for in April of the following year Gantt
and Blackwell led seventy men from St. Louis up the Platte on
an ill-starred attempt to cut themselves in on the fur trade. (See
Zenas Leonard, *Narrative.*) Gantt is of some significance to the
Bents because on his bald head legend places the onus of first
debauching the Cheyennes with alcohol. Also, he was the guide

for the army's first penetration of the plains in 1835. Variant spellings of his name obviously include Gaunt and Gant.

4. Phil Stong (*Horses and Americans*) is a proponent of the scrub theory. J. Frank Dobie (*The Mustangs*) cites a wealth of contrary evidence. Most travelers on the early plains were impressed by at least some of the horses they saw.

5. The race was held about the year 1852. The victor, Crossing Over, in another race in the 1850s easily defeated the finest runner the Osage Indians could pit against him. It was the first time the Osage, Bullet by name, had ever been beaten, and the Cheyennes collected a mountain of bets. (George Bent to Hyde, October 12, 1917.)

6. Though the Comanches might despise New Mexican goods during the 1700s, when the passage quoted in the text was written, later Americans, from Thomas James on, found the Indians eager to obtain American articles. Also, by the 1800s, the Comanches were allowing New Mexican traders called Comancheros to come among them for barter. But no Mexican settlement from San Antonio to Chihuahua was safe from their depredations—nor, for many years, were later American outposts in Texas.

7. By chance Bull Hump's Comanches found a Cheyenne village on the Platte and stole its horses. On the way home they camped at Black Lake. There a band of Yellow Wolf's wild-mustang chasers surprised them, stole the horses back, and escaped in a running battle which became famous in Cheyenne folklore. (Grinnell, *The Fighting Cheyennes*, 35–39. George Bent to Hyde, March 6, 1905; April 10, 1905; June 15, 1914, etc.) Grinnell, incidentally, gives the date as 1828; George Bent, as usual, is contradictory. If my assumptions about the time of William's arrival on the Arkansas are correct, the spring of 1830 is a much more probable time.

Chapter VII
THE NIGHT THE STARS FELL

1. Figures according to Josiah Gregg. Chittenden says 120 men, 60 wagons. Accurate appraisals are impossible. Furthermore, though there is a tendency to picture the merchants as rolling out of Franklin or Independence in a body, there were probably several different parties each year and complete records cannot be reconstructed.

2. St. Vrain to Messrs. B. Pratte & Company, September 14, 1830. Ceran names the inspector who upset pattern by riding so far out from Santa Fe as "General Biscusa." This may be St. Vrain's phonetic spelling for Viscarra, who the previous fall had es-

corted Bent's and Waldo's caravan to the rendezvous with Riley on the Arkansas.

Data on St. Vrain's and Bent's affairs during the fall and winter of 1830 come from the letter cited above and another written by Ceran to Pratte on January 6, 1831. William's adventures during the fall were described by a companion, Robert Isaacs, in the *Missouri Republican,* September 4, 1832.

3. Charles's trips can only be surmised. St. Vrain, writing Pratte on January 6, 1831, announces merely that Charles, whom he'd lent a wagon the previous August or September, is again in Santa Fe with goods. Bent thus apparently made the round trip *using wagons both ways,* in approximately four months, including time spent in Missouri buying goods and loading. This is phenomenal. A lucky caravan, like the Storrs-Marmaduke party in 1824, could make the outbound journey in less than six weeks; but bad weather such as Wetmore met in 1828 could stretch out the journey to more than two months. So Charles must have had dry weather, good equipment—and those intangible qualities of know-how which engender their own luck. Furthermore, as the text will show, he seems to have made in 1831 no less than five crossings, with a trip to Mexico thrown in. Add these journeys to the three crossings of 1830, and in less than eighteen months he covered more than six thousand miles, the bulk of them with wagons. In between trips he attended to his business. If any other proprietor during the early days of the Santa Fe Trail left that many wheel tracks in the wilderness, records do not reveal him.

4. Isaacs finishes his story of the fight by saying, "We lost no time in pursuing our course toward the nearest Spanish settlement, and although completely disappointed in our anticipations of a profitable trip, we arrived there without further molestation." In spite of being "completely disappointed," however, Isaacs shortly afterward, in July and August, received from William Sublette drafts amounting to $2260. Data from the Sublette papers, Missouri Historical Society, via Dale L. Morgan, who adds, "This must have been in exchange for beaver, and it would be interesting to know where the beaver came from."

5. Ceran's 1830 ventures were more profitable than his groan to Pratte indicates, for on February 24, 1831, Theodore Papin wrote in French to his brother, "Ceran St. Vrain with a load worth 3000 piaster which he took to the Spanish brings back 10,000, but do not judge what there is to do there by this. I believe that of 150, 100 go out and break the neck. The trips to Mexico are the most hazardous that exist"—an interesting commentary on what veteran Missouri merchants thought of the Santa Fe trade.

Papin's letter seems to indicate that although St. Vrain had written Pratte on January 6 that he planned to stay in New

Mexico, he changed his mind and was in the East before February 24. Physically the trip is possible. But a more likely assumption is that Papin heard of the beaver pelts that Andrew Carson had brought back the previous fall and had mistakenly supposed that Ceran returned with them.

6. Gregg's figures for the year 1831 are 130 wagons carrying $250,-000 worth of goods. Chittenden (II, 509 n.), usually more conservative than Gregg, lists $200,000 as the amount carried by Gregg's caravan and says that a large party (Bent's?) which followed Gregg carried a similar amount. Since Chittenden does not mention the Smith-Sublette-Jackson caravan, which had preceded Gregg, and since Albert Pike's *Prose Sketches and Poems* indicates that there were other small parties on the trail, an estimate of $500,000 for the year's trade seems conservative enough. Half a million dollars is, of course, a piddling international commerce. In evaluating it, however, one should remember that it was all carried through a hostile wilderness in wagons. Furthermore, dollars were expensive in 1831: a man like Andrew Carson would work a full day for fifty cents. Five hundred thousand dollars in 1831 would probably represent more than five million of today's dollars.

7. Dale L. Morgan thinks that Gregg must have erred in his recollections and that Charles actually was not traveling behind Gregg's caravan. Mr. Morgan argues that if Charles had gone to Santa Fe behind the other caravans that spring and had then returned directly to Missouri (where he was, beyond doubt, in late August), he would have brought back word of Jedediah Smith's death. There is no evidence that Charles did this. On the other hand, there likewise seems to be no evidence that any Missouri paper noted Jedediah's death even after the members of his party returned from Santa Fe in late September or early October (Morgan, *Jedediah Smith*, 364). Thus, though the negative evidence of Charles's apparent silence is strong, it is not conclusive enough to rule out Gregg's statement, and so I have gone along with it, meanwhile admitting that Charles must have ridden hard and fast to cover the ground in the time available. If Mr. Morgan's assumption is correct, however, my estimates in the text and in Note 3 above concerning the miles traveled by Charles Bent in 1831 will obviously have to be revised downward.

8. Forsythe to Secretary of War, October 24, 1831 (Senate Doc. 90, 22nd Congress, 1st Sess., 77). In spite of the letter's October 1831 date, Young (*The First Military Escort on the Santa Fe Trail*, 174) and others take Forsythe's phrase, "in August last," to mean August 1830, perhaps because Josiah Gregg states that 1830 was the year when oxen were first used on the trail. Perhaps they were used that year, but not by a Charles Bent train leaving St. Louis in August 1830. By that August, Charles had

reached Santa Fe. (St. Vrain to Pratte, September 14, 1830.)
Thus 1831 seems the proper date for the first full-scale use of
oxen described by Forsythe.

Whatever the date, it is strange that the step occurred so late
among a frontier people thoroughly familiar with ox-drawn
transport. Preconceptions, however, are hard to break. Because
mules had been used first on the trail, naturally mules were best.
For the purposes of this book the matter is notable mainly in
showing that Charles Bent's mind did not work in the hidebound pattern of his contemporaries. To be sure, someone else
would have thought of the move sooner or later, but Charles
happened to be the first, thanks to Riley—or rather to Riley's
harassed quartermaster, who could not get mules, reluctantly
substituted oxen, and still did not see the significance of what
he had done. As much as any of man's possessions, the patient,
plodding ox won the West.

9. Unhappily, Pike does not name or describe Charles Bent in the
brief account of the trip that he gives in *Prose Sketches and
Poems*. Fuller details, including identification of the caravan as
Bent's, come from William Waldo (*Recollections*) and from an
autobiographical sketch of Pike's reproduced in *New Mexico's
Own Chronicle*, 103–4, edited by Maurice Fulton and Paul
Horgan. After his Western adventure, Pike settled in Arkansas,
where he became famous as a journalist, lawyer, Confederate
general, and author of one of the many versions of "Dixie." During the Civil War his influence would touch the Bents again.

10. This is John Gantt. See Note 3, Chapter VI.

11. Mexican passports 78 and 79, May 8, 1832, to James M. Halli-
day and James Glenray, "with goods of commerce belonging to
the naturalized citizen St. Vrain." (Ritch papers, 108, Huntington Library.)

12. My conjectures about the beginnings of Bent's Fort are based on
the following surmises. First, so extensive an organization could
hardly have materialized, Minerva-like, from a mere thought,
though some accounts imply this. The Bents and St. Vrain were
intensely practical; an enlargement of their activities must have
been predicated on the success William had achieved on the
Arkansas before the fort was built. My assumption that his Fountain Creek stockade was indeed successful is based on statements by William's son that the four Bents had *cattle* with them
when Yellow Wolf's party stopped by the Purgatory camp.
(George Bent to Hyde, May 13, 1914; May 22, 1914.) What
cattle, unless wagons were being used? And why wagons, unless
sizable amounts of goods were being transported? The wagons
were no part of a Santa Fe train; caravans never followed that
mountainous route until after the Bents had built a road from
the fort over Raton Pass.

The statement that brothers George and Robert Bent were along comes from the letters cited above, and various others. The trip seems an excursion for the pair and not the beginning of their association with the firm; at least there is no further mention of them until a year or so after the completion of the fort.

How influential Yellow Wolf actually was in persuading the Bents to move down-river from Fountain Creek is problematical. William must have been aware of at least some of the economic factors involved. But Indian tradition makes Yellow Wolf decisive, and it may well be that his urgings helped to clinch matters.

The dates of the building of the fort need little arguing. As in the case of the earlier stockade, Charles Bowman ("History of Bent County," see Note 3, Chapter IV) seems the source of the commonly cited dates which George Bent evidently picked up and passed along to Grinnell and Hyde. Supposedly the construction of the fort spread out over four years, 1828–32, but no contemporary record mentions the fort during this period, surely a significant silence. Farnham, who visited the fort in 1839, says it was built in 1832. Matthew Field, who also visited in 1839, says 1833. William Waldo says 1833. Charles's first trading license was taken out in December 1833. St. Vrain, writing Lieutenant Colonel Eneas Mackay on July 21, 1847 (Abandoned Military Reservation Series, Box 52, National Archives, Washington), says he and Charles built the fort in 1834. To me it seems likely that planning was begun in the fall of 1832 (quite probably Charles drew up rough sketches in St. Louis during the winter); that construction was started as soon as William and Ceran could assemble workers and materials early the following summer; that the building was far enough completed for operations to start in the fall of 1833; and that the complex job was finished in the spring of 1834. (See also LeRoy R. Hafen, "When Was Bent's Fort Built?" *Colorado Magazine,* April 1954, an account that reaches approximately these same conclusions, though both studies were prepared independently.)

13. This is guesswork. The fact that William Bent went east with Charles in the fall of 1832 is established by research work of the Colorado Historical Society (Hafen, op. cit. in note above). Yet William must have returned from the East early in the spring; every tradition concerning the building of the fort puts him in charge of the construction, and the job was so huge that it must have demanded more time than would have been available if William had not left Missouri before Charles did in June. As for St. Vrain, no documentation exists to locate him during this period, but it is not illogical to suppose that he spent the winter in Taos, getting together supplies and workers (a lengthy chore

in that ill-provisioned land of *mañana*) and brought them to the Arkansas as soon as William arrived.

14. At the time I was preparing the manuscript of this book, the exact dimensions of Bent's Fort seemed impossible to obtain. One traveler said that walls seventeen feet high ran 150 feet north and south, 100 feet east and west. Garrard reduced the size to 100 feet square, perhaps the area of the inner placita, then reared back his head in amazement and declared the walls to be thirty feet high. John Hughes, marching with the Army of the West, stated that walls fifteen feet high enclosed an area 180 by 135. Ceran St. Vrain, who presumably knew, wrote (to Mackay, July 21, 1847, loc. cit.) that the fort was 180 feet square and that a corral of the same size adjoined it to the rear. Ceran, however, was offering to sell the fort and may have been careless with his figures.

That he did exaggerate was suggested by the discovery of a plan which Lieutenant J. W. Abert had jotted, September 8, 1846, on the back of a portrait he had drawn of a Cheyenne Indian. I was not privileged to see this sketch, then in the hands of a private owner (nor the sketches of Alexander Barclay, factor at the fort during the late 1830s). A summary of Abert's data was later reported in "Ground Plan of Bent's Fort," *Colorado Magazine*, July 1953. Though no ground plan was actually reproduced, the summary indicated that walls fourteen feet high enclosed an area 178 by 137. These figures suggested a rectangle, but excavations made since then by Dr. Herbert Dick of Trinidad Junior College have proved that the fort was indeed a trapezoid.

15. Grinnell says Ceran had smallpox during the building of the fort. Twenty-odd years later Ceran told Surgeon Peters of the U. S. Army of being transported in a mule litter when ill with the smallpox, but he doesn't give time or place. (DeWitt Peters to his family from Fort Massachusetts, April 5, 1855; quoted in Grant, *When Old Trails Were New*, 311.) I jump to the conclusion that the events were related.

Tradition says that Kit Carson, hauling timbers for the fort, was also stricken with smallpox. Other evidence, however, puts Kit seventy miles up the Arkansas at a shoddy log post being built by John Gantt and Blackwell, whom Kit had joined after leaving Fitzpatrick. It was at this fort that Gantt supposedly enticed the Cheyennes to drink alcohol sweetened with sugar and so turned them into a nation of drunkards. But it is hard to believe the Cheyennes had not already been introduced to liquor by other American or Mexican traders.

Whether or not Kit Carson worked on the building of Bent's Fort is a matter of controversy. In 1868 William Bent's son George visited Kit, who was ill, and bought a horse from him. Afterward they sat around in the sun, swapping stories. George says (Bent to Hyde, February 5, 1913) that Kit told him of hauling timbers for the construction and of having all the fort's horses stolen from him by Crow Indians. With a dozen men—Americans, French trappers, and two Cheyennes—Kit tracked the Crows through deep snow and bitter cold, overhauled a party of sixty, killed two in a sharp battle, and retrieved the stock. There seems no reason why George Bent would fabricate the story. Furthermore, Grinnell says, the two Cheyennes with Kit told the same version when counting their coup, a ceremony in which truth is mandatory.

On the other hand, when Kit dictated the story of his life, he said that in January 1833, when he was at the Gantt and Blackwell post, fifty Crows stole nine of the traders' horses. Carson and eleven men (but no Cheyennes) followed the thieves forty miles through deep snow and bitter cold, killed five in a battle that differs from the description given by George Bent, and recovered the stock. There seems no reason why Kit would fabricate.

Sabin (*Kit Carson Days*) thinks Kit was at Gantt's and Blackwell's post and not at Bent's Fort during the Crow episode. This disturbed George Hyde and George Grinnell, leading authorities on the Cheyennes. They accused Sabin of "begging the issue." (Hyde to Grinnell, June 1, 1917. Grinnell papers, Southwest Museum, Los Angeles.) Well, I hereby also beg the issue, though pointing out that if the construction of Bent's Fort was not begun until the spring of 1833, there is difficulty in accounting for the big snow mentioned as occurring there during Kit's adventure. (The next winter won't do; Kit was not on the Arkansas during the winter of 1833–34, as the text and subsequent notes will indicate.) Unless William returned to the Arkansas even earlier than I believe (or unless St. Vrain took Kit over from Taos with a wood-cutting crew, a not impossible event), the weather elements in the story can't apply to the construction of Bent's Fort and Kit was probably up the river at the Gantt-Blackwell post.

One more discrepant item might be added. *The History of the Arkansas Valley*, 836, says that once Pawnees stole several horses from the fort; that William Bent, Kit Carson, and a single Mexican pursued the thieves for eighty miles through deep snow and bitter cold and stole the horses back without any battle at all. Perhaps this was a different affray, but it sounds like a garbled echo of the Crow episode already discussed.

16. Senate Doc. 69, 23rd Congress, 2d Sess., *Report from the Secretary of War*. Some of the original capital expended on goods and construction seems to have been advanced by doughty old Benito Vasquez, active in St. Louis trading circles while Charles was still a boy. Vasquez, however, did not retain his interest in the firm for long. (George Bent to Hyde, April 10, 1905.) A few

years later Benito's youngest son, Louis Vasquez, would be an active competitor of Bent, St. Vrain & Company on the South Platte.

17. It was while on this trading trip for Bent, St. Vrain & Company that Carson pursued for a hundred miles a Ute who had stolen horses from Antoine Robidoux, killed the Indian in lonely combat, and brought the animals back. The next spring Carson and Lee traveled on north to the Snake River, sold the Bent, St. Vrain goods to Tom Fitzpatrick and Jim Bridger. Lee then returned to Taos. (It is not known whether he is the Stephen Luis Lee who was long a resident of Taos, or the Richard B. Lee, former West Pointer, who captained a Bent, St. Vrain train that reached Missouri on October 14, 1834.) Instead of following Lee homeward, Kit stayed in the mountains, worked briefly for the Rocky Mountain Fur Company, and then set himself up as the West's most famous free trapper.

18. Grinnell (*The Fighting Cheyennes*, 69) dates the moving of the medicine arrows against the Pawnees as 1830. Hyde (*Life of George Bent*, Chapter 11, 17 ff.) dates it 1833, the year of the great meteor shower. George Bent describes the scene at the fort in a letter to Grinnell, October 12, 1913. (Grinnell papers, Southwest Museum, Los Angeles.) Additional data concerning the arrows, the battle, and Gray Thunder's subsequent efforts to recover the charms appear in George Bent's letters to Hyde, February 6, 1905; February 20, 1905; undated, 1914; July 6, 1914, etc.

Chapter VIII
ROBES, ALCOHOL, AND DRAGOONS

1. Fontenelle to Pierre Chouteau, September 17, 1834, quoted in part in Chittenden. (I, 304–5.) After his 1831 venture in the Santa Fe trade, Bill Sublette had returned north. (His erstwhile partner, David Jackson, stayed in the South, joining Ewing Young, Moses Carson, and Charles Bent's friend, David Waldo, on a difficult, dangerous, and unprofitable mule-trading venture to California.) Joining forces with Robert Campbell, Sublette made a bold but forlorn bid to buck the American Fur Company. The fort on Laramie River was part of this operation. The establishment was only a little smaller than Bent's Fort; its initial capital, as stated in its official license, was $2957.12 as compared to the Bent, St. Vrain & Company's initial investment in trade goods of $3877.28.

Like Bent's Fort, the Sublette-Campbell post was first named Fort William, but to the mountain men it was always Fort Laramie, by which name (after it had been rebuilt of adobe on a new but nearby site) it became famous during the great emigrations to Oregon and California. Its location should not be con-

fused with the present city of Laramie; the fort lay eighty or
more airline miles farther northeast.

Sublette and Campbell did not control the post for long; in
the complicated shiftings of the trade it soon passed into the
hands of Pratte, Cabanné & Company, who had bought the
American Fur Company's Western Department on June 1, 1834.
In 1838 Pratte, Cabanné & Company became Pierre Chouteau
Jr. & Company, but in popular usage the name American Fur
Company clung to all these organizations and will in general be
used for all of them in my text.

2. On June 19, 1835, Agent Richard Cummins of the Northern
Agency, Western Territory, wrote from Fort Leavenworth to
William Clark, enclosing "a copy of a letter I received from a
Gentleman relative of an attack by Mr. Wm. Bent & others on
the Snake [Shoshoni] Indians." The gentleman is not named,
nor does his name appear on Cummins's copy of the letter. (Office of Indian Affairs, Upper Missouri Agency, National Archives.)

Cummins's informant describes the attack as taking place at
"Ft. Cass on the Arkansas River." Fort Cass is, I believe, a hitherto unrecognized post in Colorado annals. Like the American
Fur Company's Fort Cass on the Yellowstone River, it was probably named for Lewis Cass, vigorous frontier soldier who, after
the notorious Peggy Eaton affair, replaced John H. Eaton as
Secretary of War in Jackson's cabinet in the summer of 1831
and hence became a figure of importance to Western traders.
Thus the Colorado Fort Cass was probably built in 1832, after
word of Cass's elevation reached the distant Arkansas. (The Yellowstone Fort Cass was built in the fall of 1832.) But where on
the Arkansas was it erected and by whom? It was probably not
an early name for Bent's Fort, because the post was specifically
called Fort William in Charles's license of December 1833—
months before the Shoshoni murder. Fort Cass may well have
been the name of the post built by Gantt and Blackwell near
the junction of Fountain Creek and the Arkansas in the late fall
of 1832—for Cummins's informant lists John Gantt as among the
witnesses of the attack. Or perhaps Fort Cass was the name of
William Bent's early, still-active stockade in the same vicinity.
Or it may be the unknown fort in the Big Timbers so cryptically
mentioned by George Gibson of the Army of the West in his
journal, July 26, 1846: "Our camp is where Bent's Old Fort
stood, forty-five miles from the present one [more nearly thirty-
five miles; Gibson's own account shows that he overestimated],
and very few vestiges of it now remain . . . though it was deserted only about twelve years ago"—i.e., about 1834, the date
of the Shoshoni murder. Or does Gibson's journal entry perhaps
refer to one of William Bent's early stockades? Or just to one of

the cottonwood structures that traders put up wherever they wintered?

3. The story, perhaps apocryphal, is told in Favour (*Old Bill Williams*, 86–95). Though Joseph Reddeford Walker's 1833–34 expedition has been accused of abandoning its original purpose and turning into a horse-stealing party, there is nothing in contemporary accounts, especially Zenas Leonard's *Narrative*, to substantiate this. So Old Bill may not have inaugurated the "trade" in 1834. Certainly it did not become widespread until the collapse of beaver prices toward the end of the decade forced many trappers to search for new ways of staying alive. The horse stealing to which some of them turned shocked old hands in the mountains, as see Robert (Doc) Newell's Memorandum, 63–64. In November 1839, Newell says, northern Cheyennes raiding in Brown's Hole made off with one hundred horses belonging to the trappers there (including Abel Baker, trading for Bent, St. Vrain). To replace the stock some of the whites blatantly stole fourteen horses from the Hudson's Bay post at Fort Hall, Idaho, plus thirty more from Snake Indians. Another ten or fifteen trappers, according to Doc Newell, "are gone to California for the purpose of Robbing and Steeling. Shuch thing never has been known till late." Outraged, Doc named a few of the "horse thieves and banditti": Philip Thompson, Bill New, Elwen Michel, Richard Owens, and others. New, incidentally, had worked with Doc a few years earlier on the South Platte for Bent, St. Vrain. After the great horse raid in California in 1840, New returned to the company's employ as a hunter. So did Bill Mitchell, who is perhaps the Elwen Michel named by Newell. Richard Owens, occasional Bent, St. Vrain employee, became a ranching partner of Kit Carson's, and at Bent's Fort he and Kit joined Frémont's third expedition. Frémont thought highly of Richard and named for him the Owens Valley of eastern California. Probably no other district so famous recreationally and economically has been named after a horse thief.

It is almost certain that the banditti named by Doc Newell, together with Peg-leg Smith, disposed of at least some of their stolen stock to Bent and St. Vrain. By the 1840s the arrival of California horses and mules at the Arkansas fort had become a familiar, if intermittent, occurrence. Ruxton's semi-fictitious account in *Life in the Far West*, Chapter VII (in which Walker figures and which ended with the sale of the stolen horses at the fort), may be taken as a faithful composite of various raids Ruxton heard about during his visit in 1846–47.

4. The fact that Charles Bent declared goods in New Mexico on August 21, 1834 (Ritch papers, 150, Huntington Library), indicates that he was on the trail. Though no evidence proves he was in the caravan escorted by the dragoons, he would be un-

likely to eschew its protection. Certainly he knew about the recent military movements.

5. Fort Leavenworth superseded Fort Atkinson, which had stood near Pilcher's old Bellevue post, in the vicinity of modern Omaha. Atkinson, being deemed unhealthful and also too distant from the starting point of the Santa Fe trade, was abandoned in June 1827. That same spring Colonel Henry Leavenworth began constructing the famous fort which still bears his name. As the Santa Fe and Oregon trails grew in importance, so, too, did Fort Leavenworth.

6. Some of these volunteer rangers may have escorted, at least part way to the New Mexican border, the 1833 caravan which Charles Bent captained. Information is not definite. (Bancroft, *History of Arizona and New Mexico*, 335 n.; Young, *First Military Escort on the Santa Fe Trail*, 170–71.) This escort, if any, and the one in 1834 were the only times troops went with the caravans between 1829 and 1843.

7. Like the story of Bill Williams and the stolen horses, this episode of Carson and the Comanches may be apocryphal. The main authority is Joe Meek (Victor, *River of the West*), said by one critic to become occasionally "intoxicated with the ferment of his own imagination." De Voto, however, seems to accept Joe's account of the battle. (*Across the Wide Missouri*, 153.) Carson also refers to it in his autobiography, but Kit gets his dates mixed; his other known trapping activities make it difficult, but not impossible, to put him on the Cimarron at this period in 1834. (See Sabin, *Kit Carson Days*, 226–31. Also Tobie, *No Man Like Joe*.) If the battle did occur—and something like it apparently happened at some time or another—the Bents most probably knew of it. And even if it didn't happen in the summer of 1834, the partners would still have been dubious of Dodge's efforts to deal with the Comanches.

8. More history than Dodge realized was being made on the trail that summer—missionaries Marcus Whitman and Samuel Parker, headed west with a fur caravan under Lucien Fontenelle, onetime partner of Charles Bent on the Missouri. The year before, another missionary, Jason Lee, had also gone west. Soon the name "Oregon" would strike increasing chords in the land-hungry consciousness of American farmers. It conjured up pictures of trees and greenness, a country comparable to the humid East. The intervening plains, however, defied familiarity. So did the red demons inhabiting those plains. The American Board of Commissioners for Foreign Missions could envision Christian savages on the smiling coasts of the Pacific, but not, apparently, at the foot of the Rockies. Decades would pass before the zeal of the hurrying proselyters would pause to consider the Cheyennes, the Sioux, or the Arapaho.

9. Grinnell (*The Fighting Cheyennes*, 70) says without elaboration that the medicine arrow was recovered from the Pawnees in 1835 by a "trick." George Bent (to Hyde, February 6, 1905) gives the story I follow, as does George Hyde. (*Life of George Bent*, Chapter 11.) Two years later a second arrow was captured from the Pawnees by Brûlé Sioux and was presented by them to the Cheyennes with appropriate ceremony. Six arrows (the two recovered ones and the four new ones) embarrassed the medicine men. They got rid of the excess by wrapping up two of the new substitutes and depositing them on Medicine Pipe Mountain in the Black Hills of South Dakota as a gift to Sweet Medicine, the culture hero who had presented the original totem to the Cheyennes at the beginning of time.

10. The next year Dodge left the army to become the first territorial governor of Wisconsin. When Wisconsin became a state, he went to Washington as its first senator. The frontier has no better epitome than Henry Dodge: log-cabin childhood, sheriff, militia fighter, lead miner, army officer, politician.

11. The dates when George and Robert Bent and Marcellin St. Vrain joined the firm are not known. References to them are rare, especially to Robert. Marcellin apparently never became a full-fledged partner. Robert may not have. George, however, was a member by at least 1837, when the company put in a claim against the government for damages suffered during an attack by Pawnees. The claim was signed by Ceran, Charles, William, and George—not by Robert or Marcellin, though Marcellin had been in charge of the ravaged train. (28th Congress, 2nd Sess. H. Rep. 194, Serial 468.)

12. Charles's classification as surveyor, March 20, 1830, may be found in the Ritch papers, 1/4, Huntington Library. The medical lore is told without a citation of sources by Paul Walter. ("The First Civil Governor of New Mexico under the Stars and Stripes," *New Mexico Historical Review*, VIII, April 1933.)

13. Taos parish records contain nothing of Charles Bent's marriage —nor of George Bent's or Ceran's subsequent weddings. (Reference courtesy O. A. Coggiola, vice-chancellor, Archdiocese of Santa Fe.) Possibly Charles wasn't married in Taos. Possibly the clerk was negligent. Possibly Charles was married outside the Church, though his wife was certainly a Catholic and it is difficult to imagine a Protestant minister in New Mexico during that period. In the absence of records, the date of the wedding can only be guessed at from the birth of his first son, Alfredo. Allen Bent (*The Bent Family in America*) says on p. 123 that Alfredo was born in 1836; on page 211 that he was born February 12, 1837.

As for Ignacia's beauty, Garrard (*Wah-To-Yah and the Taos Trail*) is one witness, and he saw her a dozen years later, during a time of intense sorrow. William Boggs ("Narrative of a Journey to Santa Fe", mss., Coe Collection, Yale) adds a few more skimpy details about Ignacia and the Taos home.

Chapter IX
ADOBE EMPIRE

1. It is this Indian fight that has led me to join Wootton and Hobbs on the 1836 journey. In telling of their first journeys with Bent caravans, each man in his old age used different dates but similar details for the fight, though Hobbs blames Pawnees and Wootton Comanches. The fact that they otherwise talk of different events isn't necessarily a contradiction; each was remembering what impressed him most. Nor is there necessarily a contradiction in the fact that Hobbs dates his first trip as 1835 and Wootton his as 1836. Hobbs put all his dates too early, as a check with recorded events will quickly show.

   One other record of the 1836 trip comes from Robert (Doc) Newell. After having ranged the northern Rockies with various fur brigades from 1829–35, Newell had gone home for a vacation. Heading westward again in 1836, he signed up in April with Bent, St. Vrain & Company and began keeping a most laconic diary (known now as his Memorandum, preserved in the University of Oregon special collections). Concerning his trip, Newell says simply that he arrived "safely" at Fort William. "Safely" may mean that this was the only thing he thought noteworthy about the Indian fight. Or he may have been traveling in a different caravan from Hobbs and Wootton; the company sometimes sent more than one spring train westward from Missouri.

2. Raised by Cheyennes, the white captive lived to ancient age with the tribe, all knowledge of her real parents forever lost. (Grinnell, *The Fighting Cheyennes*, 40–41.)

3. Charles Bent, writing to Manuel Álvarez, December 1, 1840, concerning a man suspected of murder in New Mexico: He is "a great scoundrel we had to have him whipped at the post a year since."

4. This shooting scrape (told in Grinnell "Bent's Old Fort") may be a garbled echo of the 1834 Shoshoni murder; since the tales are completely different, however—except for the fact that in each Murray fires on a Shoshoni—I include them as separate incidents.

5. Shortly after completing Fort Laramie, William Sublette and Robert Campbell sold it to the reorganized Rocky Mountain Fur Company—Gervais, Fraeb, Jim Bridger, Milton Sublette, Tom Fitzpatrick. Soon Fraeb and Gervais dropped out, and next Fitzpatrick, Bridger, and Milton Sublette were absorbed by

Pratte, Chouteau & Company—that is, by the Western Department of the American Fur Company.

6. From south to north, downstream along the valley, they would be, first Fort Lupton, then Sarpy's and Fraeb's Fort Jackson, next Fort Vasquez, and, most northerly, Bent & St. Vrain's new post, known successively as Fort Lookout, Fort George, and finally Fort St. Vrain.

7. Garrard, roaming the Arkansas in late 1846 with Bent traders, speaks (*Wah-To-Yah*, 170) of finding William Bent and his squaws—plural—in one lodge. But the younger woman bore William no children while the elder lived.

   As in the case of Charles's wedding, the date of William's marriage is unknown. My guess at the spring of 1837 is predicated in part on the January 1838 birth of his first child.

8. Josiah Gregg thinks that Texan affairs had no influence, though certainly Santa Fe officialdom was cognizant of the Lone Star revolt. And perhaps it is only coincidence that after Texas's success both New Mexico and California experienced abortive upheavals.

9. The cartel agreement can be found in the P. Chouteau collection, Missouri Historical Society. Other data on the South Platte competition come from several letters in the same collection, some of which are cited in Notes 10, 11, 12, and from various articles by LeRoy Hafen in *Colorado Magazine*. (See Bibliography.)

   The American Fur Company account books, preserved in the Missouri Historical Society, indicate the close ties that grew up after the cartel between that company and Bent, St. Vrain—ties so close that in New Mexico Charles Bent freely drew sizable drafts on his one-time rivals (Bent to Alvarez, October 22, 1841) Some contemporaries even called Bent, St. Vrain the southern department of the American Fur Company. But it was never that. Within its far-flung area it held absolute sovereignty.

10. Frederick Laboue, in barbarous French, from the North Fork of the Platte, to P. D. Papin at Fort Pierre, December 15, 1838: "Louie Harod [as nearly as the spelling can be deciphered] . . . told me that Mr. Halsey had ordered him to . . . burn Sarpy's. This is what he did." Petulantly Laboue adds, "Dear friend, if I had to give you the details of all the bastards that are here in the fort, I would not have enough paper in all Ft. Laramie on which to write you." Trade, he grumbles, is poor, his horses are in miserable shape, he is short-handed, he wants "alcohol, as much as you can send"—and William Bent has been causing trouble, as the text will show.

11. J. Picotte, in almost illegible French, to H. Picotte, January 25, 1839. "Mr. Sinverin [St. Vrain] is drunk . . . he has swallowed whiskey like water." This was probably Marcellin, not Ceran,

although Ceran was also trading during the winter of 1838–39. (Laboue to Papin, cited in Note 10.) I cannot identify the "Black Country" (the Black Hills?) where the whiskey was being swallowed, nor the "Rivire des arcre" (sic) where Ceran was trading. The French traders used colloquial geographic names that have long since disappeared.

12. More barbarous French, to Papin at Fort Pierre, dictated by illiterate Joseph Quelte and written by John Roleta, March 1, 1839. Quelte complains that he fears Bissonnet and Vilandry "are going to find the company of Mr. Charles Bent, for the offers which he made Vilandry are most advantageous. . . . See if you can dissuade Mr. Vilandry, for I assure you that if he goes there he will be able to do you much harm." There is no evidence, however, that either Bissonnet or Vilandry listened to Charles's blandishments.

13. Farnham (*Travels*, 164–66) says sixty Comanches in July made off with forty to fifty head. Field (account in the New Orleans *Picayune*, reprinted in *Colorado Magazine*, May 1937) says three hundred Comanches garnered seventy-five head. Both are presumably repeating what was told them at the fort by Robert Bent shortly after the incident. As has been previously noted, "facts" sometimes get tangled, even in contemporary accounts.

14. The story, kept well hushed by the St. Vrains if it is true and coming to us only through cryptic allusions, is told by Sabin, *Kit Carson Days*, 283–84. Sabin identifies Félicité simply as a protégée of Ceran. The only Félicité who fits is Felix's daughter. (*Genealogy of the Family of DeLassus and St. Vrain*, 21.)

15. In 1840 or 1841, Lupton, Lucien Maxwell, Carlos Beaubien, and the Bent brothers are said to have established a settlement on Adobe Creek, west of Pueblo. (B. F. Rockafellow, "History of Fremont County," in *History of the Arkansas Valley*, 845–46.)

Chapter X
TEXIANS

1. Bent to Álvarez, December 1, 1840, concerning the murder of an American in New Mexico: "Should the diseased [deceased] have any property, it is your business to take possession of the same, and should you finde any relitives of his to pay the same over to them . . . It is your duty to make a full statement . . . to our minister in Mexico," etc.

Bent's badly spelled letters to Álvarez, almost the only writing in Charles's hand that survives, are part of the Read collection, New Mexico Historical Society, on loan at the University of New Mexico. Though not cited individually, they constitute a major source for this and the next chapters.

2. Erna Fergusson (*New Mexico*, 251) says that Armijo came of wealthy background, married a wealthy Chavez, stole no Chavez sheep. James Webb, who knew Armijo well and admired him, which most American traders did not, attests (*Adventures in the Santa Fe Trade*, 87–88) to the governor's humble sheepherding background, says Armijo taught himself to read from a Catholic primer, learned to figure by using campfire charcoal on the knees of his buckskin breeches. Webb makes no charge of sheep stealing. Though perhaps an American canard, the yarn was nonetheless widely believed.

3. The murderers seem eventually to have been turned free without punishment. (Álvarez to U. S. Secretary of State, December 18, 1842.)

James Kirker, a leader in the demand on Armijo, was one of the early American trappers in New Mexico. His embroilment with Armijo did not prevent officials of Chihuahua from offering him, a few years later, fifty dollars for each Apache scalp he collected. With a band of Americans, Shawnees, Delawares, and Mexicans, and helped by whiskey and treachery, he slew something like 170 Indians, whose scalps were publicly displayed over the main entry of the Chihuahua cathedral. One of Kirker's fellow bounty hunters was Jim Hobbs, recently ransomed by William Bent. Hobbs says that some of the raiders, annoyed over the officials' refusal to pay full price for squaw scalps, stole horses, drove them north, sold part of them at Bent's Fort. (Ruxton, *Adventures*, Hafen edition, 146–49. Hobbs, *Life*, 81–99.)

4. The "bad man" of the West may have reached the mountains earlier than is generally realized. On January 16, 1841, Charles warned Álvarez of a rumor at the fort that a gang of Americans and Shawnees were planning to waylay a caravan. And in 1842 the company itself broke up "the band of robers on the other side of the mountain. St. Vrain and George gave them some advise to be followed by actes in case the first was not attended to." Those cryptic words (Bent to Álvarez, December 25, 1842) are all that is known of what is perhaps the first instance of vigilante law in the Rockies.

5. This tub-thumping is one of the earliest schemes for the seizure of Oregon by force. Harris's letter to Grimsley and Grimsley's to Secretary of War John Bell, indicating Bent's full knowledge of the scheme, are reproduced in the *Oregon Historical Quarterly*, XXIV, 1923, 438.

6. Charles Bent was, in his own words to Ashley, a "particular friend" of John Marsh, one of the first overland settlers in California. Restless, able, and avaricious, Marsh had left Massachusetts in 1823 with his Harvard diploma to tutor the officers' children at Fort St. Anthony, now St. Paul, Minnesota. There he himself had studied medicine under the post surgeon. Marrying

the daughter of a French trader and a Sioux squaw, he stayed
on the frontier as an Indian agent and trader. Influential with
the Sioux, he led not very effective contingents of them against
the Sacs and Foxes during the Black Hawk War—and at the
same time illegally and secretly sold arms to the enemy tribes.
When a warrant was issued for his arrest because of this, he fled
from Minnesota, perhaps went to the Rockies with a party of
trappers, and in 1833 opened a store in Independence. Bent, St.
Vrain & Company evidently had dealings with him, but by early
1835 he was broke. Also, according to his biographer, George
D. Lyman (*John Marsh, Pioneer*, 193) the military had located
him and were about to arrest him on the old warrant. He nonetheless had sufficient brass to ask the government, through
Charles Bent, for an appointment as U.S. consul to Upper California.

On his behalf, Charles Bent wrote, April 26, 1835, from St.
Louis to William Ashley, then a member of Congress from Missouri, saying, "There are about fifty families in the upper part
of this state [Missouri] preparing to emigrate to that country.
There are annually a considerable number of vessels from the
U. States who visit Upper California for the purpose of commerce, and the U States having a Consul at Monterey or some
of the ports on that coast will be a great advantage to our enterprising citizens."

Ashley forwarded the letter to the State Department with a
note that "Mr. B. is a gentleman of high respectability. He has
been engaged in commercial pursuits in the Mexican provinces
for may [sic] years, & is perhaps as capable as any other man in
Judging of the regulations necessary in that country for the promotion of Citizens of the U States transacting business there."
(Record Group 59, Department of State, Appointment Papers,
1829–36—courtesy Mr. Dale L. Morgan.)

Ashley did not himself vouch for Marsh, and the appointment
was not forthcoming—nor did Marsh wait long for it. In June,
with little more than the books and possessions he could carry in
his saddlebags, he started with a few companions for Santa Fe.
(None of them, evidently, was from the fifty families supposedly
eager to go to California.) Somehow, so the story goes, Marsh
became separated from his fellows, was captured by Comanches, and classically cheated death at their hands by curing a
wound in a chief's arm. Escaping from the Indians, he at length
reached Santa Fe, tarried a few weeks, and then rode overland
to Los Angeles. After a brief period there as a physician, he
secured a huge tract of land near the mouth of the San Joaquin
Valley. From his ranch he wrote many letters fostering emigration from Missouri. He accumulated the fortune he always
wanted but in 1853 was murdered by some of his own dissatisfied ranch hands.

7. Binkley ("New Mexico and the Texan Santa Fe Expedition") says Dryden had cleared out. Bancroft, however (*History of Arizona and New Mexico,* 322 n.), reports Dryden as imprisoned in Chihuahua 1841–42. The Mexican historian Bustamante (quoted in Bancroft, 321–22) says that in August 1841 a "Julian" Workman led a gang of his countrymen from Taos to Santa Fe in an abortive attempt to assassinate Armijo.

8. When Kendall's biased, engrossing two-volume story of the ill-fated expedition appeared in 1844, it became (if the anachronism is permissible) the *Uncle Tom's Cabin* of the Mexican War and did much to stir up popular support of the conflict.

Chapter XI
KIT CARSON'S BROTHER-IN-LAW

1. Charles Hipolyte Trotier, Sieur de Beaubien, had drifted from his native Three Rivers, Canada, to St. Louis in the early 1800s. In St. Louis, where he clerked and gardened for Auguste Chouteau and joined a volunteer fire company commanded by Bernard Pratte, he probably knew St. Vrain and possibly Charles Bent. In the winter of 1823–24 Beaubien went with Antoine Robidoux and sixteen others to New Mexico. (Clark issued them passports on December 29, 1823, endorsed at Council Bluffs on February 19, 1824–Ritch papers, Huntington Library.) In Taos, on September 11, 1827, Beaubien married Paula Lobata, or, as it is sometimes rendered, Paulita Lovata.

Handsome Guadalupe Miranda, six feet tall and 220 pounds heavy, was an intense patriot. For a time he was a schoolteacher in Santa Fe, then became Armijo's private secretary and soon the Secretary of State for the province.

2. The Canadian River's name derives from its *cañudas* (canyons) and not from any association with Canadian emigrants.

3. One example (Bent to Álvarez, January 30, 1841) will suffice. Martinez, just returned from a trip, "sayes that he is considered by all whoe he had an opportunity of conversing with, as one of the greatest men of the age, as a literary, and eclesiastic, a jurist, and a philanthripist. And more over, as he has resided in one of the most remote sections of this province, intirely dependent on his one resourses, it is astonishing to think how a man could make himself so eminent in almost every branch of knollidge . . . he is a prodigy, and his greate name deserves to be written in letters of gold in all high places that this gaping and ignorant multitude might fall down and worship it."

4. Warner (*Archbishop Lamy,* 76–79) and Read (*History,* 407–8) describe Martinez's opposition to Bent and quote parts of his letters to Mexican President Santa Ana.

5. Farnham (*Travels,* 71) in 1839 met an inbound Bent, St. Vrain

caravan accompanied by a motley herd of oxen, mules, and two
hundred sheep, and intimates the sheep were customary. In the
spring of 1843, Philip St. George Cooke met a Bent, St. Vrain
caravan driving to a Missouri farm cattle "raised at the foot of
the Rocky Mountains." ("Journal," *Mississippi Valley Historical
Review,* June 1925.) Like all cattle, these sometimes grew
homesick. Frémont, reporting his 1843–44 expedition, tells of
an ox, born and raised at Fort St. Vrain, that escaped in Missouri and alone went "700 miles" back to the fort.

Dick Wootton implies he inaugurated buffalo farming; actually, calf-hunting parties by frontier Indians and settlers were
commonplace. Young buffalo were easily domesticated. Wootton says he broke some to yoke; and in the early 1830s Antonio
Barriero, trying to stimulate New Mexican agriculture, wrote,
"They [buffalo] show great docility and learn many things.
. . . They have a strength double that of the ox; therefore,
agriculture should anticipate immense advantages if buffalo
were to be employed in the place of our oxen in tilling the soil."
By the mid-1840s so many buffalo calves were being taken east
that the Indians objected violently, saying the old animals were
following the young away from the plains. The savages even
exacted tribute before allowing calves to proceed. (Solomon
Sublette, writing from Bent's Fort, May 5, 1844, quoted in *Colorado Magazine,* October 1952, 250.)

6. Grinnell ("Bent's Old Fort," 19) says the farm was acquired
   after the Mexican War. Cooke's allusion ("Journal," see previous note) and references in the William Boggs manuscripts indicate that the farm was acquired much earlier—at least by
   1842.

7. When an ambitious young attorney once charged John Bent
   with being drunk in court, Bent sleepily admitted that he was
   but said he would get over it, whereas his opponent would never
   get over being a damn fool. The sally cost John a five-dollar
   fine and attached for life to the other attorney the tag "Bent's
   damned fool." That so trivial an anecdote was remembered for
   many years in St. Louis would seem to indicate that John had
   a notable position in the city's legal circle. He was killed on
   May 18, 1845, when his carriage overturned. (Bay, *Reminiscences,* 249.)

8. The letter, dated Fort William and signed Bent and St. Vrain,
   was probably written by some clerk. The spelling, though not
   perfect, is better than either Charles's or Ceran's. Furthermore,
   Charles was in Taos on January 1. He certainly knew the letter's
   contents, however, and may have composed the rough draft.
   (Clark Letter Books, VIII, 92–93, Kansas Historical Society.)

9. Whitman had precedent for trying to dodge the Sioux. For
   months they and the northern Cheyennes had been raising gen-

eral hell. In August 1841, in northern Colorado, they killed an indeterminate number of trappers, including Henry Fraeb, Jim Bridger's partner at a new fort on the Green. Alarmed by this and subsequent raids, Old Gabe, normally not an excitable man, warned Frémont's first expedition to watch its step. Carson respected Jim's word enough to make his will, a precaution that aroused Frémont's contempt and caused temporary coolness between the two men.

Perhaps Frémont's boldness was the child of ignorance. Old hands in the mountains took Bridger's warning seriously. Tom Fitzpatrick, returning from Fort Hall with a single companion named Van Dusen, swung south through Bent's Fort to avoid the Sioux. Not that the detour did the pair much good. Pawnees pounced on them, and Van Dusen scuttled back to Bent's Fort with an erroneous report that Fitzpatrick was dead. Actually Fitzpatrick had bluffed his way through. He even talked the Pawnees into returning his horses, but they kept most of his equipment, fire-making materials, spyglass, "Indian curiosities, many curious petrifactions, mineral Specimans & cc." (Clark Letter Books, VIII, 110–11.)

10. Almost nothing is known of St. Vrain's marriage to the Beaubien girl. The Taos parish books contain no record. The *Dictionary of American Biography* and the St. Vrain genealogy ignore it, saying that Ceran's wife was Luisa Branch of Mora. Miss Branch, however, was his second wife.

Maxwell's wife, Luz Beaubien, is said to have been Beaubien's eldest child. (Stanley, *The Grant That Maxwell Bought.*) Since Beaubien was married in September 1827, Luz could have been scarcely fourteen when Lucien wed her in March 1842. Ceran could hardly have married a younger sister before then—her age would have been too tender for even a Mexican. As Frémont's account of his second expedition shows, Ceran was married to a Beaubien by the summer of 1843. I presume, therefore, considering age factors, that he was probably married in the winter or spring of 1843. Señora St. Vrain was described by Garrard in 1847 as being "languidly handsome."

Chapter XII
LAND BEYOND IMAGINING

1. Although Warfield received his commission on August 16, whereas Snively did not apply for his until the following January 28, they seem to have been acting with some concert. By January, Armijo had information of sorts about both men (Alvarez to U. S. Secretary of State, July 1, 1843), and therefore the raiders' plans must have been laid well before January. Warfield, too, was expecting Snively when he assembled his

own men on the Arkansas in late February. (Sage, *Scenes*, Chapter XXIX ff.)

Some of the plotters in Texas apparently considered Warfield as a cat's-paw to keep Armijo preoccupied while Snively swooped on the Santa Fe caravan. The picture is not complete and probably never will be. (For additional information: Binkley, *The Expansionist Movement*, 107 ff.; Cooke's "Journal," *Mississippi Valley Historical Review*, June 1925; Yoakum, *History of Texas*, II, 399 ff.; Thrall, *History of Texas*, 331 ff.)

2. Álvarez to Secretary of State, July 1, 1843: "The Prefect of the First District . . . so incensed the common ignorant class against Bent that he had to fly by night to his fort on the Arkansas. . . . He only complied with the sentence of this iniquitous judge so he could get released from confinement and flee the country for his personal safety."

The fine may have been more than the $800 Álvarez states in his letter. Writing the consul on February 28, 1843, Charles says, ". . . I have drawn on you for [illegible] Dollars. When Lee reached heare I found myself with 1800, money sent from Taos and Santa Fe."

According to Paul Walter ("First Civil Governor," *New Mexico Historical Review*, April 1933), Ignacia dug up the gold cache and ransomed her husband when Charles was captured at the outbreak of the war with Mexico. As the text will show, however, Charles was not in New Mexico when the war broke out and was never captured during that period. But since legends sometimes bear a grain of truth, I attach this one, for what it may be worth, to the Montero uproar.

3. Perhaps because of Armijo's objections Álvarez had just been relieved of his consular duties. Soon, however, he would resume them, though on a somewhat semi-official basis.

4. After holding Chavez prisoner for three days, the McDaniel gang fell out with each other. Wanting no part in murder, seven took their share of the booty (about $500 each) and returned to Missouri. The others shot Chavez in cold blood, searched his possessions again, and found another $3000 or so—about $10,-500 all told, plus some valuable furs. Chavez's fifty-two mules, difficult to dispose of, were turned loose. Eventually all the raiders were captured. McDaniel and his brother were hanged; the others received varying prison terms.

5. The exact relationship between Charles Bent and Snively can only be guessed. Yoakum (*History*, II, 401, reputedly drawing on manuscript documents) says: "On the second of June a partnership was proposed by the Bents, who offered to put in forty men then and forty more shortly after. . . . A few days later the Bents sent word they could not comply."

On June 26, after the company caravan had gone on eastward, Cooke wrote in his journal, "I ascertained this morning that some of Mr. Bent's *people* at least had communicated with the Texans: which none had given information of in the week or ten days they were with me. . . . I also now first learned that three Texan spies accompanied Bent's party until they came in sight of my tents: when on the pretense of hunting . . . they disappeared."

For Yoakum's "the Bents" substitute "some of Bent's men." The fact that Charles and Ceran wanted nothing to do with the raiders (together with the reason why Charles kept silent about the Texan spies—if he knew they were spies) is made manifest by Cooke himself in his journal entry of June 22: "St. Vrain fears the Texans, whom he considers outlaws, and he doesn't wish it known he gave information, for he thinks the American traders are in danger too." What both Yoakum and Cooke overlook is the fact that the company could not side with Texans or Mexicans or Americans without incurring the wrath of the others. Naturally they walked gingerly, and as a result pleased no one.

6. Almost the only specific information on affairs in Taos comes from letters which Charles wrote Álvarez three years later (December 17, 1845; March 4, 1846). Obviously Charles, who had not been in town at the time, was reporting hearsay when he wrote, "Has he [Martinez] forgotten the unlawful meatings that ware held in his house in the dead hours of night in june and july 1843 when they ware meditating the overthrow of Armijo?" And, "the justice Pasqual Martinise did not visit his [Beaubien's] house to *dar fay* (as it is called heare) of its having been robed in 1843, neather did he take any steps to secure the property stolen." Frémont's report adds that he learned on July 14 of a "popular tumult among the Pueblos against foreigners," in which the Indians had plundered houses and ill-treated families and had forced Beaubien to flee.

7. I assume the meeting. Kit started back from Taos approximately July 8. Maxwell had left Fort St. Vrain for Taos on July 6. Both men probably used Sangre de Cristo Pass, the quickest route for horsemen. (Raton Pass's easier trails were used by pack trains and wagons, but seldom by riders in a hurry.) The timing would normally lead to a meeting almost within the pass itself— and if they did not meet, how did Kit learn of Frémont's plans? Maxwell, incidentally, was traveling with Frémont for protection this year but was not working for the explorer.

8. After the United States appropriated the Southwest, the land grants were guaranteed. In September 1857 the surveyor general recommended that the entire St. Vrain-Vigil grant be recognized. In 1860, however, Congress limited all grants to the old Mexican standard of eleven leagues, or 97,390.95 acres.

This reduced the St. Vrain-Vigil tract by three quarters. The problem of surveys and squatters' rights led to bitter controversies; violent though these were, however, they were mild compared to the squabbles that engulfed the Beaubien-Miranda grant which Lucien Maxwell eventually controlled.

There were, of course, more grants than my text concerns itself with, and Armijo knew that nearly every one of them was made to a partnership that contained at least one naturalized foreigner. But no one else would make the effort to colonize the land, and the governor hoped that profit motives would inspire even the American-born grantees to defend their property and, incidentally, all New Mexico against gringo invasion.

9. William also held a share in the St. Vrain-Vigil grant, and his claim was recognized by Congress in 1860.

10. These short excerpts from the long memorial are taken from Keleher (*Turmoil in New Mexico*, 66–67) and somewhat rearranged in order. In passing it may be noted that Martinez's 1832 date for the appearance of forts on the Arkansas is further indirect evidence concerning the building of Bent's Fort.

11. Beaubien's pious protest to the governor that Charles had no interest in the Beaubien-Miranda grant was pure subterfuge. Soon Charles was recruiting settlers and writing Álvarez about "our grante." (April 19, 1846; May 31, 1846, etc.) In time Charles might also have acquired Miranda's share, for after Kearny's conquest Miranda offered to sell out to Bent. Charles evidently agreed, but death intervened. (Stanley, *Maxwell Grant*, 14.) That he did own substantial interest in the tract is made conclusive by the fact that Maxwell in 1866 paid Charles's heirs for their claims.

Armijo, incidentally, may have been moved to confirm the grants partly through self-interest. At least he said in his will, "I declare that I own the sixth part of the Las Animas [St. Vrain-Vigil] grant, and the sixth part of the Rayado [Beaubien-Miranda] grant." (Keleher, op. cit., 115.) I know of no serious effort ever being made by Armijo's heirs to follow up these claims, however.

12. Grinnell ("Bent's Old Fort," 32) says that Slim Face went on to Washington with his complaint. William, however, probably did not go that far—the time element almost completely precludes the possibility—and I doubt whether Slim Face did. Abert ("Journal" entry August 31, 1846, in Emory's *Notes*) implies that the Indian went only as far as St. Louis. It seems likely that Mi-ah-tose, or Slim Face, returned with William to the fort in August 1844.

1. Twenty-six-year-old James Josiah Webb was also making his first trip across the plains. In later years both Webb and Boggs wrote accounts of the journey (see Bibliography). Except for a mutual interest in eccentric Nick Gentry, the things they remember are so different that it scarcely seems they traveled together most of the way.

2. One of the leaders of the parties sent back to retrieve the stranded wagons was Jim Hobbs, recently returned from scalp-hunting in Chihuahua. He says 400 mules perished. Other accounts say 300 (*Colorado Magazine*, March 1930, 53 n.). Considering the size of the trains involved, from 150 to 175 head seems a more reasonable estimate, which is bad enough. Charles Bent and Ceran St. Vrain, hurrying their separate trains up the Arkansas, apparently missed the storm; at least there is no record that they suffered.

3. So goes the tale according to William Boggs ("Manuscript," *Colorado Magazine*, March 1930, 54; "Narrative," 26). Webb, 81–82, mentioning no bribe, says Nick accomplished nothing in his interview with the governor—yet records no trouble between Nick and the authorities over the illegal tobacco.

4. Boggs, perhaps forgetful, does not mention the eagles. Abert, however, saw them at the fort in early August 1845 (Senate Doc. 438, 29th Congress, 1st Sess.), and probably they had been captured the previous fall, for George Bent (to Hyde, March 15, 1916) says that the best time for catching the birds was when cottonwood leaves turned yellow. The ritual and methods are described in Grinnell, *The Cheyenne Indians*, 299–304.

5. He so told Emory (*Military Reconnaissance*, 13) in 1846.

6. It is a strange thing that white men, who quickly took over the trapping of beaver from the inefficient Indians, for a long time either could not or would not compete with the red men in the production of buffalo robes. Not until the 1870s did hide-hunting whites move onto the plains and systematically exterminate the bison herds, as their predecessors four decades earlier had exterminated the beaver.

7. Webb (*Adventures in the Santa Fe Trade*, 93; 111–13) was living with other traders in a back room of the Leitensdorfer brothers' store when Charles arrived with the warning. (The quarters boasted a French-Canadian cook, a dry-goods box for a table, camp utensils for dishes. They had a single glass tumbler in which they mixed eggnogs: one egg, sugar, water, aguardiente, shaken with a Spanish grammar held over the tumbler.) Charles told Eugene Leitensdorfer not to bring in more

than five or six wagons; the freebooters, knowing his many associations with the natives, would think he was hauling Mexican goods under his name and would raid him anyhow. Charles offered to do the Leitensdorfer hauling for a small commission. Webb implies that Bent was deliberately fostering a scare (a) to deter competing Mexican traders from going to the States, and (b) to get freighting business for himself. Though Charles probably would not rue injury to Mexican competition, there are too many records of his helpfulness to American traders for one to believe that his offer to Leitensdorfer was completely selfish. Leitensdorfer, at any rate, accepted the proposition.

8. In spite of the freebooters, various traders, mostly Americans, brought 141 wagonloads of merchandise into New Mexico that year.

9. Charles Bent was in St. Louis on May 9, 1845 (*Missouri Republican*, May 12, 1845) and most probably consulted with both Kearny and Frémont. He had ridden in ahead of the company train, which was not expected to reach Independence until June 1 (St. Louis *Daily New Era*, May 26). Boggs implies that William Bent was with this train. Both men apparently were back at the fort by the end of July, which means they left Missouri earlier than usual, probably because of contracts to haul supplies for the various expeditions. (Cooke, *Scenes*, says Charles and Ceran entertained Kearny's officers. No one—Cooke, Frémont or Abert—mentions William specifically, but Abert says "one of the gentlemen of the fort" was present at a Delaware-Cheyenne council; George Bent [Hyde's *Life*] identifies the "gentleman" as his father.)

10. Less is known of short-lived Fort Adobe than of any other comparable post in the West. Paul Wellman, who tells the story of Ceran's white flag in "Famous Kansas Scouts" (*Kansas Historical Quarterly*, August 1932, 347) dates its building as 1828 or 1829, much too early. Grinnell ("Bent's Old Fort," 15) dates it as prior to 1840. But Cooke ("Journal," 239), after talking to Charles in June 1843, says the firm built a "house" on the Canadian the previous fall. Kiowa tradition (Mooney, *Seventeenth Annual Report Bureau of American Ethnology*) ascribes a log house to the winter of 1843–44, the adobe to 1844–45. This is a year too early. Abert mentions no fort; if it had been in existence when he passed the site in September 1845, he certainly would have described it. By March 1846, Charles (to Álvarez, March 1, 4, and 19) was making the earliest direct references to a *fort* on the Canadian that I can discover. Implications in Charles's letters indicate that Ceran supervised the post's trading that winter, and so I ascribe the building to him. My assumption that William was with Ceran during the construction is based on the fact that throughout the firm's existence William Bent was the partner in direct charge of Indian relations and field operations.

Also, George Bent (to Hyde, December 13, 1905) says that his father was the builder of Fort Adobe.

Chapter XIV
WAR

1. Even less is known of George's marriage than of the other partners'. Grinnell ("Bent's Old Fort," 24) says that in the early 1840s George met his bride (name unknown) in Old Mexico and that she bore him a son and daughter, the son named Robert after George's Comanche-killed brother. But evidently the boy was not called Robert at home. The Bent family Bible, now in possession of the New Mexico Historical Society, has three mentions of an Elfego Bent written on its flyleaf. (He left for the United States in 1847, returned in 1854, died at Taos, 6:00 A.M., December 9, 1865.)

2. This sounds like a tall tale, but authority is Charles Bent, writing Álvarez on March 19, 1846, five days after George and Blair reached Taos.

3. During this bristly period Charles Bent penned an extraordinary attack on all things Mexican, a diatribe of the sort then filling the expansionist press in the United States. The almost illegible date on his letter to Alvarez which refers to the document seems to be 1845, but internal evidence indicates late March 1846. Charles begins his article by deriding the way the sycophantic authorities, presumably in Santa Fe, have fallen over themselves to support first the revolutionary government of Herrera, which had upset Santa Ana in Mexico City, and then that of Paredes, which ousted Herrera. Using that as a springboard, Charles continues: "They [the Mexicans] are without exception the most servile people that can be imagined. They are not fit to be free, they should be ruled by others than themselves. . . . Every speses of vice in this country is a recommendation to public office. . . . Thare religion consists intirely in outward show. . . . The Mexican character is made up of Stupidity, Obstanacy, Ignorance, duplicity, and vanity."

Just what use Charles expected to make of this outburst, or whether it was used, I cannot determine. He writes Álvarez, "I have seen your letter to Mr. Beaubean, in which you tell him, our Priest has consented to leave his press in Santafee, on the condition that thare is nothing printed against him." Then Bent adds, "I wish you to correct the article. . . . Try to get it in imeadiately . . . before the Priest can have time to renue his conditions with regard to his press." This would seem to indicate that Charles wanted the attack printed in Santa Fe on the press which Martinez had briefly used in Taos for publishing New Mexico's first newspaper. An anti-Mexican blast like that in Santa Fe by a man who had many Mexican friends and a Mexican wife? I find the whole thing inexplicable. But there it is, indubitably in Charles Bent's handwriting.

4. The figures are Charles Bent's, from an interview he gave newspapers on reaching St. Louis (reprinted in *Niles'*, July 11, 1846 —the account on which most of my surmises concerning the eastward dash are based). Josiah Gregg, however (*Niles'*, August 1), says that on June 30, 216 wagons were on the trail, with another 150 wagons and 50 carriages ready to go, manned by 1000 "traders, waggoners, loungers on and connoisseur travelers." The value of the goods carried was about $1,700,000, three or four times the amount of the best previous year. Thus the military invasion of New Mexico would seem almost an adjunct to the commercial invasion.

5. Charles reached St. Louis on July 2, phenomenal time from Bent's Fort when one considers his side jaunt to Leavenworth. On July 24 he left St. Louis. How he filled those three weeks cannot be determined. In view of later developments, it seems likely he spent some of the time in connection with political and military matters. Had Kearny left more detailed records, Charles Bent's unquestionably valuable services to the conquest would undoubtedly loom even larger.

6. Inman (*The Old Santa Fe Trail*) dates the story as 1845; internal evidence indicates that it might have occurred at any time during the 1840s. Factual details seldom restrained Inman when he launched into a story, and this has led historians to treat his material harshly. But he knew most of the people about whom he wrote and sometimes he is more accurate than his detractors are. (For one example, Chittenden, 550.) This Dale story may or may not be one of his more accurate yarns. I know of no contemporary references to it.

7. I include George among the scouts on the strength of a statement in the *Dictionary of American Biography's* sketch of Francis Blair, Jr. George certainly went to New Mexico in some capacity. Francis Parkman, reaching the fort on August 25, was entertained by Marcellin and says all the Bents were in New Mexico with Kearny.

Walker probably reached the fort with his California livestock after the vanguard of the army had gone on, for he was still at Fort Bridger on July 24. (*Utah Historical Quarterly*, Vol. 19, 52.) He was still at Bent's Fort when the convalescing Abert resumed his diary on August 26. After guiding Frémont across the Utah deserts the previous summer, Walker had grown disgusted with the Pathfinder's nervous marchings and countermarchings. Quitting him in March 1846, he gathered up stock, either by purchase or theft, and moved slowly eastward, trading with emigrants on the Oregon Trail. Jim Beckwourth may have been one of his hired hands. Jim, of course, claims that *he* was the leader and swept up eighteen hundred head; "our morals justified it, for it was war-time." Jim then went on to Santa Fe (this much rests on records other than Jim's), carried occasional dispatches to Missouri for the army, and operated a saloon which Garrard describes as "the grand resort for the liquor-imbibing, monte-playing, and fandango-disposed" soldiers. It is also on record that Jim was well liked in Santa Fe.

8. From Santa Fe, Magoffin posted south to Chihuahua, to soften up that city for General Wool, supposedly advancing from San Antonio. Magoffin was well liked in the city. He had brought his wagons there as early as 1825, had married a Chihuahua Valdez in 1830, and had maintained residence in the city until 1844. When he was arrested on his arrival from Santa Fe, he was allowed, legend says, to destroy his papers—and with them, perhaps, evidence that would reveal exactly what he had been up to in Santa Fe. The next nine months he spent in Chihuahua and Durango jails, saving his skin, legend continues, by entertaining his jailers with, among other things, 3000-plus bottles of champagne.

Eventually Congress voted to pay him $50,000, but a later administration cut the sum to $30,000. Ostensibly the money was for goods confiscated and time spent in jail. Possibly, however, it was to repay personal funds expended on Armijo and Archuleta. (Benton, *Thirty Years' View*, II, 684.) A discussion of the matter can be found in Stella Drumm's introduction to Susan Magoffin's diary. See also Cooke's *Conquest* and House Exec. Doc. 17, 31st Congress, 1st Sess.; Keleher, *Turmoil In New Mexico* 26–36.

9. Guessing is necessary here. It is extraordinary how few references to Charles Bent are contained in contemporary records of the period, probably because Charles was working out of sight of the soldier diary-keepers. Even Hughes, Doniphan's historian, had little to say of the man with whom he almost certainly worked during the preparations of the territorial laws. (Colonel Doniphan, erstwhile barrister, drew these laws, known as the Kearny code, miscellaneously from the statutes of the United States, Mexico, Texas, and the old laws of Missouri Territory. One of the colonel's chief assistants was Private Willard Hall, another Missouri lawyer and Doniphan's opponent for one of Missouri's congressional seats. While working together on the Kearny code, the rivals learned that Hall was winner of the election. Before assuming his seat, however, Hall went on to California with Cooke and the Mormon Battalion.)

Nothing from Charles Bent's own hand appears until he officially became governor. Copies of his correspondence from that time on are preserved in the so-called Charles Bent Letter Book, National Archives, Records of the War Department, Department of New Mexico, Record Copies of Letters Sent, Vol. V,

September 1846–47. These letters constitute my principal source for Bent's activities as governor.

10. The date of the ball to which Mitchell (or perhaps a Captain Johnson) escorted La Tules is nowhere given. It may not have been this one; balls were frequent. But in any event La Tules somehow got into Kearny's farewell party, as she had into others, and little Susan, a more delightful person than my text perhaps indicates, was quite properly shocked.

11. It is possible that Fitzpatrick had heard rumors of the appointment as early as July, on reaching Bent's Fort with Kearny. In July, however, he had his hands full and ignored the new agency to go on southwest with the army. His upper Arkansas and Platte Agency was, of course, a completely different entity from the New Mexico agency whose establishment (with George Bent as agent) was recommended by Charles in September.

Chapter XV
REVOLUTION

1. The persons directly concerned in breaking the revolution shed little light on how the plot was unearthed. According to Twitchell, (*Military Occupation*, 217, 314) the first information was La Tules's report to Vigil. But Sterling Price in his report of February 15, 1847, to the government, says: "About the 15th of Dec. last I received information . . ." Writing Buchanan on December 26, Charles says, "On the 17th inst. I received information . . ." All we can be sure of is that someone tattled to someone.

    Twitchell (ibid., 315 ff.) bases his story of Donaciano Vigil's warning to Durán and of Ortiz's pick-a-back escape on the reminiscences of the daughter of one of the conspirators. They may not be accurate.

2. Since Steve Lee, James Leal, and Cornelio Vigil, the principal officials of Taos, were the ones who accompanied Charles home, I jump to the conclusion that they were the ones who brought him word of the situation and thus instigated his return.

    Oddly, Ignacia seems not to have been in Santa Fe even for the Christmas celebrations. (At least lists of the travelers who went to Taos with Charles do not mention her. Also, Garrard reports that Bent went to Taos to visit "his woman.") Contemporary accounts of the entire occupation period make almost no reference to her, and it is pure assumption on my part that Charles's trip to Taos in early October was to take her back home. This silence about Ignacia may be the result of an era that tended to ignore women, or it may indicate that she was never in Santa Fe during the occupation. It is difficult to believe, however, that she did not join her husband at least for his inauguration.

3. I have adapted the details of the journey from Ruxton (*Adventures,* Hafen edition, 187–90). He preceded Bent's party by only a few days, and conditions must have been approximately the same.

4. In view of subsequent developments, it seems unlikely the Taos uprising was as spontaneous as is sometimes said. To be sure, it developed fast to fit the unexpected opportunity of Charles's arrival. But considerable plotting had gone on before, and it is probable that Montoya and Romero spent the night feverishly bringing plans up to date. If they weren't so engaged, what held back the "spontaneous" attack until almost dawn?

5. Accounts of Charles's death vary. William Boggs tells incidents he picked up from his brother Tom, who had them from Rumalda. Many years later Teresina, who was five at the time of the revolt, told her story, and in 1898 Rumalda gave a newspaper interview to a man named Thompson. Undoubtedly their memories of the morning were vivid—and, quite naturally, contradictory in details. I have tried to present a reasonable but not necessarily authentic composite.

Chapter XVI
RETRIBUTION

1. This according to Beckwourth (*Life,* 334–35). Beckwourth adds that prior rumors had already been received from an Indian. The Indian told Price that a rebel messenger from the priest in Taos, presumably Martinez, was on his way to a priest in Santa Fe. Attempts to arrest the emissary failed, but after Towne's warning a vigilant search revealed that the conspiracy was well rooted in Santa Fe.

2. This Rio Colorado, Red River (actually a creek), has no connection with either the Canadian (Red) River or the Colorado River of Arizona. New Mexican nomenclature, which often gave identical names to different streams in the same general locality (i.e., the Cimarron River and unrelated Little Cimarron Creek), has its confusions.

3. Garrard's account (*Wah-To-Yah,* 181 ff.) is ambiguous. He relates William's call for volunteers to go *with* him, but never mentions Bent as being on the trip. Many commentators have assumed from the silence that William led the detachment, though Garrard clearly mentions Maxwell and Bransford as being in charge.

Garrard's unidentified free man Tom has been taken to be Tom Boggs, although Garrard tells of having seen Boggs headed east with dispatches in January. Boggs did not leave Leavenworth on his return to Taos until March 11. (T. O. Boggs, "Dictation," mss., Bancroft Library.)

4. Garrard says Big Nigger died in the church. Ruxton, wintering on the Arkansas, learned from trappers the version I repeat.

5. As yet, of course, Polk had not heard of the costly victory of Buena Vista, Doniphan's triumph at Sacramento, nor Scott's capture of Vera Cruz. In April any victory was good news to Polk.

6. Fleeing across the mountains, Fitzgerald found sanctuary at Ponil Creek with company men, who saw nothing criminal in his having killed one of Charles's killers. Later Fitzgerald returned to the States with Ceran St. Vrain.

7. Others had second thoughts about charging with *treason* men who had risen in support of their conquered homeland. Following the Taos outbreak, four conspirators in Santa Fe were indicted for treason, but only Antonio Trujillo, father-in-law of Diego Archuleta, was convicted. He appealed and the Secretary of War instructed Blair that, although the insurgents could be punished by death for murder, the prosecution would not stand on the grounds of treason. Trujillo was pardoned. Twenty or more insurgents, in addition to the fifteen hanged at Taos, were executed for various murders committed in other parts of Mexico. Minor culprits were flogged.

8. Beckwourth (*Life,* 339) tells the story differently: "I had an order from Captain Morris . . . authorizing me to pick up all the government horses that I might find in my rambles. . . . I had found but one, the property of Captain Saverine [St. Vrain], and it I had returned to the owner."

Chapter XVII
DESTRUCTION

1. There is no documentation to prove that Ceran offered the fort for sale without consulting George or William, but the presumption is strong. Though Ceran had of course seen George in Taos during the trials, he may not have seen William that spring. We know from Garrard that St. Vrain had not appeared on the upper Purgatory ranch, where William then was, before the closing days of April; from Ruxton, that neither William nor Ceran was at the fort in the first days of May; and from Garrard again, that Ceran followed shortly behind the company caravan which left the fort on May 4. At best, therefore, St. Vrain could have seen William only briefly on the Purgatory ranch, and if he came via Sangre de Cristo Pass, as horsemen in a hurry often did, he would not have encountered Bent at all.

In offering the fort to Mackay, Ceran used the first person. Would he not have said "we" if he had the approval of the brothers? Finally, Fitzpatrick, writing agency reports from the fort while George and William were there, recommended a military post at the mouth of the Purgatory. If the brothers contemplated selling their fort, they would have told Fitzpatrick so, and it seems unlikely he would have recommended building a new fort in the vicinity without at least mentioning that Bent's was available. (St. Vrain's letter to Mackay and reports on the proposal by Thomas Swords and A. W. Enos are in the General Land Office records, National Archives. Fitzpatrick's September 1847 report from the fort is reprinted in *Colorado Magazine*, March 1920; his October report in *New Spain and the Anglo-American West*, II.)

2. H. L. Luebers, who married a granddaughter of William Bent, says ("William Bent's Family," *Colorado Magazine*, January 1936) that the baby at whose birth Owl Woman died was Charles. Other authorities (Grinnell, Hyde, Allen Bent) say that it was Julia and that Charles, the son of Yellow Woman, was born in late 1848 or early 1849. I follow Luebers. Even granting that half-breeds matured early, Charles must have been more than fifteen or sixteen when he started raising Ned during the mid-1860s. Ascribing his birth to 1847 still makes him a precocious warrior, as the text will indicate.

3. The Santa Fe *Republican* of October 29, 1847, dates George's death as October 23. Fitzpatrick, however, mentions the death, without dating it, in a report of October 19. Fitzpatrick may have started the report on October 19, then finished it several days later without changing the date.

4. Bowman ("History of Bent County" in *History of the Arkansas Valley*, 828) says that it was Charles Bent who opposed supplying Gilpin, that William then bought out Charles's interests and provisioned the dragoons. Charles, however, was dead. Accordingly, Donna May Lewis ("The Bents and St. Vrains") presumes that it was William who bought out St. Vrain. But St. Vrain was still associated with the fort in the summer of 1848. (See Note 5 below.)

Heaven knows what supplies Gilpin had. Bancroft (*William Gilpin*, 40, written from interviews with Gilpin) says food was plentiful. In his own report, written in a vein that quavers from a feeling of persecution to self-glorification, Gilpin says he "endured in tents the rigors of the long winter, subsisting . . . upon such provisions as could be obtained from New Mexico and the Indians." What he obtained undoubtedly included some Bent, St. Vrain beef; Bransford in 1857 told a congressional committee investigating the land grants that during the winter the company had fifteen hundred head of cattle along the Arkansas and on the Purgatory, then considered part of New Mexico. ("Mexican Land Grants in Colorado," Hafen, *Colorado Magazine*, May 1927.)

5. O. W. Pratt, manuscript diary, July 14, 1848: "After a hot march of 17 miles reached the celebrated place known as Bent's Fort. The owners, Messers Bent & St. Vrain, are absent in the States."

6. Frémont's figures, in a letter to Benton from Bent's Fort, November 17, 1847.

7. I assume William's objections. So far as records go, they were actually voiced by Solomon Sublette, who talked over the matter with Fitzpatrick in March 1849. But during his winter at the fort Fitzpatrick undoubtedly discussed the plan with William, and Sublette's objections are the sort any plainsman might have had.

8. The sequence of events preceding the destruction of Fort Adobe is surmise. Carson biographies do not mention Kit's trip, but George Bent had the story of it from both Carson and John Smith. (Grinnell papers, Southwest Museum, Los Angeles.) Enough is known of Kit's whereabouts to ascribe the fall of 1848 as about the only time the adventure could have occurred. Wootton dates his own venture as the winter of 1849–50, but this is manifestly impossible and so I move it ahead to 1848–49. Grant Foreman (*Marcy and the Gold Seekers*, 226), after describing the fort as having been built by the "eccentric" trader Bill Bent, adds, "Becoming disgusted one day at Indians who had killed some of his livestock, he destroyed it and went to Bent's Fort." I do not know Mr. Foreman's authority. And the fort wasn't completely destroyed. Its walls sheltered Carson's army command during the famous Adobe Walls Battle in 1864.

9. The exact date of Marcellin's flight cannot be determined. His granddaughter, Mrs. W. R. Sopris ("My Grandmother, Mrs. Marcellin St. Vrain," *Colorado Magazine*, March 1945), says the summer of 1848. Paul St. Vrain (*Genealogy*, 24) says either 1847 or 1848. I am inclined to think it was the fall of 1848.

Neither Mrs. Sopris nor Paul St. Vrain mentions the Pawnee wife. But O. W. Pratt wrote in his diary at Bent's Fort, Monday, July 17, 1848, "At this place the younger St. Vrain had kept two wives and between them they have five children." Double wives clears up George Bent's insistence that Marcellin's wife was Tall Pawnee Woman and that he saw her farming at Pueblo in 1851. (Bent to Hyde, December 29, 1913; October 12, 1917.) George never mentioned Red, nor does Grinnell. Actually, everybody was partly right.

10. In the spring Old Bill and Dr. Benjamin Kern took a party of Mexicans into the mountains to recover Frémont's abandoned baggage. Meanwhile, thirty-seven dragoons guided by Antoine Le Roux, Charley Autobees, and Lucien Maxwell soundly whipped some Utes during an annual punitive expedition. The fleeing Indians came across Old Bill and Kern. To restore face and perhaps remembering Williams's bad faith of the previous

year, they slew both whites. Thus, whether or not Williams helped cause Frémont's disaster, he paid the price in full. (Discussions of responsibility may be found in Favour, *Old Bill Williams;* Nevins, *Frémont.*)

11. The source of William's find is reputed to be Crow Creek on the plains in northeastern Colorado. (Smiley, *History of Denver,* 173.) The region was never productive of gold and the story is quite likely apocryphal, though, as the text will later indicate, William knew there was precious mineral in the mountains.

Chapter XVIII
TURN BACK THE CLOCK

1. Others continued to think so. Bancroft (*History of Colorado,* 363 n.) says that Indians captured the fort and slaughtered all the inmates except the owners, who were absent. In the fall of 1853, Carvalho (*Incidents,* 71–73) breakfasted with William on bread, venison, dried buffalo, and coffee, then wrote, "Bent's Fort . . . was recently destroyed by the Indians and has not been rebuilt from scarcity of timber in its vicinity." Where did Carvalho get that misinformation?

It was misinformation. On October 5, 1849, the Indian agent in Santa Fe wrote (Abel, *Calhoun's Correspondence,* 41–42), "One of the owners of Bent's Fort has removed all property from it, and caused the fort to be burned." (*One* of the owners? Was St. Vrain still a partner? It seems unlikely.)

The burning evidently caused more damage than the explosion. Gwinn Heap, passing through on May 31, 1853, wrote (*Central Route,* 24), "It is now roofless, for when the United States refused to purchase it, the proprietors set it on fire to prevent it from becoming a harbor for the Indians. The adobe walls are still standing." Lieutenant E. J. Beckwith of Gunnison's survey noted more damage two months later: "Its adobe walls . . . stand in part only, with here and there a chimney." Recent excavations indicate that the major destruction was limited to the east part, where the storerooms were located.

2. George Bent (to Hyde, February 19, 1913; January 29, 1914) gives William's despondency over the death of his brothers as the principal cause of the destruction. Agent Calhoun, Gwinn Heap, and others indicate that the troubled times and William's anger at the War Department were contributory. But those things alone do not explain his moving to the Big Timbers.

3. George Bent (to Hyde, February 19, 1913) gives 1852 as the year Fort St. Vrain was reoccupied. "The Siege of Fort Atkinson" (*Harper's,* October 1857) indicates that the event occurred well before 1852. George was probably forgetful again. He mistakenly gives 1852 as the year Bent's Fort was destroyed. The

close association of the two events in George's mind suggests that the reoccupation of Fort St. Vrain followed shortly after the destruction of the Arkansas post.

4. Although neither Sabin (*Kit Carson*) nor Hafen and Ghent (*Broken Hand*) mentions William as participating in the whipping incident, George (to Hyde, October 12, 1915) is definite: "At this time troops and Cheyennes put [sic] near had fight, only Agent Fitzpatrick and my father stoped it."

5. Accounts of the Council, regrettably brief, name only the main officials and dismiss the traders with remarks to the effect that there were many of them among the more than ten thousand persons present. Though William is nowhere named specifically, his absence from such a gathering would be far more surprising than his attendance.

6. William started west with Fitzpatrick, and on June 25 at Bull Creek in eastern Kansas the two men talked at length with Gunnison's railroad surveyors concerning the country ahead. (*Reports of Surveys*, II, 13.) William then seems to have pushed on in advance of the agent, for when Fitzpatrick reached Fort Atkinson in July to conclude his treaty with the Comanches and Kiowas, no traders were about to interpret for him. Illness probably made Tom travel slowly. He was so sick in Westport that just before leaving he made his will, dated June 20. On February 7, 1854, after a laborious tour of his agency, he died in Washington and was buried in an unmarked grave in the congressional cemetery—unfitting end for one of the best men the mountains ever produced.

7. Estimates of the fort's size vary. It covered an acre (Larimer, *Reminiscences*, 70). It was one hundred by 135 feet (Smiley, *Denver*, 150). It was 150 by 200 feet (Post, "Diary," in Hafen's *Overland Routes*). "There is space enough within the walls to hold 500 men." (Dr. George M. Willing "Diary," May 3, 1859, *Mississippi Valley Historical Review*, December 1927.)

Actually, the fort was almost square, the north wall being a bit longer than the south. (Quartermaster E. A. Belger to General S. C. Easton, March 20, 1867, National Archives.) The internal dimensions of the twelve rooms (accurately measured and reported in a letter from Major John Sedgwick to the quartermaster general on September 8, 1860, Box 77, Files of the Quartermaster General, National Archives) add up to a total length of 271 feet. A probable overlap of 64 feet (the rooms averaged 16 feet wide) suggests a perimeter of 315 feet, plus the width of the gates, wide internal walls, etc. Thus it is difficult to account for a square of more than 100 feet per side, yet that is certainly smaller than it appeared to visitors.

As in the case of everything else William built, the exact dates of construction are hard to determine. Inman (*The Old Santa

Fe Trail, quoting from a letter written by William's future son-in-law, R. M. Moore) says the work of quarrying the stone began in the fall of 1852. Considering the great amount of stone necessary, this seems likely, but neither Heap, who passed through the Big Timbers in May 1853, nor Beckwith, who went by in July, mentions the construction work—though both refer to the abandoned log cabins. Thus it seems that work did not begin until after July. Yet Frémont found the post occupied in the early fall.

8. The chronology of the children's education is impossible to determine, except in the case of George. He states that he was in school in Westport from 1853 to 1857, in St. Louis from 1857 to the outbreak of the Civil War, returning to Westport (and perhaps occasionally to the plains, see Note 9 below) during summer vacations. Amazingly, he does not relate a single episode from those eight impressionable years. Indeed, the man's letters, and he wrote many hundreds, are extraordinary in what they do not tell. He was caught squarely in the death struggle between his mother's people and his father's, yet if he sensed the broader implications of the tragedy, he gives no indication.

Mary might have told more if a Hyde or Grinnell had come along before her death in 1878 to take down her recollections. She seems to have been cultured beyond the ordinary white on the frontier, to say nothing of the ordinary half-breed. Since she was fifteen in 1853 and Robert twelve, it is likely that both went to school before George did. Mary was still living in Westport in 1860.

Young Charles came to Westport after 1853. Unlike the others, he was under the guardianship not of Boone but of William Bernard. Charles, too, went for at least a short time to an academy in St. Louis.

The baby of the family, Julia, seems not to have had any formal education. It is difficult to guess why not.

9. This is a hard tale to swallow, but George (to Hyde, November 28, 1913), says he saw it. Grinnell (*The Cheyenne Indians,* I, 283–88) heard of the episode from several Indians who were there and remembered it in detail. The date seems to be some summer between 1852 and 1858.

10. William Bent from Westport, dated August 25, 1856, but handed to Major Waffman in St. Louis on September 15 for forwarding to Washington (Quartermaster Files, Box 77, War Records Division, National Archives): "You will confer a favor by haveing the Provisions remaining on hand at my fort . . . removed or disposed of in Some way, as I intend Selling the fort." He did not intend leaving the country, however, for he offered to buy the goods. I assume he had already determined on building a log stockade as soon as he could dispose of his white elephant—no impetuous destruction this time!—because a

stockade is just what he did build when finally he left the stone fort.

11. George Bent, old enough by now to recall dates accurately, is definite that his father made the move in 1857 (to Hyde, February 5, 1913). But the '57 stockade was not the powerful one that William later built on the site. If the big one had been there before the summer of 1859, the gold-rush diarists who passed through would surely have commented on it.

12. The claim was made through Estafina's husband, Alexander (Zan) Hicklin. As a child Estafina had met Zan on Carson's ranch. She was still scarcely more than a child when she married him on October 20, 1856. (The date of Estafina's birth is unknown; she was, however, younger than Teresina, born in 1842. See Working, "The Hicklins on the Greenhorn," *Colorado Magazine*, December 1927.) The marriage was a happy one, and their ranch became a favorite stopping place. Though illiterate, Zan was brave, handsome, merry, generous—"the best story teller and most famous practical joker in the mountains," according to Dick Wootton.

13. Clad in her famous costume and carrying a volume of Emerson's *Essays*, Julia Holmes became, a few months after her visit at the fort, the first woman to ascend Pikes Peak. She did not go on to the Cherry Creek diggings, however, but instead wintered in Taos, then went to Santa Fe, where her husband served for a time as territorial secretary of New Mexico.

14. The headline is from the Elwood (Kansas) *Weekly Press*, September 4, 1858. With one exception the newspaper quotations in the balance of the chapter are taken from Hafen's compilation in *Colorado Gold Rush, Contemporary Letters and Reports, 1858–59*, 42–44. The exception, the September 15 *Journal of Commerce* interview with Bent, is from Hafen's *Pikes Peak Gold Rush Guidebooks of 1859*, 30–31.

Chapter XIX
THE WHITE TIDE

1. Robinson's letter to Washington announcing that Bent would accept the appointment was written on May 2. Obviously, therefore, William had agreed before Robinson, in St. Louis, could have known that the commission had been signed on April 27. This first commission was "temporary"—that is, an emergency arrangement. On December 14, 1859, Buchanan sent Bent's "permanent" nomination as agent to the Senate, where it was confirmed March 2, 1860. (Records of the Appointments Division, Office of the Secretary of Interior, National Archives.)

2. In the late 1850s (Richardson, *Beyond the Mississippi*, 255), "Col. Ceran St. Vrain, after accumulating an ample fortune, went to New York City with the determination of spending his

days. But he found life there insupportable, and soon returned."
In January 1858 he bought from Steve Lee's widow, sister of
Beaubien's wife, her interest in the Sangre de Cristo grant for
one thousand dollars and a few years later sold it for twenty
thousand dollars to William Gilpin, first governor of Colorado
Territory, when Gilpin purchased a portion of the grant. At
Culebra, Beaubien's principal settlement on the grant, Ceran
built a gristmill. In the spring of 1860 he built another mill and
opened a store at infant Cañon City. At Mora in New Mexico
he owned a store, a mill, and a distillery. During the Civil War
he would sell enormous quantities of flour and other foodstuffs
to the army, increasing his ample fortune to one still more ample.

3. Seven years of intermittent correspondence concerning the lease
(General Land Office File, Abandoned Military Reservation
Series, File of Fort Lyon, National Archives) amply indicates
that the army rented—not bought—Bent's New Fort in 1860
rather than in 1859, as is often stated. Some contemporaries,
however, thought the sale had been consummated earlier.
Charles C. Post, passing up the Arkansas on his way to the gold
fields, wrote in his diary on June 15, 1859, after visiting the fort
and finding only four men there, "It has been built four years
by Bill Bent. Bent has accumulated an immense fortune and this
spring has sold his fort to the government for $10,000." (Hafen,
Overland Routes to the Gold Fields.)

4. Frank Blair, guardian of George Bent's son Elfego while the lad
was in St. Louis from 1847–54, had risen fast after leaving New
Mexico. Elected to the Missouri Legislature in 1852, he soon
went to Congress. Once slaveholders, he and his father and his
elder brother Montgomery soon changed sides and took active
parts in Frémont's presidential campaign of 1856. They were a
quarrelsome, able, close-knit family, ambitious of making Missouri a private Blair demesne, which it almost was. In 1860 they
supported Lincoln. Montgomery Blair became Postmaster General, and Frank shared the president's confidence. It was largely
at Frank's behest that Lincoln appointed Frémont commander
of the West with headquarters in St. Louis. Soon, however, the
hotheaded explorer and the hotheaded politician locked horns.
Frémont ordered Frank arrested and imprisoned; Montgomery
ordered Frank freed; and soon Lincoln, goaded by the Blairs,
removed Frémont from a command which the explorer had certainly bungled. Frank developed presidential ambitions and
succeeded in being nominated for the vice-presidency in 1868,
only to be snowed under with the rest of the ticket by the Grant
landslide.

5. Silas Bent had served with Sloat's squadron in California during
the Mexican War and was with Perry during the opening of
Japan. His hydrographic studies of Pacific Ocean currents were
published in 1856 and 1857. In 1857 he married wealthy Ann

Eliza Tyler of Louisville, Kentucky. After his resignation from the navy in the spring of 1861 he settled in St. Louis, where William renewed ties with a brother who had become almost a total stranger.

6. Chivington's callousness is hard to believe, but such is the gist of the conversation as William reported it to a congressional investigating committee in 1865. (*Condition of the Indian Tribes,* 94.)

Chapter XX
THE LAST AGONIES

1. Satanta (sometimes Santanta, Satank, Setangya, or White Bear) is described by Richard Dodge (*Plains of the Great West,* xxvi–xxvii) as "superior in boldness, daring, and merciless cruelty . . . sharp as a briar . . . remarkable for powers of oratory, for determined warfare." In his lodge he spread a carpet for guests to sit on and served whites from small tables twenty inches high and three feet long, brightly painted and ornamented with brass tacks. He owned a French horn which he tootled vigorously when meals were ready.

   In the 1830s he is said (Wharton, *Satanta,* 67) to have taken young Jesse Leavenworth, General Leavenworth's son, to the vicinity of present Cripple Creek and there gathered gold for the boy. The encroachments of the whites soon left him less affable. Raiding in 1866, he captured, among others, a Mrs. Box, who carried an infant in her arms. When the baby's cries annoyed him, Satanta seized it by the feet and dashed its brains out against a tree, then silenced the mother's screams by beating her over the head with a rope.

2. When the news reached Ceran St. Vrain in New Mexico, he sought out Pat O'Neill and said (according to Pat's recollection in the Denver *Post,* January 11, 1920), "It isn't right, Pat, that they should starve while there's plenty in the barns . . . and good God, man, they're paying $20 a sack." For $900 O'Neill agreed to haul 300 sacks over the 350-mile stretch to the starving town. All Denver knocked off work and formed blocklong lines to buy a share. "A charitable old cuss, that St. Vrain," said Pat. "He only got $6000 for 300 sacks of flour"—less, of course, Pat's $900.

3. Ablest defender of Chivington is Irving Howbert (*Memories,* 130 ff.), who as a youth fought with the volunteers. He impugns testimony hostile to the colonel (it appears in *Condition of the Indian Tribes*) by saying that most of the witnesses were either Chivington's political enemies or jealous officers. The rest of the witnesses he waves away as "two Indian agents, two Indian traders, two half-breeds, and one interpreter," and says they joined the criticism of Chivington because the whipping at Sand

Creek meant great loss to their trade. So much, in Howbert's eyes, for William Bent's thirty-five years of devotion to the Cheyennes.

4. Mary kept her love for her wayward brother. Whenever the coast was clear on the Purgatory ranch, she put a candle in the window, hoping Charles would see the prearranged signal and visit her. (Lueber, "William Bent's Family," *Colorado Magazine,* January 1936.) But the outlaw's last visit—the price on his head amounted to five thousand dollars according to Inman— was not to chat with Mary. Theodore Davis ("Summer on the Plains," *Harper's,* April 1869, 305) repeats the story as William told it to him: "My daughter saw something that looked like an Indian's head sticking up over the bank of the main irrigating ditch . . . went out . . . and discovered Charley. He said . . . that he was after the old man, meaning me. I was off in New Mexico at the time and she . . . asked the durn'd scoundrel to come to the house. 'No,' he said; 'I only wanted the old man,' and, uncocking his rifle, he went off. That's the last we've seen of him."

5. Six thousand dollars went to each group of Charles's heirs; to Alfred's three children; to Estafina and her husband, Zan Hicklin; to Teresina and her husband, Aloys Scheurich. For some reason matters were not settled by the sale, and litigation against Maxwell's successors dragged on until 1897.

   Lucien benefited very little from his fabulous empire. After selling it, he lost heavily in a bank in Santa Fe and threw away another quarter of a million dollars in early schemes of the Texas Pacific Railroad. He bought the abandoned buildings of Fort Sumner in eastern New Mexico and completed his financial breakdown trying to create a new kingdom. In 1875 he died, almost bankrupt.

6. After the stage company abandoned the fort as a station, cattlemen used it for a corral. Then farmers began carrying away its adobes for their buildings; weather completed the dissolution until nothing remained but a dim outline on the sandy soil. Plans are currently under way to reconstruct it under auspices of the Colorado State Historical Society.

7. Ceran St. Vrain died at 6 P.M., October 28, 1870, in Mora, New Mexico. He was given a military funeral; the regimental band of Fort Union played; the commanding general and his staff were pallbearers. He was buried by the Masonic fraternity (he and Kit had read themselves out of the Catholic Church partly because of continued quarrels with Padre Martinez). More than two thousand persons attended the rites. "The service was very impressive and the surroundings of a highly romantic character; nothing equal to it was ever seen in New Mexico." (Santa Fe *Daily New Mexican,* October 29, 1870; October 31, 1870.)

ACKNOWLEDGMENTS

Much of the material for this book rests on documents assembled and microfilmed through the patient and most proficient help of several libraries and historical societies. I am deeply indebted to Miss Barbara Kell and Mrs. Frances Biese of the Missouri Historical Society; to Miss Dorothy Bridgwater of the Yale University Library, which granted permission to use materials (cited specifically in the Bibliography) from the Coe Collection; to Dr. LeRoy Hafen of the Colorado Historical Society, whose published accounts of early Colorado history must be resorted to by anyone working in this field; to Mr. Edgar Langsdorf of the Kansas Historical Society; to Mr. A. S. Gaylord, Jr., and the staff of the Museum of New Mexico and also to the University of New Mexico for microfilms of the Bent-Álvarez letters; to Miss Jane Smith, Mr. Richard G. Wood, Mr. Frank Bridger, and others at the National Archives; to Mr. Roy Basler and staff, Library of Congress. Use of the fruits of all this effort was immeasurably helped by the loan of a microfilm reader by Mrs. Mildred Spiller of the Ventura County Library, Ventura, California.

My own library searches were given direction by Dr. Robert G. Cleland, Miss Mary Isabel Fry, Mr. Ed Carpenter, and the most obliging staff of the Henry E. Huntington Library, San Marino, California; by Dr. George P. Hammond, Mr. Robert Becker, and Mrs. Patricia Bauer of the Bancroft Library, University of California; and by Mrs. Ella Robinson of the Southwest Museum, Los Angeles. As usual, Miss Ina Aulls, Western History Department, Denver Public Library, was indefatigable in providing material of various sorts. Miss Mary Helen Peterson of the Los Angeles Public Library obligingly answered random inquiries, and the Reverend O. A. Coggiola of the Chancery Office, Archdiocese of Santa Fe, searched the Taos parish records for me.

Mr. Silas Bent McKinley generously placed at my disposal materials concerning his family. Valuable aid in unraveling the penmanship and idiom of French traders' letters was given by Mr. J. B. Close of Ojai and Mr. John Van B. Griggs of the Thacher School. Mr. Roland P. Hermes of the same school and Miss Haydée Noya of the Huntington Library came to my rescue in the matter of Spanish materials.

After the fruits of these diverse efforts had been assembled, Mr. Dale L. Morgan brought his unrivaled knowledge of the fur-trade era to a reading of the entire manuscript, caught errors, generously added new material, and suggested further lines of investigation. It need hardly be said that if any mistakes still remain after this formidable array of assistance, they are completely my own.

During the research for the book Mrs. Margaret T. Hunter, Mrs. John McDougal, Mr. Homer D. Crotty, and George and Virginia Wheaton of Pasadena all helped keep the wheels rolling with the priceless intangibles of their interest and hospitality. Mr. Keith Vosburg of Ojai allowed me free run of his library, an inestimable convenience.

Finally and most essentially, the book could never have been written without my wife. Aid in research, typing, and indexing is only a small part of the debt.

BIBLIOGRAPHY

Primary Sources

I. MANUSCRIPTS

BANCROFT PAPERS. Miscellaneous manuscript items in the Colorado and New Mexico series, Bancroft Library, University of California.

BENT, CHARLES. Approximately twoscore letters to Manuel Álvarez, Nov. 1839–June 1846. Read Collection, on loan from the Museum of New Mexico to the University of New Mexico. Microfilms furnished through courtesy of both institutions.

BENT, CHARLES. Letter Book, National Archives, Records of the War Department, Department of New Mexico, Record Copy of Letters Sent, Vol. V, Sept. 1846–1847. Bent's correspondence during his governorship with Secretary of State Buchanan, Senator Benton, General Kearny, Colonel Doniphan, Commissioner of Indian Affairs William Medill (a copy of the last is also in the Huntington Library), etc.

BENT, GEORGE (William Bent's son). 260 letters to George E. Hyde, Coe Collection, Yale University Library. A few dozen more of George Bent's letters to Hyde are in the Colorado Historical Society and the Western History Department, Denver Public Library.

BENT, WILLIAM. Nine letters to A. M. Robinson, Jan. 1859–Feb. 1860, relative to the Upper Arkansas Agency. Records of the Bureau of Indian Affairs, National Archives, Washington.

BOGGS, WILLIAM. "Narrative of a Journey to Santa Fe . . . in 1844–45," Coe Collection, Yale University Library. This document adds considerable material to the William Boggs manuscript published in *The Colorado Magazine*, March 1930.

P. CHOUTEAU and P. CHOUTEAU MAFFITT collections, Missouri Historical Society, St. Louis. Miscellaneous letters, mostly in French, relate to the Bents and St. Vrain, especially J. P. Cabanné to P. Choteau (sic), Oct. 14, 1828; "Declaration of Sylvestre Pratte's Engagés," Taos, Sept. 1, 1829; papers dealing with the settlement of S. Pratte's estate; and several letters concerning the competition on the Platte.

CLARK, WILLIAM. Letter Books. Correspondence and documents of the Office of the Superintendent of Indian Affairs. Kansas Historical Society.

GRINNELL, GEORGE B. Letters (especially from George Bent), notes, and unpublished manuscripts. Southwest Museum, Los Angeles.

HYDE, GEORGE E. Life of George Bent, unpublished manuscript compiled from G. Bent's letters. Western History Department, Denver Public Library.

MARRIAGE BOOKS, 39 and 40, Jan. 1827–Dec. 1845, Taos Parish. Archdiocese of Santa Fe.

NATIONAL ARCHIVES. Miscellaneous documents, especially (1) letters of William Clark, Mar. 29 and Aug. 2, 1827, concerning appointment of Charles Bent as subagent to the Ioways; (2) letters in the records of the quartermaster general concerning claims of Bent, St. Vrain & Company, William Bent, and Ceran St. Vrain for services and supplies rendered various army groups, 1843–63; (3) several letters, Aug. 1860–Feb. 1867, in Abandoned Military Reservations Series, file of Fort Lyon, concerning William Bent's lease of Bent's New Fort to the government; (4) Records of Appointments Division, Office of the Secretary of the Interior; (5) "Ft. Lyon," from file of Historical Sketches, compiled 1889; (6) Cummins to William Clark, June 19, 1835, concerning William Bent's attack on some Shoshoni, Office of Indian Affairs, Upper Missouri Agency. Many of the above items, together with random others, are cited more specifically in the Notes.

NEWELL, ROBERT. Memorandum (Journal and Reminiscences of an early mountain man and settler in Oregon). University of Oregon.

PRATT, O. W. "Diary of an Overland Journey by Way of Santa Fe, June 9–Oct. 25, 1848." Coe Collection, Yale University Library.

RITCH, WILLIAM G. Papers. A large collection of New Mexican documents, passports, customs declarations, etc. Huntington Library, San Marino, Calif.

ST. VRAIN, CERAN. Letter to his mother from Taos, July 1825. To B. Pratte & Company, Apr. 27, 1825; Sept. 28, 1828; Sept. 14, 1830; Jan. 6, 1831. Missouri Historical Society.

ST. VRAIN, CERAN. Letter to Colonel Mackay, July 21, 1847, offering to sell Bent's Fort, and reports by Captain A. W. Enos and Major Thomas Swords concerning the proposal. National Archives.

II. BOOKS

ABERT, LT. J. W. "Journal . . . in 1845." Senate Exec. Doc. 438, 29th Congress, 1st Sess.

BECKWOURTH, JAMES P. Life and Adventures, ghost-written by T. D.

Bonner and published in 1856; reissued, edited by Bernard De Voto. New York, 1931.

BENT, WILLIAM. Agency Report, Oct. 5, 1859. *Report of Commissioner of Indian Affairs for 1859.* Washington, 1860.

BENTON, THOMAS H. "Report to the Senate Relative to . . . the Fur Trade." Senate Exec. Doc. 67, 20th Congress, 2nd Sess.

CALHOUN, JAMES S. *Official Correspondence,* edited by Annie H. Abel. Washington, 1915.

CARVALHO, S. N. *Incidents of Travel and Adventure in the Far West.* New York, 1856.

CATLIN, GEORGE. *Letters and Notes on North American Indians.* London, 1841.

CLYMAN, JAMES. *James Clyman, American Frontiersman, 1792–1881,* edited by C. L. Camp. San Francisco, 1929.

Condition of the Indian Tribes. Report of the Joint Special Committee of Congress. Washington, 1867.

Congressional Documents (miscellaneous): House Doc. 137, 22nd Congress, 2nd Sess., concerning disbursements to Felix and Charles St. Vrain on Felix's agency. Senate Doc. 69, 23rd Congress, 2nd Sess., listing an abstract of licenses to trade with the Indians in 1834. House Rept. 194, 28th Congress, 2nd Sess., concerning the claim of Bent, St. Vrain & Company for redress for depredations committed by Pawnees. Senate Exec. Doc. 325 and House Exec. Doc. 266, 27th Congress, 2nd Sess., and Senate Rept. 156 and Senate Exec. Doc. 26, 29th Congress, 2nd Sess., concerning Texan filibusters on the Santa Fe Trail. Senate Doc. 115, 29th Congress, 1st Sess., and House Repts. 34 and 37, 30th Congress, 1st Sess., concerning claims of Bent, St. Vrain & Company for furnishing supplies to U.S. troops. House Repts. 457, 254, 35th Congress, 1st Sess., concerning Mexican land grants.

CONRAD, H. L. *Uncle Dick Wootton.* (Presumably dictated by Wootton and polished by Conrad.) Chicago, 1890.

COOKE, PHILIP ST. GEORGE. *The Conquest of New Mexico and California.* New York, 1878.

————. *Scenes and Adventures in the Army.* Philadelphia, 1859.

DAVIS, HERMAN, ed. *Reminiscences of General William H. Larimer and of His Son William H. H. Larimer.* Lancaster, 1918.

EDWARDS, FRANK S. *A Campaign in New Mexico with Colonel Doniphan.* London, 1848.

EMORY, WILLIAM H. *Notes on a Military Reconnaissance.* Washington, 1848. This also contains accounts by J. W. Abert, Philip St. G. Cooke, A. R. Johnston. House Exec. Doc. 41, 30th Congress, 1st Sess.

FARNHAM, THOMAS J. *Travels in the Great Western Prairies,* etc.

Reprinted in Thwaites, *Early Western Travels,* XXVIII. Cleveland, 1906.

FITZPATRICK, THOMAS, "Report," Oct. 19, 1847, edited by Hafen, in *New Spain and the Anglo-American West,* II. Los Angeles, 1932.

———. Agency Report of 1853. Senate Exec. Doc. 1, 33rd Congress, 2nd Sess.

FOWLER, JACOB. *Journal,* edited by Elliott Coues. New York, 1898.

FRÉMONT, JESSIE BENTON. *Souvenirs of My Time.* Boston, 1887.

———. *A Year of American Travel.* New York, 1878.

FRÉMONT, JOHN C. *Report of the Exploring Expedition to the Rocky Mountains in the Year 1842 and to Oregon and North California in the Years 1843–44.* Washington, 1845.

———. *Memories of My Life,* 2 vols. Chicago, 1887.

GARRARD, LEWIS. *Wah-To-Yah and the Taos Trail.* First published in 1850, reprint edited by Ralph P. Bieber. Glendale, Calif., 1938.

GIBSON, GEORGE R. *Journal of a Soldier under Kearny and Doniphan,* edited by Ralph P. Bieber. Glendale, Calif., 1935.

GILPIN, WILLIAM. Report of the Campaign of 1847–48. House Exec. Doc. 1, 30th Congress, 2nd Sess.

GRANT, BLANCHE C., ed. *Kit Carson's Own Story of his Life.* Taos, 1926.

GREGG, JOSIAH. *Commerce of the Prairies.* (In Thwaites, *Early Western Travels,* XIX–XX. Cleveland, 1905.)

GREGG, KATE, ed. *The Road to Santa Fe.* Albuquerque, 1952. (The letters and diaries of George Sibley.)

HAFEN, LEROY R., ed. *Pikes Peak Gold Rush Guidebooks of 1859.* Glendale, Calif., 1941.

———, ed. *Colorado Gold Rush: Contemporary Letters and Reports.* Glendale, Calif., 1941.

———, ed. *Overland Routes to the Goldfields, 1859.* Glendale, Calif., 1942. (Particularly, for this book, the diaries of C. C. Post and H. M. Gass.)

HAMILTON, WILLIAM. *My Sixty Years on the Plains.* New York, 1905.

HEAP, GWINN H. *The Central Route to the Pacific.* Philadelphia, 1854.

HOBBS, JAMES. *Wild Life in the Far West.* Hartford, 1872.

HOLMES, JULIA A. *A Bloomer Girl on Pikes Peak,* edited by Agnes W. Spring. Denver, 1949.

HOWBERT, IRVING. *Memories of a Lifetime in the Pikes Peak Region.* New York, 1925.

HULBERT, ARCHER B. *Southwest on the Turquoise Trail*. Denver, 1933.

HUGHES, JOHN T. *Doniphan's Expedition*. Cincinnati, 1850.

JOHNSON, A. R.; EDWARDS, M. B.; FERGUSON, P. *Marching with the Army of the West*, edited by Ralph P. Bieber. Glendale, Calif.

KAPPLER, CHARLES J. *Indian Affairs, Laws, and Treaties*, 3 vols. Washington, 1903, 1913.

KEARNY, STEPHEN W. "Report of a Summer Campaign . . . 1845." Senate Exec. Doc. 1, 29th Congress, 1st Sess.

KENDALL, GEORGE W. *Narrative of the Texan Santa Fé Expedition*. New York, 1844.

KENNERLY, WILLIAM. *Persimmon Hill*. Norman, Okla., 1950.

LARPENTEUR, CHARLES. *Forty Years a Fur Trader on the Upper Missouri*, edited by Elliott Coues. New York, 1898.

LEONARD, ZENAS. *Narrative of Adventures*, edited by W. F. Wagner. Cleveland, 1904.

LOWE, PERCIVAL. *Five Years a Dragoon, 1849–54*. Kansas City, 1926.

MAGOFFIN, SUSAN. *Down the Santa Fe Trail and into Mexico*, edited by Stella Drumm. New Haven, 1926.

MAJORS, ALEXANDER. *Seventy Years on the Frontier*. New York, 1893.

MARCY, RANDOLPH B. *Border Reminiscences*. New York, 1872.
———. *The Prairie Traveler*. New York, 1859.
———. *Thirty Years of Army Life on the Border*. New York, 1866.

MARSHALL, THOMAS M. *The Life and Papers of Frederick Bates*, 2 vols. St. Louis, 1926.

MELINE, JAMES. *Two Thousand Miles on Horseback*. New York, 1872.

Message from the President of the United States Concerning the Fur Trade and the Inland Trade to Mexico. Senate Exec. Doc. 90, 22nd Congress, 1st Sess. Washington, 1832. (This contains Pilcher's letter on the trade to Secretary of War Cass and also Alphonso Wetmore's diary of a trip to Santa Fe in 1828.)

Message from the President . . . Relative to the British Establishments on the Columbia, etc. Senate Exec. Doc. 39, 21st Congress, 1st Sess. Washington, 1831. (This contains Pilcher's letter to Sec. J. H. Eaton on his 1827 trip to the Rockies.)

NIDEVER, GEORGE. *The Life and Adventures of George Nidever*, edited by William H. Ellison. Berkeley, 1937.

PARKMAN, FRANCIS. *The California and Oregon Trail*. New York, 1849.

PATTIE, JAMES O. *Personal Narrative* (in Thwaites, *Early Western Travels*, XVIII. Cleveland, 1905.)

PIKE, ALBERT. *Prose Sketches and Poems Written in the Western Country.* Boston, 1834.

PILCHER, JOSHUA. See under *Messages from the President.*

"Report on the Expedition of Dragoons under Col. Henry Dodge." *American State Papers, Military Affairs*, VI, 24th Congress, 1st Sess. Washington, 1835.

Reports of the Commissioner of Indian Affairs, various years from 1835 through 1867.

Reports of Explorations . . . For a Pacific Railroad. Senate Exec. Doc. 78, 33rd Congress, 2nd Sess. Washington, 1855.

RICHARDSON, ALBERT. *Beyond the Mississippi.* Hartford, 1867.

ROBINSON, JACOB S. *A Journal of the Santa Fe Expedition under Colonel Doniphan.* Princeton, 1932.

RUXTON, GEORGE F. *Adventures in Mexico and the Rocky Mountains.* London, 1847.

———. *Life in the Far West* (semi-fiction, edited by L. R. Hafen.) Norman, Okla., 1952.

SAGE, RUFUS. *Scenes in the Rocky Mountains.* Philadelphia, 1846.

VICTOR, FRANCIS F. *The River of the West.* (Joe Meek.) Hartford, 1870.

WARE, EUGENE F. *The Indian War of 1864.* Topeka, 1911.

WEBB, JAMES J. *Adventures in the Santa Fe Trade, 1844–47*, edited by Ralph P. Bieber. Glendale, Calif., 1931.

WETMORE, ALPHONSO. See under *Messages from the President.*

WISLIZENUS, A. *A Journey to the Rocky Mountains in 1839.* St. Louis, 1912.

III. PERIODICALS

"Bent's Fort, 1844–45." *Colorado Magazine*, Nov. 1934. (Excerpts of newspaper accounts, travelers' reports, etc.)

BERNARD, WILLIAM R. "Westport and the Santa Fe Trade." *Kansas Historical Collections*, IX, 1905–6.

BOGGS, WILLIAM M. "Manuscript." *Colorado Magazine*, Mar. 1930.

Bulletin of the Missouri Historical Society, VI, Oct. 1949. (Newspaper and diary reports of the cholera epidemic of 1849.)

CAMPBELL, ROBERT. "Correspondence, 1834–45." Missouri Historical Society, *Glimpses of the Past*, VIII, 1941.

COOKE, PHILIP ST. G. "A Journal of the Santa Fe Trail," edited by William Connelley. *Mississippi Valley Historical Review*, June 1925.

DAVIS, THEODORE R. "The Buffalo Range," *Harper's New Monthly Magazine*, Jan. 1869.

———. "A Stage Ride to Colorado." Ibid., July 1867.

————. "Summer on the Plains." Ibid., Apr. 1869.

————. "Winter on the Plains." Ibid., June 1869.

DENIG, EDWIN T. "Of the Arickaras." *Bulletin of the Missouri Historical Society*, Jan. 1950.

EVANS, HUGH. "Journal of a Dragoon Campaign of 1835." *Mississippi Valley Historical Review*, Sept. 1927.

FIELD, MATTHEW C. "Sketches of Big Timbers, Bent's Fort, and Milk Fort in 1839." *Colorado Magazine*, May 1937.

FORD, CAPTAIN. "Journal of an Expedition to the Rocky Mountains." *Mississippi Valley Historical Review*, Mar. 1926.

ISAACS, ROBERT. "Perils of a Mountain Hunt." *Missouri Republican*, Sept. 4, 1832.

KENNERLY, JAMES. "Diary" (1824). *Missouri Historical Society Collections*, VI.

KINGMAN, SAMUEL. "Diary" (1867). *Kansas Historical Quarterly*, Nov. 1932.

LANE, WILLIAM C. "Letters." Missouri Historical Society, *Glimpses of the Past*, 1940.

MARMADUKE, M. M. "Journal from Franklin to Santa Fe in 1824." *Missouri Historical Review*, Oct. 1911.

Niles' Weekly Register, Vol. 23, 1822 through Vol. 70, 1847. Published in Baltimore and Washington, this early-day newsmagazine reprinted considerable data from western newspapers.

O'NEILL, PAT. "Reminiscences." Denver *Post*, Jan. 11, 1920.

PIKE, ALBERT. "Narrative of a Journey in the Prairie." *Arkansas Historical Association*, IV, 1917.

PRATTE, BERNARD, JR. "Reminiscences." *Bulletin of the Missouri Historical Society*, Oct. 1949.

Publication of the Nebraska Historical Society, XX, 1922. Excerpts from contemporary newspapers concerning the Missouri River trade, etc., during the early nineteenth century.

ROBINSON, DOANE. "Official Correspondence Pertaining to the Leavenworth Expedition of 1823." *South Dakota Historical Collections*, I, 1902.

SMITH, E. WILLARD. "Journal." *Colorado Magazine*, July 1950.

SOPRIS, W. R. "My Grandmother, Mrs. Marcellin St. Vrain." *Colorado Magazine*, Mar. 1945.

STORRS, AUGUSTUS. "Answers to Certain Queries . . ." *Niles' Weekly Register*, Jan. 15, 1825.

WALDO, WILLIAM. "Recollections of a Septuagenarian." Missouri Historical Society, *Glimpses of the Past*, V, Jan.–Mar. 1938. Reprinted from "Recollections of the Bent Family," *Western*, St. Louis, Vol. 6.

WAUGH, ALFRED S. "Desultory Wanderings, 1845–46." *Bulletin of the Missouri Historical Society*, Apr. 1950–Jan. 1951.

WILLING, DR. GEORGE M. "Diary of a Journey to the Pikes Peak Gold Mines in 1859," edited by R. P. Bieber. *Mississippi Valley Historical Review*, Dec. 1927.

WOLF, CAPT. L. B. "Diary" (1860). *Kansas Historical Quarterly*, May 1932.

Secondary Sources

I. BOOKS

ALSOP, FRED W. *The Life Story of Albert Pike*. Little Rock, 1920.

ALTER, CECIL J. *James Bridger*. Salt Lake, 1925.

BAKER, JAMES and HAFEN, LEROY. *History of Colorado*, 3 vols. Denver, 1927.

BANCROFT, HUBERT H. *History of Arizona and New Mexico*. San Francisco, 1889.

———. *History of Nevada, Colorado and Wyoming*. San Francisco, 1890.

———. *History of North Mexican States and Texas*. San Francisco, 1889.

———. *Life of William Gilpin*. San Francisco, 1889.

BAY, W. V. N. *Reminiscences of the Bench and Bar of Missouri*. St. Louis, 1878.

BENT, ALLEN H. *The Bent Family in America*. Boston, 1900.

BENTON, THOMAS H. *Thirty Years' View*. New York, 1856.

BILLON, FREDERICK L. *Annals of St. Louis in Its Territorial Days*. St. Louis, 1888.

BINKLEY, WILLIAM C. *The Expansionist Movement in Texas*. Berkeley, 1925.

BOWMAN, CHARLES. "History of Bent County," in *History of the Arkansas Valley, Colorado*. Chicago, 1881.

BRYAN, WILLIAM, and ROSE, ROBERT. *A History of the Pioneer Families of Missouri*, rev. ed. St. Louis, 1935.

CHITTENDEN, H. M. *The American Fur Trade of the Far West*, 3 vols. New York, 1902.

CLELAND, ROBERT G. *This Reckless Breed of Men*. New York, 1950.

COMAN, KATHERINE. *Economic Beginnings of the Far West*, 2 vols. New York, 1912.

CONNELLEY, WILLIAM E. *Standard History of Kansas and Kansans*, 1922.

———. *Doniphan's Expedition*, etc. Kansas City, 1907.

CUTTS, JAMES MADISON. *The Conquest of California and New Mexico*. Philadelphia, 1847.

DAVIS, W. W. H. *El Gringo.* New York, 1857.

DE VOTO, BERNARD. *Across the Wide Missouri.* Boston, 1947.

———. *The Year of Decision: 1846.* Boston, 1943.

DICK, EVERETT. *Vanguards of the Frontier.* New York, 1941.

Dictionary of American Biography. New York, 1928–36.

DODGE, RICHARD I. *Our Wild Indians.* Hartford, 1883.

———. *The Plains of the Great West.* New York, 1877.

DRURY, CLIFFORD. *Marcus Whitman, M.D.* Caldwell, Ida., 1937.

DUFFUS, ROBERT L. *The Santa Fe Trail.* New York, 1930.

DUNN, J. P. *Massacres of the Mountains.* New York, 1886.

FAVOUR, ALPHEUS. *Old Bill Williams.* Chapel Hill, 1936.

FERGUSSON, ERNA. *New Mexico.* New York, 1951.

FERGUSSON, HARVEY. *The Rio Grande.* New York, 1933.

FOREMAN, GRANT. *Marcy and the Gold Seekers.* Norman, Okla., 1939.

———. *Pioneer Days in the Early Southwest.* Cleveland, 1926.

FRITZ, PERCY S. *Colorado.* New York, 1941.

FULTON, MAURICE, and HORGAN, PAUL, eds. *New Mexico's Own Chronicle.* Dallas, 1937.

GARWOOD, DARRELL. *Crossroads of America, The Story of Kansas City.* New York, 1948.

GHENT, W. J. and HAFEN, LEROY. *Broken Hand, The Life Story of Thomas Fitzpatrick.* Denver, 1931.

GRANT, BLANCHE C. *One Hundred Years Ago in Old Taos.* Taos, 1925.

———. *When Old Trails Were New: The Story of Taos.* New York, 1934.

GREENE, J. EVARTS. *The Santa Fe Trade,* etc. Worcester, 1893.

GRINNELL, GEORGE B. *The Cheyenne Indians,* 2 vols. New Haven, 1924.

———. *The Fighting Cheyennes.* New York, 1915.

HAFEN, LEROY. *Colorado and Its People.* New York, 1948.

HAFEN, LEROY, and YOUNG, F. M. *Ft. Laramie,* etc. Glendale, Calif., 1938.

HALEY, J. E. *Charles Goodnight.* New York, 1936.

HALL, FRANK. *History of Colorado.* Chicago, 1889.

HILL, JOSEPH J. *The History of Warner's Ranch.* Los Angeles, 1927.

The History of Jackson County, Missouri, 3 vols. Chicago, 1893.

HODGE, F. W. *Handbook of American Indians.* Washington, 1907.

HOWBERT, IRVING. *The Indians of the Pikes Peak Region.* New York, 1914.

INMAN, HENRY. *The Old Santa Fe Trail.* New York, 1899.

JACKSON, W. TURRENTINE. *Wagon Roads West . . . 1846–69.* Berkeley, 1952.

JAMES, MARQUIS. *Sam Houston.* Indianapolis, 1929.

JENNINGS, SISTER MARIETTA. *A Pioneer Merchant in St. Louis, 1810–20 . . . Christian Welt.* New York, 1939.

KELEHER, WILLIAM A. *The Fabulous Frontier.* Santa Fe, 1945.

———. *Turmoil in New Mexico, 1846–68.* Santa Fe, 1952.

LEWIS, DONNA MAY. The Bents and St. Vrains as Pioneers in the Trade of the Southwest. Unpublished Master's Thesis, University of California, 1924.

MORGAN, DALE L. *Jedediah Smith, And the Opening of the West.* Indianapolis and New York, 1953.

NEVINS, ALLAN. *Frémont, Pathmarker of the West.* New York, 1939.

PELZER, LOUIS. *Henry Dodge.* Iowa City, 1911.

———. *Marches of the Dragoons in the Mississippi Valley.* Iowa City, 1917.

PETERS, DEWITT C. *The Life and Adventures of Kit Carson.* New York, 1858.

PRINCE, L. B. *A Concise History of New Mexico.* New York, 1883.

READ, BENJAMIN. *Illustrated History of New Mexico.* Santa Fe, 1912.

RICHARDSON, RUPERT N. *The Comanche Barrier to South Plains Settlement.* Glendale, Calif., 1933.

RISTER, CARL COKE. *The Southwestern Frontier, 1865–1881.* Cleveland, 1928.

RIVES, GEORGE L. *The United States and Mexico, 1821–1848.* New York, 1913.

ROCKAFELLOW, B. F. "History of Fremont County," in *History of the Arkansas Valley, Colorado.* Chicago, 1881.

SABIN, EDWIN L. *Kit Carson Days,* rev. ed. New York, 1935.

ST. VRAIN, PAUL A. *Genealogy of the Family of DeLassus St. Vrain.* Kirkville, Mo., 1943.

SCHARF, JOHN T. *History of St. Louis City and County,* 2 vols. Philadelphia, 1883.

SEELEY, CHARLES L. *Pioneer Days in the Arkansas Valley.* Denver, 1932.

SMILEY, JEROME C. *History of Denver.* Denver, 1901.

———. *Semi-Centennial History of Colorado.* Chicago, 1913.

SMITH, JUSTIN H. *The War with Mexico.* New York, 1919.

STANLEY, F. *The Grant That Maxwell Bought.* Denver, 1952.

STEINEL, ALVIN. *History of Agriculture in Colorado.* Fort Collins, Colo., 1926.

STEVENSON, R. M. "History of Pueblo County," in *History of the Arkansas Valley*. Chicago, 1881.

SULLIVAN, MAURICE. *The Travels of Jedediah Smith*. Santa Ana, Calif., 1934.

TOBIE, HARVEY E. *No Man Like Joe: The Life and Times of Joseph Meek*. Portland, 1949.

TRIPLETT, COL. FRANK. *Conquering the Wilderness*. New York, 1883.

TWITCHELL, RALPH E. *The History of the Military Occupation of the Territory of New Mexico*. Denver, 1909.

———. *Leading Facts of New Mexico History*, 3 vols. Cedar Rapids, 1912.

WARNER, LOUIS H. *Archbishop Lamy*. Santa Fe, 1936.

WEBB, WALTER P. *The Great Plains*. New York, 1931.

WHARTON, CLARENCE. *Satanta, The Great Chief of the Kiowas*. Dallas, 1935.

WHITNEY, CARRIE W. *Kansas City, Missouri, Its History and Its People*. Chicago, 1908.

WILLIAMS, CHAUNCY P. *Lone Elk: The Life Story of Old Bill Williams*. Denver, 1935.

WISSLER, CLARK. *The American Indian*. New York, 1931.

YOAKUM, HENDERSON. *History of Texas*. 2 vols. New York, 1856.

YOUNG, OTIS. *The First Military Escort on the Santa Fe Trail, 1829*. Glendale, Calif., 1952.

ZOLLINGER, JAMES P. *Sutter, The Man and His Empire*. New York, 1939.

II. PERIODICALS

ATHERTON, LEWIS. "Business Techniques in the Santa Fe Trade." *Missouri Historical Review*, Apr. 1940.

BIEBER, RALPH P. "The Southwestern Trails to California in 1849." *Mississippi Valley Historical Review*, Dec. 1925.

BLOOM, LANSING. New Mexico under Mexican Administration. *Old Santa Fe Magazine*, I, II.

BINKLEY, WILLIAM C. "New Mexico and the Texan Santa Fe Expedition." *Southwest Historical Society*, Oct. 1923.

CHACON, RAFAEL. "Campaign against the Utes and Apaches in Southern Colorado, 1855." *Colorado Magazine*, May 1934.

CHEETHAM, FRANCIS T. "The Early Settlements of Southern Colorado." *Colorado Magazine*, Feb. 1928.

———. "First Term of the American Court in Taos." *New Mexico Historical Review*, Jan. 1926.

COFFIN, WILLIAM H. "Settlements of the Friends in Kansas." *Kansas Historical Society Collections,* Vol. VII.

COX, ISAAC J. "The Opening of the Santa Fe Trail." *Missouri Historical Review,* Oct. 1930.

DUNHAM, HAROLD H. "Sidelights on Santa Fe Traders, 1839–46." Westerners' *Brand Book,* Denver, 1951.

———. "Lucien B. Maxwell." Ibid., Denver, 1950.

FLYNN, ARTHUR J. "Furs and Forts of the Rocky Mountain West." *Colorado Magazine,* Mar. 1932.

GRINNELL, GEORGE B. "Bent's Old Fort and Its Builders." *Kansas Historical Society Collections,* XV, 1919–22.

HAFEN, LEROY R. "Andrew Sublette." *Colorado Magazine,* Sept. 1933.

———. "The Early Fur Trade Posts of the South Platte." *Mississippi Valley Historical Review,* Dec. 1925.

———. "Colorado Mountain Men." *Colorado Magazine,* Jan. 1953.

———. "Fort Jackson and the Early Trade of the South Platte." Ibid., Feb. 1928.

———. "Fort St. Vrain." Ibid., Oct. 1952.

———. "The Fort Pueblo Massacre and the Punitive Expedition against the Utes." Ibid., Mar. 1927.

———. "John D. Albert." Ibid., Mar. 1933.

———, "The Last Years of James Beckwourth." Ibid., Aug. 1928.

———. "Louis Vasquez." Ibid., Jan. 1933.

———. "Mexican Land Grants in Colorado." Ibid., May 1927.

———. "Old Fort Lupton and Its Founder." Ibid., Nov. 1929.

———. "Tom Fitzpatrick and the First Indian Agency in Colorado." Ibid., Mar. 1929.

———. "When Was Bent's Fort Built?" Ibid., Apr. 1954.

HAFEN, L. R., and YOUNG, F. M. "The Mormon Settlement at Pueblo." *Colorado Magazine,* July 1932.

HALLOCK, CHARLES. "The Siege of Ft. Atkinson." *Harper's New Monthly Magazine,* Oct. 1857.

HILL, JOSEPH J. "Antoine Robidoux," etc. *Colorado Magazine,* July 1930.

———. "Ewing Young in the Fur Trade of the Far Southwest." *Oregon Historical Society Quarterly,* Mar. 1923.

HUDNALL, MARY PROWERS. "Early History of Bent County." *Colorado Magazine,* Nov. 1945.

LOUNSBURY, R. G. "Material in the National Archives for the History of New Mexico." *New Mexico Historical Review,* July 1946.

LOYOLA, SISTER MARY. "The American Occupation of New Mexico, 1821–1852." *New Mexico Historical Review,* Jan. 1939.

LUEBERS, H. L. "William Bent's Family and the Indians of the Plains." *Colorado Magazine,* Jan. 1936.

McHenrie, A. W. "The Hatcher Ditch." *Colorado Magazine*, June 1928.

———. "Origin of the Name of the Purgatoire River." Ibid., Feb. 1928.

Mead, James R. "The Little Arkansas." *Kansas Historical Society Collections*, X, 1907–8.

Montgomery, Mrs. F. C. "Ft. Wallace and Its Relation to the Frontier." *Kansas Historical Society Collections*, 1926–28.

Palmer, Capt. H. E. "History of the Powder River Expedition of 1865." *Nebraska State Historical Society*, II, 1887.

"Peg-Leg Smith—A Short Sketch of His Life." *Daily Alta California*, Mar. 8, 1858.

"Peg-Leg Smith." *Hutchings' Illustrated California Magazine*, V, July 1860–June 1861.

Perrine, Fred S. "Military Escorts on the Santa Fe Trail." *New Mexico Historical Review*, Apr. and July, 1927.

Russell, Carl. "Picture Books of Fur Trade History." *Bulletin of the Missouri Historical Society*, Apr. 1948.

Seabrook, S. L. "Expedition of Col. E. V. Sumner against the Cheyenne Indians, 1857." *Kansas Historical Society Collections*, XVI, 1923–25.

Shields, Lillian. "Relations with the Cheyennes and Arapahos in Colorado to 1861." *Colorado Magazine*, Aug. 1927.

Stephens, F. F. "Missouri and the Santa Fe Trade." *Missouri Historical Review*, Apr. and June 1917.

"The Story of an Old Trapper" (Peg-leg Smith). San Francisco *Evening Bulletin*, Oct. 26, 1866.

Taylor, M. L. "The Western Services of Stephen Watts Kearny, 1815–1848." *New Mexico Historical Review*, July 1946.

Thompson, Albert W. "Thomas O. Boggs, Early Scout and Plainsman." *Colorado Magazine*, July 1930.

Walter, Paul A. "The First Civil Governor of New Mexico under the Stars and Stripes." *New Mexico Historical Review*, VIII, 1933.

Wellman, Paul. "Famous Kansas Scouts." *Kansas Historical Quarterly*, Aug. 1932.

Working, D. W. "The Hicklins on the Greenhorn." *Colorado Magazine*, Dec. 1927.

Wyman, W. D. "Bullwhacking." *New Mexico Historical Review*, Oct. 1932.

———. "Freighting on the Santa Fe Trail." *Kansas Historical Quarterly*, Vol. 1.

———. "The Military Phase of Santa Fe Freighting." Ibid., Nov. 1932.

————. "Kansas City, Missouri, Famous Freighting Capital." Ibid., Feb. 1937.

YOUNG, F. G. "Ewing Young and His Estate." *Oregon Historical Quarterly*, Sept. 1920.

(Various minor sources that are cited in the Notes do not reappear in the above tabulation.)

INDEX